THE
WHITE-BONED DEMON

Mao: A Biography

The China Difference (editor)

The Future of China: After Mao

Flowers on an Iron Tree

R. H. Tawney and His Times

800,000,000: The Real China

China and Ourselves (editor)

THE WHITE-BONED DEMON

A BIOGRAPHY OF MADAME MAO ZEDONG

ROSS TERRILL

WILLIAM MORROW AND COMPANY, INC.

NEW YORK 1984

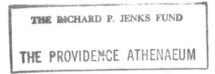
Copyright © 1984 by Ross Terrill

Library of Congress Cataloging in Publication Data

Terrill, Ross
  The White-Boned Demon.

  Includes index.
  1. Chiang, Ch'ing, 1910–   . 2. Statesmen—
China—Biography. I. Title.
DS778.C5374T45 1984   951.05′092′4 [B]   83-13316
ISBN 0-688-02461-0

Printed in the United States of America

First Edition

1 2 3 4 5 6 7 8 9 10

Chinese characters have been romanized in the *pinyin* way, used by the Chinese and by most foreigners, except for the following places and names known very well to foreigners in their pre-*pinyin* form: China, Canton, Chiang Kai-shek, Hong Kong, Peking, Sun Yat-sen, Tibet, and Whangpu River.

Acknowledgments

I wish to thank the following people for various types of assistance: Kyoko Arakawa, Anne Bernays, Tom Bower, Creighton Burns and Ray Blackburn, Donald Chang, King-yuh Chang, Chang Shang Pu (Kang Jian), Yenshew Lynn Chao, Timothy Cheek, Jack and Yuan-tsung Chen, Chen Suimin, Chen Wen, Chen Jiying, Cheng Pai-kai, Chu Hao-jan and Mrs. Chu, Chung Hua-min (Zhao Cong), Ding Ling, Ding Wang, Y. T. Feng, Bryce Harland, E. F. Hill, Joan Hill, Steven Goldstein, Jeffrey Kinkley, Warren Kuo (Chen Ran), C. M. Lau, Steven Levin, Li Tianmin, Smarlo Ma (Si Malu), Michael Mao, Charles Nairn, Neil Newnham of the *Melbourne Herald*, Malkah Notman, Pam Painter, Pei Mingyu, Rulan Pian, Robert Scalapino, John Stewart Service, Madge Slavin, Su Fei, Mark W. Tam, Gerald Tannebaum, Audrey Topping, Nym Wales (Helen Foster Snow), Paul S. C. Wang (Wang Sicheng), Eugene Wu, Joseph Wu, Tatsuo Yamada, Chieko Yamashita, Yu Ta-wei, Zhang Suchu, Zheng Yongzhi—and numerous Chinese who cannot be named.

For particularly important help my special gratitude to the following: Ch'en Li-li, Cui Wanqiu (Tsui Wan-chiu), Kichinosuke Ihara, Lois Snow, Wang Tingshu—and two sterling Chinese who cannot be named.

—R.T.

Shanghai, October 1983

THE
WHITE-
BONED
DEMON

Contents

1

Prologue: "I Was Mao's Dog"

From Ibsen's A Doll's House:

HELMER (to his wife, Nora): But this is disgraceful. Is this the way you neglect your most sacred duties? . . .
NORA: I have another duty, just as sacred.
HELMER: You can't have. What duty do you mean?
NORA: My duty to myself.

It was a cold November afternoon. A stone's throw from the Peking Hotel, the black cars with curtained windows snaked their way through a phalanx of bicycles, whose bells trilled like cicadas, along a narrow old street of ornate mansions called Street of Righteousness. They turned noiselessly through a gray brick archway, whose heavy steel gates seldom open; this secluded compound, smelling of dust and stones and administration, is part of the city's Police Headquarters.

Here during the week, righteousness, new China style, is upheld, and on Saturday nights, in the compound's Public Security Ceremonial Hall, unrighteousness flourishes as law-enforcement officials watch movies of a kind not considered safe for people outside the steel gates to see.

Nine men, most in khaki uniforms but without the red collar tabs that are a mark of active military service, climbed unsteadily out of the cars and were led like docile goats up the stone entrance steps. Then a woman, dressed in black, spectacles dominating her ivory-colored face, her neatly combed black hair gleaming, a suggestion of a smile at her purposeful mouth, was led after them. She walked erectly with slow, almost regal steps into the Ceremonial Hall, which was set up for a trial, with a green rug, a row of ten boxes for the accused, and six hundred invited guests whose role was to be "the public."

Jiang Qing, last wife of Mao Zedong and movie actress of another era, was to be tried by a special tribunal for counterrevolution, framing innocent people, generally throwing her weight around as a

13

senior member of her husband's government, and, not least, insulting the pragmatic new leaders of post–Mao China. ("Deng Xiaoping is a quisling and a fascist!" she had shouted.)

The stately widow came last into the hall because of all the ten defendants—the Gang of Four, the military associates of the former defense minister, Lin Biao, and Mao's amanuensis, Chen Boda—she had behaved worst in the pretrial interrogations. Had she not tried to ask, instead of answer, the questions? Did she not one day take off all her clothes to force her male interrogators to withdraw from the room? To put her in the number ten position was the all-male court's way of slapping her on the wrist. It was safer, too, to put at the front Wang Hongwen, youngest member of the Gang of Four, who before the trial had shown his compliance by confessing even to crimes he did not commit, rather than risk an unseemly outburst from a Jiang Qing who might have used the number one position to rumbustiously express the utter contempt she felt for the tribunal, the current Chinese government, and anyone who dared to oppose her.

Looking a decade younger than her sixty-six years, Jiang gave off more life and spirit than all the other defendants put together. On the faces of the military guards who dotted the chamber, one could read shyness, embarrassment, even guilt, all in sharp contrast with the haughty fearlessness of Jiang's expression. Not one wrinkle broke the chiseled grandeur of her face. Rumors over the years that her hair was false seemed laid to rest; no wigmaker would turn out a coiffure so perfect lest it *look* like a wig. Yes, Jiang Qing had looked after herself in her time as China's First Lady; sipping the liquid from eight boiled chickens each day had been good for her complexion and the sheen of her hair.

"Not so," she retorted to the presiding judge's assertion. The voice was deep but feminine; a *confident* voice. "I really have no idea," she declared grandly to an awkward question. Tossing her head up, she seemed to revel in the courtroom's anxiety at what her breathtaking defiance of convention might lead to next.

"Defendant Jiang Qing, what is your reply to this charge?" the tribunal president rasped after a projector flashed onto a screen a photocopy of a document that suggested Jiang Qing had intrigued against Premier Zhou Enlai. A furrow on her brow, Jiang leaned forward gravely, pressed a pair of earphones closer to her head, and looked up at the president. "I am a little deaf; I did not catch what you said." The voice cracked high with an actress's cadence.

"I wish to go to the toilet." Escorted by two young female soldiers, she sailed slowly to a side room. For an eternity she remained in the cubicle; the escorts, and after a moment others, too, wondered if the unpredictable woman would ever come out.

Was Jiang Qing, called now the "White-Boned Demon" by Peking's official press, in some strange way mistress of the bleak situation?

"Everything I did, Mao told me to do. I was his dog; what he said to bite, I bit." Nervous laughter rippled across the room at this devastating rejection of the charges piled up against her.

Jiang's real audience was larger than the thirty-five judges and the six hundred invited guests (gathered like so many pieces of scenery from various provinces of China, housed together, virtually sealed off from the rest of Peking, in the labyrinthine comfort of the Xi Jing guesthouse). Elsewhere within the Public Security compound, in a small room equipped with a row of closed-circuit TVs that showed the tribunal proceedings close up and from every angle, senior government figures huddled by the sets to see the White-Boned Demon without being seen by her. And Jiang Qing was addressing, too, the TV audience of millions who each night of the trial saw selected portions of her latest, perhaps her last, struggle against one more bunch of the "enemies" who had beset her all her days.

Having felt, since she was a small girl, subject to shackles of one kind or another, Jiang Qing had seldom borne any shackle with more dignity than, on this day in court, she coped with the handcuffs at her wrists and the railings that framed her like a picture in her defendant's box. She did not look as if she belonged within the pinched, staged ritual that began to unfold in the Ceremonial Hall. She seemed to be appearing before a crowd of millions in Tian An Men Square, watching for the cues, alert to each camera's position, making an appeal to some absent, suprapolitical force that could acknowledge her for what she believed herself to be.

There are people who find the world outrageous; Jiang Qing was one of them. Society had allocated no reserved seat for her. Few people seemed to be able to speak the language of her deepest emotions. Life itself was neither logical nor fair. Why do people kill each other? she asked herself. Why is China, with all its long centuries of greatness, such a barbarous place? Why do women have to put up with more than men?

It was a major puzzle to her that the world so blatantly failed to conform to her ideal imagination of it. She was far too confident to think that any part of the problem lay within herself. But she was disarmingly aware of the gap, and her life was one long effort to bridge it—through fantasy, in the theater, by blowing up her own individual will into a universe of its own, finally in a surge of political action relevant only to the imperious demands of her personality.

"You're talking like a child," the husband says to Nora in *A Doll's House,* a play that deeply influenced Jiang Qing from girlhood. "You don't understand the world you live in." And Nora, confused but stirring to assert herself, replies: "No, I don't. But now I mean to go into that . . . *I must find out which is right—the world or I.*"

The White-Boned Demon was sentenced to death, suspended for two years to "see if she repents." Long before that formality, the propaganda pens, the street cartoonists, the upright mothers and dutiful fathers and filial children of the Middle Kingdom had declared her a "traitor," a "witch," a "murderer," and a "prostitute." None of these charges she admitted.

"We've explained that she is a bad woman," a high Chinese official said to me with irritation. "Why are you interested in a bad woman? Write about a good woman!" To Jiang, it never seemed possible for a moment that anything she did was bad.

Born to a troubled family, Jiang Qing had tried to put behind her the memory of a violent father and a mother whose work as a domestic servant bordered on prostitution. Jiang made a fantasy world for herself, and it seemed natural that she went into the theater. Hardly less so that she gave herself briefly to a string of men, who all felt the power of her smoldering will: a conventional young businessman in Jinan; a brilliant radical of high family position in Qingdao; a theater writer of romantic character and cosmopolitan culture in Shanghai.

When the artistic world of Shanghai collapsed as Japan attacked, Jiang Qing again chose adventure. She presented herself at the dusty wasteland where the Communists were keeping out of Chiang Kai-shek's way as they tried to win the future by standing for Chinese nationalism in the war against Japan. Mao Zedong, a lecher and a country bumpkin, fell for the new arrival from Shanghai's bright lights. Accepting a drastic change in her free-wheeling life, Jiang married him—a man more than twenty years older than she, already twice married and the father of eight children, the top figure of the Chinese revolutionary movement. Mao treated Jiang as a "Nora," his playmate and supporter. Jiang accepted the role, biding her time.

The theater, politics—for Jiang the two realms were not very different. In both, her life mattered more than her art. When the time was ripe and Mao woke up to the fact that he needed her (as FDR came to need Eleanor Roosevelt), Jiang Qing used the same methods to make her mark on Peking's politics that she had used to make her mark on Shanghai's performing arts. She did not wait to be spoken to; she made the approach. Flashing her puzzling but arresting smile, she had her say—and often got her way.

When Mao sank toward death, Jiang thought it the most natural thing in the world that she should step up to be empress. Wu Zetian had proved thirteen hundred years ago that a woman could rule China effectively. Had Jiang not done an apprenticeship of thirty-eight years at the side of the brilliant, elliptical, overbearing Mao? She had always thought that big, smart, and powerful people took her for granted; now she could prove them wrong. Her final act of personal fulfillment would take the form of an empress's beneficent rule over the backward but adoring Chinese masses.

Jiang Qing failed her climactic test. To her bitter surprise, she joined the fixed array of the Chinese pantheon of demons. The masses of the Middle Kingdom began to curse the woman they had yesterday honored above all others. "The Chinese are not a very civilized people," Jiang said.

In our time a few nations have torn themselves to pieces of internal volition; Cambodia after Pol Pot took charge, and Uganda under Idi Amin are among the saddest cases. But only one of the world powers has over the past three decades worked itself into such a frenzy over power, policy, and personality as to cause loss of life in the hundreds of thousands, and years of diversion from rational purposes, out of a fixation on settling old scores—China.

In the story of Jiang Qing's career we watch men and women pursuing goals that led to this chaos and suffering. We come upon events and customs that suggest China is still a world apart, for all the superficial comings-together announced in recent years by politicians and the media. A world where children pay for the sins of their parents; truth means nothing compared with ritual; merit gives way to connections; revenge is a way of life; and the greatest transgression is to step out of line from the tribe.

China tended to view a willful woman in a leading political

post as a high-class prostitute who had used her feminine charms to get power. Having risen with Mao, whom she is alleged to have corrupted, Jiang fell with Mao. The power she won was never to be credited to her account.

If sex was in Jiang Qing's generation virtually the only route by which a woman could gain power, it was a hopelessly perilous route. A woman's power could be seen only as an extension of the power of some man. The prostitute may enter the halls of power—many have in Chinese history—and achieve great deeds there, but the nature of her route to power is never overlooked by the image-makers. At her trial, Jiang Qing, having lost power, was in the dock as a prostitute.

Her story is one of extraordinary will. Wolves, men, illnesses—she was always doing battle with an enemy. At the age of nineteen, she cut all past ties to go alone to one of the world's biggest, most dangerous cities and try her luck in the arts. Always she felt poised on the tightrope of her will. Fame and power lay waiting on one side; infamy and subjection glared from the other.

Like Joan of Arc, she was focused upon herself and she saw visions. Like Eva Perón, she watched almost as a spectator her performances before the masses who were her audience. Like Eleanor Roosevelt, she displayed single-mindedness and belief in herself in picking up power that slipped from a weakened husband.

In Jiang Qing, we Westerners, used to seeing the old civilizations of the East mainly as a museum of relics, come face to face with a living personality of universal dimensions, whose spirit speaks to the heart of ambitious women—and not a few men—everywhere.

"Let us not go too much into it," a current Chinese leader said of the Mao-Jiang Qing relationship. "Members of the Communist Party are not saints," Hu Yaobang went on. Indeed, they are not. A moment later, though, Hu lambasted a fallen and dead leader, Kang Sheng, for the "depravity" of his liaison with Jiang Qing. "I cannot find words to tell you about their personal relationship. . . ."

For the truth-makers of the Communist Party, the personal relations of the leaders are never deemed proper for the public to know about—*until* a particular leader is disgraced, and then the "depravity" of the fallen one is laid out in vivid detail. This is hypocritical, but that is merely its outward sheen. The really disgusting thing is the calculated effort to hide the basic workings of Chinese politics from scrutiny, foreign *and* domestic.

"Personalities don't count in our political life," the Chinese official told me. It has turned out in recent years that the personal relations of the leaders are more important in China than in any other major country. In this book about one remarkable personality who came to wield more power than any woman in the history of Communist politics anywhere, we see how the Mao-Jiang marriage shaped the lives of a quarter of mankind and how family feuds and personal grudges made playthings of policy issues.

"It is all water under the bridge," another Chinese minister said to me testily. "Now all we're interested in is economic development." Not so. Politics still eclipses economics in Peking. The newspapers of China and the speeches of its leaders are filled with the past for a very good reason: The legitimacy of the present powerholders depends (given the absence of elections) upon the "truth" about the past. If Peking's version of Jiang Qing's story should be a lie, then today's Chinese regime is based on a lie.

The Chinese have their ways of communicating, even if they are not the West's ways. The Chinese habit of saying nothing frontally about momentous occurrences gives the impression of a "deaf and blind history." When Jiang Qing exercised power, the newspapers gave no information on her past career, her previous marriages, her children. When she was arrested, nothing was reported of the circumstances, not one word of what she said to her assailants in her own defense. At her trial, the long indictment with its account of Cultural Revolution maneuvers *never once mentioned the Red Guards,* who were the shock force of that event.

Of course, no one, except the naïve foreigners, was expected to accept such silences. Subterranean networks of information filled the vacuum. In Chinese history it has long been thus; the unofficial story was called "outside history" or "wild history." It turns out that in the Communist era, hardly less than under the dynasties, the real story never appears in aboveground organs.

Apart from a date here, a selected fact there, the story of Jiang Qing will never be published in Communist China. This book tells Jiang's story on the basis of the eloquent "unofficial" voices of China: oral eyewitness accounts from the grass roots; testimony of those Chinese now outside China who watched, knew, hated, or loved Jiang Qing; documents of the Peking elite that were directed at a small readership but have reached me in the West.

For the Peking mandarins, history is moral judgment. In *The White-Boned Demon,* history is part at least of the story of what actually happened.

2

Growing Up, Reaching Out (1914–33)

I did not even have any underclothes.
　　　　　　　　—Li Yunhe (Jiang Qing)

In a lane of dust and dogs and gossiping neighbors, rich with the smell of vegetables being carried on carts, an attractive but harassed-looking woman of about thirty gave birth to a daughter. There was none of the hubbub that usually surrounded the arrival of a baby in this lane off a main street of low brick-and-wood shops, in a county town of northern China. A friend of the woman's served as midwife; the father was not present. The mother was fed a gruel of glutinous millet and brown sugar. In a ceremonial feeding, the baby's mouth was opened with a few drops of water. She began to cry fiercely.

It was 1914. The last dynasty of Confucian China had fallen three years before, but no fresh order had arisen. Traditionalists were sad at the passing of a settled world; moderns were angry at the obstacles on the path to a freer world. There was chaos within the land and the smell of war at its doorstep. The common people, not able to shape events, took refuge in family and economic activities. Their own tasks and troubles were quite enough to fill the day, leaving little time and energy for trying to understand the strange new talk about a "revolution."

Yet the baby girl was going to have a lot to do with the Chinese Revolution. Her cries now were purely personal; one day they would become the cries of political battle.

Zhucheng was a sleepy town of thirty thousand inhabitants, enclosed by ancient walls and gates. The surrounding countryside is rich in corn, peanuts, tobacco, and wheat. These people of Shandong Province are tall, sharp-featured, and dry in manner. They tend to be dogged in their ways and conscious of a long, brilliant past, which embraces the lives of China's two greatest sages, Confucius and Mencius.

Life here was more prosperous than in most towns of poor, crowded Shandong, though deteriorating since a railroad was built two decades earlier between the province capital of Jinan and the coast, bypassing Zhucheng. The town was near enough to the Yellow Sea to be influenced by foreign trade. And when China began to be carved up like a melon by the knives of more masterful nations at the turn of the century, the area felt the intrusion of Japan, which pushed Germany out of Shandong soon after the baby girl's life began.

The infant, whose first given name was Shumeng ("Pure and Simple"),* was born into an odd, troubled family. Decades later, when the child had become a woman of power, and such a legend in her own lifetime that the facts of her childhood were overlaid by myth, she remarked to a laborer in a receiving line during a visit to the city of Tianjin: "Your father was an oil worker, mine was a carpenter—we're both of the working class." But it was not quite so. The father was a carpenter who managed to start his own wheelwright's shop, acquire a small inn for overnight travelers, and later buy farmland.

Dour at best, her father, Li Dewen, drank heavily, and enjoyed a poor reputation in Zhucheng. A man of sixty when Shumeng was born, Li took little interest in her, leaving a totally negative impression on her memory of him. His relation with Shumeng's mother, ambiguous from the start, was remote when it was not stormy.

Shumeng's mother, much younger than the father, was one of two children, both daughters, of a school official in Jinan, a city some three hundred kilometers inland to the west. She cared doggedly for Shumeng, and left a much more favorable image in the daughter's mind than the father. Yet she remained a puzzle to Shumeng as a girl, and in later life the daughter's remarks about her mother were devoid of affection and included no comment on her character. People in Zhucheng thought of Shumeng's mother as a tender but worn and harried woman.

She was not the first wife of Li Dewen. The age difference was too great (almost thirty years), as was the age gap between Shumeng and various older brothers and sisters—the youngest of whom was a dozen years older than Shumeng.

* This was her "small name" (*xiao ming*), used until a more formal name (*xue ming*) was allotted to her when she went to school.

At one stage the household contained nine people, of whom Shumeng was by far the youngest. When Shumeng was at primary school, one of her father's sons (Li Ganqing) was a senior police officer, and a daughter was already married. It is also remarkable that Shumeng's grandfather, the school official in Jinan, should have allowed his daughter to cohabit with a craftsman in a small town three hundred kilometers away.

Shumeng was puzzled at her mother's irregular nocturnal comings and goings and defensive about her mother's motives. The child's reaction was understandable, for her mother was not the regular wife of her father. She was Li Dewen's concubine, or "little wife." To this day, her name is unknown, as are the date and circumstances of her death.

The family as a whole was not poor. Shumeng's father employed a full-time laborer, two blind men to do grinding, and occasional extra labor. His workshop did well enough during Shumeng's early childhood for him to sell it a few years later at a price that enabled him to buy a substantial piece of land outside the town.

At home, conditions were crowded when all the father's children by his regular wife were under the roof, but the house was comfortable enough. It was of whitewashed plaster, with brown wooden beams and fragile paper windows. There were three or four rooms, including a large kitchen, with its never-cold stove, greasy black woks, and dried vegetables hanging from the rafters. The floor was packed mud, the furniture was plain and solid in local wood, and oil lamps gave light.

When Shumeng lacked proper food and clothing, as she sometimes did, the cause was family quarreling, and to a degree the social disorder that threatened the entire province, not insufficient family income.

In Chinese, one word (jia) covers the meaning of the two English words "family" and "home," so basic in Chinese tradition is the idea of a family's physical togetherness. Childhood was supposed to be one's Golden Age. The whole meaning of life was contained in family relationships. When a young person got married, to a partner generally chosen by the parents involved, this was a terribly important event, at which one set of binding family ties was reinforced by a new set of family ties. Shumeng's life was to be most untraditional in all these respects.

Her first problem was that she was a girl. So earnestly did parents in old China hope for the birth of boys that it was not unusual to express disappointment at the arrival of a girl by giving it a first given name such as Xiao Cuo ("Little Mistake"). A daughter was not reared to remain in the household, as a boy was. She was a short-term blossom, to be plucked by anyone who wanted her, then taken off to *his* family hearth. Shumeng once heard her father curse the bad luck of having female children. She felt that was strange; her father himself was born of a woman; could it be so wrong to be a woman?

Shumeng's feet were bound, which was not too surprising in Zhucheng before 1920. The compressing of a girl's feet with tight swaddling was meant to make her look dainty and to signal that she was destined not for work but for marriage alone. "She hated the whole idea of it," a classmate recalled of Shumeng. "She took off the binding! So we always called her 'Renovated Feet.' Of course, the binding of her feet left its ugly mark—and gave a bandy-legged look to her walk for the rest of her life."

If Shumeng's parents would have preferred a boy, the fact that Shumeng's mother was her father's concubine made matters worse. The new wife was resented as an interloper. Her presence created complexity in the all-important matter of the inheritance. That she could hardly have been much older than Li Dewen's eldest children must have added to the strangeness of her (and Shumeng's) position.

Shumeng met with violence as well as causing some herself. Her father beat her, and so did a stern half sister. Yunxia, much older than Shumeng, had the same strong, longish face as Shumeng, but she was less wild. Shumeng was cheeky toward Yunxia, and her love of fantasy led her into pranks that annoyed her older half sister. In retaliation, Yunxia chased Shumeng around the house with a feather duster, beating her bottom in fury whenever she could catch up with her.

One evening when Shumeng was about five years old her father, whose nicknames included "Thieving Wolf" (*Lang Zei*) and "Master at Cursing," excelled even his reputation. It was the Lantern Festival, when the town was gaily lit and people drank and ate special fare, including cakes so large it took two people to lift one.

Perhaps Li had grown tired of his concubine. Perhaps the tensions between her and Li's regular family became too great for him to endure. Even if Shumeng's mother was not as "immoral" as official Chinese accounts assert, she was so much younger than Li that she may well have associated with other, younger, less bad-tempered men. For whatever reason, Li flew into a rage and ran after

Shumeng's mother with a spade. Fiercely he beat her on the back, then on the hands, breaking a little finger. Shumeng sprang to her mother's defense, according to her own story. Her father's flailing spade banged into the child's mouth and broke a tooth.

Fleeing this nightmare, played out in the open streets of Zhucheng, with Shumeng strapped to her back, the mother also fled from the life of the "Thieving Wolf."

"There was family pressure on the father," related an observer of the relationship, "to pay the concubine, Shumeng's mother, a sum of money in order to get rid of her." This must have been part of the background to the Lantern Festival fight. The parting between the young concubine and the older man did not seem to be sudden and complete, however. Shumeng was seen at her father's farm, bought in 1920, after the climactic fight between her parents. Her mother retained some contacts with Li Dewen's family, no doubt out of some hope for her "inheritance rights."

Shumeng and her mother had often seemed to be a group of two—the half brothers and half sisters were not present at the street fight—and now Shumeng was alone with her mother.

The mother slowly sank. Despite some continuing links with Shumeng's father's family, she spent most of the following years as a domestic servant, moving with Shumeng from one household, after mysterious ructions, to the next. For Shumeng, violence gave way to pathos, family tension to loneliness.

It was rare for a woman to be sent away by—or walk out on— her husband, and Shumeng's mother found herself in a sad state. Alone with her child, she was far from her own parents and hometown, open to all kinds of exploitation, an easy target for gossip about the ways of a wandering single woman. Soon after the split with Shumeng's father, mother and daughter retreated to the home of the mother's father in Jinan.

They soon returned to Zhucheng, because the mother was not ready to give up her tenuous claim to an inheritance (that is, financial support) from Shumeng's father. But dealings with the father's family proved hopelessly difficult, and whatever additional money the mother got from this direction, she still took to the road looking for work.

At two primary schools, which she attended with interruptions due to family exigencies, Shumeng's image and character began to take shape. She was a tall girl, a bit gawky, with a mouth a shade too large but a winning smile. Her hair was in two long pigtails, which brought her agony because the ordinary mode was a single pigtail, and two were considered newfangled, things fun to pull at.

More embarrassing were her clothes, which were neither new nor girls' clothes, but castoffs from her half brothers. Some fellow pupils at the second (and better-class) school laughed at a broken-down pair of shoes she used to wear. "Big Brother," they called the big toe that stuck out of one shoe. "Duck's Eggs" they cried in mockery of her protruding heels.

She was usually quiet, opening up rarely but impressing others when she did so. She was easily upset and quick to say what she thought, or to burst into tears. Her appearance could change strikingly from one day to the next, as her emotions made a plaything of her body, and illness began its lifelong *pas de deux* with her moods. In school as in the town at large, she was the target of the epithet, "girl without a father."

Particularly at the second school, which was a good one run by the county for the daughters of the relatively well-off, together with some "scholarship pupils" like Shumeng, she was an awkward, controversial child. This was probably because her family background did not equip her to look and behave as the other girls did and as the school expected.

She often fought with other pupils, perhaps because they bullied her for her appearance and her odd family background. Several teachers found it necessary to hit her; after she had daydreamed in class, one dragged her to the toilet and gave her five blows on the hand with a board.

Society did not set a good example on questions of violence and cruelty. Shumeng learned to count how many criminals were shot each night by listening to the number of rifle shots that cracked against the brick town wall. At the Little East Gate, quite near her home, she saw public executions by decapitation, and walking home from school she watched in terror as heads were carried dangling from a shoulder pole, still dripping blood. All this was done with the legal authority of the state, which made some people wonder if the existing state would last long.

After one semester, Shumeng was expelled from the county-run school, probably for fighting with other pupils. "I vowed never again to let anyone bully me," she later said of her experience at school, indicating that she had transmuted her awkward social situation into a sense of personal grievance.

Shumeng's mother, meanwhile, was leading an almost nomadic life in some kind of service to wealthy households. Even if one draws a veil over today's official Peking view of her as "immoral"— it is too automatic a condemnation—Shumeng's own later remarks about her mother, positive as they are, lead us close to the conclusion that sex was involved in her domestic service.

Years later, Shumeng told an interviewer that a landlord "who had a wife and several concubines but still no male offspring asked [her mother] to join his family as a servant"; and she conveyed mixed feelings about her mother's acceptance. "When I was only five or six," she said several times, "I learned to walk in the dark in search of my mother" (a remark that left the astute interviewer "wondering just what her mother's nocturnal employment was"; a resident servant, after all, is not habitually out late at night). She recalled staying in villages with her mother, and occasions when she was alone in Zhucheng because her mother was "away."

Why *was* the mother often out at night? Why would a hard-up, separated woman make trips out of Zhucheng? Why the moves from one household to another? These are not easy questions to answer on the assumption that Shumeng's mother was simply a domestic servant.

She was probably giving sexual favors as well as doing household work, a common occurrence in the establishments of the gentry. Perhaps she had been doing this for many years and met Shumeng's father in the course of a transaction.

By the mid-1920s life in Zhucheng for mother and daughter was insupportable. Contacts with Shumeng's father's family—the father himself died of typhus about this time—were empty of benefits to the needy pair. The social situation of a mother not living either with her husband's family or with her own parents was excruciating; the rumor mill ground on.

Nor was life in the houses of the gentry very stable or tranquil. Shumeng grappled with a landlord's daughter who had tugged at her pigtails, and she struck the sister of another on the breast for an insult. She tormented a gentry's dogs until they turned on her and bit her. In her traumas she concocted a fantasy with wolves cast in the role of her ever-present enemy.

The mother, in poor health now, gave up. She wrote a letter to her parents in Jinan, expressing anxiety about Shumeng's future and stating her desire to return to her own family's embrace. The parents were willing to care for both mother and daughter. It was unusual for a couple to assume responsibility for the daughter of a daughter. But they were old and in need of care and company. They had only one other daughter and were happy to "take a peach in place of the pear," a phrase for the building up of a family with substitute elements. And they had grandparents' curiosity at how Shumeng, whom they hadn't seen for four years, was turning out.

The mother sold some possessions, apparently including a portion of a house she had acquired from Li Dewen's estate, bought train tickets, hired a man to help prepare and carry the luggage, took Shumeng around to say farewells, and the two of them began a long walk northeast to the railroad town of Jiaoxian.

It is said that during their walk north, a handsome carriage came within an ace of running them down, and a fat man shouted from the carriage window: "Are you looking for death?" He leered at mother and daughter hatefully and went on: "You're just like dogs there on the road." To his own child, sitting beside him in the carriage, the elegantly dressed fat man said, sneering: "One is a woman dog, and one is a girl dog."* Shumeng's mother, in tears, murmured to her bitterly: "Who made you to be a girl?"

At Jiaoxian, Shumeng and her mother boarded the 9:30 P.M. train, supplied with *man tou* (steamed buns) and pieces of vegetable, and by next evening they were settled into the grandparents' house. The provincial seat of Jinan was a big, grand world compared with Zhucheng.

Lying in calm possession of itself nine kilometers south of the Yellow River, Jinan was a city of ancient Chinese-style houses and brick shops with open fronts. The street names reflected the city's political role: Judicial Yamen Street, Provincial Treasury Street, West Magistrate Street. There was a generous sprinkling of temples, theaters, and "flower houses" (brothels). The whole was set off by natural springs due to outcroppings of sandstone, and one of China's loveliest urban lakes, called Daming (Great Brilliance).

"A festive city, a commercial center and also a political pillar, which in its vanity has not yet cast off the air of the late Qing dynasty." The contemporary guidebook's description was apt, though warlordism had unsettled the city's life, its handicraft economy was holding it back economically as other Chinese cities began to modernize, and the population of four hundred thousand now included five thousand Japanese.

The grandfather's house was a comfortable low brick one built

---

* The sneering remark (*Zhe shi i ji mu gou he i ji gou nu*) could be translated, "One is a bitch and the other is its little bitch."

around a courtyard on Control Department Street, in a quiet but central part of the city. Shumeng resumed her education at Number Two Primary School Attached to Number One Teacher's Training College, on a graceful corner of the same street as her grandfather's house. She was given a new name, either by the family or at school, to mark a new phase of her life—Yunhe, "Crane in the Clouds,"* a rustic name.

"The name did not suit her," said one of her classmates. "She had very little of the harmony and serenity that 'Crane in the Clouds' suggests." The name also had a literary flavor which, in the classmate's view, was beyond the scope of the girl's narrow mind; perhaps the grandfather devised "Yunhe."

In additional ways the grandfather's help was important. Yunhe was able to leave behind the turmoil, violence, and gossip of her family's life in Zhucheng and set her feet on a path that potentially could lead to a settled life in a city of culture and refinement. There were only twelve thousand primary-school pupils among Jinan's four hundred thousand people (twenty-five hundred middle-school pupils); "Crane in the Clouds" was among the fortunate of Jinan's children.

Yunhe said she studied hard, yet her personal ordeals and the sharp gusts of her likes and dislikes seemed to dominate her life. Once a boy hit her, and some girls who were standing around clapped him for it. Yunhe did not fight back, despite her mortification, knowing she was isolated, yet neither did she ask for mercy as more blows came upon her. She clenched her teeth and stared at the ground. That night, members of her household scolded her for coming home late and then noticed a bruise on her face and a broken strap on her schoolbag. But Yunhe would say nothing of her ordeal; too proud to complain, she preferred to endure in silence the pain of her maladjustment.

She abhorred discipline. The Confucian "three obediences and four virtues" seemed to her inventions of the devil designed to prevent self-expression. (She had a point, for the three obediences were: A woman in her maiden home is to obey her father, a married woman is to obey her husband, and a woman after her husband's

---

* The Chinese attach great importance to the naming of a child. There is no set list of given names (Joan, Bill, Mavis, Horace . . .) as in the West. Any two characters (occasionally just one) can be chosen to form a child's given name. They may come from a poem, the classics, or family tradition; they may be inspired by the appearance of the child or the circumstances of its birth. So there is more flexibility to name giving in China than in the West and hence more significance to the name chosen.

death is to obey her son.) Yunhe's family argued, as was the custom, that she should study hard in gratitude to the family, but Yunhe felt unusually little family loyalty. Anyway, it was far more difficult for a girl to bring honor to the family than for a boy.

Still more fluidity entered Yunhe's life in 1926 or 1927, when she and her mother went north to the port city of Tianjin, to stay for a while with a half sister of Yunhe's. She did not go to school there but helped in the household, cleaning the rooms, washing clothes, shopping. Already a hater of housework and of the confinement of female members of a Chinese household in the 1920s, she sought a job with a tobacco company, in the ranks of the children who sat in rows hand-rolling cigarettes. But the family vetoed the scheme.

Back in Jinan, during 1928, Yunhe's mother faded from her daughter's life, so much so that many people who knew Yunhe thought her mother had died. It seems likely that the mother married again. Yunhe did not lose all contact with her (and later on, when she got a job, she sent money to her mother), but the close relationship between mother and daughter was over.

For years Yunhe's mother had been her protector. Often Yunhe had sat at home, alone and forlorn, waiting for her mother to come home, terrified that maybe she had fallen foul of a cruel man and would never return. It was not that Yunhe really understood her mother's world, or admired what she did understand of it. She did not express to others any heartfelt sympathy with her mother; the remarriage in 1928 probably added to Yunhe's reticence in talking to friends about her. The mother had doggedly fulfilled her duty to Yunhe, and yet there was not much in Yunhe's childhood years for her to look back on fondly. Her mother was a victim of old Chinese society, unable to be a truly free person, as Yunhe was determined to be. Yunhe's strongest reaction to her mother's sufferings was a passionate determination to get out of the world her mother had been trapped in. She wanted to throw herself into something fresh and different.

Yunhe, in her fourteenth year, was virtually an orphan in a strange city and a disordered epoch, a girl of fantasies with no clear plan or prospects for fitting into the world she found herself in. The grandfather wanted to see her better educated. But Yunhe was not one who liked to be disciplined; nor was it easy for a girl to gain admission to a middle school.

In Shandong, a province famous for its theater, there were, in addition to established, prestigious theater companies, a number of

low-grade, underground troupes. They performed vivid excerpts
from local opera. Often connected with secret societies, these
troupes obtained talented recruits from kidnaping outfits on the
lookout for footloose youth. "Golden boys and jade girls," as the
most attractive of the available young people were called, were supplied at a price by the kidnapers to families who needed a domestic
servant or who sought an attractive adopted child; to the brothels
that were numerous in the Daming Lake area (girls as young as sixteen could register as prostitutes); and to the theater.*

During 1928 Yunhe became part of one such underground
troupe, based at Licheng, a suburb of Jinan. Either Yunhe had been
kidnaped; or, confused, alone, and yet hungry for a fantastic adventure, she willingly joined the troupe to try her luck and earn her
keep without having to rely on her grandparents.

During many months (perhaps more than a year) with the
troupe, Yunhe appeared in small roles, and she did manual jobs, as
a new recruit was required to. She was living in the company of
people who were tough but also intriguingly different from any she
had previously encountered.

Did not boys and girls of the troupe find an excuse in the demands of their roles to slide a hand against each other? Did they not
glimpse more of each others' bodies, while pulling off their gaudy
costumes, than an ordinary Chinese man and woman saw of each
other's body in a lifetime of marriage? Did not the applause turn the
heads of these golden boys and jade girls for whom modesty was
supposed to be a great virtue? It was all true, and it changed
Yunhe's life.

She loved new things, she was drawn irresistibly to fantasy, and
the period in the theater troupe gave her a proof of an alternative
world, with fewer constraints than in the household or at school. In
this alternative world she could be an extrovert, which was the impulse of her own personality; it was as natural to be so in the theater
as it had been unnatural in more conventional grooves of society.

"Like a melon not ripe but soon to be ripe," Yunhe was attractive and yet still possessed an alluring air of innocence. She was con-

---

* Here is an account from that epoch of the way concubines, prostitutes, theater children,
and household servants were recruited: "Then, when the purpose of their visit was finally discussed, the girls would be brought in, nicely dressed for the occasion, their faces beautifully
powdered and painted. But the buyers were very cunning businessmen and could not be
cheated, and often they would compel the girl to lift her long, broad trousers or her gown that
they might see the color of the skin on her legs. Now and then a man would take a cloth, wet it,
and rub the powder off a girl's face to make certain the skin was fair beneath. And there were
times when he would feel her body here and there."

sidered a girl who "spoke well" and was capable of elegance when she was able to avoid impulsiveness. Her breasts were large for a girl of fourteen, her eyes were "glassy in their brightness," and she was often taken for an eighteen-year-old. "Her confidence in her attractiveness made her haughty and vain," said one observer. "At the same time she was sensitive to her poor upbringing, and there was a streak of servility, together with a gradually growing anger at the world." Some of the men in the troupe found her highly appealing. Others found her forward, a flower not content to await the attentions of the bees and butterflies but waving itself high and wide to meet them.

Yunhe loved the stage, finding excitement in the makeup, costumes, and bright lights, and she began to see in it a possible career. Still, a whiff of prostitution hung over the underground troupe, in which the jade girls were not only free of family supervision but also subject to the whims of moneymaking bosses. This gave Yunhe further experience of the predicament of a female in a situation—however appealing in its trappings—of fundamental powerlessness.

One night Yunhe's grandfather and his wife took an evening off from sitting around in anxiety over Yunhe's disappearance to see a performance of *Beating the Princess,* a Peking opera about a princess who is beaten because she doesn't want to attend a birthday party for her husband's father. Who should they see onstage, playing the main role of Duke Fengyang's beautiful but hapless wife, in a brilliant blue silk dress and a hat encrusted with pearls, her face powdered white like a freshly baked loaf, but their own lost granddaughter!

Did Yunhe want to go home? In recent weeks the hard-bitten, shady middleman who controlled the troupe apparently had begun to maltreat her. Future prospects were bleak in such a low-class circle where a young girl was not free. Yunhe's first taste of the theater had enticed her, but she also saw the troupe as a battleground of sex and money and male power. Although she probably had mixed feelings, she agreed, under her grandfather's persuasion, to go back to Jinan.

The grandfather scraped up the exorbitant sum that the troupe's boss, viewing his golden boys and jade girls as "money trees," demanded for her release. Yunhe bowed three times before this sinister figure, then departed in silence with her grandfather. The old man wished her to go to a conventional school again, but somehow the bees and the butterflies had turned the flower's face toward a fresh horizon; Yunhe had tasted the potency of fantasy as an answer to life's frustrations.

For Yunhe, home now was Jinan, an old city facing the challenge of reform. A new wave of leftism, nonconformity, and feminism pitted the progressive fringes of Jinan against the city's establishment. The conflict had a sharp personal meaning for Yunhe. Very likely her grandparents were seeking to arrange for her a marriage with a young man who would draw her off into a solid, secure household. Was there a way of avoiding such a fate by swimming with Jinan's new wave of modernism?

Yunhe heard about a newly formed Experimental Arts Academy, subsidized by Shandong Province, that was offering places for young people to pursue a career in art, music, and drama. She put down her name for the entrance exam. There was nothing to lose, she told friends. Unlike a try at the examinations for becoming an official, there was no loss of face if one did not succeed at an arts exam. And for a girl, more than for a boy, the risk of failure was less because everyone's expectations of a girl were less. To her delight and surprise, she was accepted as a student for the spring 1929 session.

"Kerosene has to go in the kerosene flask," the grandfather said with a sigh of pessimism, taking the view that some flaw in Yunhe's character was pulling her down to an inferior destiny.

Theater people had always been looked down upon socially, yet the reforming waves of the May Fourth Movement washed away some of this prejudice. The Experimental Arts Academy was a respectable, serious place. Its weekend performances by advanced students became events of note in Jinan. It was a sign of the new situation that the school was financed by the provincial Department of Education. Each student received an allowance of six yuan a month as well as free tuition and meals.* "We had chicken, duck, fish, and meat [a set phrase meaning an abundance of food]," recalled one student. Without the subsidy, Yunhe would not have been able to enroll. Her decision to seek entry was in part a decision to escape her grandparents' control, and this was possible only if she could dispense with their financial support.

Housed in an old Confucian temple, the Experimental Arts Academy taught classical music and drama, but it also was a harbin-

* For most of Yunhe's time in Shandong and Shanghai one yuan was worth about thirty U.S. cents.

ger of a new approach to the performing arts in a Shandong under Nationalist Party sway. Teachers such as Zhao Taimou, a well-known man of the arts who was the academy's head, and Wang Bosheng, whose drama classes influenced Yunhe, knew Western culture and believed that China's progress required a blend of Eastern and Western values.

"On opening day she was jumping around with vigor and excitement," an observer recalled. "She wore a white shirt, black skirt, and her two long pigtails. A sweet, innocent girl. She was given the nickname 'Little Rabbit.' " Soon she was rising at dawn to practice her scales and trills, and using the long mirrored wall of the rehearsal room to work on her gestures and facial expressions.

Recruits to the academy were supposed to be middle-school graduates—"or equivalent." Little Rabbit, not a middle-school graduate, crept in under the ropes of "or equivalent." A classmate called Wang Tingshu recalled: "Yunhe was one of only three girls, and because girls were in short supply for the performing arts, the standards were lower for them than for the men." There were two entrance exams for the academy, one held in Jinan, and one in Peking. The Peking route brought in some of the best students, and these recruits spoke a clearer Mandarin, the speech required for the stage, than the Jinan recruits.

"Yunhe passed the Jinan exam," classmate Wang explained, "and she would not have succeeded even in that but for an accidental factor." She had long, flowing hair, common in southern China but rare in northern China. One of the teachers, Wu Ruiyan, worried because she lacked girls with long hair who could play the part of saucy maids, was delighted when she saw Yunhe's flowing locks. This helped Yunhe "pass" the exam.

But once admitted, Yunhe cut off her hair! Influenced by the "new wave" of modern social thinking in Jinan, she wanted to show that she was a professional, just like the men, and not a pretty, helpless creature who would wait on the sidelines until a man came to scoop her up.

Wang, a dashing, stylish man, thin and energetic, who entered the academy by passing the Peking exam, went on: "Teacher Wu was terribly chagrined when she saw the long hair of her new student cut off, but Li Yunhe was not the kind of girl to be obedient if it didn't suit her to be so." Yunhe would have been perfect for the role of the saucy, rural maid in modern dramas. Shorn of her hair, for the time being she wasn't suitable for any role.

In old China the arts were seen in functional terms, as cement to keep in place the bricks of the Confucian social order. The plots of the operas reinforced filial piety. Storytellers were the common people's history teachers. Songs were meant to be sung as one worked.

But at the academy Little Rabbit studied plays that were weapons in the war of social change—"antifeudal plays," in the Communist cliché of a later day. She read foreign literature that, in contrast to Chinese tradition, celebrated individual will. Ibsen's *A Doll's House* was to color her thinking for life; "as soon as she read it," a classmate recalled, "she wanted to play the role of Nora and began to *think* of herself as a Nora who knew very well that she wanted to smash the door of the doll's house."

Yunhe did not learn any foreign language or receive any of the social or scientific teaching of a university education. But the studies at the Experimental Arts Academy were potent and exciting. They opened the students' eyes, changed their lives by turning them from ordinary youths into performers of potential star appeal, and put them into the Bohemian avant-garde of a society torn between the bonds of a crumbling tradition and a raw passion for reform.

It was a Westernizing education. In the music department—the other two were acting and playwriting—each student had to choose a Western or a Chinese instrument. Yunhe chose the piano. This meant putting a foot outside Chinese tradition; she learned music as individual self-expression. As for drama, the very idea of a country girl being taught to dress up and perform on a stage was inconceivable without the Western influence that came through Wang Bosheng and Zhao Taimou.

It was not that Yunhe shone as a student. "In Peking opera she used to get out of time with the music," Wang Tingshu explained, "and she'd reach for a certain pitch and fail to stay on it. Then there was the curse of her broad Shandong accent." Wang gave his interviewer a wry smile. "I'm sorry to say we laughed at her." At the piano, Yunhe's tempo was irregular, which led the teacher to hit her wrists with bamboo sticks to force her to play with more control.

Although Yunhe was a bit crude, she was sexually attractive to many of the men students. "She was definitely the prettiest of the girl students," said Wang enthusiastically. "She had a friendship with a music student called Tan Wen and an affair with a student of Peking opera called Wei Heling." That she quarreled noisily with some other male students, including Gao Yonghui, a specialist in modern drama, suggests either that she was a tomboy or that an aura of sexuality hung over her.

The centerpiece of the innermost chamber of the temple building was a grand, forbidding statue of Confucius surrounded by his seventy-two disciples and adorned with a ceremonial headdress. "We were all young and new to this old temple," Wang recalled, "and the place reeked of superstition. The buildings awed us, and although we thought we were 'moderns,' to a degree they scared us." No one dared to go into the innermost chamber, and especially at night it was considered spooky. "One day, one of the students announced a really terrifying competition. He said the aim was to discover which of the men really had guts. The prize would go to the one—if indeed there was one—who would steal into the inner chamber after midnight, approach the statue of Confucius, climb up, remove his ceremonial headdress, and bring it out into the light to prove his courage to his classmates." The offer remained open for several nights; no student was able to conquer his inhibitions. Then one night the dormitories erupted in amazement. A *girl* came out of the inner chamber clutching the ceremonial headdress, a look of brassy triumph on her face. It was Li Yunhe.

"After that, she was unforgettable," said Wang Tingshu. "It *amazed* us that a girl had done that. We men were really too frightened to do it, and it never crossed our minds that one of the girls would do it—it was Confucius himself, after all. But that girl just went and *did* it. She was a shocker, she made storms, she drew attention to herself."

During her one year or so at the Experimental Arts Academy, Yunhe learned quite a bit, developed her taste for self-expression, and eventually won praise for some intense, if melodramatic, acting. In the traditional operas, Yunhe played *qing yi* roles. These were mature leading-lady parts, of serious, tragic figures (as distinct from the *xiao dan* roles, portraying servants, younger sisters, or flirtatious girls). Those who liked Yunhe's acting—and not everyone did— liked the vivid, wild colors she brought to her *qing yi* roles of tragic heroines.

But as she advanced—the more so as she advanced—Yunhe felt herself to be living in a jungle where struggle was at a premium. Each day she girded herself for the next insult, and tried to plan a way to deal with it. Like almost any girl of talent in the China of that time, she was faced with a contradiction. Not expected by her family to earn money or bring much honor to the family, but merely

to catch a man, she was encouraged to make herself pretty, even coquettish. Yet that very coquettishness in a girl of spirit was easily
taken for pushiness, and her talent was viewed maliciously, virtually
as a prostitute's offering. So if Yunhe was an angular spirit, the reasons lay not only in her own personality but also in the situation that
she, as a girl from a humble family in a college of mostly well-off
boys, found herself in.

"She was obviously from a fairly poor family," said Wang
Tingshu. "Most of the students received money each month from
their parents—but not Yunhe. In the case of Yunhe's family, no one
asked about them, because knowing their situation was a lowly one,
we had no desire to meet them."

The three girls shared one dormitory room, which, like the
classrooms, was part of the former Confucian temple. Yunhe fought
with both her roommates. There were disputes over roles in plays
and because Yunhe felt slighted by remarks about her odd clothes.
And tensions arose from the fact that one girl was a sister of Professor Wang Bosheng, and from Yunhe's habit of seeing more boyfriends than the other two did.

One evening Yunhe seized a chance to turn the tables on one of
her privileged girl classmates. At the popular weekend performance
of *Tragedy on a Lake,* a play by Shanghai writer Tian Han, the
leading role was being played by the student who was the sister of
Wang Bosheng. But on this Monday, at an additional show, Yunhe
was given the role. Though the audience was smaller than at the
weekends, she saw an opportunity to vindicate herself.

Yunhe hurled herself into the role of the tragic heroine so fully
that nearly everyone in the auditorium cried. Whether in the moment's emotion, or in excitement that she had struck back at her enemies with a triumphant performance, tears began to stream from
Yunhe's own eyes. Backstage, as she wiped off her makeup, the
academy director and her drama teacher strode in to praise her.
Overcome by jostling, disparate emotions, she again burst out crying
and rushed from the dressing room, leaving her mentors open-
mouthed.

In late 1930, the Shandong Province Experimental Arts Academy closed its doors, a victim of political change that sliced away its
budget. The half-trained students had to face a precarious world.
The arts in Jinan were being pinched and pressured by warlords and
the Japanese. A few students were taken on by Peking theatrical

companies. Others found work in the more modernized world of Shanghai movies. Many abandoned the performing arts for mundane jobs.

"Yunhe and I and some others went to Peking," Wang Tingshu recalled. "Our teacher Wang Bosheng took us. He included us in a 'Singing Society' that he formed, and he helped us get small roles in the theaters of the capital." But Yunhe did not succeed in Peking, despite brief appearances in *Beating the Princess* and an opera about an ambitious prostitute. "She just wasn't abreast of the Peking style," explained Wang. "With her local ways and speech, she was not accepted by Peking audiences or theater companies."

Back in Jinan, no one offered Yunhe a position. Nor did she have a comfortable, acceptable family world to return to. She knew at that moment that she was handicapped by the lack of a regular advanced education and a secure family background. It seemed to her that only what she could grab by her own talent, personality, or scheming would ever be hers.

A young man called Fei, a middle-school graduate who liked Peking opera and modern plays, went to the Arts Academy to see a performance of *Tragedy on a Lake*. Yunhe happened to be appearing that night. Fei, the son of a Jinan merchant, was transfixed by Yunhe's style and her beauty. Some years older than Yunhe and quite presentable, Fei was a practical man of filial character. Yunhe was pleased that her appearance in *Tragedy on a Lake* had electrified a man in the audience. She and Fei met several times.

As the academy closed its doors, Yunhe was at a loose end and hard up, her semesters at the academy having put her even farther at a distance from her remaining family members than previously. More than one friend advised her to bend before the prevailing wind and accept security: "One must not let the golden turtle get away" was the maxim for a girl in the face of a "good offer." At the end of 1930 she married Fei and went, as custom dictated, into residence as a captive daughter-in-law in the merchant Fei's house.

It seemed a backward, very traditional step. Perhaps Yunhe's grandparents reasserted their influence—Yunhe still was only sixteen—and played a role in encouraging Mr. Fei. "There was a wedding price to be paid by most brides," Wang Tingshu recalled. "At the academy we all assumed it was impossible, for this reason, for Yunhe to marry at that time. Perhaps family members paid the wedding price for her to marry this young man."

Or perhaps Yunhe made the decision entirely by herself, simply seeing no alternative until another door opened in the world of the arts.

The marriage lasted only several months, the last weeks full of turmoil and recriminations. Gossip had it that Yunhe was lazy, "sleeping until the sun rose to the height of three sticks" (about 10:00 A.M.), sitting around "like a rich madam" who expected "others to go to the kitchen and bring dishes to her." She was accused of lacking respect for Fei's mother, being unaccustomed to household rules, always away at a party or with questionable friends, and unable to grasp that she was no longer on the stage but in the real-life situation of a newly married woman who ranked lowest in the Fei family.

Life in the Fei household was economically comfortable, but that was not what mattered most to Li Yunhe.

As tensions mounted, Fei is supposed to have blazed at her: "You make even the chickens fly and the dogs run." Before the marriage, the idea of living with an actress was exciting to Fei, but afterward, exercising his prerogative to possess his wife body and soul, he expected the flightiness to give way to homely virtues. Yunhe, for her part, on this occasion as in later life, did not see why marriage should be allowed to stunt her personality. The common old saying, "When you marry a chicken, stick with the chicken, when you marry a dog, stick with the dog," was altogether too stoical for her nature.

On a stone park bench beside Daming Lake, as pleasure boats glided across the porcelain-blue water and ducks cried out a mad message, the unhappy pair transmuted anger into grim negotiations. Yunhe is said to have demanded a "small household" (*xiao jia ting*), which would have meant splitting up the "stem family" (a two-generation family) and living with Fei as a household of two. She told Fei to choose between a wife (herself) and a home (*jia*—the larger Fei family).

A simple nuclear household was unusual for China in 1930, and it was outrageous for the young wife (as distinct from the parents of the husband) to propose it. Fei concluded, surely correctly, that such a demand was a tactic; that "his" actress was no longer his and that she wanted a divorce. Probably Yunhe wanted Fei to propose divorce; that way the property settlement would be more in her favor.

In the modern fringe of Jinan society, it was almost fashionable, if still a bit daring, for an educated young woman to seek a divorce. It was like opposition to foot-binding, prostitution, and the custom of a wedding price, and like support for free marriage and celebration of Women's Day on March 8—a badge of emancipation.

Yunhe consulted a close girlfriend, a modern and Bohemian person. The girlfriend went to Fei and bargained on Yunhe's behalf about the terms of the divorce. An "unconditional divorce," meaning that the husband's side would make no claims upon the wife, was arranged. Yunhe, confused, relieved, having made a mistake and corrected it, and beginning to realize that she was attracted to normally forbidden realms, enjoyed a momentary and melancholy freedom. The divorce was a great embarrassment to Yunhe's grandparents; it cut her off even more than before from family moorings.

Yunhe's mind turned to Shanghai, China's largest city and the hub of its entertainment industry. Tan Wen had gone there, and she was quite fond of him. Wang Tingshu was also there; she knew he liked her, and if she concentrated on him, perhaps she could like him. But Shanghai was 560 kilometers to the south, and Yunhe had no connections outside Shandong Province and too little money to wander anywhere for long. She had experienced much for a girl of sixteen, but her feet were set on no clear path, and a gap yawned between her daily life in Jinan and the dreams she had begun to have for her future.

Yunhe inquired about the former Arts Academy director, Zhao Taimou, who had praised her acting in *Tragedy on a Lake*. She heard he was in Qingdao, as dean of its new university, and academy classmates told her that this port city, eighty kilometers east of her home town of Zhucheng, was a lively spot for the arts and politics. Perhaps Zhao could help her.

She bought a train ticket, bundled up her few possessions, carefully secreted in her clothing the money she had received from Fei at the time of the divorce, and feeling she had little to leave behind in Jinan, went east to Qingdao.

Each time Yunhe broke up with a lover, she left town and started a fresh life in a different city. It happened with Mr. Fei; it would happen in identical fashion with her second and third husbands.*

Qingdao was a newer city than Jinan. With its cotton mills and German cobblestones, Qingdao was an ocean-minded, industrial

* Later in life, Yunhe would have cause to reflect wistfully on how much more stable the childhood of her fourth husband, Mao Zedong, was than her own. Mao never left his native village in Hunan Province until the age of sixteen. By that age, Yunhe had resided in three towns and numerous houses, lived away from her family, and had had boyfriends and one husband. Mao's father was strict, but not violent and uncaring like Yunhe's. His mother, a devout Buddhist, was a simpler and calmer woman than Yunhe's mother. Nor did Hunan in the 1900s experience the social upheaval and imperialist intrusion that Shandong did in the 1920s.

city of some four hundred thousand inhabitants, a creation of the Treaty Port era that had brought China and the West jarringly yet seductively into contact. If Jinan belatedly had begun to modernize under the Nationalists, Qingdao was in its bones a modern city. In avant-garde culture, socialist ideas, and nationalist agitation against Japanese aggression, it was ahead of the Shandong capital. In atmosphere and layout it was a semi-Western city.

Yunhe wrote a note on a card to Dean Zhao, who was also a professor of literature, identifying herself as his former performing arts student from Jinan. But Zhao did not offer her a job or a place as a student at Qingdao University—either of which she would have jumped at—even when she burst into tears at his desk. All she got from the dean was a temporary room in a dormitory, where she sat around wondering how she might break into Qingdao's cultural life.*

Yunhe decided to use the back door and approach Zhao's wife. Boldly she took a horse-drawn carriage (*ma che*) to the house of Yu Shan, who was a specialist on Peking opera, equally as distinguished as her husband. An elegant woman from a social class several notches above Yunhe's, her family influenced by Protestant Christianity, Yu Shan was taken by the girl's spirit and sympathetic toward her plight as a wandering divorcee in a family-minded society. She helped in two ways.

Qingdao University library employed a host of minor clerks, as Chinese libraries do, and Yunhe soon found herself one of them, thanks to Yu Shan's intervention with her husband. The library building, on a hillside with a sea view, was in Germanic concrete (the campus had been a German military base), with red tiles, and glassless windows of an attractive lattice pattern, painted red to match the roof. Yunhe sat at a tiny wooden table inside the front doorway, its top decorated with a half-moon portico, in a cotton dress of Western style, and wrote out book borrowing cards in her stylish handwriting. The library was in the middle of the campus, lecture halls to one side, neat Western-style dormitories to the other. Yunhe met people and felt the pulse of campus life. She was a girl who drew attention to herself. She gossiped intelligently; when news reached her, it went in one ear and out her mouth.

As a library clerk she had the right to audit classes. She went to

---

* Years later, Yunhe made no mention of her lack of qualifications in speaking of her disappointment with Zhao; she explained her clash with him in terms of his timid reformism as opposed to her full-blooded revolutionism.

lectures on the history of literature, Chinese and foreign, and on creative writing, most of them given by professors of left-wing views who had studied in the United States and, returning to a China in flux, were now immensely influential on the minds of a questing generation of Chinese intellectual youth. She wrote stories and poems in the zealous style of the time. She even wrote a play, *Whose Crime?*, about a young leftist whose political activities brought about his mother's death and his own arrest. But none of them were good enough to make anyone feel she had a career ahead of her as a writer. In reaching up to the field of literature, Yunhe showed her brassy way of knocking on any desirable door, however much it may have seemed to be above her level.

As always, Li Yunhe made a striking impression on some people, but marred her prospects by fighting with others and overreacting to small setbacks; she was quite unable to find a middle path between outbursts that were unfair to others, and wounded retirement that was unfair to herself. Professor Yang Zhensheng, author of a famous novel, "humiliated" her, she said. Her drama teacher, Professor Zhao Binge, laughed at her as a political fool. Dean Zhao marked her down as a troublemaker. Many of her fellow students, moreover, often found her aggressive, awkward, or unpredictable. Never mind; at Qingdao University Yunhe's days were soon full of things more delightful and important than academic details.

Yu Shan's second contribution was to introduce Yunhe to a brilliant student and political activist, Yu Shan's own younger brother Qiwei.* "He was fairly tall for a Chinese," said Nym Wales, the wife of Edgar Snow, "a little unkempt in his long Chinese gown. His face was handsome and expressive, with an easy smile." Mrs. Snow, like many others, was greatly impressed by Yu Qiwei's character and ability. "He was cool and calm and gentle and tolerant. He had the quality of leadership—it permeated the room as he walked in, even though his manner was quiet and rather shy." Women liked him.

Yu Qiwei was a leader of the Communist underground which, in Qingdao as elsewhere, enjoyed complicated, ambiguous links with aboveground performing arts and literary circles. He was an upper-class youth who had leaned down socially to aid the Commu-

* It is possible Yu Shan took this step out of anxiety that Yunhe and her husband, after a poor start, had become all too friendly for Yu Shan's comfort, and because she was unwilling to make a fuss with Zhao for fear of the consequences to them all if he should lose his job as dean.

nist cause. Yunhe was a girl of humble origin who was looking upward for any cause in which she could fulfill herself.

After being frequent guests together at Dean Zhao's house, on a leafy hillside where the two-story brick villas with red tiles, tall chimneys, and green-painted window frames recalled a seaside city in Europe, the pair grew closer.

The city's center of attraction is Qingdao Pier, long and handsome, with chains hanging gracefully between its steel posts, each one holding up a magnolia lamp, and a pavilion in traditional style at the pier's far end. Yunhe and Qiwei went there at sunrise, when the smell of salt and fish filled the nostrils and the city began to present itself like a German painting against the hills. More often they went to the pier at night. As moonlight made a silver field of the sea, they would huddle together against the railing, watching the boats, whose lights twinkled like stars in a black velvet sky, or go for long walks by the seashore, chatting about the women's movement, socialism, free love, *Dream of the Red Chamber* and other novels, and China's peril in the face of imperialism. Qingdao is a city of beaches, and Qiwei would go swimming, while Yunhe, who did not know how to swim—she had never seen the sea until she came to Qingdao—would sit in a boat and watch him in his brief, modern swimsuit. They went for long walks on the fine white sand of the seashore. They combined business with pleasure by going as a couple to seminars and progressive cultural events.

"The pair fell in love," a close relative of Yu Qiwei's recalled, "and during 1931 they began living together." It was a modern marriage, without a certificate and apparently without any ceremony.

Yunhe had found a partner light-years ahead of Mr. Fei. A young man of wit and knowledge, a biology major whose grades would have been even better if he had not spent so much time on politics, Yu was from a family that combined idealism with social prominence. His involvement in radical politics gave him, in Yunhe's eyes, an attractive aura of mystery, of having a sense of mission. Living with him in the modern, antifeudal mood of Qingdao at the time brought no daughter-in-law's servitude and few household chores.

Thanks to Yu, whose job in the university's Communist group was chief of propaganda, Li Yunhe entered the circle of the Communist Cultural Front. Apparently she was able to join the League of Left-Wing Theater People and the League of Left-Wing

Writers, on the strength of a few manuscripts, much enthusiasm, a forceful approach to older men, and Yu's influence. After the "September 18 Incident" of 1931, which led to Japanese seizure of three provinces of northeastern China, and at Qingdao University brought class boycotts and faculty struggles (over how radical the modes of resistance to Japan should be), she joined the emotionally red-hot Anti-Imperialist League. She threw herself into the Seaside Drama Society, a group typical of the times, which pitted the power of dramatic art against that of Japanese guns, taking to rural communities plays such as *Lay Down Your Whip,* a patriotic story of Manchurian refugees suffering under Tokyo's rule. She felt a part of history, caught up in a movement that promised to lead China—and herself—to a new high land.

Yunhe's feelings of national indignation were strong and genuine, yet her political knowledge was meager—she did not even know the difference between the Communist Party and the Nationalist Party. She was becoming an actress of some accomplishment and an asset to Communist-front circles, yet this activity gave her little status and was second best to creative writing and academic studies, in which areas she did not shine. She was really an appendage to the dynamic Yu Qiwei.

Yu charmed her, lifted her eyes to new horizons, not least the gathering cloud of the Communist movement, and introduced her to interesting people who were socially of the elite even as they moved to the verge of being political outcasts. For months Yunhe did not know that Yu was a Communist; if he returned very late to the apartment, she would accuse him of being out with another girl, when in fact he had been at a cell meeting. But gradually Yu as a committed political activist worked an influence on the malleable Yunhe.

"Yu was really a superior kind of person," Nym Wales recalled, "and so I have always thought that [Li Yunhe] could not have been terribly different—otherwise he simply would not have linked up with her."

One chilly day in February 1933, as a fog lay over the harbor, Yunhe walked with her arm around a thin male student along a cobbled street in the industrial quarter, inconspicuous amid the pale, drawn faces of workers making their way home from breweries and cotton mills. The pair moved slowly, heads inclined together in amorous talk.

Yunhe had worked hard for this moment and paid money for

it, though she barely knew the man whose arm held her tight—it was not Yu—and she did not know the destination of this late-afternoon stroll. Near a small park with cypress trees, pruned shrubs, and a pavilion housing a marine exhibit, they turned into an alley. The man swept his eyes to the rear, then they disappeared into a warehouse. Half an hour later Li Yunhe was registered, sworn in, and commissioned as a member of the Communist Party of China, Qingdao branch.

For all the danger involved, which called for subterfuge in dealing with key Party figures, Yunhe had taken this step out of a fuzzy motivation. It was true that she had come to hate the old Chinese social order—a natural, if not sufficient, springboard into the Communist faith—yet had it not been for Yu Qiwei she would not have found herself in the warehouse, signing on with the Chinese Revolution. Even as she crossed that threshold her heart remained set on the liberty and fantasy that could be found in the theater. Given the mood of the time, when the arts were left-wing virtually by definition, an ardent young person did not have to choose —yet—between the self-expression of the stage and the self-abnegation of the Communist Party.

Party member Li Yunhe sometimes looked like a scarecrow, yet she was not without style. It was *de rigueur,* when it was not unavoidable, for young political activists to look down-at-heel, eat irregularly, and flout all conventions; Yunhe was no exception. "Two Stalks" she was nicknamed, for her skinny legs, short dresses, and lively gait. But she stood out as a girl of unusual attractiveness when, at a special event or during an evening of relaxation, she would appear in a blue silk *qipao,* with its high mandarin collar and slit skirt.* She would smile enticingly and listen intently, flatteringly, to the passionate political utterances of the men in her circle, only now and then adding in a resonant voice a brief, modest remark of her own.

Suddenly Yunhe lost Yu Qiwei. The Nationalist government began a crackdown on "the fifty most influential Communists of the city." Qingdao University was under pressure to squeeze out the Communist students; apparently some were offered fifty yuan as an

---

* *Qipao* means "banner robe," and it was the Manchus, called bannermen, who brought the garment into Chinese life. The Manchus were somewhat nomadic, and the women were wild and tough. Reaching the Chinese court, the Manchus felt they should feminize their women. The *qipao* was the result. As well as a high collar, it has a crescent-shaped opening on the right side extending from under the chin to the armpit, a fitted waist (to prevent unladylike movements), and slits at the side that permit a gliding walk (but not long strides). The color blue in a *qipao* stood for loyalty.

inducement to leave. In the tightened political atmosphere, Yu Qiwei was tracked down and arrested while conferring one evening with two Communist colleagues in a park on Sun Yat-sen Street. He was put in prison, and Yu Shan sent for Yunhe to tell her the news. Yunhe was devastated. She cried, and she lost her grip on herself. For weeks she remained deeply shaken and began to wonder if the Communist path was for her.

After some months, Yu was released. His family was the type that could bring political influence to bear. Yu Shan contacted Qiwei's uncle, Yu Dawei, a senior official in the Nationalist government at Nanjing. Yu Dawei intervened on his nephew's behalf. "Be of quiet mind and not agitated," he cabled Yu Shan, quoting Confucius. Yu Dawei felt that his nephew and his circle were "really just eager patriots . . . They were young, and opposed to foreign bullying of China. I did not feel that they belonged in prison."

After Yu Qiwei came out of prison, he left Qingdao. The Communist Party evidently assigned him to new tasks; at any rate, he went to Peking to work in the radical student movement there. Yunhe was bereft. Only when Qiwei was imprisoned did she realize how deeply fond of him she was. Perhaps she felt that he could have stayed on in Qingdao had he really wanted to. While Qiwei was in prison she had eased her loneliness by taking a boyfriend—a student of physical education called Qiao—and this may have turned Qiwei against her. It is also possible that Yunhe "betrayed" Qiwei politically, whether knowingly or not, when she was questioned about him by the police.

Or perhaps Yunhe began to think that the entire Yu family—Qiwei the Communist, Yu Shan the elegant woman of the arts, Yu Dawei the uncle who was an important minister in the Chiang Kai-shek government—dwelled in waters beyond her depth.

At a low ebb, she decided to leave Qingdao. As in Jinan, the end of a marriage made her wish to change her entire environment. Nothing held her back from an effort to make a fresh start in a different city. Why not head for the bastion of self-expression, China's New York, the bitch-goddess city of Shanghai?

Yunhe's lonely childhood resulted in an almost un-Chinese individualism of spirit. She resembled the young Eleanor Roosevelt, who was also a lonely child, not close to her parents' other offspring, orphaned early (at age ten), and often embarrassed by the inappropriate clothes she was given to wear. Both women turned the traumas of their early years into sources of creativity and independence of spirit.

Most of the people around Yunhe were brought up to be, and *sought* to be, like everyone else. As average Chinese children, they traveled a road from indulgence during infancy to harsh discipline during youth. Yunhe was different. With her blazing will and her stock of what she considered to be especially unhappy memories, the last thing that Yunhe wanted was to be like other girls.

She did not have the experience—or the problem?—of a father pushing her into an ultrafeminine role, molding her into a dependent little girl, preparing her as a doll for a future master's amusement. On the contrary, she lacked the constant love of a male protector into her adolescence, just as she missed out on the give and take that close brothers and sisters provide.

After the early years of her mother's coddling, Yunhe, instead of being sharply reined in, was left much to her own devices. Her self-esteem was not struck down, in the usual Chinese style, by a heavy weight of parental authority and group pressure. She was terribly alone—for better or for worse—which is the last thing a young Chinese expects to be.

Along with independence of spirit, there grew in Yunhe a conviction that she would be required to struggle if she were not to be trampled upon. Disorder and strain in her upbringing led to anxiety about what might befall her if she was unwary. She had to resist older men (her father, the underground theater troupe boss, Mr. Fei); she dealt with and meted out violence; she was conscious of living in a disintegrating society that could not promise justice or certainty. It did not seem natural to Yunhe—though it was the Chinese family and social way—to seek peace at any price and "put into her stomach" (hide) any feelings of hostility. She would make a polarization even when the ingredients for it were hardly there; far from masking her feelings, she used them as weapons of struggle. Her experience of family quarreling probably gave her personality a narrow-minded, scheming streak.

Feeling deprived, Yunhe sought revenge, and so a third basis of her personality (together with independence of spirit and the impulse to struggle) had shown itself as she grew up and reached out in Shandong. Filial piety and a general ingrained deference to authority were supposed to make a young Chinese person stoical about trials. Yunhe, however, often hit back at her enemies; and when she could not do so, she stored up the grievance for a future accounting.

"Her career seems amazing to me," said Wang Tingshu, Yunhe's Jinan classmate, "when I think back to the Li Yunhe I saw day by day. She eventually became a 'theater lord,' spinning the artistic life of China around her little finger. But I know she's a naïve person. Tough, yes, and very passionate, but simple and narrow." Wang's eyes shone with the memory of those times together in Shandong. "Should I feel pity that a lofty label has been put on such an ordinary piece of goods? Or should I be comforted that she made it, that the Yunhe I knew rose so high?"

3

Onstage in Shanghai (1933–37)

All I knew was that I wanted to feed myself
and that I adored drama.
         —Li Yunhe (Jiang Qing)

Sailing down the coast from Qingdao to Shanghai, cooped up in a tiny berth, Li Yunhe worked herself into a high state of nervousness, wondering how she would fare when faced with the new levels of talent, beauty, and toughness of the "city for sale." When the dumpy steamer eventually left the East China Sea and entered the winding yellow strip of the Whangpu River around which Shanghai clusters, she felt weak from the assaults of two of her perennial enemies: illness and the male sex.

She vomited most of the way, for the sea was rough, and she had never been on an oceangoing boat before. Worse, an unwelcome activist from Qingdao, Wan Laitian, formerly of the Arts Academy in Jinan, where Yunhe met him, had been assigned by united front circles in Shandong to keep an eye on her during the voyage. He paid more attention to her than she wished. He took advantage of her seasickness to try to dragoon her into sharing a hotel room with him on arrival at Shanghai. What a tedious pig he was, she felt.

As the steamer docked amid the sailboats, foghorns, cluttered wharves, and impatient crowds of China's largest city, Yunhe fled the deck as fast as she could, her high heels hardly keeping pace with the scramble of her long legs down the gangplank, so desperate was she to put her sickness out of mind and the presumptuous male escort out of sight. Would Shi Dongshan be there, as planned, to meet her?

Her eyes searched the pier for this movie director, a friend of Dean Zhao's and Yu Shan's, at whose house he met Yunhe. Anxiety almost brought on another fit of vomiting. Suddenly Shi appeared, with a silver-colored Morris taxi, and whisked her (minus a piece of luggage that in her agitation she left behind) to his room in a crowded section of the inner-city district of Hongkou (Mouth of the Rainbow).

Shanghai was just past the peak of its spectacular career as a Western toehold in China and a magnet for the Chinese entrepreneur. Exciting but heartbreaking, hedonistic yet full of Christian missionaries, corrupt and at the same time a nest for left-wing idealists, rich in opportunity and rife with injustice, a congenial base for cocky Europeans doing business in the Far East but poised for the destruction of its freewheeling old ways by assaults from Japan, Shanghai was a cauldron of contradictions, a city that wore its heart on its sleeve and took in its stride the epoch's kaleidoscope of greed, thrills, and death.

If Peking was politically minded, Shanghai more often had money on its mind. The Nationalists ruled harshly and inefficiently. Even people who closely followed politics took little notice of the recently decimated Communist Party. Virtually no one outside the thin ranks of the Party faithfuls had heard of Mao Zedong, the "peasant Communist" who was in the inhospitable mountains of Jiangxi Province raising an army.

The Shanghai headquarters of the squabbling Communist Party espoused an "urban path" to power, while Mao and others who had been driven out of the cities by warlords and Nationalists in 1927 resisted the urbanites and trod a "rural path." Shanghai's Communists, who disapproved of Mao's guerrillaism and bowed a knee to Moscow, worked underground; yet as in Qingdao—and on a grander scale—they wielded enormous if indirect influence on literature and the performing arts.

The girl of nineteen arriving to try her luck in Shanghai, like the city itself, had no awe for the past or long-term vision of the future, but only an eye for what the present moment could offer. Insofar as she was a leftist, the "urban path" suited her, since she couldn't tell millet from sorghum, or pick a mule from a water buffalo. Young and energetic, aspiring to be an actress, she had come to the one city where success, if it was within her capacity at all, could be won; and where failure, for a woman of humble origin seeking work in the arts, would very likely bring the bitter alternative of prostitution.*

---

* In 1934, 1 person in 130 in Shanghai was a prostitute (the respected newspaper *Shen bao* reported), compared with 1 in 960 in London, 1 in 580 in Berlin, and 1 in 430 in Chicago.

"You could see she had a rustic background," recalled Kang Jian, a movie actress whose career unfolded in the same years as Yunhe's. "She was a frugal girl, not especially dressed up, as people later accused her of being. She was quite attractive, but her clothes hung on her, and her legs seemed too long."

Of her acting potential, the very successful Kang Jian, who had arrived in Shanghai from Nanjing and who was to have boyfriends who were also at one time or another Yunhe's boyfriends, had a mixed view. "Not bad as a stage actress, but she lacked a good camera face: too bulgy in the jaw, teeth too prominent. I, from Nanjing, wasn't up to Shanghai sophistication. Li Yunhe, when she first came, was very far from it. If you weren't 'Shanghai,' people could tell—and you *had* to be 'Shanghai' to get the top movie roles."

Shanghai women shocked Yunhe at first. To a Northerner—even one like Yunhe who fell short of Peking restraint and taste—the females in the upstart city of Shanghai were brash, loud-mouthed, flirtatious, gaudily dressed, and overly made up. Yunhe was amazed to see Shanghai women snarl and scratch at each other in a street quarrel and to hear the prostitutes of Nanjing Road shout for customers like boys selling newspapers. She did not think of herself as a sheltered wallflower. But perhaps she would be too sedate for Shanghai, after having been too pushy in Shandong?

Shanghai seemed a liberated place for a young woman to live; Mae West was a cult figure among the tizzy shopgirls flocking to the movies, whereas women still were viewed as chattels in most of rural China. Yet appearances were deceptive. Quick changes had bred anomalies and brought dislocations.

In the 1920s a feminist movement sprouted in China's cities; women paraded in men's trousers, swore never to marry, and gave support to firebrands such as Han Ying, who urged a "system of hate" and said the entire male sex was the enemy of the women's movement. Women fifteen or twenty years older than Yunhe, shaped in this "Mary Wollstonecraft era," developed attitudes to men, marriage, and work that were far apart from hers.

In the 1930s the feminist movement, in Shanghai at least, was overtaken by a rising wave of general political radicalism ("the chief enemy is not men but capitalism and imperialism"). Equally it was compromised by the sudden appearance of a "Mae West syndrome," the seductive image of a Western-style liberated woman who could be casual about men, do without men most of the time, find them fun on occasion—but never be obsessed by them either as boss or enemy. Trousers and close-cropped hair and manly ways gave way to *qipaos* and flowing hair and high-heeled shoes.

Yunhe was a young woman of the 1930s, and she felt in her own life the ambiguities of the Mae West syndrome. Unlike women of the previous generation, she had enjoyed some modern education and not been "pinned to a marriage bed" for life. So she had not felt the full brunt of feudal oppression. She did not hate men. She had arrived in Shanghai untrammeled and open-minded, wanting only to feed herself and pursue drama.

Yet Yunhe was to learn sobering things about being a woman in the "liberated thirties." Shanghai was an enclave, but not one that could remain impervious to what transpired in the rest of China. Independence was fine, but Shanghai was a social and economic jungle whose inhabitants were not born equal; many a young woman's pleasure at being "free" was clouded by the pain of encountering male supremacy at every turn. To be an actress, in particular, was to walk a fine line between being a "star" (in control of affairs) and a "doll" (the plaything of one's patron or director). Could one in the end be *sure* that a man's support was not desirable?*

On her first evening in Shanghai, Yunhe dined alone with Shi Dongshan. This director and writer, now in his thirties, had been in the Shanghai theatrical world since 1921. He was active in left-wing cultural circles though not a Communist Party member.

At a small brown table in the vast restaurant of Dai Sun Department Store, a landmark amid the shopping paradise of Nanjing Road, the experienced director told the hopeful novice about the League of Left-Wing Theater People and its personalities. A key group for one with Yunhe's interests, the League, as a needle's eye, caught up many of the tangled threads of art, politics, passion, and feuding that made up Shanghai's left-wing Bohemia.

As they ate Western dishes with a Chinese personality, a name that recurred in the conversation was Tian Han. A playwright who had studied in Japan, he wrote *Tragedy on a Lake* in which Yunhe had played the heroine's role on a memorable evening at the Arts Academy in Jinan. Her main teachers at the academy, Wang

* Lin Yutang, writing in 1935, caught the ambivalence: "Today the salesgirls in the department stores of Shanghai still look with eyes of envy on the married women with their fat handbags and wish they were buying instead of selling. Sometimes they wish they were knitting sweaters for their babies instead of counting the change, and standing for a stretch of eight hours is long and tiring in high-heeled shoes. Most of them know instinctively which is the better thing. Some of them prefer their independence, but the so-called independence in a man-ruled society does not amount to much."

Bosheng and Wu Ruiyan, were both associates and admirers of Tian. By the time the couple strolled out of Dai Sun into Nanjing Road, which pulsated with life as no street Yunhe had seen before, the young actress had decided to present herself to Mr. Tian.

Tian Han was a brilliant, opinionated man, older than the young Bohemians who were gathering in the new world of the theater and with an established reputation as a playwright. He was a romantic. "Wine, music, and cinema," he remarked, "are man's three greatest creations." At the same time he was a secret member of the Communist Party. For some days Yunhe stayed in the large Tian family tenement house opposite the China Bookstore in Mouth of the Rainbow district, so that Tian's entourage could look her over for talent and reliability. But Tian Han took little interest in Yunhe. Occupied with a hundred projects—once he was still revising the third act of a play as the cast began the opening night's performance of the first act—he appointed his young brother to help Yunhe.

Yunhe was disappointed. She did get a role in a minor troupe doing plays for working-class audiences. She began to earn her living with part-time teaching jobs. But brother Tian Hong was objectionable. He was too interested in her as a pretty girl and too little interested in her as a professional artist. "He traded on his brother," said Yunhe's future husband, agreeing with her low view of Tian Hong, "and made a nuisance of himself. He followed Tian Han everywhere, poking his nose in. He wasn't an artist, he was an idiot."

Later, Yunhe would come to know Tian Han on a more equal plane, thanks to her future husband. For the moment she had to be content with a meager place on the fringes of Shanghai's left-wing theatrical life. With courage, persistence, and charm she tried to bore her way farther into the honeycombed tunnels of this world.

She was not bent on "contacting the Party," as she would later put it. The Communist Party, after its catastrophic experiences between 1927 and 1930, was a dangerous organization to be in. Few people, especially of Yunhe's interests and personality, sought to join it in the early 1930s. And after she lost Yu Qiwei, her appetite for Communist Party work declined.

From Tian Han's side, caution was the policy. Chiang Kai-shek's White Terror was such that the Communist Party had to be extremely careful about taking in new members for fear of spies entering the ranks. Yunhe could serve the cause as an actress in left-wing plays, but she did not seem a suitable recruit for Party organizational work.

For Yunhe, membership in the Communist Party was not necessary for her artistic and personal purposes. Her Communist sympathies existed, a legacy from her time with Yu Qiwei. But in Shanghai they were just another string to her bow, not at the center of her concerns, like acting, meeting interesting men, and exploring the city's life.

Still, there was a hard political streak in Yunhe. She wanted to throw herself into politics as well as the theater. She thought it was the right thing for the times, and she also loved the self-expression it afforded. If Tian Han was unsure that she was serious and reliable, she would make her militance so unmistakable that he would *have* to take her on board as a Communist.

The days and nights were a merry-go-round of rehearsing, handing out antigovernment leaflets at street corners, and performing under conditions that were often grueling, makeshift, and dangerous. Yunhe conversed earnestly in Hongkou coffeehouses with other young, idealistic Bohemians about the role of art in society. She audited classes at Shanghai University. She joined in theatrical events to harness the rising tide of patriotic fervor against the encroachments of Japan. There was time out for sleeping around, and time spent on the gossip and heartbreak that resulted from the revolving-door romances common in the Shanghai theater world.

As a teenage newcomer, Yunhe was a very small fish in the murky if alluring pond of Shanghai theater. The large fish mostly cruised by her with unseeing eyes. The lesser specimens (of male variety) saw a chance to bully or toy with her (envy and rivalry held her back from friendship with females in the pond of theater-plus-politics). All the while her allotted task was mundane maintenance work on the dirty bottom of the pond, far beneath the real vocation of a first-class cultural fish, which was to leap and turn in the clear surface water, where the lights caught every wriggle, and spectators nodded appreciation at the pond's edge.

Yunhe's political activity during 1933–34 was carried out as a member of the Communist Youth League, in which her guide was Xu Yiyong, a plain woman with a rasping voice and moles on her face. "Sister Xu," as Yunhe came to call her, considered her new charge interesting but flighty, and the pair were to have a close but checkered association.

A position which Yunhe gained at a night school for women workers and peasants in the fall of 1933 probably was due to Sister Xu and the Youth League, not to intervention by Tian Han and other moguls of left-wing culture. This interesting school was supported in part by the YWCA, from its big British-style building on Bubbling Well Road. The job was humble, tough, and far removed from Yunhe's real love of work in the theater.

She taught basic language and general education—two classes a day to fit in with the hours of shift workers—to shop assistants, seamstresses, and operatives in sock workshops, cotton mills, and cigarette factories. The women were raucous, smelly, and (being exhausted by the day's labors) hard to teach.

"There was no one to take charge of our singing class," a woman from a Shanghai cigarette factory recalled. "Night school teacher Xu asked the Communists if they could help out. So Li Yunhe arrived as our teacher of singing. Twice a week she came, always punctual. She used to introduce a new song by playing it on the *erh hu* (two-stringed violin) while singing the lines in her lovely, wide-ranging voice."

Struggling as she was, Yunhe did not consider herself a "proletarian" like these women—the presumed backbone of the Communist cause she was on the fringes of. Was she not a girl of some education? Were the bright lights of the stage not beckoning her?

She did not dress in a worker's tunic, as her pupils did, but in the Western-style dress of a middle-class or intellectual Shanghai woman. She occupied a room of her own, at the back of the school premises, while the women worker-pupils were packed in several to a room at the front.

In money matters, Yunhe, though not penniless, was at times in difficulty. She had no funds from family members—unusual for a nineteen-year-old—but in addition to the pittance she earned from the night classes and a lesser amount from other bits of part-time teaching, paid by the hour, apparently she still had money from the divorce settlement with Mr. Fei, and savings from her two years' work at the Qingdao University library.

Yet there was a moment when she lacked even a few cents* for a tram ticket, after having impulsively bought a top-price seat at a play (when she could have made do with an inferior seat for one-sixth the cost). A year later, after Yunhe had left the YWCA night school, a roommate called Ai Gui, who worked as a household servant, scrounged boiled rice and an egg from the table of her employer to feed her, a day after she had just bought a fine blue silk

---

* The Chinese yuan is divided into one hundred *fen,* and ten *mao,* but for simplicity I refer to fen as cents.

qipao with a fancy white embroidered hem. One month she could not muster the rent for her attic and had to pawn a wristwatch given her as a keepsake by a lover to pay some basic bills, having splurged at an expensive eatinghouse, where she perched at a window table, observing and on display.

As at Qingdao, there were puzzling financial transactions between her and some political figures, with the lines of obligation far from clear. Her second short-term living place, after she left the Tian home, was with another member of the League of Left-Wing Theater People, Liao Mosha.

Why she moved into Liao's garret, when she had to sleep on a tiny table and evidently was the subject of bickering between Liao and his wife, is not easy to fathom. Even less so is why, in order to escape from the suffocations of the household, she paid this left-wing notable the substantial sum of twenty yuan. Perhaps she feared Liao was out to "control" her, as she felt the Tian brothers were. Perhaps, as Liao himself hints, she was attracted to Liao—which caused her to leave Tian Han's house for Liao's garret, and provoked bickering between the Liaos.*

For all the vagueness of her political beliefs, Yunhe possessed revolutionary idealism and took political risks. For a while, she worked as a part-time clerk, virtually without pay, in a movement that sought to bring knowledge to the villages far from Shanghai. The leader of this enterprise, which was in the Russian tradition of intellectuals "going to the people," was Professor Tao Xingzhi, a kind, persistent man bent upon doing good. Yunhe would go to his office, often tired from her other activities, and file papers, send out letters, and make travel arrangements. This greatly impressed some of her friends, including her future husband.†

One night she acted in a play to benefit striking tobacco workers. *The Murder of the Babies* was a drama in the service of social justice, and Yunhe played the role of a harassed, battling working-woman. All afternoon people had been arrested in Shanghai for

---

* "We were both living in Tian Han's house," Liao recalled years later. "But my room was larger and better furnished than Li Yunhe's. She became jealous (*yan hong*)." Liao moved out to his own place. "Inexplicably, Li Yunhe came round, said Tian Han's place was too small and noisy, and asked to live with us." There was only the kitchen (not garret, according to Liao) for her to sleep in. Soon she quarreled with Liao's wife. It was typical of Yunhe, who hated the way men controlled women through finances, that four decades later she complained indignantly that the "loan" to Liao still had not been paid back. Liao suffered during the Cultural Revolution. He in turn put the knife into Yunhe at her trial (see pages 384–85).

† It was an irony of Yunhe's later political career that she crusaded against the reputation of Wu Xun, who was just such a "going to the people" idealist as Tao Xingzhi (see page 194).

demonstrating against the management of the British-American Tobacco Company. Proceeds from the evening would go to the struggle against this firm. As she put on her makeup, Yunhe felt the danger and excitement of theater that was also politics. Everyone knew that the Indian Sikh policemen of the International Settlement may well storm the theater during the performance and arrest cast and audience alike. Yunhe acted well, spurred by the special attention to her art that came from the risk of the situation, seeking vindication against those who thought she lacked guts. When the final curtain fell on *The Murder of the Babies,* actors and audience filed out a tiny back doorway into a main street and joined the swelling ranks of the continuing demonstration. Yunhe was exhausted, hungry, penniless, and immensely excited.

Street demonstrations, circulation of leaflets, antigovernment plays—all were subject to the penalty of law as interpreted by a Nationalist government that was almost as opposed to Chinese communism as to Japanese encroachment on China. In some ways a girl of stunning naïveté—not least about her own impact on other people—Yunhe often was unaware of the high risks she was running. Nevertheless, she gradually learned the arts of deception and discretion that were part of the mental uniform of a left-wing activist in the Shanghai of the early 1930s.

When she spotted a team of police sniffing for a raid, as she traveled on a tram or a bus with a companion or a document judged subversive, she learned how to slip off the vehicle with an innocent face; or, if the bus was flagged down and a confrontation with the police became unavoidable, how to charm the surprised officers with elaborate courtesy and how on desperate occasions to shout and scream so outrageously that the police would be paralyzed by sheer embarrassment.

As an actress dabbling in politics, while working as a teacher to make both ends meet, she seemed to be leading her disjointed life in front of a mirror. To a substantial degree she was sincere; if comfort and pleasure had been her goals, after all, she could have sought out a businessman and become his mistress. Yet the drama of a dangerous moment was more real to Yunhe than the danger itself; the sense of hurling herself vigorously into a cause was more compelling to her than the cause itself. The cause was left-wing politics, a life-and-death one for many people, and of inestimable importance to China's future, but for Yunhe the point of it seemed to be her self-expression as a person trying to command a response from the world.

In Shanghai—as recurrently in later life—Yunhe mixed up in her own mind "political persecution" and personal affront. It was not always clear in her reminiscence, or perhaps in her original perception, whether an unwelcome man had come to her room to rebuke her for an error made in trying to push the Communist cause, or to rape her; whether troubles encountered by her night school students were due to a Nationalist crackdown, or to an attempt by enemies within the left-wing camp to "get at her" by making a scapegoat of those under her guidance; whether an eruption of contention in a left-wing cultural group had to do with a disagreement over political tactics, or with a bitter chase after her affections by a crowded field of lustful actors, directors, and editors.

This was the kind of person Yunhe was. "She didn't stand for much then," recalled movie actress Kang Jian. "She didn't know much. But she was able to dramatize things."

"If she came to dinner," recalled a male artist who knew her then, "one found oneself quarreling with one's wife when she had left."

Whether out of exhaustion due to a tough routine, or dissatisfaction at her low status, or personal turmoil in the wake of rocky affairs with men used to nibbling any candy within reach, or simply because the chill of October made her quarters at the night school bleak as never before, Yunhe left Shanghai in the fall of 1933 to take a look at Peking.

During several months in the northern city she did not participate in any theater. She hung around Peking University, going to lectures in the social sciences—neither her chief interest nor a realm in which the fruits of any serious study ever became evident. Her purpose was to contact Yu Qiwei. If only out of nostalgia, her lover of Qingdao days, now an important figure in the Communist underground at Peking University, might be willing—she apparently surmised—to help her gain a better foothold in Shanghai. She needed an entrée to top cultural circles in the entertainment capital of the kind Yu had provided for her in Qingdao.

If Yunhe hoped to resume the marriage, that did not occur. If she expected a job, that did not materialize either; she existed on an allowance of seven yuan, probably arranged by Yu, which after the rent was paid for a miserable room left less than five cents for each meal. No clear purpose was fulfilled by Yunhe's winter in Peking. She contacted some former classmates from the Arts Academy in Jinan, now working in the Peking theater, but she really had no business in the capital if the embers of the affection between Qiwei and herself were beyond a resurgence.

It may be, as an important source declares, that she became pregnant by Qiwei (ending in an abortion) but then quarreled with him. The relationship, at any rate, did not pick up.

In early 1934 Yunhe took the train back to Shanghai. New opportunities—and perils—faced her, for Yu (whose family was even better connected in Shanghai than in Shandong), negative as he may have felt about a resumption of the romance, wrote letters to some of the fractious, haughty comrades in Shanghai on her behalf.

Yunhe was caught in a vicious circle during late 1934. Yu's contacts provided a way to a better foothold on the crowded ladder of Shanghai society. Yet she was far from adept in the realm of left-wing politics and, particularly because of her impulsive ways, she was exposed to hair-raising dangers.

Major trouble came through contact with a handsome young man, an old friend from Qingdao, who had a double motive in wanting to associate with her. A cashier in the Shanghai post office, the Qingdao man ran into Yunhe on the street and soon asked her help in some "progressive" cause he said he represented. He also invited her for meals and strolls in Zaofen Park.

Problematic as the dashing cashier's blending of political and personal attentions was, and despite her recollection years later that he worried her, Yunhe met with him repeatedly and accepted a copy of a radical magazine called *World Knowledge* from him. This young woman of ardor and curiosity permitted, as so often, the pleasantness of being sought after to blur her judgment of the relationship that was taking shape.

Immediately after one meeting with the "old friend," two plainclothes Nationalist police nabbed her, marched her to a police station, confiscated the issue of *World Knowledge* she was carrying, and announced that she must leave the territory of Shanghai city proper that night. It was in character that Yunhe's first emotion was not fear, but anger that she had allowed herself to fall into the clutches of unreasonable brutes. For the moment, she was locked up in the women's cell on the second floor of the station.

It happened that Wang Tingshu, the classmate from the Jinan theater school, now in a Shanghai drama company, walked into the police station. "So many theatrical people were leftists," Wang recalled, "and one of my friends had been arrested—I went there to see him."

Wang entered the large gray building, which was brightly lit for the processing of the crimes of the night. One of the clerks at the reception desk turned out to be an acquaintance of Wang's from Shandong. "You know, we've just had a young miss from Shandong brought in," the clerk remarked to Wang. "Immediately I thought to myself that must be Li Yunhe," Wang recalled. He soon verified her identity.

Wang Tingshu stared down the cheerless corridors in indecision. "I was afraid of contact with Yunhe. I knew she had become a leftist, since she quit Jinan and came under Yu Qiwei's influence in Qingdao. And that was dangerous." Wang wanted to visit his male theatrical friend, but to do this he would have to pass by the grille of the long women's cell. "I was afraid Yunhe would see me," Wang explained, "and call out to greet me by name—she was that kind of person. Then the whole police station would turn eyes of suspicion on me." Wang walked out of the building without seeing either prisoner.

Yunhe's account of what happened later that night suggests that the drama of the situation eclipsed fear and anger alike (and perhaps colored her memory of what the police actually did to her). She was not "suitably dressed" to walk to the fringes of the city, she remonstrated, whereupon the resourceful police found for her a "gaudy Chinese gown made of velvet." There was apparently a consensus that this *was* suitable attire for the journey.

While the policemen covered their eyes, she took off her Western dress, donned the velvet gown, put the Western dress back on over the top of the gown, and, as if to make herself larger than life in every respect, struggled into a wool knit waistcoat to cover gown and dress. This created an effect that allowed her to be released from the police station, and she began a walk through the night toward the vegetable plots of Shanghai's suburbs.

That the police were taking Yunhe seriously as a revolutionary may be doubted. That Yunhe feared posterity might not take her seriously as a persecuted Communist is suggested by her addition to the story of a quite unbelievable item: Before heading out into the night she took from her discarded underclothes a "secret application form from the Party organization" and tucked it into the corner of her waistcoat (by widespread testimony, no such form existed in the Shanghai Communist Party of 1934, nor did Party members or followers carry any document of Party identification).

As she strode westward, more than one strange man tried to

"waylay" her; she ate the Party application form while sitting in a rice paddy field; she was again kidnaped by Nationalist plainclothes agents (the same breed that had released her earlier in the evening). Whatever the truth of these recollections of Yunhe's, it is a fact that in October 1934 she found herself in prison. She had fallen under suspicion for her diverse associations with people the Nationalist government considered subversive. "You ought to spend your time catching real Communists!" she shouted to the wardens as they locked her behind bars. The remark may have been melodramatic, but it rang with truth. It was a terrible setback, and shame, at any rate, for Yunhe to find herself in prison.

"Suddenly she stopped coming," the former student from Yunhe's night-school class of cigarette workers recalled. "Teacher Xu came in with a very sad look on his face and told us that Teacher Li had been arrested. . . . We took up a collection to buy biscuits and other foods and supplies and asked Teacher Xu to try and pass it on to her in prison—to express our respect and condolences."

Yunhe recalled her "eight months" in prison as a time of violence, oppression by men, and betrayal, yet ultimately of her own triumphant struggle against her captors. Her menstrual periods ceased, the afternoons brought on chills and fever, one guard slapped her face in a rage at her impudence, another flicked his whip at any woman (in this women's prison) who dared to cry. But Yunhe sang arias from Peking opera (would these not convince the wardens that she was no Communist?); coached fellow inmates in how to reply to interrogation; received from the Party organization (which she had never been able to contact!) gifts of bread, bed-clothes, and money; went so far in her defiance as to cry, "Why don't you shoot me?"; and in the spring of 1935 was released when a foreign YWCA official turned up to vouch for her innocence.

There is another version of Yunhe's "three months" in prison, less heroic, nearer to the truth, according to which she did indeed often prevail, but less by political shrewdness than by skillful use of her feminine charms, and at the end was released simply because she confessed.

She chatted and drank with the guards (Chinese sources from the period say) and gave them photos of her stage appearances. She sang her favorite Peking opera highlights, *not* in order to prove herself nonleftist but to charm the guards into treating her leniently. She gossiped so much during the interrogations that she implicated a man called Shao Zheng and others as Communists, which caused their arrest. She was slowly won over by the guards' argument that she was "young and beautiful" and would find her "golden years ahead of her" if she denounced communism as nonsense and declared her unshakable belief in the Nationalists' "three principles of the people." After writing a confession (*zi shou*)* she was released in early 1934.

"I told her, 'Your case is really simple,' " one of her former prison guards recalled. " 'Just turn over a new leaf and everything will be all right.' " This guard prided himself on not striking Li Yunhe—he says some other guards did—but on speaking kindly and reasonably to her. "She had a most pitiable look on her face when I told her all would be forgiven if she converted herself. Soon she wrote out a confession."

That Yunhe recalls the prison experience with overtones of melodrama—indeed experienced it that way—doesn't mean that she did not suffer privation, humiliation, and injustice. If her menstrual periods ceased, she must have been weakened through weight loss. Being half spectator of her ordeal did not mean that its pain passed her by, or that she did not realize what was happening; rather that she was deeply unsure how much of her outward political identity was the real, inner Yunhe, and that she was still trying to construct a reality out of her impulses and the external events she was caught up in.

While still behind bars she asked a fellow inmate who was being released to assure the Party organization that her "*true* identity was still undiscovered" by the prison authorities. It was still undiscovered by Yunhe herself.

What is a "real Communist"? Yunhe wondered. She felt herself to be one, in a vague way, because she was expressing the passions of the era in her nationalism and in her sympathy for underdogs. It was not fair, she thought, for people to look back with hindsight and judge Shanghai, where the Communist Party really was a propaganda organization, by the standards of the Soviet areas (Mao's territory), where the Party was a political and even a military organization. Was the battle in Shanghai not one of ideas? And who was more militant in her instinct for injustice than Yunhe?

When a delegation of progressive Japanese writers visited Shanghai, Yunhe was among a group of Chinese theatrical women leftists who met with them. "She was thin and graceful, but there

---

* A *zi shou* is not quite a confession, but an explanation of one's wrongdoings and an undertaking to behave better in the future.

was something strong inside her," recalled Tokyo writer Seiko Nishi. Each of the Chinese wrote a message on a piece of paper for the Japanese delegation to take home and share. Yunhe wrote: "Please stop making movies that disgrace China."

Whatever compromise Yunhe had made with the Nationalists, she took fewer risks and was less politically minded after her imprisonment than before. A shift in her priorities occurred, from public affairs to personal, and from political organization to the performing arts. Her idealism still existed, but her methods of expressing it became more prudent.

The left-wing politics of the day was made up of a network of contacts, every relationship a vertical one involving discipline, none a horizontal relationship of equals who could relax with each other. A comrade sent to meet another comrade would recognize him or her by a cunning signal—the first and third buttons on the jacket would be left open, a hat would be held in the left hand at a certain angle—and the keynotes of such activity came to be wariness, furtiveness, and self-importance.

It was a world without friendship, and Yunhe found it chilly. In her life and work she wanted, in addition to fewer risks, more emotional satisfaction.

She did not return to the night-school residence, where she had been surrounded by political activists, but went to live with a theatrical friend in the French Settlement. For a fresh start, almost a re-molding of her persona, she chose for herself yet another name, Lan Ping, which means "Blue Apple."

Her former teacher, Wan Laitian, observed to her that "Yunhe" ("Crane in the Clouds") not only suggested a passivity and retirement that did not suit her ardent nature, but even had the flavor of a Taoist nun about it (*dao gu qi*). Wasn't this the moment to bury Yunhe and become a more forceful person?

She thought of going back to "Shumeng" but told friends it was too rustic a name for Shanghai. She also thought of using "Luan," a name which figures in her family background, but dismissed it on the ground that theater fans, of which she was determined to have an army, had difficulty with names that took so many strokes to write (Luan takes twenty-two).

She settled on "Lan" ("Blue") as a new family name, either because its sound reminded her of "Luan," or because of her liking for the color blue (especially in clothes). To it she added "Ping" ("Apple"), perhaps recalling the town of Yantai in her native

Shandong, famous for its crisp, delicious apples. At twenty, Lan Ping was born.*

"You must see her," Hong Shen, a distinguished producer who had studied in the United States, and a close friend of Yu Shan, the sister of Yu Qiwei, said to Cui Wanqiu (Tsui Wan-chiu), Shanghai's leading literary journalist. "She's a newcomer, from your own province of Shandong. She took some classes from me in Qingdao— she's very good." Cui, a sharp, elegant, bright-eyed man, took a taxi with Hong to a shabby hall in the French Concession, where Lan Ping was rehearsing Ibsen's *A Doll's House.*

There was a break in the rehearsal. Cui and Hong watched the actors and actresses milling around, sipping tea and smoking, some chatting in groups, others sprawled across the auditorium seats in repose. Hong pointed to an actress who was by herself, pacing along a corridor by a window, her head in a script, murmuring her lines. "That's Lan Ping."

Cui turned to see a slender girl in a dark blue *qipao,* her hair cut in a fringe. "She looked rustic," Cui recalled, "not at all Shanghai." Hong beckoned Lan to come over to the edge of the stage. She came quickly, with a shy smile, her script clutched at her side. "This is Mr. Cui, editor of *Da wanbao.* He's a senior fellow provincial of yours."

"Oh, I've read your articles," Lan Ping said respectfully, "and some of your books." Cui could tell that she had been coached in Mandarin for the theater, though a Shandong accent twisted it as she pronounced "Zhucheng," the name of her home county. "Already when I was working at the library of Qingdao University, I knew your name."

"I pray for your success," Cui said, riveted by the charm and courtesy of Hong's young student and friend.

"When this play is over," Lan Ping said sweetly, "I would like to come and visit Mr. Cui, to learn from you and also to chat about our native places."

"I don't know about learning from me," Cui replied, "but you are welcome to come and chat any time you like."

Later, Lan told a friend about the introduction. "It was important to meet him," she said evenly. "And he's quite handsome, too."

Cui recalled: "I was impressed from the start by her serious attitude—going over her part while the others were relaxing or gos-

---

* That Jiang Qing changed her name twice (and used one or two additional temporary names) was not especially unusual in the artistic and political circles she moved in. All four of her husbands used more than one name.

siping." As for her appearance, Cui, known as a ladies' man, summed up: "You could not call her a beauty. But with a slender body, clean-cut face, bright eyes, and nice red lips, and being so clever and quick in manner, she was a pretty girl." Alluding to a famous phrase for a beautiful girl in China—"bright eyes and white teeth"—Cui detected a flaw. "Bright eyes, yes, but I couldn't add white teeth, because one of her front teeth was a yellow color."*

"As a Shandong man," Hong said to Cui as they took their seats to watch a scene of the rehearsal, "you'll be able to help her, to give her moral support (*peng*)." Cui said he would be delighted to do anything he could, through his paper and in other ways. "She's promising," Hong concluded. "And there's just something about her personality . . ."

The director, Zhang Min, signaled the start of a scene, and Lan Ping began her Nora, filling the character with rebelliousness.

The League of Left-Wing Theater People, the umbrella organization of politicized arts circles, combined characteristics of Shanghai, Bohemianism, nationalism, the romanticism of youth (virtually all those Lan became involved with in work and personal life were in their twenties), and communism.

Fault her as we may for not seeing the incompatibility of being a "revolutionary" yet also an "individualist," Lan Ping was typical in wishing to be both. Fuzzy as she was about the boundary line between theatrical art and political goals, she was little more so than a host of others in the League.

Nor was the flightiness of her way of life—especially prominent during the second half of her four-year stay in Shanghai—terribly unusual for an actress in her early twenties trying to claw her way up the ladder of the performing arts. Many a director expected "his" actresses to sleep around. Lan knew, as did others in her circle, that Zhou Yang, the leading Communist Party intellectual, was living with a young girl. Colleagues hardly raised an eyebrow. Outbursts of temper, declarations of eternal love, nights of weeping and fighting—these were the very proofs of an actress's dramatic capacity. To confuse the two realms of life and drama, as Lan often did, was to demonstrate a magnificent absorption in one's art.

Lan met a football star called Li. Theater people and sports people often sought out each other's company—they still do in

---

* This is the tooth that, according to Lan, her father broke in the course of attacking her mother with a spade.

China today—and the two were living not far from each other in Lafield Street in the French Concession.

"Whenever I had a match at the Yi Yuan or the Jiao Zhou [two sports grounds in the French Concession]," Li recalled, "she would always turn up, and cheer to spur me on." He remembers Lan as a coquettish girl, fairly slender, of medium height, and good at presenting herself in social situations. She as an actress and he as a football player were dubbed by some friends, "the beauty and the knight."

Their meetings were fleeting, awkward, and never really private, until one day they both found themselves invited to a reception at the Rich Harvest Gardens, an entertainment complex on Nanjing Road. They were seated together, and after an abundant meal, and some wine, they stole away to the Carlton Theater, on Jingan Temple Road. This teeming movie house was famous for its customer couples who came to sit close to each other as much as to watch the screen. They settled into back seats to watch *A Beauty's Heart,* a romance from Mingxing Studio starring the beautiful Hu Die and the handsome Gu Meijun.

"When the story hit an enticing moment," Li said years afterward from his exile in Hong Kong, "she turned her strange, yearning eyes on me. During a sexy scene, she would lean a little more firmly against my body."

Making a bid for the dashing football player, Lan Ping was misjudging the degree of aggression suitable for the man and the moment. "After all," Li said, "I was a man with some prior experience and not bursting with inquisitiveness about sex with a girl. To her fantastic enticements I made no response."

"Perhaps you don't care?" Lan's gentle question was almost an accusation.

"No, no," Li answered with a hiss, "I'm just absorbed in the movie and Hu Die's great acting." A moment later he cried out "Well done!" in the general style of Chinese audiences of the day as Hu Die saved her situation with a cunning maneuver.

Lan Ping pushed her "soft jade arm" around Li's tight warm waist, trying to inflame him before the movie ended and the lights came up.

Soon the crowd poured out into Nanjing Road, some misty-eyed, some chatting animatedly. "Her intention had already become solidly rooted in my mind," Li recalled. He felt he understood Lan well. She was young, fairly new to Shanghai, and on the rise—but palpably eager to rise *faster* and to clasp fame almost viciously like a gem in an anxious palm.

Even to a football star, her ambition and exhibitionism were flagrant. "What a risk-taker," the aroused if slightly puzzled Li marveled.

As dusk fell, and the red and green neon signs of Nanjing Road lit up their excited faces, Li and Lan strolled with few words to Champion Gardens restaurant, where at a corner table they ate an early dinner, in the Chinese style, of fish and rice, together with a few glasses of sweet red wine.

Darkness found them in a fourth-floor room of the Hui Zhong Hotel. Sedate in wood and silk, it was luxuriously furnished, with an ample bathroom and brocade lamp shades shedding a dim, soft glow. The bustle of Nanjing Road seemed infinitely far below. "All this added up to a suitable atmosphere for sexual activity," Li noted with Chinese practical sense.

"No sooner did I close the door and sit on the sofa than she was passionately upon me, with warm words and hot kisses."

"Are there any matches this week?" Lan inquired in an urgent whisper as she put both arms around Li's neck. She moved against his chest like a child clinging to a parent. "Which team will you be pitted against?" Her words were beginning to seem irrelevant.

"No match this week—but I have to go to Suzhou [Li's hometown]."

Lan clucked in mock despair. "You mean I'm going to have to do without you for so long?"

"One week will pass swiftly. And then I have a match next Sunday."

"I love your vigor and courage on the field," Lan said ardently. "Especially your skill in shooting," she added with a gasp, her cheeks blushing. She began to adopt positions from scenes in *A Beauty's Heart*, her body as hot as a bowl of steamed rice.

"All of a sudden, she took off everything except her underwear and hopped with a springing step into the bathroom." The bathroom was not fully closed off from the bed and sitting area, and Li, lying on the bed, flushed with the red wine and amazed at Lan's aggression, watched her reflection in the mirror over the washbasin. He saw a lithe form, a snowy complexion, "flat, lovely eyes," and firm, round breasts. Near her right nipple was a pea-sized black mole.

Lan returned to the bed, where Li had undressed himself, and "the beauty and the knight" came together. Able, as always, to unstabilize a man with a shaft of mystery or outrage, she murmured as Li began to kiss her "pink lips," "I am going to give you unsurpassable pleasure."

"She left me with the impression," recalled Li (who did not sleep with her a second time), "of a promiscuous woman, capable of going to extremes." It was almost as if her masterfulness was too much the center of the encounter, eclipsing the shared pleasure of the lovemaking. Her "unique skill" in bed left Li "half dead and half lost." Yet she was too conscious of herself as a performer, too busy *telling* Li about her charms, to be as good a lover as she promised. "She rendered me great joy but not complete satisfaction."

Lan Ping at any rate made a mark on football player Li's memory. "More than thirty years have passed since that night in the Hui Zhong Hotel," he recalled in Hong Kong. "Her enticing power may now have gone. But I will never forget her."

Lan was a great success as Nora in *A Doll's House,* playing opposite the popular actor Zhao Dan, later a prominent figure in Communist cultural politics. It was her breakthrough into professional acting.

The sparse, powerful Ibsen drama, whose theme is the gradual, surprising growth of Nora's resolve to leave the domesticity of a conventional marriage to Torvald Helmer, a lawyer, for something—anything—else, had been Lan Ping's favorite play since her days at the Arts Academy in Jinan. "I threw myself into the part," she said of the rehearsals, to which she devoted long hours each day for two months.

For the opening night the Golden City Theater was jammed. Every beacon in the sky of the Shanghai theater was there, including Lan's "mountain," Shi Dongshan, and all the leading critics, not least the handsome Tang Na of *Da gongbao,* who watched and said nothing. Cui Wanqiu took his seat expectantly. Before the night was out, Lan had the audience at fever pitch by the challenge to Chinese tradition in the words falling from Nora's lips. Lan found a submerged aspect of her personality in turning herself into this "woman *rebel*" (her own phrase, when she later boasted—with some reason—of having gone "beyond Ibsen's original conception of the character").

Lan was able to shout across the footlights her own private message to Mr. Fei: "We must both be perfectly free. Look, here's your ring back—give me mine." She was able to explain her resentment of male directors: "I've lived by performing tricks for you, Torvald."

Lan Ping *was* Nora. For the rest of her life she continued Nora's habit of humming to herself when something pleased her or when she wished to appear enigmatic.

A Doll's House ran for two months—unusually long for a left-wing play. Lan's performance brought high praise—allowing for the fact, as one must do, that as Nora and Torvald pitted themselves against each other, some of Zhao Dan's established glory rubbed off on Lan Ping.

"Miss Lan Ping has made us know the real Nora for the first time," a leading critic wrote. "When she cried, everybody felt miserable; when she smiled, the whole theater was happy."

Another prominent critic (not left-wing) later wrote: "[In the Shanghai theater] 1935 was the year of Nora."

"Nora made her famous," Cui Wanqiu recalled. "You see, it was breathtaking, she took Nora as such an extreme *rebel.*" Cui added, with the fond but resigned smile of one who liked Lan but not her politics: "And being her, she said this was all very *revolutionary.*"

As Nora, Lan had given those who cared to take note a glimpse of her personality. "This young star," Cui murmured to a colleague as he left the theater, "could never make a good wife. Anyone who marries her will have a tough time." Less than a year later, speaking to a man who was in love with Lan and who had been present at the opening night of *A Doll's House,* Cui would repeat his opinion, advising him not to marry this "brilliant rebel" but "inadequate wife. . . ."

Cui went to his office at *Da wanbao* (which carried on its masthead an English version of its title, *"China Evening News"*) and planned a series of articles on Lan Ping and her acting. Full of praise, they filled the theater page for days on end. "Was Lan grateful for this coverage?" Cui was asked (in English) years later. He merely smiled. "You used too nice a word," Cui's charming and witty wife, Zhang Junhui (Chang Chun-hui), observed to the questioner. "Just say she was *great.*" Cui's smile broke down a little. "Don't go into that," he said evenly.

The director of *A Doll's House,* the brilliant Zhang Min, a cosmopolitan man who was an exponent of Stanislavsky's doctrines, was impressed with Lan not only professionally but also personally.

Hong Shen had brought her to his attention. From a number of fine actresses, some very well known, Zhang Min had chosen the unknown Lan Ping for the role of Nora. From now on Zhang would pay more and more attention to Professor Hong's talented, striking "find" from Shandong.

One critic dissented from the storm of praise, and it was typical of Lan Ping's career that this man, writer and director Zhang Geng, was reacting personally as well as professionally to the "woman *rebel*" she had made of Nora.

Zhang Geng, a smooth, confident man in his late twenties, had been Lan's boss at the work-study troupe in 1933. "She's my girl, so don't touch," he would say of his new young charge from Shandong. Furious at being treated as his possession, Lan had battled to "keep him at bay," refusing his constant offers to take her home after evening rehearsals or political meetings. Surprised at the spirited resistance of this minor actress who seemingly had no cards to play, Zhang Geng cut through the knot of her obstinacy by announcing that he wanted to marry her. She refused him point blank. These were the days when Lan collected marriage refusals the way her friend Li, the football player, collected trophies.

A year later, gazing coldly at Lan Ping's portrayal of Nora, the distinguished director and critic found it rough, crudely assertive, and objectionably rebellious. He drawled his verdict: "Too naturalistic."*

Lan Ping's second detractor was Wu Mei, a well-known artist who had auditioned for Nora but lost out to Lan. "She's a bitch," the pretty actress said, her face a mask of hate. "She flattered Zhang Min from beginning to end." Wu Mei, a member of Tian Han's "Southern Society," went into a black fury when director Zhang Min cast her only as Nora's neighbor in *A Doll's House.* She refused to attend rehearsals. Only the day before opening night did some of her friends, begging her to take into account the "overall situation," succeed in persuading her to swallow her pride and play a minor role alongside Lan Ping's Nora. Lan had made another enemy.†

Despite Zhang Geng's negative judgment—which Lan Ping

---

* With the hindsight that allowed her to put a political coloration on every personal or artistic feud, Lan later claimed that Zhang Geng spread the rumor that she was a Trotskyite (a terrible indictment in Communist circles) and tried to cut her off from the League of Left-Wing Theater People.

† Decades later, during the Cultural Revolution, Wu Mei's home was ransacked five or six times by Red Guards representing the dominant political forces of the time.

could have avoided by sleeping with him, if she had been bent purely on artistic and political advancement at whatever cost to her pride as a person—and despite the growing dislike of women rivals more polished than she, Lan's Nora was her ticket to the movie roles she desperately wanted.

After the success of *A Doll's House* and through the dogged help of Shi Dongshan, who felt a loyalty to their mutual friends in Qingdao and also was attracted to her, Lan Ping landed a three-month contract with the Dian Tong Studio at a wage of about twenty-five yuan a month.

Dian Tong was a left-wing outfit in which the Communist Party had a heavy influence, whose movies, done on a shoestring yet often lively, were meant to raise social and patriotic consciousness.

"The difference between Dian Tong and a commercial studio like Mingxing," observed a leading critic, "was that Dian Tong was new, underfinanced, run by the artists themselves, and committed to social justice." Dian Tong's films were "intellectual films," not terribly popular among ordinary people, who preferred the "ice cream for the eyes" of Mingxing films. "You see, Lan Ping was not an ordinary actress," said a young colleague, Su Fei, who was later to have a long career in the Communist movement. "As a Dian Tong girl, she was really simple, straightforward, and rather serious, compared with the pop actresses. Lan didn't cover herself with rouge, lipstick, and eyebrow paint the way a Mingxing girl would." Kang Jian recalled that she earned seventy yuan a month at Mingxing, nearly three times Lan's pay at Dian Tong.

Lan Ping would still have to battle to secure roles, but she had launched a career as a "progressive" movie actress. She worked for a year at Dian Tong, from spring 1935 until spring 1936. Her assignments during the first months were humble—sewing costumes and erecting sets while waiting for a part. She was thought of as a girl whose life was as likely as her work to win the world's attention. She was known as a gregarious young recruit who would swing through the studio gate on the arm of a director, or chat intimately with a handsome actor in an all-night noodle restaurant after a late movie at the Carlton Cinema.

One evening Lan went out for dinner with a group of friends that included Wang Ying, a well-known actress, and her actor boyfriend Zhou Boxun. They dined well at Peaceful China, a Russian restaurant just off Lupan Road, and drank much vodka. Later, when most of the group had dispersed, Zhou Boxun found himself with Lan Ping and his own Wang Ying, both drunk. Before taking Wang Ying home to his place, Zhou escorted an unsteady Lan Ping to the front gate of Dian Tong Studio, where he asked the gate-keeper to make sure she got safely to bed. The elderly gatekeeper thought it best to fetch a studio colleague of Lan's, a male actor and director, to carry her upstairs.

The young man did a thorough job. Next morning Lan awoke to find herself naked, her clothes in a pile in one corner of the room. Glancing down her body, she saw red marks on her stomach. It was writing! Done in her own lipstick, which sat uncapped on the bed-side table, was this message: BE CAREFUL NEXT TIME, GREEDY DRINKER. Lan threw on some clothes and went to see Wang Ying.

"My dear, I was drunk too," Wang Ying said to Lan. "I never knew Russian liquor was so strong."

"Ying, how did I get home?"

"Zhou Boxun asked the gatekeeper to carry you upstairs." Hardly able to believe that the old janitor could be so mischievous, Lan went to see him. "Yuan Muzhi took you to your room," the old man explained.

Lan Ping summoned the brilliant young director to her room. Closing the door behind him, she cried, "How could you!"

"You're angry with me, but you should thank me." Lan's mood moved from anger to coquettishness as her handsome colleague spoke. "If you really don't think I should have written the message," Yuan said with a broad smile, "take off your clothes and I'll wipe it off." It was not the end of Lan Ping's roller-coaster dealings with Yuan Muzhi.

The world of Shanghai movies was, in a reflection of Shanghai itself, extravagant, tough and yet sentimental, cosmopolitan to the point of being un-Chinese,* and as recent (by the measure of China's long history) as mushrooms after spring rain.

Talent and excitement existed in abundance. Shopgirls squealed and ricksha pullers sighed at the sight of the star per-formers, even left-wing ones, and devoured trashy movie magazines with the concentration of brokers reading stock tables. In a young industry a talented young actor or actress or director could fashion a

---

* During 1929, 90 percent of the movies shown in Shanghai were American.

career in months. Budgets were low, the technical level was abysmal, yet the magic of huge audiences made up for much.

Artistic standards were not high. There were no steady traditions to give definition and perspective to the present. Political imperatives often whittled art into propaganda. Many movies seemed neither fish nor fowl—cut off from Chinese tradition yet too imitative of the West to be truly cosmopolitan.

Lan Ping, rootless and confused, was in an apt realm, where her weaknesses were almost strengths; her mentality, in turn, flowered through experience in this plastic realm.

In movies, the smile and the snarl were twins, poverty and glitter seemed to breed upon each other, and realities—from China's national agony at the hands of Japan, to the creaking social order, to Lan Ping's exposed situation in the jungle of Shanghai—could be crowded out of mind by fantasy, impulse, an evening of passion, or flickering images on a screen ("silver dreams" was Tian Han's term for movies). Was it not a perfect place for Lan Ping, who had little to lose, to aspire to satisfactions that life had so far denied her?

But she would have to walk a tightrope between fame and vilification, between freedom and exploitation. Women in particular were tossed about by the contradictions and short-changed by the illusions of the performing arts world. On the screen an actress was a "jade girl," adored, envied, the focus of each audience's dreams. When the lights went out, she was on a level, in Shanghai society, with vagrants, butchers, and prostitutes.

Surely the actress was as liberated as a woman could be, free of the drag of family, expressing herself on an equal basis with men? That was one aspect of her life, like the crimson of a roll of silk viewed from one angle; but a darker color hit the actress's own eye, like the brown of the silk when looked at from a different side: She was always under pressure to be a "doll" of the director, to whom she owed her role, and she was a slave in the whimsical kingdom that men of power liked to make of the entertainment world.

Lan Ping could see both colors in the roll of silk. But unlike Ding Ling, the writer and feminist, who toyed with the idea of acting in movies but rejected it because of the sexual exploitation of women involved, Lan Ping's options were few, and her drive to assert herself by whatever means was so fierce that she could stomach—for the moment—many an insult to her own integrity.

If Shanghai was an enclave within rural, tradition-bound China, the Bohemians of Shanghai formed a liberated enclave within the crass commercialism of their own city.

Underneath Lan's easygoing buoyancy was a determination not to let anyone "control" or "possess" her; her charm could turn to fury if she suspected that an actor or director was trying to manipulate her—as Zhang Geng did—into a situation at odds with her own goals. If a man paid for her at a theater or a restaurant she would insist, the next time they met, on paying for him, even if she had to scrape the bottom of her purse to do so.

Some people underestimated the intense will inside this pretty girl. The promiscuity that earned her the nickname "Rotten Apple" (*lan ping guo*, a play upon her name) hid from easy view a streak of purposefulness.

Theater colleagues would see her sitting in an expensive cafe, ordering only a cup of tea or a bowl of steamed rice, and assume she was waiting for a man friend, old or new. And often a man would come in to join her. Yet that was not the only significance of Lan's bold ways. There was also in her behavior a self-confidence that was not manipulative, but an end in itself.

Most people prefer to be constrained by duty and routine, it is said, than to be free. Perhaps that is true, and, if so, it is truer in China than in most places. Yet Lan Ping was an exception. She was happy to be by herself. She had no craving to be really dependent— on a man, a director, a teacher, on anyone.

While colleagues (and rivals) took her for a confident, even brazen woman, Lan burned with a sense that virtually everyone she dealt with despised her as an upstart without "class" or qualifications. Self-possessed as she seemed to be, a person more of calculation than of impulse, in fact she was emotionally a fragile flower. She did not work well in a team with others, especially women, and despite her toughness, the turmoil of her life brought its suffering.

Cui Wanqiu was poring over proofs in his office at *Da wanbao* at 3:00 P.M. when the phone rang. It was Lan Ping. *A Doll's House* had just finished its run, and she wanted to thank him for the shining notices she received in the theater pages of *The Torch*, the arts supplement to *Da wanbao* (*China Evening News*). Perhaps she could drop by for a chat?

Cui had a date for dinner with Ah Ying, a screenwriter for Mingxing Studio, but both men were happy to have Lan join them; this Nora seemed intriguing. While Ah Ying finished up a piece of business at the studio, Cui took Lan to Avenue Joffre for predinner coffee in the fashion of the time.

Lan wore a pale blue *qipao* and plain shoes. She had put on a touch of lipstick, rouge, and powder. Her manner seemed an odd blend of Bohemian, proletarian, and girl of pleasure.

At dinner in the Jinjiang Restaurant, a crowded landmark in the French Concession, the talk turned to Peking opera and Lan offered strong, antitraditional views. Mei Lanfang was "conservative," she said, in a reference to the leader of the most celebrated school of opera. Cui and Ah Ying disagreed. Lan illustrated her point by ridiculing the portrayal of women in *Heavenly Maidens Scattering Flowers* and other such Mei Lanfang operas. "Sentimental women," she said with distaste. "Now they titter, now they are hysterical." She did not like the idea of a beautiful woman "so delicate that the wind could blow her down," the type who "always needs a man to hold her up."

Cui was taken aback by Lan Ping's forcefulness. "I don't understand," she added as a parting shot, "why so many men *like* this kind of *tubercular ghost.*"

As empty dishes piled up like the results of a battle, the three diners quoted bits of operatic verse. Lan knew much less than Cui and some say she could not sing the arias (*jing xi*) in the professional manner, despite her hints that she could.

Cui asked if she often went to movies. "Movies are like textbooks for us," Lan replied. She expressed no preference for Chinese or foreign films, saying she devoured both. When they talked of the merits of the two most famous Chinese film actresses, Hu Die, the one whom Lan and football star Li had seen in *A Beauty's Heart,* and Yuan Lingyu, an extremely spirited woman who committed suicide when she felt depressed about being treated as a plaything, Lan spoke up for Yuan.

Hu Die is a "wooden beauty," Lan said, "just like a statue." Cui and Ah thought that was unfair. "And she danced the night away with Zhang Xueliang," Lan remarked with a frown, "the very night of the 'September 18' incident" (when Zhang, who commanded the forces in the Northeast, should have been on duty resisting the Japanese invaders).

"Lan Ping and I arrived in Shanghai at exactly the same time," Cui recalled with a smile years later, "she from Qingdao, I from Japan." After Hong Shen's introduction they had a pleasant acquaintanceship, he as a leading editor, she as a junior actress. Briefly, perhaps, there also flowered a personal friendship. He knew her well enough to introduce her proudly on many occasions to visiting Japanese intellectuals. Lan would often utter fierce anti-Japan sentiments when she met Cui's acquaintances from Tokyo, but that did not deter him from showing off his "junior provincial."

"She wrote a few articles for my literary supplement," Cui said. "They were not terribly mature—she was delighted to have something published." Payment to her was three yuan per thousand words. Guo Moruo, Xia Yan, Liao Mosha (whom Lan had quarreled with), and the other big stars got ten yuan per thousand words.

No political collaboration existed between Lan and Cui. Cui was not a leftist but a member of the China Youth Party, a group then critical of the Nationalists but far closer to them than to the Communists. It was true that Lan, now a modest success in the theater, was less preoccupied with revolutionary politics than before her capture and imprisonment. But it was not the case, as Peking now asserts, that Cui was a "Nationalist spy" and that he lured Lan, after her release, into "secret work" for the Chiang Kai-shek cause. Cui was kind to Lan, not out of political cunning but because he liked her and felt her acting was worth encouraging.

One man who had liked Nora very much was the brilliant, sentimental arts critic for the newspaper *Da gongbao*. Tang Na had a handsome, open face, a little flat, with a large expanse between mouth and nose. His big eyes danced with humor and excitement. Natty in a Western suit of light cloth, his gleaming black hair slicked down, he was seldom without a cigarette bobbing up and down in his gesticulating hand, or relegated to the corner of his mouth so as not to interrupt his rapid talk. That night in the Golden City Theater, he had sat entranced with Lan Ping's acting. He found her strong, exciting, and sexually attractive. Meeting her was only a question of time.

It was a warm evening and Tang Na was walking to the studios of the Dian Tong movie company, where he had supplementary work as editor of its magazine and as a director. Huai Hai Boulevard in the French Concession was crowded with strollers, food sellers, entwined couples, beggars. Suddenly Tang saw her walking briskly in the steamy night, her hair cut in a girlish fringe, the silk of her blue *qipao* lit from the neon rays. Only a very careful eye could notice the too-heavy ankles and the slightly bandy-legged walk, legacies of childhood foot binding that were never to go away. Lan knew who he was, just as he knew who she was.

They both paused. Tang smiled broadly like a handsome cat, and Lan put out her hand. Tang said how much he admired her

Nora. Of course, Lan said, she was well acquainted with the writing of Mr. Tang Na. "I'm a revolutionary," she burst out to the man-about-town of Shanghai's cultural left wing. She looked wonderful. Her strange, unsynchronized self-assertiveness did not deter but entranced Tang.

"It was enormously exciting to me," Tang Na recalled, "that this new actress from Shandong, very seductive, said to me right there on Huai Hai Boulevard that she was a committed revolutionary."

Socially, culturally, and economically, Tang Na was several notches above Lan Ping.

Born in Tianjin, Tang Na as an infant lost his father, a railway clerk who died after swallowing medicine meant for external application, and at the age of fourteen months Tang was sent to live with a widowed, land-owning aunt in Suzhou. He took the name "Tang" from the nurse, Miss Tang, who took him down to the lovely garden city; "Na" came from the phrase *rong na*, "to be tolerant," a suggestion of his aunt's. His mother and brother remained in Tianjin; like Lan Ping, Tang Na came from a broken family.

"My first article was for a local Suzhou paper," Tang Na recalled. "How excited I was when the editor accepted it. My topic was chain letters—I attacked them. You know, all that superstition, if you didn't send off a letter, something terrible would happen to you. And if you did, and enclosed one yuan, you'd become rich. Silly nonsense."

A live wire as a teenager, Tang hated the Confucian education administered to him by the tutor his aunt employed. "I had to recite the Classics. If I got a word wrong, the teacher hit me with a bamboo slat." It amused Tang to recall his tactic of rebellion. "Every few minutes I said I had to take a piss. My teacher knew it was just to escape from the monotony of the lessons. His fury rose."

"What do you like about Suzhou?" Tang Na asked a friend years later.

"The bridges, the gardens—and the people are good-looking."

"I don't think Suzhou girls are as beautiful as people say," Tang came back, with his tendency to see another side to a question. "Look at me," he added with a grin, "I haven't always selected Suzhou girls."*

---

* Tang Na's present and longtime wife, the beautiful and talented Chen Renqiong, is from Fujian Province. Her family later moved to Peking, and her father became Nationalist Chinese ambassador to France and later foreign minister.

The dashing rebel of Suzhou became, in Shanghai's conditions, an unprogrammed leftist. At St. John's University, a foreign-controlled school, he was taught Chinese literature by an American. "It wasn't so much a humiliation as plain stupid," he felt. "Two things in Shanghai made me a leftist: foreigners lording it over Chinese, and the gap between rich and poor."

Tang Na did not get into Communist Party politics, as Lan did in Qingdao. "I just never thought of joining the Communist Party," explained this Bohemian of effortless talent. "We were a group of *artists.* We had the same ideas, we felt passion over the issues of the time. We used our pens, our voices, our bodies to help China. It didn't seem to require being in the Communist Party." Nor had Tang ever read a single book by Marx or Lenin. In politics, Lan Ping had a harder, more calculating, perhaps more serious streak in her than the charming critic she met on Huai Hai Boulevard.

The next day, Lan went to see Tang Na at the Dian Tong Studio, where he was under contract. She was open to an affair. She had not lived with a man since losing Yu Qiwei, and she still was adrift in the human sea of Shanghai. Her approach was to confront "Mr. Tang," as she addressed him, with a lofty wall of elaborate respect, which could not but please him, and also to permit an occasional, sudden shaft of flirtatiousness to play on the soft underbelly of his personality.

Should a man already so accomplished have to come so often to the office to work? Lan Ping allowed herself to inquire. Inspired by her effort to turn an acquaintanceship into a mutual baring of the soul, Tang explained that he worked hard and also played hard. Was Miss Lan perhaps the same?

Indeed she was, the young actress purred, putting plenty of stress on work, as if to bring into more enticing relief her flirtatious sallies. Pleasure could not be tasted at its purest by those who did not also work to their limit. Did Mr. Tang not agree? And yet, Lan ventured, a slight frown joining forces with a warm smile, just as each year offers only one spring, and not every day is a lovely day, so pleasure has its moment; it does not hang in midair, available always and automatically, but must be grasped on the rise, or it has a way of disappearing. . . .

Lan Ping may have been pushy, but she was fresh and exciting, and Tang Na found himself falling for her.

In old China, a girl could only hint at her availability—showing her tiny red shoes beneath the wooden partitions of a home, stand-

ing on a veranda at sunset, playing on a stringed instrument (the
qin) so that a young man down the street could hear it. In the Shanghai of the 1930s, a girl could be bolder.

"Even in Shanghai, she was exceptional," Tang Na observed.
"Don't think of her as a timid Chinese girl. Perhaps you are used to
Chinese girls being retiring. Well, Lan Ping was not like that. She
was one who did not hesitate to go up and talk to a man, to take the
initiative, to put herself in a man's path. Oh, she was a bold girl!"

Lan strode in the gate at 405 Jingzhou Street, in Mouth of the
Rainbow district, to the Dian Tong Studio. She looked smart in a
blue *qipao* split to the thighs, her long hair gleaming in the afternoon sunlight. The Western-style property, formerly a middle
school, comprised a three-story hostel of suites for the professional
staff,* and courts for basketball and tennis, as well as offices and
workshops for sets and costumes. (Being left-wing did not prevent
the acquisition of pleasant premises.)

The gatekeeper escorted Lan to the tennis court, where actor Ci
Zhao was in the middle of a game of doubles with three colleagues.
Was Mr. Tang Na around? inquired Lan Ping, who as a new member of Dian Tong was unknown to the four playing tennis. He was
not (in fact, Tang did not play tennis). Nor were Wang Ying, the
leading actress, and Yuan Muzhi, the actor and director (who had
applied lipstick to Lan's stomach), whom Lan then asked about. She
sat down to watch the game, a conspicuous presence, because of her
appearance, and the mystery of her identity and what her business
with Tang Na might be. Within a few minutes her busy, magnetic
smile had won her an invitation from Ci Zhao to try her hand with
the racquet.

Soon, a long driving shot by Ci struck Lan in the chest. She fell
to the court, by the net where she had been positioned, and lay there
in a dramatic heap. Massage by various eager hands revived her to a
degree, and for the next half hour she watched from the sidelines as
the others resumed playing. Only that evening, in the studio dining
room, when the Dian Tong manager, Ma Dejian, introduced Lan as
the studio's newest recruit, did the tennis players of the afternoon
learn the name of the striking visitor.

For days Ci Zhao talked only of Lan Ping—while never daring
to look directly into her face—but there were other actors striving to

---

*It seems that some members of the company, including Tang Na, also maintained an
apartment in the city.

get to know more of the girl with the bruise on her breast. During a slack period just prior to the shooting of *Free Spirit,* an unremarkable film starring Wang Ying in which Lan had a small role, she was the focus of attention for the worldly yet slightly childish Dian Tong actors. If it wasn't Tang Na asking her to a movie at the Carlton Cinema, it was Ci Zhao strolling with her in Lotus Park, or Yuan Muzhi huddling with her in a sustained whisper, or the solidly built actor Zhou Boxun begging her to go out for a midnight snack at the open-air food market near the Park Hotel.

One night, at 2:00 A.M., she was lying in bed checking over the lines for the next day's scene of *Free Spirit* when a dark shadow at the window made her cry out in fright. Her breathless "Who's there?" brought no reply. An hour later, after having dozed off, she suddenly awoke to see a man's hand reaching through the doorway of the room. This time Lan's screams brought half the company rushing in nightclothes to her room. As the victim related her horrible experiences, some earnest expressions gave way to fleeting grins. Was she really in danger of her life, or merely of relentless attention from one or other of the quartet of actors who found her sauciness appealing?

The next morning, she saw outside her door a body sheathed in a quilt. Whipping off the quilt, she discovered Zhou Boxun, fast asleep, his moon face like a baby's in the morning sun's rays. "What are you doing here?" she blazed. Having languished in the course of passion's pursuit, the disheveled Zhou could only smile weakly, gather up his quilt, and beat a retreat to his own room.

Even in the bathroom Lan Ping could not escape the presence of the four suitors (if escape was really what she wished). A wave of "toilet literature" began. One piece of roughly written doggerel stared down at her from the cubicle wall:

> Little Ci halfway through the night unbolts the door,
> Old Zhou has turned into a piece of the ground by
>   sleeping always on the floor,
> Muzhi three times each night to her room is seen
>   to steal,
> Tang Na for three days has not felt able to eat a meal.

Meanwhile, as if to show that the men friends of the frustrated four could match the low levels of the mischievous girl colleagues of Lan Ping—perhaps Wang Ying had penned the poem?—various declarations of affection ("Miss Lan Ping, I love you") appeared on the wall of the males' bathroom, "signed" with the name of Ci, Tang, Zhou, or Yuan. When a letter reached Lan's mailbox, purportedly from the solidly built Zhou, arguing that his extra flesh amounted to a guarantee of extra passion, Lan, by turns angry, amused, flattered, and bewildered, decided to take advantage of the completion of shooting of *Free Spirit* to stay away from the studio as much as she could.

She enjoyed the excitement of being chased, if these accounts from movie magazines are to be believed, though it irritated her when the label "loose" was draped on her.

Among the young men interested in Lan, it was Tang Na who interested her most and annoyed her least.

After a period of absence from the studio, Lan was seen, one spring afternoon, strolling out of the compound with Tang Na, their hands clasped, their shoulders touching. That night both failed to return to their rooms at the hostel. The company was agog. When the couple did not show up on the second night, Lan's other admirers died a thousand deaths. At 6:00 P.M. on the third evening Lan and Tang walked through the gate, arms interlocked and faces flushed. Saying nothing, they went directly into the office of the manager, Mr. Ma.

At dinner Mr. Ma rose to say he had good news to announce. "Our colleague Mr. Tang Na, and Miss Lan Ping, in mutual understanding and a meeting of wills, have decided to live together." The dining hall erupted. All the actors and actresses—there were three exceptions—laid aside their chopsticks to clap, gather round the shining pair to offer congratulations, and in Chinese style to demand details of how and when love had arrived.

That night Yuan was found distraught on a couch to which he had set fire, in some mad experiment to take his mind off Lan Ping; Ci Zhao ended the evening in a drunken fit under a table in the dining room; and Zhou, his layers of flesh heaving with grief but not devoid of lust, began a three-day stay in a nearby brothel. Tang Na swept his unofficial wife off to Arden Mansions, in the International Settlement, where the couple set up house in Tang's Western-style apartment of three rooms, easily the nicest living place Lan had known during three years in Shanghai.

It was a glamorous match that caused some excitement among the Bohemians because Tang was influential, Lan was new and promising, and both were young, smart, and in the movies.

* * *

In Tang, Lan Ping had found not only one of Shanghai's leading young left-wing cultural figures but also a man who, despite lacking the organizational involvement that Lan had had with the Communist Party, was progressive and anti-imperialist.

Communism and the performing arts climbed into bed together in the Shanghai of the 1930s. It was a natural partnership in that Nationalist repression offended the impulse to free expression, and foreign trampling on China made the Communist Party's antiimperialist position appealing.

Was it not Chiang Kai-shek, mortal foe of the Communists, who was shooting writers? Did not the passions of nationalism prompt one to reject "art for art's sake"—just as the Communists did—and use art as a rapier against the injustices of the Japanese? For these reasons many persons in the theater, like Lan Ping and Tang Na, were "natural Communists" even though ignorant of Communist doctrine.

One night Lan and Tang were strolling home after an evening of café talk over Shaoxing wine and dancing at a parlor on Bubbling Well Road. Suddenly the sound of a fight rent the humid night air. Tang pulled Lan nearer to have a look. A towering White Russian was kicking and beating a ricksha puller. Both Tang and Lan were purple with fury. A crowd gathered as the White Russian interspersed his blows with accusations that the ricksha man had asked too high a fare.

Tang took the lead in speaking up for those in the crowd who were angry with the European, because Tang spoke good English, the language in which Chinese in Shanghai had to deal with foreigners. "Let's fix a fair price," said Tang as calmly as he could while Lan Ping stood by with fire in her eyes. Knowing the area well, he suggested one yuan, when the White Russian stopped his attack long enough to say where the ride had begun.

"Ten cents," snarled the White Russian. It was an impossible sum for ten minutes in a ricksha. The bleeding ricksha man began to fight back with extraordinary force. Tang and Lan led a movement among the crowd to escort both parties to the nearest police station. Once there, Tang and Lan found they had not reckoned fully with the bias against a Chinese protagonist on the part of authorities within a European concession. "What right do you have to arrest this European gentleman?" the police sergeant inquired icily to deflect the issue to fresh ground.

"We are Chinese," Tang said with grim fury. "We cannot stand by and watch such injustice toward one of our people."

But a friend of the White Russian had arrived, a European surgeon who was part of the informal network of informers that the police in the concessions depended upon. Tang and Lan had lost. A fine was levied against the ricksha man. Tang and others chipped in to pay it. Tang and Lan spoke some quiet words of encouragement to the crowd, as young intellectuals holding the banner of mass radicalism, then they walked quickly home, agitated, depressed, reinforced in their conviction that Shanghai was becoming ripe for revolution.

Tang and Lan were night owls. Often they ate late at Russian-style restaurants off the Avenue Joffre in the French Concession. A generation of Chinese cooks, many from Lan's own province of Shandong, had been apprenticed to White Russian restaurateurs, and having learned how to make borsch, chicken *à la Kiev,* and other Russian dishes, they carried on Russian cooking without Russians. "It was cheap," Tang recalled. "For twenty cents you got a meal of soup and a main dish, and the tea was free. We bought a package of six tickets for one yuan, saving a bit by quantity."

They both smoked, Lan lightly, Tang heavily, favoring an American brand, Washington, that came in a can. They drank a lot of *bai gan,* a strong spirit, and *huang jiu,* a yellow wine of the mellow Shaoxing kind. They were young, they had energy, and night after long night there was much to argue and compare notes about in left-wing artistic circles.

After dinner, sometimes they would dance at a parlor in Bubbling Well Road, or go to the racier scene on the fourth floor of Sincere's Department Store (the fourth floor was not, like the top floor, a haven for prostitutes, but it was dark, steamy, and intimate). Generally, Lan and Tang went dancing in a group. "Everyone danced with everyone," Tang said. "At the parlors in Bubbling Well Road, you bought a ticket for one yuan, and this gave you three dances with a taxi girl." Apparently Lan rested when Tang waltzed off with a taxi girl. "They sat in rows around the room," Tang recalled of these pale, shining professionals. "The mediocre ones prominent at the front, the really good ones, in our Chinese style, in the back rows."

Tang Na did not have much money, yet he and Lan saw themselves as part of an elite. A maid came in to clean several times a week. They usually traveled on buses or tramcars, but they quite often took rickshas, and when necessary they could afford one of the silver, brown, or blue taxis of the various cab companies.

"Did you ever go to the Great World?" Tang Na laughed at the idea that the "artists" would be seen in this gaudy entertainment palace. "It was for the lower classes—nothing to learn there." How could Lan and Tang care for shooting galleries, snake charmers, and fortune tellers? "Our maids went there," said a pretty young journalist who was on the fringes of the Bohemian circle. "They adored the jugglers."

It was a hot Saturday afternoon, and Nanjing Road swirled with shoppers and young couples out for a stroll. Lan and Tang arrived at the entrance to the Carlton Cinema with two bundles of crudely cyclostyled leaflets. "We were there to demonstrate against an American movie, a corrupting movie, full of violence and capitalism." Its topic was American business life in the Orient. Lan and Tang were aroused because Hong Shen, the producer, famous in Shanghai for his translation of *Lady Windermere's Fan,* told them the movie was an insult to laboring people and also to China.

"If you're Chinese, don't go in," Lan said to the bemused crowd. "Are you *real* Chinese?" Roughly dressed, her ankles bulging in cloth shoes, but tall and passionate amid the thrall, she thrust a leaflet into each available sweaty palm. Neither Lan nor Tang had seen the movie; that mattered no more than that the Western student demonstrators against the Vietnam War of the 1960s had never seen Vietnam. "Hong was older than we were," Tang recalled with a laugh, "and he was a professor, educated at Harvard. Lan and I trusted his judgment."

Sikhs in turbans rushed through the crowd. They were policemen of the International Settlement, in which Nanjing Road lay. Lan, Tang, and others were arrested. It was quick and without violence. Lan swore a bit; Tang quieted her. They had to spend a night in prison, but they won their battle. The movie was taken off two days later.

"Our lives were full of that sort of thing," Tang Na recalled. "I think we were right.

"Of course, we saw Shi Dongshan," Tang Na recalled of those months. "One evening," he said of the talented artist who had eased Lan Ping's way into Shanghai theatrical life, "he brought around a script he'd written about relations between women and wanted to know if I thought it would work." Being a lodestar of critical judgment, with access to foreign culture through his excellent English, Tang often was consulted. "Some director asked us to come and have a look at Bai Yang," he said of the actress soon to be famous, who was then trying out for the movie *Crossroads.* "We went along to a rehearsal at a guild hall. We thought that her acting was good but that her face was too flat."

On one occasion, Tang played in a movie himself. *Escape** was a melodramatic tale of a rural hero arriving, innocent and expectant, in Shanghai. "He told me," Tang recalled of Yuan Muzhi, who wrote and directed the film, "to turn my head this way, smile now, point my cigarette there—it was all very easy and great fun." While Tang was away in northern China on location for the shooting of *Escape,* he and Lan missed each other keenly. Lan told friends she felt as if Tang were a soldier, her soldier, who had been sent away on duty to a far "border country."

One afternoon, Lan and Tang were at Tian Han's place. The rambling tenement served as a salon for young artists to talk about the theater, speculate on politics, and trade gossip. Tian Han knew who Lan was by now. Tang had lifted her up, and the notoriety of her private life had put a spotlight on her. Tian Han had never really disliked her, as she felt he did, but simply had not taken much notice of her prior to her role as Nora and her coupling with Tang Na.

"Oh, I've got a dinner appointment," Tian Han exclaimed, interrupting his role as the sparkling host. "If you're free, come along with me." Tian, in his aboveground life as a playwright, had many friends among wealthy merchants. One such had invited him to dine, and to edify him and some of his friends with cultural conversation. Lan and Tang were pleased to join in, not least because the dinner party was at the Great Elegance (*Da Ya*), their favorite restaurant. Tian Han summoned five rickshas. Dressed casually, chatting happily, Tian, Lan, Tang, and two others sped off behind their grunting ricksha men to Nanjing Road.

"I've brought four friends," Tian said airily to his host as they all stared at a round table prepared for the exact number of guests invited. The merchant smiled bravely and waved his well-manicured hand in acceptance. Tian Han and his four young Bohemians enjoyed the "capitalist" dinner party enormously and left some traces of left-wing influence on the mind of the host.†

---

* "A very silly movie," Tang Na's subsequent wife commented. *Escape* was also released under the title *Scenes of City Life.*

† Ding Ling said of a visit to a Tian Han open house: "I went one day to visit Tian Han, the leading dramatist in China. . . . At his house I saw his friends dancing with many 'modern girls' and some of the men were dressed as women. This nauseated me and I ran out."

If a new play was on, Tang and Lan never would miss it. Plays were known as "people's theater" (*ren min xi*). They were a new thing in China, which has little tradition of spoken drama. Older Chinese, and most Chinese of any age outside Shanghai, considered it vulgar to have people using everyday speech on the stage. But for Lan and Tang, plays were badges of a militant, forward-looking way of life; they went to them as Chinese of the hinterland might go to a temple.

"The play about Wu Zetian is said to be powerful," Lan remarked to her husband. "Can we get tickets for the first night?" After coffee at a shop in North Sichuan Road where they were regulars, they took their seats at the Golden City Theater. Empress Wu was the only woman in Chinese history to ascend the throne. By brilliance of mind, coolness in a crisis, and the use of any weapon at hand, she ruled China for fifty years. The play portrayed her as a great person, though flawed by excesses.

Lan became absorbed in the play, more so than Tang, but after it was over she was irritable. At the cast party she criticized the actress who had played Wu Zetian to her face, at first mildly, then as she became worked up, trenchantly. It wasn't clear, even to Tang, what Lan felt was specifically wrong with the portrayal of Wu. She was simply annoyed that she herself had not been given the role, because she felt she could have been a stronger, more convincing Wu Zetian than the other woman.

Young, provincial, with no involvement in Shanghai's Western-oriented business community, Lan Ping had not mixed with Americans or Europeans. She has never in her life visited the West, mastered a Western tongue, or had a close friendship with a Westerner.

Yet in taste and temperament Lan Ping seemed for a while to be a paragon of the Westernized Chinese.* She wore Western-type dresses and high-heeled shoes. She liked foreign movies. The YWCA, epitome of Western-sponsored internationalism, had provided her first job as a teacher in the night school for women factory workers.

Lan was a modern, cosmopolitan woman in style but not in substance. She adored Hollywood while knowing nothing of the United States. She tilted toward Western literature without know-

---

* The paradox came to a head in the Cultural Revolution, when the ex-actress, anti-Western as she was in political line, reformed the performing arts in a "Westernizing" direction, defending the use of the piano, favoring Tschaikovsky-like musical scores, and opposing anything traditionally Chinese as "feudal refuse."

ing the West or its languages. The theater gave Lan Ping a coloring of cosmopolitanism (nothing to do with any pro-West political attitude). Chinese movies, especially, were a virtual transplant on Chinese soil of Hollywood norms and techniques—it was the least traditionally Chinese realm she could possibly have chosen to work in. The pronounced individualism of Lan Ping's personality, with its roots in her childhood experiences, also made her seem more akin to a Western woman than to an obedient, discreet, childbearing woman in a tradition that stressed the group and crimped the individual.

Lan was akin to a Western person in that she always looked forward, seldom back. With her social origins, she had little to cling to, nothing to save her from the necessity of standing on her own two feet, as a Western woman had to do. And she could enjoy being alone, which was more typical of a Westerner than of a Chinese. She felt she must ultimately rely on her own efforts; leaning on other people had quite often failed to produce for her the hoped-for results.

Tang Na's impact was a third reason why Lan Ping in Shanghai was less narrow and traditionalist than might have been expected.

At St. John's University, Tang was fed on Western culture. Lan's education had not included experience at a foreign-run school. Living with Tang, some of his cosmopolitanism rubbed off on her. Tang could see the influence, and he felt it made her a broader person.

Tang introduced Lan to her first European acquaintances. He taught her some English, enough for her later on to teach a dozen English words to others. With him, she better understood Western plays, because he was imbued with some of the individualism that flavors Western literature.

In Qingdao, Yu Qiwei had made a great impact on Lan, giving her a political sense and left-wing values. In Shanghai, Tang Na's impact was at least as great; it was cultural, and it was internationalizing, pulling her beyond the purely Chinese realm.

For the time being, Lan did not feel that there was a clear-cut difference between what was Chinese and what was Western. She didn't have to *choose* (as in Peking after 1949). As far as her knowledge went, the world—especially her world of the theater—was a cultural unity that rose above national boundaries. Absolutely Chinese as she considered herself to be, she found it natural in 1936 to wear the same kind of dress as her idol Greta Garbo was wearing.

* * *

After a few months together, Lan Ping and Tang Na entered a stormy period of tears, slammed doors, and physical scuffling, for the moment made bearable by intervals of warmth.

Moving a step away from Tang, Lan rented a small room of her own on the second floor of an apartment house within the International Settlement. On the floor below, in an equivalent room (these *ting zi jian** were servants' rooms, tucked between floors of tenement houses), a tailor worked far into the night, the purr and staccato rhythm of his machine providing a backdrop for Lan's late-night reciting of her lines for the next day's shooting or rehearsal. In the same type of tiny room above her, the tenant was Ai Gui, a working-class girl who had come to Shanghai to find work as a domestic servant. Lan and Ai became friends, being kindred spirits, to a degree, as single women set adrift in the "city for sale."

Ai Gui, homely and practical, helped Lan clean her room and wash her clothes, and tided her over with food when Lan's chaotic schedule left her short of time, money, sleep, or all three. Once when Lan was hungry, Ai went out into the street, bought two catties of tomatoes, washed them, and without fanfare put them on Lan's window ledge.

Lan, of quite a different temperament from her plodding neighbor and having more glamor than money, would tell Ai interesting stories about the theater and sometimes, in gratitude for practical help, give the Good Samaritan upstairs a photo of herself onstage.

One night, probably in early March 1936, Ai was in the middle of a dream when a piercing cry from Lan's room woke her up. Sounds of fighting alarmed the dazed Ai Gui. "Save me! Save me!" Lan shouted into the night. Ai scrambled down the ministaircase that connected the box-rooms, bruising herself in her haste, and burst into the second-floor room to find Tang Na and Lan Ping fighting each other. Ai's arrival (according to her own account) brought the fracas to an end. The "weapons" (unspecified) were laid aside. Apparently Tang left. Lan was "saved."

Soon after, to celebrate International Women's Day, Communist circles put Lan Ping in charge of an amateur theatrical production, for which the parlor of a hotel was rented. It was something of a chore, and a throwback to her political, preprofessional days; yet it was the kind of hearty, propagandistic theatrical organization that

* Tang Na lived in a *ting zi jian,* just off Huai Hai Boulevard, on first coming to Shanghai.

she excelled at. However, she was tired, ill, and vexed by the ambiguities of the relationship with Tang Na; she also said that she and Tang were in economic difficulties at that time—but this is hard to credit, except in the sense that Lan, whatever her income, had a tendency to expand her expenditures to exceed it slightly.

Members of the cast failed to appear for rehearsals, which led Lan to think her old suitor, and foe, Zhang Geng, was practicing sabotage (no nest of singing birds, these leftists) to prove that she could not manage without him. Stage sets that had been promised did not arrive, so Lan, at once resourceful and melodramatic, strode out bristling from the rehearsal to arrange for replacements personally, only to slip on the stairs, in her haste and anger, and go hurtling like a missile down into the hotel lobby.

Eventually an audience gathered; Lan Ping could not, would not let them down.

As if gazing at her troubles in a mirror, Lan Ping turned affliction into art—or at least into a good cry for her working-class audience. Staggering onto the improvised stage for her own role in the production, she was too much of a wreck to remember her lines. "My head was as if lead were being poured on top of it," she recalled. Nor, as she began to sob uncontrollably (in no way part of the script), could she hear the earnest whispering of the prompter. The audience, moved by her emotion and reacting, she believed, to her intense misery over and above any reaction to the play itself, began to cry too.

But her fellow cast members failed her. "They did not realize the seriousness of my condition," she said later, "so they did not help me." Indeed, one actor was so unimpressed by the situation that, making a temporary deviation in the character he was playing, he pretended to be drunk, moved swiftly toward Lan, and struck her a tremendous blow on the back to try to snap her from her fantasy. The play ground on shakily, and Lan's fever of 104 degrees and her maudlin mood continued to feed recklessly upon each other.

Summoning back the event over thirty-six years, she claimed that by the time the show ended, a low-grade infection had turned into pneumonia and that friends rushed her to a hospital, where she remained a patient for several days. However, an account she wrote at the time is not the same.

"I took a ricksha back home," she related, adding, "During that period we [she and Tang Na] spent much time at South Ocean Road." This address was Tang Na's apartment in Arden Mansions;

it was there, not to the hospital, that Lan, sick and distraught as she may well have been, repaired after the curtain came down on her efforts to celebrate International Women's Day on March 8, 1936.

Inside the apartment, Lan was in such a state that she lost her bearings and forgot why she had come back to Arden Mansions, rather than to her own *pied-à-terre,* or to the Dian Tong hostel. Idly slumped at the living-room table, she noticed a letter placed within a pile of books at one end of the table. Something made her reach weakly to see whose it was. She found two letters, one a love letter from Tang Na to a "young girl" he had supposedly gotten rid of in favor of Lan, the other a cascade of sweet nothings from this girl (her name was Ai Xia) back to Tang.

"Heavens," Lan exclaimed, "can you possibly conceive of any human being suffering the torments I suffered at that moment?" The triple horrors of illness, "misunderstanding by friends," and her lover's alleged infidelity joined forces to beat like an "iron rod" upon her skull; she swooned. Coming to, she cried out, whether in relief or in the vanity of being a spectator before her own ordeal, "I am still Lan Ping!"

Would she leave a crisp message for "Na" and depart from his life in that summary way? No; she reasoned that she was not of that inconsiderate sort of temperament. She sat there pondering that she had "no place to go." It seemed—for there *were* places to go (such as her own *pied-à-terre*), if getting away from Tang Na was her goal— that her spirit could not but wrestle on with Tang.

She pulled herself together, left a short message for Tang, and took a bus to a theatrical club, where she thought she might run into friends who could comfort and advise her. She installed herself in a room available to actors during periods of rehearsal. Soon the door opened and in walked Tang Na. The dance of love and fury resumed. He begged her to return with him immediately to his apartment at Arden Mansions. She replied that in the circumstances she could not do that: "We cannot again tread the same path." But he cried terribly, like an abandoned baby. Could they not at least go back, he asked, quavering, talk matters through, and on that clear-cut basis part company?

As she stood firm in her wounded pride, the pair came to the brink of one of their scenes of shouting, crying, and scuffling. Then Lan gave in and agreed to go home with Tang. "I was afraid of a dreadful incident erupting within the theatrical hostel," she explained. They took a taxi to Arden Mansions.

Unable to reconstruct trust, yet unable to split up, they talked in circles. Futility and fatigue enveloped them. "At dawn I attempted to leave," Lan said. "But, alas, how bitterly this poor creature cried! Till the end of my days I will never forget his pitiful face." Tang asked her forgiveness for philandering with others instead of making her the center of his life. She did not grant it. He turned on his heel and rushed from the room.

Uneasy that his mood had been terribly "irregular" (*bu dui*), she "jumped out of bed" (from where she apparently had conducted her conversation with him) and went into the reception room that he shared with two or three other tenants. On the table was a folded piece of paper. She picked it up and recognized the large, neat characters of Tang's handwriting. It was a message for her: He was going to kill himself.

Throwing on a scanty dress, she rushed "with every ounce of strength in my body" into the steamy night to look for him on the crowded sidewalks. She found him and asked him to come back. But Tang in his misery was a man with a will for one act alone. Rooted to the spot, he asked her to give immediate balm for his wounds. Did she love him or not? he inquired as the pair stood awkwardly amid the swirl of passersby. Would she forgive him or not?

"My God," she said later, "to have a man about to commit suicide standing in front of me talking this way!" At her limits, grabbing at the imperfect to avoid the disastrous, Lan Ping gave in. "I told him I loved him! I told him I forgave him!"

If Lan Ping's resistance to Tang Na's entreaties shows that she was a woman of spirit, not easily controlled or bought for favors, her unreadiness to cut him out of her life entirely is also remarkable and requires explanation. Perhaps she clung to a lingering hope that she could reform him? Perhaps she still counted on his help with her movie career?

The immediate crisis over, Lan relapsed into a 108-degree fever, mad talk (*hu shuo*), cursing people without reason and pounding her bed with her fists, in a general physical and spiritual breakdown. Tang was extremely kind and looked after her every need. In this way he won her gratitude, and to some degree her affection. At his suggestion, she decided to leave Shanghai, with all its strains, and stay in the Tang family home in Suzhou, the ancient garden town two hours inland by train. There, amid willows and graceful stone bridges, tended by Tang Na's aunt and visited weekends by Tang, Lan Ping rested and reflected for seven weeks.

* * *

Not all of Lan's dramatizations of Tang's faults were based on reality, and it may be that no one could have given all she was asking.

Many of the Bohemians who knew both Lan and Tang were doubtful about the match. "She is so strong," Cui Wanqiu said, "and he is rather soft and refined (*tai wen ya*)." A number of people felt that Lan had hooked Tang in part to have his eloquent pen and influential voice buttress her acting career.

"She'll do a real Nora," it was whispered behind the back of Tang, who was almost universally admired. "She'll play the role in Tang Na's apartment, just as she did at the Golden City Theater! When the time is ripe, she'll walk out on him just as Nora walked out on Helmer."

Non-Bohemians who knew Tang were even more skeptical. "A strong woman could be stronger than he," Chen Jiying, a journalist on *Da gongbao* said of Tang. "People like him were brought up in a hothouse," continued Chen, who was then a general reporter and not an artistically inclined man, "so removed from the real world as to let their lives twist and turn according to their passion for a woman."

Cui went to see Tang and talked indirectly about love and marriage. Character, Cui said offhandedly, is more important in a marriage than is beauty. One has to take into account, added the *Da wanbao* editor, who was not then married, that a beautiful flower will attract every bee and butterfly in the sky. . . .

"A great love between a man and a woman," Tang replied passionately, his large eyes fixed on his smaller, less dashing friend, "outweighs all other considerations." Cui thought of Lan's willfulness and of the merry-go-round of romances in Shanghai's Bohemia. He looked into Tang's trusting face. Unwilling to hurt him, Cui said no more.

"In all the time I lived with her," Tang was later to tell a friend, "I knew nothing of Lan Ping having been imprisoned and having made a confession." Whatever the exact truth of this matter, Lan was more politically minded than Tang. To become involved in the Communist circle, in however amateurish a way, was to invite a shadow upon one's life.

"A traitor is a traitor," Tang said with hindsight of Lan's confession, though how far Lan renounced her Communist beliefs to the Nationalist prison authorities remains unclear.

Tang Na denied that the letters to his former girlfriend Ai Xia were "love letters." Lan Ping denied that the meetings she had begun to have late at night with Zhang Min, who had directed her in *A Doll's House,* amounted to a sexual affair. Whatever the degree of these infidelities, they were consequences, more than causes, of Lan's and Tang's falling out.

Both Lan and Tang were individualistic, career-minded, and passionate, all of which were common among actors still in their twenties. It is certain that one man would not have satisfied Lan Ping, and it is possible that one woman would not have satisfied Tang Na.

Lan's conduct made her difficult to deal with, yet she was not purely opportunistic in her approach to Tang. He did write nice reviews of her work, as she no doubt expected him to. Her money problems were for a time eased by the proximity of Tang's ampler purse. Yet pure opportunism is ruled out by the fact that Lan quarreled with Tang, almost from the start of their relationship. She would have been crazy to provoke him as she did if all she wanted was help for her career. She did care for him. She was too proud to sell out her feelings for her career; Lan Ping wanted vindication of herself as a person—her talents *and* her emotions.

But Lan was not fair to Tang, because she wanted from him a loyalty she was not prepared to return. Many people in movie circles saw this, and Lan herself acknowledged a "widespread feeling" that she had failed to match Tang's commitment.

The outrageous demand she made on Tang was not for nice reviews and help in securing bigger roles, but for his acceptance of her as an independent spirit, while at the same time expecting him to nestle contentedly in the palm of her hand—and see no other women.

It was a glorious spring day, and the compartment full of colorfully dressed young artists was in high spirits as a morning train from Shanghai to Hangzhou puffed through the green paddy fields. The chatter was about movies, romances, and favorite spots in the ethereally beautiful lakeside city ahead of them. China's many troubles, which were often on the minds of these politically tilted Bohemians, for the moment seemed far away as they approached a place that Marco Polo in the thirteenth century found so pleasurable that "one fancies oneself to be in paradise."

Zheng Junli, an actor-director known among cosmopolitan movie fans as "the Chinese Leslie Howard," and a close friend of

Tang Na's, was ribbed by the others for not having a lover with him. "My lover is still part of the vast human sea," he said in self-defense.*

It so happened that almost all the other travelers were not only paired off but also on their joyful way to an exotic, three-couple, collective wedding.

One couple was Zhao Dan, the actor who played opposite Lan in *A Doll's House,* and the pretty young actress Yie Luxi. A second was the popular actor-director Gu Eryi and a very young actress named Du Lulu. The third was Tang Na, pleased with himself for having softened a wild spirit into a beaming bride, and Lan Ping, relaxed and apparently at peace with herself after her stay in Suzhou.

After hiring a boat to glide around the porcelain-blue waters of West Lake and making a picnic lunch at Yellow Dragon Spring, on a rocky slope high above the lake, the party strolled to the Pagoda of Six Harmonies. There the "six who would be harmonious" assembled quietly.

Acting as a witness was Shen Chunju, a lawyer and a close friend of Tang's and Lan's. Zheng Junli—later the director of the epic film *The Spring River Flows East*—was best man. He orchestrated the six, with his sense of style and timing, and Shen Chunju helped him. The pair moved their finely attired friends from this rock to that mound as directors would move their actors. Each couple, using a variety of wordings and documentation, stepped forward and made a modern and Bohemian betrothal. The collective wedding reflected the techniques of a studio publicist, and the fantasies of actors who spent half their days onstage, more than the family-minded values and sacred references of an ordinary Chinese marriage.

That evening the young party took a train back to Shanghai. The wedding became the talk of Shanghai's Bohemia. Ten days later, another reception was held in the YMCA at Bridge of the Eight Immortals. Friends and relatives of the six who married in Hangzhou gathered for a second bite at the cherry of celebration.

"It was just a picnic," Lan said. "We wanted to make a symbolic act," Tang Na recalled, "that our relationship was stabilized, an act that our friends could recognize."

Only Lan and Tang, among the three couples, omitted a mar-

---

* He soon married Huang Chen, who is still alive in Shanghai and who is one source for this account of Lan Ping in 1936.

riage document. They talked about the matter thoroughly, and according to Lan they both felt that a marriage certificate (*jie hun shu*) was not appropriate for them. "If love is not there," Lan said, "a marriage certificate is not going to help" (*mei you yong de*).

Lan was more reluctant to marry than Tang. Many times he had raised the issue; many times she had said no. Only after the International Women's Day crisis, and the ensuing retreat to Suzhou, where the low-key atmosphere of the Tang family hearth may have softened her feelings, did she change her mind and marry the man who, she claimed, had recently driven her to the brink of madness.

"We married for economic reasons," she later told friends. "There was no feeling of passion." She claimed that she and Tang, who were short of money "because of unemployment and illness," felt getting married would enable Tang to "get a bit of money from his family."

It was Lan's third marriage, and she was one month past her twenty-second birthday.

In the city of Guilin a few years later, as a group of literary and theatrical friends, including Tian Han and the leading actress Wang Renmei, were reminiscing about the "Hangzhou wedding," one of the group came up with the quip, "From the Pagoda of Six Harmonies came six disharmonies."* Indeed, none of the three marriages lasted long, and Lan's and Tang's was the shortest of all. It is doubtful that Lan expected an enduring union, a settled life, or children. She did not believe that her future happiness would come mainly from her marriage.

"At that time," she wrote of the period immediately after the wedding, "although I had forgiven him, each moment I thought about that night, and those two [love] letters, my heart jumped around as if to break with grief."

One of the suitors who lost out to Tang Na, "lipstick" Yuan Muzhi, remarked to Lan as her affair with Tang bumped along, "If one of you doesn't submit, there'll be a tragedy." Tang adored Lan, and his life was disrupted by the passions of their affair, but it seems he wasn't ready to close his eyes to all other women, let alone to conquer his alleged strain of passivity in order to meet Lan's image of what a man should be. Lan Ping was too self-willed to submit (as she was to do in the different circumstances of a later marriage). Yuan Muzhi had seen the problem; but there was no solution to it.

* Difficult to translate, *liu he ta qian liu bu he* literally means "in front of the Pagoda of Six Harmonies, six disharmonies."

"Mention Zhang Min," a movie magazine commented, "and everyone thinks of Lan Ping." Zhang Min was Shanghai's great exponent of the ideas of Stanislavsky, two of whose books he translated into Chinese from an English translation of the Russian. Zhao Dan and other prominent actors held him in high regard as a director and a theorist of the theater. He was married to a schoolteacher, a pretty but quiet woman who could not always keep up with him, and the pair had an eight-year-old son, Kelin (perhaps copied from the English name Colin). It was the spring of 1937 before Lan and Zhang Min lived together, but their affair began sometime in 1936.

The Dian Tong Studio collapsed in mid-1936, due to government pressure and limited audiences for its strident movies. "They just stopped paying us," Tang Na recalled. For some months, until she won a contract at the bigger, broader Lian Hua Studio, Lan Ping was floundering for stage or movie roles and for money. She may well have hoped for help from Zhang Min, whom she knew was fond of her. At any rate, she got it, winning the lead in his stage production of *The Thunderstorm* by the Russian dramatist Ostrovsky, which did well.

Tang Na felt cheated by Lan's liaison with Zhang, of whom he would forever hold an icy view, as did Zhang Min's wife, whose friends rallied around her and denounced Lan in loud, effective whispers. Lan was not deterred. She must have realized the hazard she was creating for her marriage. She simply told Tang she felt she had the "right" to see Zhang Min on the side. Later, in the spring of 1937, when Mrs. Zhang cleared out and Lan moved to Zhang's apartment, she met the son, Kelin, and boasted of how well she and the boy got along.*

It was only five weeks after the wedding at the Pagoda of Six Harmonies that Lan and Tang had a big quarrel. Zhang Min was an issue, as was Tang's "young girl," Ai Xia, and Lan's "right" to do whatever came into her mind at any moment.

Distraught and lacking work, Lan decided to take a break away from Tang and Shanghai. She took a train to the quieter world of Jinan, where she saw relatives and friends and perhaps contacted Mr. Fei, her first husband. Tang Na, "love-mad," as one observer described him, went after her. He earnestly wanted to bring Lan back to Shanghai and to win from her a clear declaration that she loved him, and him alone.

* Perhaps because Mrs. Zhang left rather than making a big fuss, her marriage with Zhang resumed after Lan Ping left Shanghai.

"Although I doubted they would live together for a lifetime (*bai tou xie lao*)," Cui Wanqiu said, "I never dreamed they would fight and split like that so quickly."

Tang Na arrived in Jinan by train on the evening of June 27 and went to the Railway Inn not far from beautiful Lake Daming. He sent a note to the house of Lan's aunt, the sister of her mother, where apparently she was staying. Lan replied with a melodramatic message about her sufferings and said she could not possibly see the man who was causing her such turmoil. Tang Na read the wild note with despair. That night he took an overdose of sleeping pills in his room at the inn. The owner of the inn discovered Tang in time. Shocked and amazed that the well-known critic from Shanghai should be reduced to such misery, he managed to contact Lan. She came to the inn, took charge, and the pair went back to Shanghai together.

Lan and Tang could not live smoothly with each other; neither could they live without each other.

Tang Na's suicide attempt made Lan Ping far better known than ever before. By July the magazines that reported on the Bohemians were telling the story of how Lan's beauty, elusiveness, and unsubservient spirit had driven the sensitive, affectionate Tang to try to take his own life. If Lan's art had not yet brought her top fame, her life was filling the breach.

Tang Na was dining alone with Zheng Junli in Zheng's spacious, chaotic apartment in a tenement house. The director's wife, Huang Chen, also an actress and writer, was away. Lan Ping during this week was flying in her own realm. The grotesque incident at Jinan had warded off divorce without bringing stable harmony. Tang, wounded in spirit but ever an optimist, was hanging on, sustained by his loyal circle of friends and his love of the theater.

After dinner, Tang and Zheng sat back to chat and drink a few glasses of *bai gan*. Zheng Junli, who knew almost every kiss and curse of the Lan-Tang marriage, waited for Tang to unwind and offer his brilliant *aperçus* on the new plays, as he loved to do. "I have something to give you, Na," Zheng said during a pause in the conversation.

Zheng Junli went to his bureau and came back to the armchairs with a letter. "You know who it's from," he said gently, handing Tang a pale blue envelope on which his name was written in Lan Ping's bold, slightly childish characters. "She told me to give it to you—I use her words—when you were in a good mood."

A pleasant talk with his dear friend Zheng Junli turned, for Tang Na, into an evening of anguish, and before the night was done one more effort to escape from his marriage in the starkest possible way.

"You've been waiting a long time for these pages," Lan wrote in her two-thousand-word letter. "I'm sure you will understand the bitter turmoil that I've had to endure," she said to the man who had just tried to kill himself over her.

Lan was writing to say she had to leave Tang, and to confess to an ambition that made it impossible for her to settle down, either to be Tang's wife, or to be part of the Shanghai Bohemian world he loved.

"After going into movies," Lan stated, "I felt a contradiction, growing sharper each day, between words and deeds." The agony of the contradiction, which once led her to the brink of suicide, was "forgotten" when she met Tang. He alone had made her feel good as an actress and as a woman. Yet Tang had lifted her up only to dump her down to an even more horrible predicament than she had known before their love soared.

She had tried so hard to love him, she said. "Before I planned to go back to Jinan, just in order to please you, I agreed to try again for some happy days together." But she could not forget the fighting, and the aching regret she always felt afterward, when she would wander in the rain, unspeakably unhappy, in an agony that ended only when a fainting spell engulfed her.

"When I realized that I would have to leave you," she wrote in lines heavy with a sense of the drama of her own response to sufferings inflicted upon her, "and when I thought back over the things you told me, it seemed my heart was jumping into my throat, choking me. My body trembled fiercely. I couldn't move a step." She staggered into a taxi, she recalled, and went around to Zhao Dan's apartment. Confused images danced in her mind—of her married life together with Tang in the apartment on South Ocean Road, of how *stubbornly* she had loved him.

The "contradiction" had tortured her, she pointed out. To have to say one thing, and yet feel another. To pretend to values that in the depth of her heart she was not attached to. To give Tang the impression that she could make her life with him, when in fact she knew she must turn her face elsewhere.

But she would not give in to suffering, she explained. She, Lan Ping, would struggle, she would take her life back into her own hands. She had found a way to "resolve the contradiction" and make her death worthwhile—by leaving Tang Na, and with him the glamor and comforts of his way of life.

"Your terrible bad temper in our last period together," she wrote, "really did me a good turn." Otherwise she would not have been pushed to make the decision to leave him and to try to plan a life that would transcend the environment of the Shanghai performing arts.

She and Tang had quarreled over whether she should "settle down," alike in the Shanghai Bohemian life and in a stable household with him. "You were right, but I was also right," Lan said. "Your truth holds true only for your own world, the world of you and Zhao Dan and the others. But I myself, I know another world. For three or four years, I tasted a different life." Lan was recalling her political activity and telling Tang, whom she saw as a child of the theater alone, that she had an additional point of reference that she could not deny herself.

"Didn't you say I had made a great leap?" Lan continued, her letter a march of "I's" that is most untraditional in Chinese writing, where feelings seldom are expressed so directly. "You're absolutely correct." Nothing is more bitter, she explained, than to return to the past after having made a great leap ahead. In moving quickly into the Shanghai Bohemian world, she had proved herself, but she confessed that it was in her nature to have to *keep on leaping*. Lan was telling Tang Na that she wanted to "leap" beyond marriage and beyond the theater.

At one point she hoped she might be able to prise Tang away from movieland, she recalled, in order for them to find happiness together in another realm. "But after long examination of you, I find such an idea impossible." If she could not put him first, she accused him of the same shortcoming toward her. "You love the life of the theater more than you love me. In your pretty talk about love, one has to insert a few question marks." Lan said Tang had once stated that he wanted to take charge of her. "But if so," she inquired, "what reserve of strength do you possess in order to accomplish this?"

It was hard for Tang, or anyone else, to love such a woman. In her candor, Lan acknowledged this. "I have not been a good wife," she admitted, "and also I have not been a good lover." Although her letter was full of accusations flung at Tang, Lan did not hide the main problem. "As for me, I do love my work more than my lover."

Lan's dreams were soaring beyond the capacity of any marriage to contain them (or any marriage that was possible in the China of the 1930s). "You probably think I am being selfish." But had she not warned him "at the beginning of your love for me" that "to love me would be to suffer"?

Tang had said he was quite prepared to put up with tribulation in order to have her. "If it ever becomes necessary for you to leave me," she had asked, "please do not hate me." Tang had responded: "Till my death I could never hate you." Now, as she wrote what was intended as a farewell letter, she told Tang how moved she was by his remark and how she would never forget it.

For a woman of twenty-two who had considerable feelings for Tang and much to gain from her link with him, Lan was astonishingly resolute in protecting her independence. If it were possible to combine success at work and success as a woman, surely a life in movieland, with Tang as her partner, was the way to do it. Yet she was saying no to such a life. Within Lan Ping there was already a demon driving her to reach beyond success (in career and marriage alike) for something grander.

"In all my troubles," she wrote, "confidence in myself and a drive toward fame were the forces that enabled me to pull myself together."

"Several friends have said I worked an influence on you," Lan went on. "In the first period, yes, there was some. For at that time you burned with love for me." She raised the question of his influence upon her. "At times I have tried to receive an influence from you and to fit in with the shape of that world, but the result was worse than before I tried." She felt that the demands made on her had cramped her.

Lan said she ought to point out Tang's faults. There were three, she realized as she looked back. He was promiscuous, as indeed "you men" tend to be. "You always said you loved me, but when a wave of licentiousness came over you, you forgot all."

Tang's second fault was a passivity of character. "You just let things go, if they can be let go." Where was his ambition? she wondered. Where were his ideals? Wasn't it a sign of weakness that he would write his reviews at the last minute, only when the task could not be postponed any longer?

"You cover up your shortcomings," Lan wrote, reaching Tang's third fault. "At times you know you're wrong, but you say you're right—and you claim I misunderstand you."

"These three faults have blocked our advance," Lan declared. Perhaps they could be rectified? "At any rate," she said, "unless you correct your faults, *you will not be worthy to say you once were my lover.*"

Lan put down her stick, smiled, and said Tang, for all his weaknesses, was nevertheless a "sincere and warm child" who had "no bad feelings toward any human being." She observed, "Sometimes you are kind even to your enemies"—not one of her own traits. "I believe," she declared, "that given effort, and if you heed what I say, you will achieve great things."

"What matters," she laid down to Tang, "is that you should remember me as a vivid, spirited woman—one who never caves in before men, who will never bear to be treated as inferior to men." Poor Tang was asked to think of the problem as some kind of triumph.

"Darling, don't be sad. In our respective future lives, we will be able to overcome the contradictions that we have been facing." He would find another wife, she felt sure, and she would be able to pursue her higher ambitions. "The future does not deceive human beings—you'll get a reward for your efforts." For her part, Lan said she would go back to teaching for the time being.

Lan made a rare reference to the person who for years had been closest to her. "As for my mother, I have made arrangements for her in the countryside [at Lan's half sister's place]. There's no need to worry about her." Perhaps Lan's mother's new husband was dead by now.

"Forget me now, darling. Go your own way—you have selected it. I congratulate you in advance on your success. Good-bye from your dearest Ping."

Lan asked for Tang's fountain pen and watch as keepsakes. The pen, she told him, would serve her in writing down her life's experiences (she did not say writing poems or plays). The watch surely would spur her to more regularity in her work. In turn she offered him an album of photos of herself, in poses of performance and relaxation, and a favorite white knitted pullover, as "memorials" and to make him "strive harder."

By the time Tang Na had finished reading Lan's letter, he was in despair, and soon he tried to take his life again. Lan Ping had returned to Jinan for a further stay with relatives. Tang did not reply to the letter. "I did not even know her exact address at that moment." Yet, whether because Tang Na was "love-mad" or because of Lan Ping's capacity to deceive herself, the marriage was not at an end. The two of them spent most of the rest of 1936 in a stable if not ardent attachment. Lan's expectations were reduced. After her letter, the marriage was alive only as an interim compromise.

One reason for a lowered temperature was that her own friendship with Zhang Min, and perhaps other men, put her in a weak position to upbraid Tang for his philandering. One day she found in a book Tang had been reading a newspaper clipping of a love poem he had written for Ai Xia, his "former" girlfriend, during the period of Lan's stay in Jinan. Tang denied that the poem was directed to a particular girl. But the demons of doubt came back to haunt Lan. She threw herself to the floor in despair. "I lay there like a mental defective," she recalled. "I stared through the window at the trees trembling in the wind and the clouds against the blue sky." Yet Lan did not leave Tang, or even confront him immediately, over this "outrage," as she had done on similar previous occasions.

Lan was also afraid, she told friends, that if she walked out on Tang the result would be another attempt to kill himself, and more gossip against her as the cause of his sadness.

"If I took the knife and cut the thing into two pieces," she wrote of this period, "[we] were afraid he wouldn't be able to stand it and would try suicide again." Indeed, she said that at one point she and "three friends" had to beg and persuade him not to make another attempt. She felt she had to establish "a calm phase, to allow him to build up some hope. . . ." She realized the marriage had entered its downward slope, but she hid this feeling from Tang, as she admitted, so he could be sustained by a hope that "an opportunity for the resumption of their love" would come.

One reason for a new stability in the relationship was that Lan put her work first. "This is the Year of Reading for Lan Ping," she wrote on a strip of paper and pasted it to the wall of her bedroom at the start of 1937. She was seeking to deepen her knowledge of the theater and dramatic technique. In the spring she was offered a substantial role in a film that did well. As the suffering wife in *Blood on Wolf Mountain*, from Lian Hua Studio, she was in her element. She portrayed an embattled woman who was terrified of wolves (a symbol for the Japanese invaders) and who battled heroically against wolves (which were always for Lan a symbol of enemies at once vaguer and more personal than the Japanese).

Months earlier, when Lan was filling her idle hours at Dian Tong Studio complaining to Tang about the film industry and declaring once more that she must leave its sordidness and seek some fresh air elsewhere, Tang had made a suggestion. Make one really good film, he urged her, then leave.

Lan replied, after careful thought, that this was an unworkable suggestion. A good film would lift her from frustration and obscurity, and then she wouldn't *want* to leave movieland.

Success in *Blood on Wolf Mountain* and even more so as the female lead in *Old Bachelor Wang* some months later, put Lan Ping precisely into the situation she had imagined. Meanwhile, the praise from critics and audiences for her vivid performance in *Blood on Wolf Mountain* made her a happier woman and made Tang Na happier to be with her.

In *Old Bachelor Wang,* a harrowing film set in a slum, Lan played the role of a poor but determined young woman who meets bachelor Wang, and marries him, not because she loves him as he loves her, but out of gratitude for his kindness when her father dies. Poverty, alcoholism, and Japanese invasion add up to a life of suffering, but the woman struggles, and in a sense triumphs over the weaker Wang by outliving him—survival was just about the only realistic goal in such a life. The movie ends with Lan bent over his dead body, unfazed by tears and blood, swearing defiance toward her own and China's enemies.

Word spread as the film was being shot that Lan was brilliant as Wang's plucky wife. "Her performance made a deep impression on me," said Wang Tingshu, the Jinan classmate who now was in the Shanghai theater. Lan's morale rose. But, alas for Tang, "one really good film" led her to leave not the movies, but Tang Na!

Tang wrote a review that praised *Old Bachelor Wang* and Lan Ping's performance in it, but his stamp of approval meant less to her than in the previous year. Just as during 1936 her career frustrations made her difficult for Tang Na to deal with, so during 1937, after she had two major movie roles to her credit, her success reduced her need for Tang as a "mountain to lean on" in society and emotionally.

One frigid winter night late in 1936 a big crowd gathered at the Golden City Theater, Shanghai's premier playhouse, for the opening night of a play by the accomplished playwright Xia Yan, a colleague of Tian Han and an acquaintance of Lan Ping. *"WITH HER LITTLE TONGUE,"* the billboard cried, *"OUR HEROINE SAVED 1000S OF INNOCENT PEOPLE IN THE CITY OF PEKING."*

Sai Jinhua was a dramatization of the story of a bold woman of the era of the Boxer Rebellion, when women were expected to "smile without showing their teeth and walk without showing their feet." At first a prostitute, she became for a while a political figure and was later disgraced and impoverished. Her life (1874–1936) became one of those legends that the Chinese love to fashion out of a blend of history and romance.

Sai was the sort of woman who preferred to be independent as a prostitute than to be a meek appendage to a conventional man—as Lan Ping had preferred to seek her way in a risky profession rather than be an obedient wife to Mr. Fei in Jinan. Sai, like Lan in her later political career, showed a natural talent for politics; quite ignorant of theories, she nevertheless was brilliant at maneuver and at the dramatization of issues.

Sai was, like Lan Ping, a woman who, given the vagaries of Chinese politics and the obsession of Chinese culture to put a person in a category, could over a period of time be vagrant, toast of the establishment, and traitor.

Lan Ping wanted the part of Sai (Xia Yan made a heroine of Sai) as she had wanted few parts in her life. She spoke to Tang Na about it, and also to Zhang Min. Her desire to portray this colorful woman outweighed her unease at some aspects of the comparison between Sai's life and her own. What mattered to Lan was that here was a woman who had struggled for a lifetime against her bad reputation and yet made an *impact,* alike on the politics of her time and on the imagination of the Chinese people. And the male lead in the play was the famous Jin Shan, "Golden Mountain," the Clark Gable of the Shanghai stage.

But Xia Yan, a prominent left-wing figure who had studied in Japan, was not an admirer of Lan's. He gave the role of Sai to the enticing Wang Ying, who often had been leading lady in his plays and his Dian Tong movies. When she heard the news, Lan's fascination with the play turned into "fury" that a "traitorous whore" like Sai should be made the subject of a drama! How could such a bitch be permitted to "speak for China" and eclipse the role played by the "heroic mass movement" of the Boxers? She went to such extremes in her opposition to the play—which she had previously set her heart on starring in—that members of the "1940s Society," which put on the play, made threats on her life in an effort to stop her shrill outbursts.*

* In her phase of political dominance, during the 1960s, Jiang Qing said the play was "soaked with bourgeois poison" and called Sai a "100 percent anti-Communist traitor."

*   *   *

As if both were too bloodied by past crises to face many more, Lan and Tang began to slide fairly calmly toward divorce. The love and the splitting up seemed to be parallel parts of the same drama, a serial in a hundred installments with a new twist each week.

Arguments about each other's rights replaced outpourings of the heart. Lan came under criticism in Bohemian circles for stringing Tang on while caring for him less than he cared for her. Her version of events was that Tang was weak and unstable, but she admitted that she no longer loved him and that she was seeing Zhang Min.

One day he stormed into her *pied-à-terre*. He was suffering too much, he said; he wanted to "clarify matters" (*qing suan*) with her. He pulled out a page of a letter from Ai Xia, just back from Japan, in which this former girlfriend grieved that Tang had spurned her (for Lan). Tremblingly, Tang showed it to Lan as proof of his single-minded devotion to her.

But there was no prospect of "single-minded devotion" from Lan's side. She made her position clear that day: "I did not love him anymore." She was prepared to be "good friends" with him, she said.

For Tang this was almost worse than nothing.

She asked if he wished to have news of a separation published in the press. Tang replied that if it were necessary for Lan, they would, but it was not necessary for him. She didn't see the need for it either, so they made no announcement. Tang decided to leave Shanghai for a time.

Some weeks later, Tang appeared on her doorstep and began to curse her for "seeking to advance her position" and "tricking" him by sleeping with "a man" (Zhang Min).

"You mean to say that, when we've settled matters, I then can't love another?" Then Lan went one crucial step farther. *"Even if we hadn't settled matters, I still have the right to love another!"*

"He cursed me," Lan recalled. "I remained silent and let him curse. When he had cursed to his fill, he left." She resolved that if he came back again, she would strike him.

He did come back. "In my apartment," she wrote of that evening, "apart from a small fruit knife and a pair of scissors, there were no available weapons. There was nothing to be afraid of. Let him come! I'm not going to budge."

Closing the door behind him, she struck him a swift blow. He hit her back. A servant woman and friends heard the blows, but they could not get through the door that Lan had securely locked. When Tang left, he took some letters he had written to Lan, she claimed, and two notebooks in which she had recorded episodes from their life together. But Lan felt her pride, if not her apartment, was intact.

"He said he was going to publish an announcement of our separation," she observed, "but he didn't do it."

In a moment of black despair over Lan, Tang Na sprang from a parapet into the Whangpu River. It was daytime, his leap was seen, and he was rescued. *Da wanbao* and other papers briefly reported the incident, but Lan Ping's name was not mentioned.

A divorce was finalized—it was made easier by the absence of a legal marriage agreement—in May 1937. Lan left a loan unpaid at a Shanghai bank; Tang Na had to pay it off. She pawned Tang's watch and pen.

During the affair with Tang Na, professional theater work became the center of gravity of Lan's life. The consequences were great. Her money problems were solved. The fees from movie companies did not make her wealthy by any means, but poverty was behind her. People noticed that she spent more money on clothes and cosmetics. And her desperate awkwardness was essentially conquered. The heartaches of her life, the oddity of her ways, the willfulness that constantly brought her trouble, all could be transmuted, onstage or before the cameras, into emotions that were cathartic for Lan Ping and moving for her audiences.

Although "art and literature" always were coupled in left-wing Chinese phraseology, in Shanghai during the 1930s the foot soldiers of the performing arts, such as Lan Ping, were on quite another level from the writers, of whom Lu Xun was the most famous.

Lu Xun insisted on a distinction between propaganda and literature, but the distinction between propaganda and the performing arts was harder to make. Sheer emotion could capture a theater audience, but on the printed page sheer emotion counted for less. Lan Ping was far more effective in front of an audience, using the full range of her intense personality, than she had been writing stories and poems in Qingdao.*

Equally the actress's way of life—declaiming rather than sitting

---

* She realized that her writing was not successful. Perhaps, when she became a politician years later, there was an element of the "failed writer" behind her ambition, as there was of the "failed painter" behind Hitler's.

down with a book, on show for all to see, taking on one persona today and another tomorrow, brushing shoulders with a variety of people—was quite different, and far more Lan's cup of tea, than the writer's way of life, with its requirements of isolation, patience, and consistency.

There crystallized in Lan's mind a quite amazing identification, which later colored her political ideas, between *audiences* and *masses.* She came to think that those who watched her perform were "the people" in the same sense in which the Communist Party's constituency of workers and peasants were "the people." Both were her heroes; to both she would be a guide. Obsessively she talked of her "grass-roots work"; this did not mean political organizing, but an artist's cultivation of admiring fans.

Lan forged an amalgam of theatrical and political passion that, years later, would fuel her crusade to obtain, and wield, the supreme power of the Chinese state. Was the wolf who pursued her, as she played the role of the harassed wife in *Blood on Wolf Mountain,* an animal from the dark recesses of her childhood memories that she could summon such emotion in fleeing from it? Or was she equating the wolf with the Japanese (as the critics said), or with the "capitalist class enemy"? It was difficult to tell.

Lan Ping was an elemental person, not given to concepts. The roles she played, because of the passion she felt as she threw herself into them, shaped her own values as a wife and lover, and as a citizen of China in the 1930s. The wolves in *Blood on Wolf Mountain* became wolves in the landscape of her own life. The enemies she did battle with onstage and on the screen were readily transmuted into the "class renegades" who were to be the targets of her political crusades. It is quite possible that her keenest feeling of economic deprivation and of hatred of Japanese aggression occurred not in her own life but as she acted in *Old Bachelor Wang.*

Yes, she poured the passions of her experience into her art; but her life was also deeply colored by her memorable artistic moments.

In observing anyone who moves from acting to politics, as Lan Ping was to do, it is hard to pin down the actor-politician's own ideas, because he or she has become accustomed to giving passionate expression to a variety of *other* people's ideas. One may look at a Lan Ping movie of the 1930s, aware of Jiang Qing's career during the 1960s—as at an old Ronald Reagan movie from the vantage point of the 1980s—and ask, "Which is the real person?" Both are real. It is the same woman—in more than the sense that the same flesh and blood is moving this way and that—for the passion that grips her on the two occasions is of a piece—to get even, to ward off nasty or lustful men, to move a crowd, to vanquish enemies by sheer assertion.

"She would never make a good wife," Cui Wanqiu murmured to a friend as he watched Lan play the role of Nora. "Just see how strong, how convincing she is in denouncing Helmer and declaring her independence!" Seeing Lan Ping's Nora, he felt he was understanding something of Lan Ping herself.

"I cannot bear it any longer," Lan Ping wrote in the magazine of Lian Hua Studio. "I am going to tell the truth." The newspaper talk and gossip among Tang Na's friends about her "cruelty" toward him provoked her to tell the theatrical public her side of the story. It was May 1937 and she was living with Zhang Min, not having seen Tang for some time.

"At first," she said, "I was just going to be patient with this nuisance. In heaven's name, do I deserve to be bothered *yet again* by Tang Na?" Then she realized that if she didn't speak out, people would conclude she was guilty. "And they would only insult me with added ferocity."

No longer were there any murmurs from Lan's corner that she had been inadequate as a lover and a wife. The fault lay entirely with Tang. "What was his method of loving me?" she wrote. "It was to ardently love someone else, while at the same time loving (?) me. That was his method."

She had been naïve, she said. "Everybody knew he was in love with another girl when we first met, as friends, at Dian Tong Studio." She never asked him about Ai Xia until much later, and he said that affair was merely a "smoke screen" to turn prying eyes away from the love that was developing between Lan and himself. "The matter flashed away from my mind like a shooting star," Lan wrote. But Tang was not finished with Ai Xia, she told the readers of *Lian Hua Pictorial*. "My self-confidence was wounded. For I used to believe that when a man loved me, he would not betray me."

Really she had married him to avoid hurting him. "Neither he nor I," she now asserted to the world, "took the wedding seriously." It was the same in Jinan, after his first attempt at suicide. "My main idea," she said of that anguished night in the inn near Daming Lake, "was that I should get him to respect himself, and then I could leave him." She felt that in Jinan, her heart "unbelievably softened," she had given in to him. "Out of sympathy and compassion," she said, "I did the most shameful thing of my life—I came back to Shanghai together with him."

To Lan, the same pattern was evident when the marriage ran off the tracks in late 1936. "My best friends felt I should not divorce Tang abruptly, for that would have driven him crazy." Alas, the period of detachment itself had a bad effect on Tang. "He was not resolute enough to reform himself," Lan explained. "Mind you, I am not saying that if he *had* reformed himself I would have loved him again! No, Lan Ping could *not* love him further. The scars were too deep."

Lan said Tang made a further attempt at suicide after she began living with Zhang Min. This drove some of Tang's friends, she claimed, to threaten her with physical violence. "God, if these people would only show such courage and boldness toward the Japanese aggressors," Lan commented, "China could still be saved. How pitiable that they vent their fury instead on a poor girl!"

"Why Tang Na and I Split Up" was an arrogant, devious essay. Lan was defensive, saying more times than seemed natural that she was convinced she had done no wrong toward Tang. She did not mention the name of Zhang Min and went out of her way to say that Fei Mu, another producer, had given her the breaks at Lian Hua Studio, which wasn't the whole truth. She presented her rejection of Tang as a necessary, long-delayed step to preserve her own mental and physical health. Many times she thought of suicide, she said. But Tang was actually driven to attempt it.

"I told him," she said of the period after his third attempt to kill himself, " 'If you do kill yourself, I will go on with my own life even more resolutely than before.' "

Of course, Lan Ping was not the type to commit suicide. "I must respect myself!" was her battle cry, whatever the season, the circumstance, the adversary. "I have never given in to an attack; this is one thing in my life I am proud of."

She contrasted herself with Yuan Lingyu, the beautiful actress who at the age of twenty-five killed herself in despair at gossip about her divorce and her promiscuity. "I was absolutely not going to be like Yuan Lingyu," wrote Lan, who was uncomfortably aware of the comparison as criticism swelled about her conduct toward Tang Na and her romance with Zhang Min, "and kill myself out of terror at gossip. I will not yield. I will not give in one inch." Whether it was physical attack from Tang Na, or verbal attack from Tang's friends, and in the movie magazines, she would brave it all.*

"Do they take me for a pitiable worm, to be trampled on at random by whomsoever? Well, I am not! Lan Ping is a human being. She will never yield in a thousand years, especially in the face of these miserable tricks [of the gossipmongers who sided with Tang Na]."

She wanted a strong-willed man. Yet Lan and such a man would have been like two tigers in a cupboard, an excess of strength for the situation. She kept lashing Tang Na to "think better of yourself." Yet would a prouder, more resolute Tang Na have found Lan Ping any less difficult?

Political pressure, augmented by the chaos that followed Japan's full-scale attack on Shanghai in the summer of 1937, crippled the city's movie industry. Lan Ping made one more film at Lian Hua, an anti-Japanese short called *Twenty Cents,* in which she won respectable notices as the female lead. But Lian Hua's operations soon spiraled down to a halt.

Lan's personal life, too, had come to the end of a cycle. She was divorced. The publication of "Why Tang Na and I Split Up" made her a controversial young woman, even among the Bohemians. She was widely thought to have "crossed the limits" in twisting Zhang Min's arm to get the lead in *The Thunderstorm.* In Zhang Min's drama troupe she was criticized for haughty behavior, trading on her link with the boss, such as eating alone in a private room while troupe members ate communal dishes in a cafeteria.

Yet there really was no future—even if she hoped for it—in the affair with the complex and overcommitted Zhang Min. Above all, Lan was an actress in a city where the professional stage and screen were being dismantled by the week. Like many others in the performing arts, she now had to reckon with politics as an overriding fact of life.

Shanghai would not long remain politically safe for Lan. "All those who had been arrested by the Nationalists," a young actress who was later close to Lan observed, "knowing they were on the Nationalists' books, grew anxious in 1937 to depart for another po-

___

* Many years and several phases of her life later, she would still work herself into a passion when recalling the "humiliations" dealt her by those who disparaged her in Shanghai. "Read that," she said to an American visitor, pointing to a copy of Lu Xun's essay "Gossip Is a Fearful Thing" (which was inspired by Yuan Lingyu's suicide), "for in it you will find clues to my own life."

litical environment. I think this is one reason why Lan Ping left Shanghai."

On the occasion of one of Lan Ping's preliminary "farewells" to Tang Na, she had proposed a scheme for easing the social pain Tang would feel at the separation. "Say I am dead." It was a fantasy that suited both her sense of melodrama and her sense of her own fragility. "Anyway," she wrote, as if safeguarding a connection between the real and the imaginary, "I am leaving this Bohemian environment—isn't that a death?" The plan called for Tang to say she had succumbed to meningitis. "It will be a secret only between you and me that I actually live on." Her magnanimity flowered: "I am confident of your ability to keep the secret."

Now the fantasy was not needed; Lan Ping was indeed "dying" to her Shanghai world. In July 1937 she packed up her belongings, including a collection of photos of herself in performance, and left the city. As for Tang Na, he heard that she was moving, but he was not sure of her exact reasons; she was Zhang Min's worry now, not his.

The apparent mysteries and paradoxes of Lan Ping's four years in Shanghai—her endless difficulty in "contacting the Party," her hot-and-cold relationships with Tang Na and other men, the blend of self-indulgence and courage in the pattern of her activities—are less puzzling when seen against the backdrop of her inner goal: to escape exploitation by the "big ones," to be mistress of her environment, to express herself freely as an individual. Everything else— whether organizations, ideas, or people—was merely the arena for her self-conscious personal struggle.

These four years were in a way her Golden Age. "I was not a brilliant actress," she said years later, "but I stood out rather prominently among the new actresses." Indeed, for all Shi Dongshan's connections, Tang Na's warm reviews, and Zhang Min's subjective casting policy, for all the protective cocoon of Communist-led arts groups, she advanced in large part because of her own will, energy, and talent, because of an exciting passion in her approach to life.

Little of all this can be said of some of her later periods, when she rose higher and looked back with embarrassment at the 1930s; but it can be said, to her credit, of her years onstage in Shanghai. Perhaps Lan Ping was Jiang Qing at her best.

Before leaving Shanghai, Lan wrote an essay called "Our Life," which summed up the values she embraced in Shanghai, expressed some unchanging traits of her personality, and foreshadowed her method of handling a fourth marriage that lay ahead, and the political career that the marriage would ultimately lead to.

In characteristic style she began by placing herself in a position contrary to common opinion. "How fascinating, how wonderful to be an actor or actress," people often say. But Lan felt they miss the point. "Ah, but she's one of those immoral actresses!" people also say. This infuriated her.

Drama is a tool of social betterment, she maintained, and in the Shanghai of 1937 it must be anti-imperialist. So it was not surprising that people of the theater were feeling insult and attack on all sides. The "tentacles of imperialism" (a moment later, as her taste for animal imagery proved irrepressible, the "hunting dogs of imperialism"), in an attempt to "cling on to the old world," were making a target of the "new theater movement" and the "sparkling fresh flowers" it had brought forth.

In such a chilly clime, the actor and actress (each time Lan used the character for "he," she put "she" in brackets after it, to make clear that she was talking as much about women as about men) must train and discipline themselves, philosophy and will no less than the body, to become "as unbreakable as steel rods." *They are not mere dolls,*" she almost shouts.

She seemed to be thinking of Zhang Geng ("She's my girl, don't touch"), perhaps with less ferocity of Zhang Min, and of her own struggle against being taken for granted as a mere pretty face, without a mind and will of equal worth with those of the male directors and writers.

The playwright and director must rise to "penetrating social analysis" if the theater is to fulfill its true social function. Even if a script is good, a director whose social analysis is inadequate—or "incorrect," she added, in a chilly foretaste of the dogmatism that later engulfed her—can ruin the play. But *the actors and actresses,* Lan Ping insisted, are a third component of equal importance in the creative process. They must have minds of their own and make original (and "correct") analyses of society.

They must not be just dolls with pretty faces, as in "capitalist theater." They must not merely recite passively the lines that have come from the playwright's pen—adequate as that may be in a bourgeois scheme of things—but invest their own spirit in the play, creating an amalgam of their own values and the playwright's intention. Indeed, they have to be *just as bright* as the playwright and director, she avowed. They are engaged in a "common endeavor" with these two, and they are to be judged by the "same measuring rod."*

The prose is flowery, the mood passionate, the stance subjective, and the viewpoint trenchantly left-wing. "Our Life" is a battle cry on behalf of the values of strong will, creativity, and independence of mind and spirit.

"Many people think acting is an easy business," Lan Ping went on, "that it's just a case of learning the lines, a smile here, some tears there, a twist of the waist or two—and after all, can't anyone smile, cry, and twist their waist?" Well, she may be young, and new to the craft, but she will shoot down that nonsense. "An actress may have talent, but unless she exerts her energy, unless her will is strong, the talent will wither and even become *refuse.*"

Nor is "beauty and liveliness" enough if energy and will are lacking, she declared—perhaps recalling Yuan Lingyu and other pretty young actresses who met tragic fates (and, I think, confusing the personal success of the actress with the fulfillment of the theater's social function). Was not Lan Ping telling the world that she herself possessed more than beauty and liveliness, that she had needed great energy and will to survive as far as she had, and that she would deploy these in whatever realm the future placed her?

Meanwhile, at the tender age of twenty-three she felt able to give guidance to the aspiring actor or actress. If you discover you have dramatic talent, Lan advised, set about resolutely to educate yourself. The task, she said, in a phrase that seems to have come from reflecting upon her own past conduct, "is to deploy both your spirit and your body, now one and now the other, to suit the various situations you are in."

In her life so far she had done just that, and it had given people the impression that whatever sphere she was in—the theater, left-wing activity, a marriage—her eye was on more than the object of immediate attention, that her own persona always transcended the task or loyalty of the moment.

With bows to Stanislavsky now and then, Lan went on to dissect the craft of acting. No two personalities are completely alike,

---

* One cannot but think of that later "theatrical production," the Cultural Revolution of the 1960s, when Jiang Qing put the principles of "Our Life" into practice; Mao was the scriptwriter and producer, to be sure, but his wife, long a standard-bearer for the rights and dignity of actors and actresses, saw to it that she and other players in that political drama were not mere passive recipients of the director's shouts but creators with him of a daily-unfolding "new politics," in the end as much theirs as his.

she observed, and one cannot go onstage and simply act as oneself. Role A may suit an actress better than role B, but it is always a creative act to put oneself into any role.

"Acting is an art," she burst out, "not a way of life."

With that declaration Lan rebuked the directors who viewed her as a doll, onstage and offstage, rejected the tired image of the "immoral actress," and held high the banner of the actress as a creator.

As she lambasted the Shanghai theatrical environment for being "evil," she found her fundamental theme: She would insist, regardless of contrary pressure, on the separation of her theatrical art and her life. Into the theater Lan had put her acting skill; but she had not and would not put her life at the disposition of the theater.* The creative talent she poured into her portrayal of Nora, and Wang's wife in *Old Bachelor Wang,* and the woman fighting wolves in *Blood on Wolf Mountain* was hers, Lan Ping's. She was a different person from these three women; she held in her own hands the ingredients of that difference.

She was a young, questing, malleable individual in the maelstrom of revolutionary China. Her "art," these past years, had been directed to the stage, but it need not in the future be confined to the stage.

Just as a young man who is brought up in a religious household, finding that he has oratorical talent, might fuse his drive to express himself in front of others with a vocation to be a clergyman, Lan Ping had, for a season, harmonized her vaulting ambition with a vocation as an actress.

But her drive to assert herself eclipsed her attachment to any art, any cause, any man. As "Our Life" rejected the idea of an actress as a semiprostitute—a doll to titillate the audience, or be played with by the director—so Lan Ping struggled to reject the role of a semiprostitute as her destiny in life. Her struggle—"deploying both my spirit and my body, now one and now the other, to suit the various situations I am in"—was far from over.

"She realized she had to get out of Shanghai," Tang Na said to a friend. "Her essay 'Our Life' is her meal ticket to Yanan," he added, in a reference to the Communist base in northwestern China.

Lan Ping had been too strong for Tang Na, and her ambition was swelling too large for the theater to contain it. Her next man

---

* "I would like people," Ingrid Bergman once said, "to separate the actress and the woman." It was a natural wish of the actress with a colorful private life.

would have to be extremely strong; her next realm would need to take her beyond words and images, beyond emotions expressed for one night's audience and then gone, to actual control over big events. "Never forget," she once said, "that beauty is not as important as power."

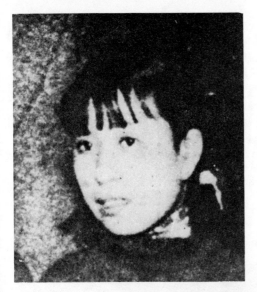

◄ Li Yunhe (Jiang Qing) at age nineteen, about the time she left Qingdao for Shanghai, her hair in *liu hai* (bangs) style.

▼ Li Yunhe (Jiang Qing) as an ardent, rebellious Nora in Zhang Min's production of *A Doll's House,* 1935.

Lois Snow

◄A historic photo, unearthed from the files of Edgar Snow, of the third marriage of Lan Ping (Jiang Qing) at the Pagoda of Six Harmonies in Hangzhou in 1936. In the front row are the six who were wed: Yie Luxi and Zhao Dan, Lan Ping (Jiang Qing) and Tang Na, Du Lulu and Gu Eryi. Shen Chunju, the lawyer, is in the middle of the back row and Zheng Junli, the best man, is at left.

The wedding party ► after returning to Shanghai.

Tang Na (inset) and the Railway Inn at Jinan, site of the first of his suicide attempts in despair over Lan Ping (Jiang Qing). ▼

Lan Ping (Jiang Qing) in ▶
a movie (perhaps *Scenes
of City Life*); "Urban
Shadow" reads the Chinese
inscription.

◀Lan Ping (Jiang
Qing) the actress on
the cover of a maga-
zine in 1936 or 1937.

◀Roman Karmen's photo of Jiang Qing on horseback in 1939.

Jiang Qing at work in Nan-▶ niwan in 1939.

▲Jiang Qing (second from left) with Li Lilian (Otto Braun's wife), Edgar Snow (second from right), and Indian medical friends at Yanan in late 1939.

Lois Snow

▲ Mao with his previous wife, He Zizhen, just before their divorce.

◀ The chairman and his wife in Yanan in the early spring of 1945.

▲ Wartime: Mao and Jiang are soon to leave their cave at Yanan as renewed civil war rages, 1947.

◄Kang Jian, Cui Wanqiu, and Mrs. Cui, in a photo taken in Tokyo in 1955 after all three had left China.

Jiang Qing and Mao with► Madame Hartini Sukarno, 1962.

▼Zhou Enlai and his wife, Deng Yingchao, with Madame Sukarno.

An extraordinary ▶ glimpse of Peking in the leadup to the Cultural Revolution: (from right) Wang Guangmei (hostess), Madame Sukarno, Zhu De, Liu Shaoqi, and Mao Zedong·

◀Wang Guangmei with President Sukarno on the fateful trip to Jakarta, 1963.

▲ After her fall, Wang Guangmei is mocked in a cartoon, 1967.

▲ At the height of the Cultural Revolution, Jiang appears on the Gate of Heavenly Peace with Kang Sheng (to her right), Zhou Enlai, Lin Biao and her husband, Mao Zedong.

Jiang Qing receives Red ▶ Guards after a performance of *Shajiabang* in 1967.

▲ Jiang Qing, Zhou Enlai, and Kang Sheng receive the applause of a Red Guard rally in December 1966.

4

Mao's Housewife in Yanan (1938–49)

Sex is engaging in the first rounds, but what sustains
interest in the long run is power.
　　　　　　　　　　　　　—Jiang Qing

Far from Shanghai, the town was a dust bowl in a valley beneath golden hills. Buildings in brown clay and wood with paper windows sat around a curving river. Chickens scratched in peace along the main street as donkeys slouched by with bundles on their backs. Smoke curled up from coal stoves on which millet was steaming. From the highest hill a pagoda built during the Song dynasty (960–1276), thin and neat like a pencil, blessed the scene.

Only the uplifting slogans on the mud-brick walls, wiry soldiers practicing boxing and swordplay on a school sports field, and guards with Mausers by the homes of Mao Zedong and the other leaders on the hillside hinted that this cozy community in northwestern China was not simply a center for surrounding farms but an outpost of determined political pilgrims.

As sunset came, turning the hills purple, a girl sat on a rock by the muddy ripples of the Yan River. Khaki fatigues rolled up to the knees, long legs wide apart and feet in the gurgling shallows, she held a lump of soap in one hand and her soiled uniform in the other. For a while she did not notice the man standing to one side, Jack Chen, an artist newly arrived in Yanan. Chen said hello, and the attractive girl managed a quick smile. There was a wry look on her face as she stood up, straightened her back, and contemplated her finished laundry. Preoccupied, she did not pursue the conversation with Chen but took her wet clean clothes back to the Reception Center for fresh arrivals, where she was staying.

For Lan Ping, the past few weeks had been ones of reassessment. As Shanghai crumbled under Japan's assault, the Communist

Party tried to pick up the pieces of the politically influential performing arts groups and reorganize them into National Salvation Theater Troupes, to fan out and present anti-Japanese shows to an anxious, suffering China. But as Lan's own unit, the Amateur Experimental Drama Troupe, run by her boyfriend Zhang Min, took a train west to Nanjing, the Nationalists' capital, Lan wondered if she really wanted to go on to Sichuan Province, where many of the Shanghai circle were headed.

Lan's outspokenness, and the nasty taste left in many mouths by her breakup with Tang Na, had created enemies. Nor was she a *top* actress, for whom any door would fly open and any role would be there for the asking. Shi Dongshan had been enigmatic; at times she suspected he judged her mediocre. "Lipstick" Yuan Muzhi, a powerful figure in the Central Film Studio being set up from Wuhan, had become a straight-out detractor (he had not enjoyed seeing Tang Na pluck Lan from under his longing gaze at Dian Tong Studio).

She reached Wuhan, about halfway between Shanghai and Sichuan, and hesitated there for a week or two. "Lan Ping asked to see me about a job," recalled Zheng Yongzhi, then a director in the Central Film Studio in this city on the Yangzi River, "approaching me through Yang Hansheng, secretary to Guo Moruo." Zheng Yongzhi twice declined to receive her because he could not help her. "I had no vacancies for actresses in July 1937. The second problem was that Tang Na was in my company. He had a terrible resentment against her—I couldn't have considered employing her, for Tang Na did not wish to set eyes on her again. I think she soon left Wuhan."

In a declining industry, Lan realized she might lose out.

She was as capable of putting up with hardship as the next person and was at least as outraged at Japanese aggression. Yet she also was a seeker after the limelight. Some friends felt there had already sprouted in her mind the idea of playing a personal—as distinct from a purely artistic—role in the Communist movement. "Look," said Tang Na to a friend, "she had to get out of Shanghai, and once that was decided she began to think of hooking someone in Yanan." One cannot be sure. But she certainly itched for a new adventure.

Lan had a dream that she could join her art and her life into a combination that would dwarf the separate possibilities of either. In Yanan she would work in the theater. At the same time she would reach beyond the theater and press her personal drive for self-fulfillment within the Communist political community.

There were two men, both important Communists, who might help her get a start. Her husband from Qingdao days, Yu Qiwei, was at this time also going to the Northwest; Lan had kept in touch with him and probably knew this. And her fellow townsman Kang Sheng, whom she had met when he became headmaster of Zhu-cheng primary school, after graduating from her own alma mater, Qingdao University, was heading back to the Northwest after study-ing in Russia. Surely Lan could lean on this "mountain."

So she set her face toward the loess hills, there to deploy her tal-ents, "now one and now the other," to gouge a niche in a world that would be different—as different from Shanghai as Shanghai had been from Zhucheng—and which just might have the future on its side. At the very least, it would be fun and a change from Shanghai.

Xian ("Western Peace") is an ancient city of broad, straight boulevards and low, sprawling buildings with courtyards. Buddhist pagodas rise above the flat geometry of the streets, as if keeping watch over this strategic gateway between the heart of China and the fringes of Eurasia. As the Japan-China war began in earnest and the Nationalists and Communists nibbled with each other, from their bases in different parts of China, in a supposed "united front" against Japan, Xian became a political bridge. It was the transit point for traffic between Chiang's "White Area" (in which Xian lay) and Mao's "Red Area" (headquartered from January 1937 at Yanan, "Extended Peace").

Lan unpeeled herself from a hot and sticky railroad carriage one day in late July 1937. Carrying her two bundles and a purse with her savings, she took a *ma che* to the Liaison Office of the Com-munists' Eighth Route Army, a sort of embassy of Mao's China in the territory of Chiang's China. In the courtyards of these low, whitewashed barracks, pilgrims to the red desert farther north had to check in and be appraised.

Lan had traveled part of the way to Xian with an actress who also felt herself to be taking a step away from the theatrical center. Li Lilian was soon to marry Otto Braun, the reclusive German who, as Comintern delegate to the Chinese Communist Party, was a tool in Moscow's effort to control the Chinese Revolution. The future Mrs. Braun saw the nervous, gossipy, curiosity-ridden, very femi-nine side of Lan Ping.

Lan was not an ordinary pilgrim, any more than she had been an ordinary schoolgirl, an ordinary housewife to Mr. Fei, an ordinary actress, or an ordinary wife to Tang Na. No one had sent her to the Northwest. She had not arrived with a Party mandate in her blouse, or a defined mission ahead of her, but on spec, to see what might turn up. "I asked to go there," she admitted.

In Communist China, everyone belongs to a "unit." The individual lives and moves within the cocoon of the unit. He or she speaks of it as a Westerner might speak of a secure but stifling large family. Lan had a tendency to occupy a twilight zone among a number of units, moving from one to the other with an almost un-Chinese restlessness. In wartime as in peace, married or single, while holding down a job and also when drifting, Lan always was fundamentally a unit of one.*

In her two weeks at Xian, she seemed at a tangent, strangely separated from any co-workers, to all externals without a purpose. She was a confident wanderer. Her floating condition aroused suspicion in some people, attracted others.

At the hostel of the Eighth Route Army offices, Lan found Sister Xu, her plain and slightly sinister political mentor from Shanghai. In a new political season, Xu had replaced her previous given name of Yiyong with Mingqing. She had not seen her flighty charge for a while, and she marveled, with a slightly uneasy laugh, at how her "little sister," Li Yunhe, had become the well-known actress Miss Lan Ping.

It was the scheming side of Lan that Xu saw and evoked. Shrewd in her calculations as to what the looming switch of roles would require from her, Lan already felt some anxiety lest her unstable and Bohemian past go down badly in this stern new environment. How much would be known in Yanan about her time in prison? There was that damn "confession" she had written in a weak moment. Still, the newly minted United Front between Chiang and Mao would surely put her contacts with the Shanghai Nationalists in an improved light. At least she hoped so. Some people, however, might point a finger at her promiscuity. And would she be able to convince the arbiters of proletarian virtue how tough—and so, in a way, proletarian—her childhood had been?

Older Sister Xu and Younger Sister Lan, fueled by some kind of attraction between opposites and conscious of the possibilities of mutual help, sat around in the bone-dry heat, sandals off, hair awry, eating fruit and chatting about future plans. Lan was drawing nearer to the maelstrom of politics, and she needed the loyalty of her former "organizational leader" if she was to succeed.

---

* Years later she described herself as "a unit of one" (see page 364).

Many of the women in the hostel were dumpy; Lan was slender. It was the norm to neglect one's appearance; Lan was very conscious of hers. In the lassitude of midsummer, she moved with a Girl Scout's vigor, humming to herself (as Nora did in *A Doll's House*), asking a hundred questions about life in the Northwest.

She was quick to smile, seemingly full of the *joie de vivre* that finds something to comment on or chuckle at every ten minutes. When pleasure came to her face, the large bright eyes gave radiance to her features, and her calm, vibrant voice made people take notice.

Onstage Lan had become skilled—as revolutionary women fighters never were—at putting on a particular garment in a particular way to create a particular effect. In discarding the *qipao* in which she arrived at Xian, she by no means discarded her instinct for clothes. She tied the cloth belt around the waist of her unisex jacket and trousers with a decisive flourish. Her clothes were battleship gray, but her shining black hair lit them up. The hair still was long—one could not, despite Sister Xu's urging, change everything overnight—but instead of allowing it to fall in a riotous cascade to her shoulders, she had disciplined it into two braids. She chose blue ribbons that lent a touch of color without looking showy. Even without makeup, her face stood out among those of the women pilgrims.

A male chauvinist atmosphere, which can make women hate each other when they are potential rivals, also can draw noncompeting women closely together. Sister Xu, plain as a bulging sausage in her uniform, lapped up Lan's tales of how her fans in Shanghai cheered her, wrote her letters, sent her flowers. Lan allowed her style and charm to work for her, at the same time punctuating the conversation with self-deprecatory remarks and stressing that although she happened to be an actress (perhaps the point of appeal for Xu), her cause in life was revolutionary politics. The pair ate lunch, and sat on their hard wooden beds speculating about the future of the war and the revolution. Their permission to go to Yanan in hand, they decided to travel together. One shimmering morning at 6:00 A.M. they climbed into a truck for the first leg of their journey.

For Lan, everything was fresh and new. There were black mountain sheep. The farmers wore blue denim, sunglasses to keep out the dust, and towels on their heads in the Shaanxi manner. In Shanghai, this China had seemed as far away as the moon and certainly farther from Lan's thoughts than Hollywood was. Compared with the Shandong Province of her childhood, the farmers here looked dirty, the animals scrawny, and the dusty terrain inhospitable to crops.

A storm hit the hills and turned the red loess soil into torrents of caramel sauce, pouring down to block the truck's path with rocks and mud, dissolving half the dirt road before the travelers' eyes. They tried to continue by mounting some scraggy horses produced by the copper-faced farmers. Some managed, but Lan managed only to mount a spectacle. While the country folk knew how to talk to a horse, Lan did not even know how to get on a horse's back.

"I had no idea how to ride it," she later confessed merrily after her life-style had changed and she had come to "adore riding."

The horse she found herself on top of kept its head to the ground, as if humiliated by its exotic burden, and would not move. Embarrassed to ask instructions—that would type her as a Bohemian in this unBohemian part of China—Lan dismounted in silent fury, grabbed a willow branch, clambered back up like a child getting for the first time into an upper bunk, and began whipping the horse's buttocks with the branch.

"That made him wild and he galloped away madly," she said, almost as if she were talking of one of her husbands.

But the blows served no great purpose. In the soaking rain, horse and woman flew nowhere in particular until the horse, raw from the blows of Lan's willow branch, became exhausted as well.

Lan, Xu, and the other pilgrims, skin splashed red from the mud, continued the trip in their army truck after the storm gave way to an eerie blue stillness and the road was cleared of its flotsam, arriving at Luochuan in the third week of August 1937.

In a low mud hut on a barren hill of this small town, the leaders of Chinese communism sat smoking at a long wooden table. An enlarged Politburo was discussing a report entitled "For the Mobilization of All the Nation's Forces for Victory in the War of Resistance," written by the most powerful man in the room, Mao Zedong.

Xu had been able to escort Lan via Luochuan because her husband, Wang Guanlan, a senior figure with a Shanghai background, now chief of the United Front Department, was taking part in the meeting, and she was to meet him there. Installed in one of the residential mud huts, the women—only men sat at the long wooden table—waited for the meeting to end and the trip to Yanan to resume.

The next day Lan awoke early. It was a morning to remember.

The air was so still a donkey's bray could be heard from miles away. The brilliant sunlight put color into the loess hills, as electricity transforms a neon tube. They didn't look so miserable after all. And there was a wonderful blueness in the atmosphere Lan felt she could almost touch.

News came with breakfast's millet soup—no toast, as in Shang-hai—that the Politburo meeting had ended halfway through the night and that everyone, including hangers-on such as Lan, would begin the fifty-mile drive to Yanan at seven.

The political pilgrims piled into trucks. Lan sat with Xu and her husband, Wang, waiting for an order to set the convoy crawl-ing into the morning calm. Some VIPs, fountain pens in their important-looking pockets, came out of the low mud hut, taking their time as they conversed among themselves, and got into a wait-ing sedan. Lan Ping was fascinated by the self-confidence of these Communist leaders—rustic as was the stage, and rude the sets and costumes, for the political drama they were rehearsing. She wanted to check her hair, but there was no mirror in the truck.

One sedan in the convoy remained empty. As all eyes in the trucks looked toward the mud hut for the last arrivals, Mao Ze-dong, as the star who comes out last, emerged—a fairly tall, lean fig-ure with long hair and the face of a satisfied associate professor.

"That's him," Wang Guanlan whispered to Lan. It was not right to point or stare, but the hangers-on felt like doing so, for there was a glamour to Mao's entrance and an air of excitement that *made* it an entrance. Lan suddenly felt appalled at her youthfulness and political ignorance. In this world of the Communist leadership there seemed to be nuances, secrets she might never learn. Would she be out of her depth? Was she a fool to be headed for Yanan?

Years later Lan would claim that at Luochuan "all the leading comrades of the Central Committee had come out to greet me." That was nonsense. Yet Mao's top colleague and rival, Zhang Guo-tao, who was present, was only half correct to say of Lan that "she was then an artiste who did not attract much attention." No one knew who she was, but she did attract some quick, admiring glances. The leading comrades may not have greeted her, but some of them did *see* her.

When the glances were over and the vehicles began to move, Lan tried to look at the Shaanxi countryside as she felt a serious ob-server should. She pushed her eyes toward the terrible eroded fis-sures that scarred the hills with too few trees. But her mind ran back to the scene of the quietly confident Communists coming out of their mysterious meeting. Mao Zedong looked more than forty, she found herself ruminating; to her, at twenty-three, that seemed intimidatingly old. Where is his wife? she asked herself.

Lan was still lost in her wary, yet oddly leaping thoughts when the snaking dragon of a convoy reached the outskirts of Yanan. At the south gate of the city wall she noticed an old inscription: "Calm the Waves." Whose waves? Whence the calming force?

Facilities in Yanan—a makeshift coordination center for the Communists' guerrilla war against the Japanese, superimposed on a sleepy market town of some five thousand people—would shame a European village. Industry did not exist. A car was as rare as a stegosaurus. The airport was a cloud of dust. Most Yanan people confronted with a flush toilet would not have known what it was.

The surrounding villages of Shaanxi Province were among the most backward in China. Their people were said to bathe only twice in a lifetime, at birth and at marriage. During the famine of 1928–29 some three million people in the province starved. Of the survivors, many were so ignorant that they did not know the location of Peking, who the Japanese attackers were, or even their own birthdays.

As Lan Ping had to wash her own clothes in a muddy stream, so each hour of the day she had to hide her shock and pain at the absence of amenities and entertainments that in Shanghai were taken for granted.

In Yanan you were supposed to live for things of the spirit. In her own way and for her own motives Lan, as much as most people, was able to look beyond dirty clothes, foul toilets, and lice in the bed to intangible satisfactions and long-term goals.

If her motives in coming to Yanan were mixed, so were many other people's. Parts of the Nationalist areas offered much danger, little personal freedom, and uncertain prospects for education; many a young person came to Yanan to escape an arranged marriage, to be free of the family, to go to a college that he or she could not afford to do in Shanghai, or just out of curiosity.

The Yanan Communist commitment, like the Shanghai Communist commitment, was flecked with ambiguity. In Shanghai, individualism fueled the cause of communism—and would later seem the antithesis of communism. In Yanan, a sense of adventure on the frontier fueled the cause of communism—and equally would later seem subversive of the wary-eyed conformism of post-1949 Communist China.

Among the young people who flocked to Yanan in the late 1930s, Lan stood out for willpower but not for political sophistication. Her knowledge of Marxism consisted of phrases, wispy ideas, and militant opinions. When she talked about the issues involved in the revolution and the war, it sounded like a tale of heroes and villains in a Peking opera. "We are right and they are wrong" was all she knew. She felt the passion of it all and the sense of struggle, but history was a closed book for her. Her mind was the wrong shape for social analysis. It was a mind geared for maneuver.

Lan Ping engaged in two maneuvers over the next six months. In the realm of her "art," she needed a green light from the Party to start work or a course of study that would enable her to resume a career. In the realm of her "life," she wanted to make her mark as a woman who could bring to drab Yanan a touch of Shanghai excitement.

At the canteen of the Reception Center, Lan tackled her rations with what she supposed was jaunty proletarian enthusiasm. Eating a breakfast of millet gruel, she declared it delicious, though she hated the coarse fiber of the millet and missed the sweetness of Shanghai-type gruel. When her turn came for military training—no pilgrim was exempt from this—she moved her body nimbly and with an actress's grace. She handled weapons a little ostentatiously but with relish.

Something of the rural girl came to the surface. Perhaps the simplicities were welcome, to half her spirit, after the insecurities, rivalries, and revolving-door romances of her life in Shanghai. In Yanan, the rustic Red Army soldiers collected photos of Shanghai movie stars and White Russian ballet dancers from coupons in cigarette packs. None thought of Lan as one of those stars.

In a larger sense Lan Ping was not well placed to meet Yanan's demands. In the Northwest, whatever one's special skills, a fine or at least sound political record was the key to acceptance. Lan did not have one. Going to Shanghai in 1933, she had entered a vast, tossing ocean in which each person made his or her way as that person wished. Going to Yanan in 1937, she was knocking on the door of an armed camp in which the duties were fixed and admission was only by means of the Communist Party's approval.

Lan was not accepted as an established Communist, as were women who had made the Long March (like Mao's wife, of whom more in a moment, and Kang Keqing, "Backwoods Boadicea," the wife of the Red Army chief Zhu De) and those who had studied abroad and done labor organizing or education work in the 1920s and 1930s (like the spirited Cai Chang, the wife of Li Fuchun, and the dedicated Deng Yingchao, the wife of Zhou Enlai).

Nor was Lan accepted as an established intellectual, to be assigned work in editing or teaching, as was Ding Ling, by then a much-published writer of stories who was made literary editor of *Liberation Daily,* the Communist newspaper.* Lan had to start at the bottom. She considered herself a revolutionary idealist. Yet her two main assets lay elsewhere: Shanghai style, and a talent for getting men to pay attention to her.

As in the early days in Shanghai, she was thrown back, in part by circumstances, in part by her own will to independence, on her resources as an attractive young woman of striking personality. She would not have been human—at any rate, she would not have been Lan Ping—if she did not realize, once more, that her "life" mattered more than her "art," that Lan Ping as a woman was a greater force than Lan Ping as an actress or a Communist.

One day Lan met Zhu Guang, a twenty-seven-year-old Shanghai man in the Party Propaganda Office, and an affair began. "They were always together," a resident of Yanan recalled. "In the autumn of 1937 everyone thought of them as a couple." Zhu, good-looking and voluble, had been a student at Shanghai University, where one of his teachers was Tian Han. Lan and he found a lot to talk about.

"When Lan Ping was applying to regain her Party membership," said the official who first handled her application, "she always came to my office together with her friend Zhu Guang." On those visits Lan wore simple Chinese pants, and a plain work jacket in the Cantonese style. She and Zhu, with vivacious faces and Bohemian manners, were Shanghai wine poured into Yanan bottles.

The romance with Zhu Guang did not last long. Some say he was not effective enough as a "mountain" for her to lean on. We cannot be sure of her feelings about him. When the affair was over, at any rate, Lan still was living at the Reception Center, still waiting for Party approval and an allotted task.

As winter approached, two loftier "mountains" came to Lan's aid. Wang Guanlan, Sister Xu's husband, went to talk on Lan's behalf to Li Fuchun, husband of the distinguished woman revolutionary Cai Chang, and the senior authority dealing with new,

---

* It was galling to Lan that Ding Ling, and also the actress Chen Boerh, a rival of Lan's, were allowed to enter the Party School as soon as they reached Yanan, on the basis of their past political work, while she herself was kept waiting many months.

untested arrivals from Shanghai and other White Areas. None other than Yu Qiwei also talked to Li about Lan's desire to "join the revolution." Now fat, Yu had lost the air of a half-starved student rabble-rouser and carried himself like a mandarin. He did not live in Yanan but was on an extended visit to report to Mao and other leaders on Communist activity in the White Areas.

Lan needed a good word from Wang Guanlan and Yu Qiwei. Her worries expressed to Sister Xu in Xian were well founded. At best, her political activity in Shanghai was seen as vague; at worst, the stench of collaboration with the Nationalists hung over those years. But Yu Qiwei could speak of Lan's work in the Qingdao years. She had indeed joined the Communist Party there in February 1933, and no one was in as good a position as Yu to relate the details. As for Lan's period in Shanghai, well, Yu really didn't know enough to be sure. . . .

Sister Xu testified on Lan's behalf about the Shanghai period. True, Xu had also been released from a Chiang Kai-shek prison after writing a disavowal of communism. But with Wang Guanlan as her husband, her pushy personality, and an apparent willingness to embroider the truth, she was able to help Lan, whose glamor and strength of will awed her.

As the wheels slowly turned in Li Fuchun's office, Lan went to see Zhang Guotao. "She approached him," recalled a Yanan resident, "because she was impressed with his high status." But Zhang, now defeated by Mao, wielded no power despite his high post as head of the border government. A second factor worked against the flowering of a relationship between the veteran and the starlet: Zhang Guotao's wife, Yang Zilie, a distinguished revolutionary, suddenly arrived in Yanan to rejoin her husband at the end of 1937.

"Lan Ping is a licentious woman," Yang Zilie snapped. "She simply does not seem to be able to exist without a man."

"My husband's office was in Yanan's only Western-style brick building," Yang recalled, "very comfortable with a bed and a stove." She described an odd situation. "Lan was often with an actor named Wang, and when she knew that my husband wasn't in, she would take Wang there. They would keep warm by using the bed and the stove." Perhaps Yang Zilie arrived in Yanan just in time. Or perhaps Lan was just playing games, knocking on doors, spreading herself thin, making her presence felt in a general way as Shanghai's latest gift to Yanan. She knew Zhang Guotao well enough, at any rate, to come in and out of his office as she pleased.

Li Fuchun reached a decision. Lan Ping was admitted to the Party School. "Li was reluctant about this," said one who dealt with him on the matter, "but Yu Qiwei influenced him." This was a step ahead for Lan. The school was not then, as it became later, an elite institution for fine-honing those already admitted to the Party, but a place for short-term further education for those still being tested. For Lan it was a niche, however modest. She took her place, one of ten women among the three hundred students, in the school's classroom, a former Catholic church. She was a bit like a goldfish among trout as she pored over Engels' *Anti-Dühring* and Mao's *Report on an Investigation of the Peasant Movement in Hunan* and listened with apparent absorption to lectures on military tactics.

"Lan Ping didn't say much," said a woman cadre who taught her. "She couldn't, because her understanding of politics was shallow." Some of the other women, veterans or with academic credentials, "looked down on her."

One day at the Party School, Lan Ping, who was in Class 12, joined several hundred other students in the school auditorium for a talk by a "leading comrade." Notebooks readied, feet tapping defensively in the chilly afternoon, they awaited the speaker. When it turned out to be Mao, who came onto the stage from the left at precisely 2:00 P.M., people stood, beamed, and applauded. Some say Lan drew attention to herself by pointing at Mao and clapping a few seconds longer than anyone else. (She herself, with hindsight, recalled the afternoon a little differently; Mao "sought [her] out personally and offered [her] a ticket to a lecture he was to give at the Marxist-Leninist Institute.")

That night Lan wrote to Mao. She recalled her past glimpses of him, introduced herself further, lamented that there were numerous gaps in her knowledge of ideological questions, and said that only a face-to-face meeting with him could supply what she wanted.

Lan's detractors say she almost forced her way to Mao's three-room cave on Phoenix Hill. Without waiting for a reply to her letter, she turned up like a house on fire, cracking jokes, treating the guards as old friends, calling out a greeting to Mao before she had been told to enter. When she finally confronted Mao, these accounts say, he was cold to her, reading a document as she asked him questions, and answering her only with the titles of books and essays she should read to fill in the "numerous gaps."

If Mao did talk with Lan that day in the early spring of 1938, it was his decision to do so. Lan certainly was a bold young woman, and she often marched into a man's place unannounced. Yet Mao's residence was not a bus station, for all of Yanan's informality. Indeed, it was heavily guarded with Mausers.

During the early spring of 1938, Lan's thoughts did not seem to center on Mao. She still hoped to make her way in the performing arts, and on this path she met a fresh Bohemian lover in the Shanghai mold.

There was in Yanan a Lu Xun Arts and Literature College, a natural place for Lan Ping. She said years later that she had not been interested in it, but that was not true. She made efforts to transfer there from the Party School. Yet she did have pangs of doubt about working at Lu Xun College. Could she make the shift from the theater of glittering Shanghai to that of wartime Yanan? Would her old enemies and rivals push her down?

Lan knew that Yuan Muzhi, together with other former associates of hers, most of whom thought poorly of her, often for personal reasons, was setting up a Communist-sponsored film studio in the Northwest. She was not asked to join. When it began work in Yanan, its star actress was the lovely Chen Boerh, of whom Lan Ping was jealous. It must have seemed doubtful to Lan that she would be successful, or even welcome, in the left-wing movie establishment.

She looked upon Lu Xun College much as an injured ballerina might look upon her favorite pair of ballet shoes. Perhaps this explains why she later disavowed ever having wished to go there.

"She simply was not a success as an actress," said an observer of a performance Lan gave in a play called *The Trampled People*. In a commemoration of an incident involving Japan, this anti-Japanese play was produced for a "January 28" festive evening in Yanan's best hall. Lan auditioned but won only a minor role. The leading actress was Sun Weishi, who had just returned from the Soviet Union, where she studied acting in the Stanislavsky style. "This beautiful girl was brilliant," recalled one who watched the performance.

"After this 'January 28' commemoration evening," said the same eyewitness, "Lan was not rated highly by audiences. She was never onstage again." Perhaps the role did not suit Lan. Perhaps she was overshadowed by Sun Weishi, gorgeous and seven years younger than she. Perhaps she was out of touch with stage work, or unsuited to the Yanan variety.

For all her doubts, Lan Ping in March or April 1938 applied to go to Lu Xun College, if only to get away from the analytic rigors of the Party School. She was interviewed by Chen Yun, an able, methodical man, later a high economic policymaker in Peking. He did not take to her. Lan made the mistake of talking about Marxist concepts that she did not understand, fearful lest the unartistic Chen Yun think the theater was all she was any good at. It also seemed pushy of her to arrive for the interview with her luggage in her hands, in an effort to show her eagerness to begin her studies that very day.

A major "mountain" came to Lan's aid. Kang Sheng, back from Russia, had become deputy head of the Party School. In China, people who come from the same district feel a close affinity, and they quietly help each other. If there are few of them within a larger grouping, they act almost like brothers and sisters. So it was with Lan and Kang. Some sources in Shandong say that one of the households in which Lan's mother toiled as a servant was Kang Sheng's. Whether or not the Kang-Lan association was as early, as intimate, as poignant as that, in Qingdao days Kang Sheng introduced her to left-wing activists and recommended her to her lover Yu Qiwei.

Lan went to see Kang. In their local Zhucheng accent, the two of them gossiped about Shandong. Perhaps they slept together once or twice. Soon afterward, Lan was not only admitted to Lu Xun College, but also appointed an assistant teacher there. "With Kang Sheng as a dependable friend," she was heard to remark, "no enemy can really hurt me." Chen Yun, not given to back-door ways like Kang Sheng, resented the interference with proper procedures that brought Lan Ping to a post at Lu Xun College. Before long he took an opportunity to criticize Lan's acting in an internal college play.*

"She was at Lu Xun College in the summer of 1938," recalled the Party official who had first received Lan's application to regain her membership, "and during that time, she fell in love with Xu Yixin." Xu was a man of the arts, dashing and brilliant, a senior teacher at the college. He was the kind of man Lan was used to, and Lan was the kind of younger actress Xu was used to. "With Xu, Lan was coquettish," said an observer of the brief romance. "This showed she loved him (later, with Mao, she was quiet, which showed she respected rather than loved him)." Xu was in the mold

---

* When Lan and Chen later came into contact in politics, they always thought as badly of each other as it was possible to do. Chen and Kang were also enemies for years.

of Tang Na and Zhang Min, and a big step up from Zhu Guang.

To Lan's fury, Xu Yixin paid more and more attention to Sun Weishi, the pretty, extremely young actress who had outshone her at the "January 28" theater evening. There were loud scenes. Whether or not Lan would like to have settled down with Xu, the choice was not hers. His infatuation with Sun Weishi was not to be stopped. They soon married.*

Lan picked herself up, busying herself with her duties as a teaching assistant. The college was a *carrefour* of the performing arts as sopranos, Peking opera exponents, cellists, folk singers, and devotees of European drama all worked at their craft. Lan was in the modern drama section. To friends in Shanghai, she wrote a letter, saying she was teaching drama and also serving the college as "counselor on life" to the students.

One of the movie magazines that used to report the latest twist in her love affairs wrote an article about the new Lan Ping, based on her letter, which gave the impression that her life had simmered down and that what now bubbled up was her "revolutionary art." But it was not quite so. Lan did not feel she had reached a satisfying plateau as a junior teacher at Lu Xun College. Nor had she gotten there purely on her own merits. Once more she had turned to a man as a "mountain to lean on." Was this the only way for a woman to advance?

Of course that had been true in old China; then a woman could really enter public life only through her husband or her son. But this was supposed to be revolutionary China. Surely in the new society taking shape among the red hills of Yanan a woman would be able to fulfill herself and be her own person, have a career, and choose to marry or not to marry according to what suited her?

One day Lan Ping would be free of the need to "lean on a mountain," but that day had not arrived.

Her work in the drama section of Lu Xun College was criticized, some sources say, because she was not well enough versed in dramatic technique to teach well, impressive as she could be in performance. It didn't matter, as it turned out.

Mao Zedong felt the arts were important politically (though his personal tastes ran only to established items from the Chinese tradi-

---

* Years later, Lan took revenge on both Sun and Xu. In the Cultural Revolution, both were unreasonably accused, and Sun died in prison. Sun's later years (she outlived Xu) were spent as the wife of none other than Jin Shan, the Clark Gable of the Shanghai stage, who had starred in *Sai Jinhua* in Shanghai in 1936. So Lan Ping had multiple reasons to harass Sun Weishi in the 1960s.

tion), and one day he arrived at Lu Xun College to lecture on the subject. As he rose to speak, looking not unlike a shaggy priest, a smile flickered on Lan's face, which was several shades paler than those of most of the students, who were of peasant origin or had been in the rural Northwest longer than she. In the applause she was to the fore. At the end she asked a couple of very innocent questions. And before Mao left she exchanged a few remarks with him at the front.

If she had to have a mountain, let it be the loftiest peak in northwestern China!

Yanan was a small place, an "elbow-to-elbow world," as Nym Wales (Mrs. Edgar Snow) called it, and Mao, whom Lan had glimpsed at Luochuan and met after his visit to the Party School, was in 1938 a human presence in the town, not yet a distant god veiled from view. People would see him stroll down from his cave on the hill to sniff the twilight air and look around the commercial district at the belly of the valley before he began his night's work. Everyone knew his car—there were so few others—with its surreal inscription: "Ambulance: Donated by the New York Chinese Laundrymen's National Salvation Association." Most people who asked to visit him were able to do so.

Now Lan Ping knew him. It was true that she had twice drawn attention to herself in his presence; that was her style. But Mao could have looked the other way had he wished. He did not. The two of them met several times over the next few weeks, at Mao's cave, owned by a Farmer Wu, on a slope of Phoenix Hill. It was not Lan, a girl from the rank and file, who was singling out Mao, but Mao, the most powerful man in town, who, in his loneliness, was singling out Lan.

Perhaps Lan Ping was fiercely attracted to Mao Zedong. Even in China, where love and marriage seldom coincided, that cannot be ruled out. Yet Lan was twenty-four and Mao was forty-five. This monk of politics and military arts was totally unlike the dashing, romantic, fast-talking Bohemians Lan had been attracted to in Shanghai and during her first months in Yanan. It is hard to imagine two Chinese as different as the brooding Mao and the sparkling Tang Na, and all Lan's lovers since Tang had been of Tang's type.

One evening after dinner Zhou Enlai, who like Mao worked much at night, received a disturbing cable from Chiang Kai-shek. It carried the danger of an especially serious dispute between the Communists and the Nationalists, who were supposed to be resisting Japan jointly. Zhou read it again and murmured gloomily to his secretary. A rejoinder must be sent that night, and Mao would have to decide on its wording. Zhou took the cable and walked along the ridge to Mao's cave on the side of Phoenix Hill. The chairman wasn't in, and, most unusually, his staff didn't know where he was. Zhou sat down outside the cave to wait. But soon he grew anxious, alike about the reply to Chiang and about Mao's whereabouts. Mao's bodyguards, for their part, felt bad about Mao's unexplained absence.

It was decided to go out over Phoenix Hill to look for the absent boss. The two bodyguards and Zhou, each carrying an old-style Chinese lantern, its flickering light encased in paper, headed into the dark, still night, past scraggy trees that rose like drunken sculptures against the inky sky.

It was Zhou who spotted the pile of bags on a grassy bank. The bodyguards advanced with their golden lanterns thrust forward. But it was not a pile of bags—it was the reclining forms of Mao Zedong and Lan Ping. Zhou, then as later a master at quick-thinking diplomacy, blew out his lantern with a strong, quick puff. He tersely ordered the bodyguards to blow theirs out, a split second, he hoped, before they had recognized their boss in his off-duty pose. In silence the three retraced their steps back to Mao's cave, to await the return of the chairman from his late-evening break.

It was in August 1938 that Lan obtained a transfer from Lu Xun College to a pleasant post as secretary of the archives at the Military Commission, near Mao's office.

"I don't think it was just Mao's initiative," Tang Na observed from afar. "I think Lan Ping did to him what she did to me. She was attractive, and she presented herself as a revolutionary—the combination hooked Mao." Lan's previous husband went on: "I am convinced that if Lan Ping had not just come out of the Shanghai world, Mao would never have been enticed by her as he was. You see, our Shanghai life, and Mao's life in the hinterland, where the peasants looked up to him as a god, were two different worlds."

Nine months before, on a chilly afternoon in late 1937, when Lan was still at the Yanan Reception Center, waiting for Party credentials and an assignment, a twenty-eight-year-old woman checked into the hostel of the Eighth Route Army in Xian. It was He Zizhen, mother of five of Mao Zedong's children and still in theory his wife. She was sick and unhappy. She had fled from Yanan, together with her third daughter.

A few months earlier, the same hostel had been a staging post for another young woman who was buoyant, aspiring, and on the way in. But He Zizhen was tired, bitter, and on the way out. Like the political spies who filled the graceful old market city, Lan and He, one after the other, walked the same streets but dreamed of different things. Lan Ping had been seeking adventure and a man; He Zizhen was sick of adventures, men, and childbearing.

A bright and lively girl of eighteen when she and Mao began to live together in 1928 (her eyes were "a pair of crystals," one of Mao's commanders said at the time; to meet her "gave you a feeling as sweet as honey"), He Zizhen now was pale, wild-eyed, and thin as a scarecrow. Her body throbbed with the pain of shrapnel wounds from a bombing attack during the Long March. Her mind at times deserted her as she tried to make sense of the events of the past two years and to decide where to go from the transit point of Xian.

On a tiny stool in her room off the courtyard of the Eighth Route Army compound, Mrs. Mao tried to align feeling and reason as she pondered her husband . . . that first meeting in the mountains at Yongxin, when after a political rally at which Mao spoke, they chatted and ate a supper of two chickens and two bottles of wine . . . Mao's announcement to some colleagues, a few days later, "Comrade He and I have fallen in love" . . . the ardent years as Mao, whom she then worshiped, despite his lack of respect for her in any context except the bedroom, forged a peasant army that would one day march on China's cities . . . the excitement and the pain of the children, one after the other, five in seven years, as Mao seemed not to have the slightest interest in birth-control measures . . . the questions that had jumped around in her mind about Yang Kaihui, Mao's first wife, murdered in 1930, whom he never talked about . . . then the terrible fights of recent months.

In despair He Zizhen staggered from the stool to the wooden bed and cried herself to sleep.

She awoke as two women came into the room, one of them carrying luggage that she put beside the second bed in the room. Turning her head, He recognized the woman without luggage as Deng Yingchao, the plain, sharp, cheerful wife of Zhou Enlai. Deng seemed to be escorting the new arrival.

He sat up on the bed and managed a smile of greeting. "This is Comrade He Zizhen, the wife of Comrade Mao Zedong," Deng said quickly to the tall, good-looking woman who had arrived to share the room. She was Yang Zilie, the wife of Zhang Guotao, who was now on the brink of a break with Mao. The roommates shook hands.

The next morning He and Yang awoke at the same hour, washed together, and began to talk over a breakfast of buns (*man tou*) and soup. It could have been an explosive encounter, if the record of their husbands' dealings with each other was any guide, but some cord of mutual sympathy bound them together. They got along well and talked all morning.

He seemed dazed and hardly understood the purpose of Yang's trip to Xian (which was to rejoin her husband, whom she had not seen for seven years, in Yanan). "Why are *you* here?" Yang asked He. "Why aren't you up in Yanan?"

"I am in poor health—I may be going to Moscow for treatment."

"But the arrangements for that would take time, and you don't want to be waiting here. Isn't it better to go back to Yanan? We can travel together."

He, feverish, embarrassed, anger at Mao rising in her again, had to explain to Yang what Mrs. Zhou Enlai had given no hint of. "I shall *never* go back to Yanan! Zedong treated me horribly. Oh, we quarreled, we scuffled. . . ." He Zizhen was becoming overwrought. "He would grab a bench and lunge at me. I would grab a chair. Things are absolutely at an end with that man." She heaved and sighed pitiably.

"Don't see it that way. How could it be over? You're both good comrades in the Party, you've been together in hard days. Try not to be so sad. You know, it's quite common for a couple to have quarrels." Tenderly, naïvely (she had not been in Yanan), Yang volunteered to talk to Mao when she could. "I'll get him to write a letter to you and take you back."

He Zizhen bowed her head and said nothing. Her tortured mind seemed to have foundered against the rocks of a revolution's paradoxes. How was it *possible* that a love forged in the midst of heroic struggle could prove so fragile? Could a man really be so great in his work and such a monster in his personal life?

"You're lucky," He Zizhen murmured, looking up at Yang. "Comrade Guotao has stayed faithful to you."

Yang Zilie slipped out of the room. Later she ran into Liu Qunxian, a Long March veteran and the wife of the senior leader, Bo Gu, who knew the Yanan situation. They discussed He Zizhen. Liu told Yang in strict confidence that there was a certain young woman on the horizon. "She dresses nicely and can act—Lan Ping is her name. Since she arrived in Yanan, old Mao has had an eye on her and spoken well of her. He Zizhen got jealous. . . ."

He Zizhen, her health worse, left for the Soviet Union. Her daughter went with her. Still Mao's wife, she was pregnant with a child who had been conceived in Yanan in the early summer of 1937. Born in Moscow, the boy died soon after.

So it was that Mao Zedong's marriage came apart during 1937. But what Bo Gu's wife told Yang Zilie in Xian was not the whole story. By the time Lan Ping met Mao, He Zizhen was already starting to reject him sexually. Lan was not the first Shanghai actress who caught Mao's eye in Yanan.

The fifty women who made the Long March stood high in Yanan. Whether career heroines of the original Communist generation, such as Kang Keqing, Zhu De's wife, or those who had become revolutionary lovemates to top male leaders, such as He Zizhen, they were tried and tested. And they had scarcity value.

These "Amazons" could throw their weight around. Their great weapon—used by the revolutionary lovemates and career heroines alike—was to withhold sex from their man. So total was the monopoly of the Amazons that they did not have to care about their appearance. Makeup never occurred to them. When their hair grew so long as to be in the way, they hacked it off with a knife.

Little rivalry to the Amazons came from the timid, politically unawakened Shaanxi village women. But the influx of educated girls from Shanghai and other White Areas—"the princesses"— shook the Amazons. Business soared at the Divorce Office, Nym Wales noticed. "Mao says," Agnes Smedley wrote to Edgar Snow after a talk in Mao's cave, "all the women [that is, the Amazons] are against dancing because they can't dance." It is not easy to dance on feet that were once bound, as many of the Amazons' feet were.

Smedley became an evangelist for some modern ideas that were a threat to women such as Kang Keqing and He Zizhen. She spoke of love. She talked alone with Chinese men in their caves. She promoted dancing. "The Amazons," Snow noted in a private memo, "began to notice a stir of rebellion among the menfolk and they held her responsible." In particular, a personal antipathy began to brew between Smedley and He Zizhen that was to rise to a terrible climax.

Without Smedley's role in Yanan, it is quite possible Mao's fourth and final marriage would never have come about.

"I haven't 'corrupted' Mao yet [by dancing]," Smedley wrote gleefully to Snow, "but I shall do so soon. He says that if he ever goes abroad he will study dancing and singing." Smedley added a remark that startled Snow: "I think he should leave his wife here if he does."

It happened that Smedley was allotted as her interpreter the most spectacular princess who ever came to Yanan. Lily Wu (Wu Guangwei) was a poet, a divorcee, and an actress. To this unusual combination of traits she added nice curves, large liquid eyes, and a sexy voice. With her long hair and lipstick she brought the spirit of Shanghai close to many a Yanan warrior. Nym Wales called her "the Bernhardt of the local theater."

Lily Wu was born to make the Amazons grind their teeth.

"Mao often came to the cave where I lived with my girl secretary," wrote Smedley, dryly recording Mao's affair with Lily Wu. It began in the spring of 1937, more than three months before Lan Ping's arrival in Yanan.

Sitting over a glass of wine at the Smedley-Wu cave, in a quiet spot on a mountainside, Mao would write couplets—for Smedley, yet really for Lily Wu. Wu would write a reply in matching rhyme and meter, which delighted Mao, as Smedley scrambled to write down some rough English equivalent. Wu was able to get Mao to laugh and sing and drink as He Zizhen would never do. "Certainly," Smedley told Snow during the month when Mao was infatuated with Wu and neglecting He, "his poetry has become better in the last few weeks."

Again using the hostess as a tool to work upon the "girl secretary," Mao would ask Smedley, his Chinese words addressed to Wu, who turned them into English for Smedley, about love and the meaning of life. Did she have any experience of romantic love, he wondered, love as he had read of it in translations of Byron, Shelley, and Keats?

"Agnes told him of her marriage to Dr. Chattopadyaya," Snow wrote in his private memo, based on a deathbed talk with Smedley in London, "a distinguished scientist with whom she had lived both as lover and as collaborator in the Indians' efforts to win freedom. 'Chatty,' she told Mao, had been the one true love of her life. He then wanted to know exactly what the word 'love' had meant to them, how they had expressed it in their daily life, and, if it had been a true marriage of minds, how it was that they had quarreled and parted."

"I was amazed at his childlike curiosity," Smedley related. "He told me that he had often wondered whether the kind of love he had read about in Western poetry and novels could really exist, and what it would be like."

Mao's marriage with He Zizhen was not love of this kind; Zizhen was a lapdog, a sex machine, a mother to his children, but not, in Mao's mind, an individual spirit meeting him on equal terms. "He said," Smedley went on, "that I was the first person he had met who seemed to have experienced such a [Western romantic] love. He seemed to feel that he had been cheated somehow." Smedley had the impression, as the three of them discussed romantic love, that Lily Wu was "the very embodiment of the subject."

Once, during these long, passionate evenings, Mao even recited a poem he had written in memory of his first chosen wife, Yang Kaihui, which was a clear message to Smedley—but really to Wu—as to how little he thought of his present wife, He Zizhen, who was at home in the Mao cave a mile away.

Meanwhile, two thousand miles away, in Shanghai, Lan Ping was living with Zhang Min and trying to resist the tide of criticism directed against her for her behavior toward Tang Na.

The Amazons had their information networks, and an Amazon, narrow as she may be, did not lack stubbornness and single-minded strength. Word reached He Zizhen that one night Lily Wu grasped Mao's hand, that he let her do so, and that a romance flowered with the apple blossoms during that Yanan spring.

It was past midnight on an early summer night, and Smedley was in bed in her part of the cave when she heard footsteps outside her door. She recognized Mao's "soft southern voice." She heard a knock on the door to Lily Wu's part of the cave, where a light still was burning, and then the sound of a door opening and closing. Smedley turned over and tried to sleep, but suddenly she heard a scramble of footsteps rushing up the hill to the front of the cave. Lily's door was hurled open and a woman's voice pierced the night.

"Bastard! Son-of-a-pig! Whoring good-for-nothing!" It was He Zizhen, and she was addressing her husband, the chairman of the Communist Party of China. "How dare you sneak up here to sleep with that dancing, bourgeois bitch!"

Smedley threw on a coat and rushed into Wu's room. Mrs. Mao was striking her husband with a long flashlight. Mao remained on his stool, in his greatcoat and cotton cap, not resisting the blows. A bodyguard, bewilderment on his face, stood transfixed in the doorway. Mrs. Mao kept on shouting and wielding the flashlight, her face awash with tears, until she subsided out of sheer exhaustion. Mao stood up.

"Stop it, Zizhen," he said in a stern, even voice. "You're ruining yourself, you're disgracing yourself as a Communist. Go home before your comrades learn about this."

Mrs. Mao now turned on Lily Wu. "Dancing whore!" she bellowed as she pinned the pretty girl to the mud wall. "How dare you try your dirty tricks even on our chairman!" Wu froze, like a kitten before a tigress. With one hand, Mrs. Mao battered Wu, scratching her face, pulling her hair, her flashlight all the while swinging madly from the other hand. Wu managed to rush across to Smedley and crouch behind her legs. Mrs. Mao then confronted the foreign orchestrator of all the modern nonsense that had turned the mind of her man.

"Imperialist bitch!" screeched the sick worn veteran of the Long March. "Get back to your own whorehouse cave!" With that she landed a heavy punch on Smedley's neck. The American journalist was not one to turn the other cheek. She paused, took aim, and dealt a blow to Mrs. Mao that sent her crashing to her knees.

He Zizhen turned her attention back to Mao, howling into the dark blue night: "What kind of man are you, what kind of husband, what kind of Communist! You let an imperialist tart beat me before your very eyes!"

"You attacked her," Mao said, "and she had done nothing to you. She had a right to defend herself." Still quite calm, he added: "You're behaving like a rich woman in an American movie." He told the bodyguard to pick up his wife and take her home. But when the young man bent down to gather her up, Mrs. Mao tripped him and knocked him down. The bodyguard, his embarrassment now turning to anger, called for help from two other guards waiting outside, and the three of them mastered the hysterical woman. As they carried her down the hill, Mao walked silently behind them, and startled faces appeared at hillside caves to watch the procession.

It was just as Lan Ping arrived at Yanan that the resulting furor approached a climax. At first by chance, later consciously, she profited from the breakdown of the Mao-He marriage. And she built upon the ruins left by Lily Wu's fall; Lan became a shrewder and luckier successor to Wu, a fresh "embodiment of Western romantic love."

Mao reported the incident to the Party. Differing views were expressed, but the Central Committee decided to regard the matter as "closed." However, it was not closed. He Zizhen kept it open. Moreover, the marriage was at an end. He Zizhen would not open her heart to Mao anymore; and it was only a matter of time before Mao looked elsewhere.

He Zizhen complained formally to the Party that Lily Wu had "alienated the affections" of her husband. And she rallied her Amazons to a relentless campaign on several points: Wu should be banished; Smedley should find work away from Yanan; the bodyguard who often stood idly by while Mao philandered should be disciplined; dancing should cease.

"Either you stop gossiping about this matter," General Zhu De said in exasperation to Kang Keqing, who sided passionately with He Zizhen, "or I swear I'll divorce you. Give me your word."

Mrs. Zhu De did. But He Zizhen was different. She was Mao's wife, nothing more nor less, and her rights as Mao's wife were an absolute for her. She won the departure of the two women, but she lost the larger battle, thanks in part to Lan Ping. The prize weapon of the Amazons—"I won't go to bed with you"—would no longer work for He Zizhen in the Yanan of 1937.

Agnes Smedley and Lily Wu found themselves far from Yanan by late September 1937. Smedley was persuaded to search for news on the battlefront. Wu was sent to the front with a theatrical group. On the eve of her departure from Yanan she was seen crying, and burning the poems Mao had written for her.

Lan Ping's and He Zizhen's presence in Yanan overlapped for several months. During this period an encounter between Mao and Lan apparently upset He Zizhen. "When she found out about it," Chen Ran, then a senior official, recalls, "she ran after him with a knife. He escaped by hiding in Zhu De's cave." Perhaps He Zizhen was reacting to Lan's call on Mao after his lecture at the Party School.

He Zizhen was at her wits' end and ill, and after much quarreling and scuffling, she walked out on Mao toward the end of 1937. It was shortly afterward that Mrs. Zhang Guotao ran into her in Xian. Mao did not kick He Zizhen out. Nor did the question of a divorce arise at this stage.

For some months in the first part of 1938 Mao lived alone.

Yang Zilie remonstrated with Mao, as she promised He Zizhen in Xian that she would. "It's all your fault," she blazed at him. "You should write her a letter straightaway." Mao, who possessed a fiery temper, did not blow up at Mrs. Zhang Guotao. A few days later he ran into her and said: "I've written a letter to He, but she won't return." Yang Zilie could not be certain that Mao had appealed to He Zizhen, though pro-Mao sources say he did send a letter (or telegram) to her, in mid-January 1938; she replied that she wanted nothing more to do with him.

Indeed, that was probably how He Zizhen felt. She was the kind of Amazon who would have required Mao to *beg* her to come back. And even if he had done that, she probably would not have agreed. Whether He Zizhen regretted her decision later in life, we do not know.

Lan said she never met He Zizhen. Her remarks on her predecessor are flecked with opportunism,* and reflect little awareness that He's behavior was in large part a natural response to the exhilarating but terribly dangerous fate of being married to a man who was the Marx, Lenin, and Stalin, wrapped into one, of the Chinese Revolution.

He Zizhen failed Mao, Lan said, because her background in the landlord-merchant class made her "used to living in cities" and "scornful of manual labor." True, He Zizhen did come from a well-off family, more so than Lan Ping's, but He was a hardworking, obedient, politically militant woman, a Communist Party member since 1927, whose experience of "living in cities" was zero by comparison with Lan Ping's.

Did Lan really believe any woman should have been *more* submissive to Mao than He Zizhen had been? Did Lan really want to find in a woman's class background the parameters of what she could and could not be in taking hold of her own life?

Yet Lan was correct to say He Zizhen was "unable to understand the political world of Chairman Mao."

We cannot say—could the participants themselves?—what was the exact catalogue of reasons for the breakup of the Mao-He marriage. Certainly Mao was becoming vainer, more conscious of a high destiny. He may well have felt he had outgrown He, who was in any case in poor physical and perhaps mental shape.

Yet Mao's friendship with Lily Wu was the immediate cause. Just before it unfolded, many visitors to the Mao-He household

---

* It is not the case, as she stated to Witke, that He left Mao as soon as the Communists reached the Northwest (the end of 1935); or that Mao and He were already divorced by the time Lan Ping arrived in Yanan in August 1937. That she should have predated these events suggests defensiveness about her own possible role in completing the breakdown of the Mao-He marriage.

found the atmosphere good (if patriarchal; Edgar Snow said He Zizhen "seemed completely under her husband's spell and domination"). Once it was under way, Mao and He began their physical scuffling. And a longtime Mao bodyguard testified that the collapse of the marriage was sudden.

He Zizhen was nearer to being a Nora, in the Communist style, than Lan Ping would ever be able to be. He Zizhen was a family woman; she worked in women's organizations; she was not at all a prima donna. In her sincerity and in her narrowness she took her love for Mao seriously, and when it was betrayed, she was unable to compromise. She was Mao's revolutionary lovemate; she was not willing to be a political wife.

In his personal evolution, influenced by the evolution of the Chinese Revolution he lead, Mao passed He Zizhen by. She could, perhaps, have caught up with him and become a political wife. But it was Lan Ping who, in a new era, proved better able to "understand the political world of Chairman Mao."

Lan wanted a strong man, all the better if he was a truly extraordinary man, with great power in his hands. A weak man she despised, as she made clear to Tang Na. For a strong man, she would make allowances. She would never throw up a brick wall over one of his extramarital affairs, as He Zizhen did.

Perhaps some streak in Lan despised He's very submissiveness—rather than the stubbornness in He that she shrilly denounced. Asked what explained He's troubled mental state after 1937, Lan gave an answer at variance with her earlier portrayal of He as a hand-wringing daughter of privilege: "Depressive reaction to the harsh circumstances of her life." It was as if there were two compartments in Lan Ping's mind when it came to He Zizhen. From one she viewed He as a rival; from the other she viewed her as a woman, to a degree a victim of her times, of Chinese society, and of Mao Zedong's manipulative attitude toward women.

In the confusion of her youth, Lan Ping did not realize that some of what He suffered she, Lan, would suffer too. Yet Lan's response to the problems of being Mao's wife would prove quite different from He Zizhen's.

It was after Lan and Mao began sleeping together that Mao's marital scandal reached its second climax.

Lan Ping "was among our guests at first," wrote Braun of the weekend parties he gave with his wife, Li Lilian, the actress who traveled with Lan to Xian, "but she soon stayed away. She had sound reasons for this. A scandal was threatening which touched on Mao Zedong's intimate life and caused quite a stir among the top cadres in the Party."

Opinion in Yanan was very much against Mao's new living arrangements, in part out of sympathy for He Zizhen, in part out of disapproval of Mao's having chosen an actress to replace her. "He's a sex maniac," a very senior military commander said of Mao on hearing of the switch, "abandoning a comradely wife of long standing to marry a despicable actress." It was a common view. There was even a student strike at the Shaanxi public school to protest the Mao-Lan cohabitation.

He Zizhen's relatives made trouble. It happened that He's sister had married Mao's youngest brother, Mao Zetan (after Zetan had left his first wife). Zetan himself was murdered by the Nationalists before Mao Zedong reached Yanan, but his widow, He Yi, suddenly appeared on the Yanan scene. With her was her new husband, Tu Zhennong, a senior Communist official. Vigorously, adamantly, He Yi and Tu protested Mao's "abandonment" of their close relative, He Zizhen.

"Chairman Mao is becoming physically weak," Tu said of Lan's impact on him. "The proof is he has started drinking liquor during meetings as a stimulus." Tu was also annoyed that he, in seeking to divorce his previous wife to marry He Yi, had met with great resistance and long delay from the Party, whereas Mao seemed to be getting away with a very rapid change of mates.

Furious with Tu Zhennong and He Yi, Mao not only turned a deaf ear but also had Tu transferred to southern China, separated from He Yi, to intimidate the couple and stop their clamor against his new liaison with Lan Ping.

But Lan Ping was not yet Mrs. Mao. Just as Chinese politics is a strange mixture of bureaucratic formality and back-door deals with "whom you know" (*guan xi*), so Lan's new marriage was both complicated and casual.

The Amazons, He Zizhen's relatives, and the striking students were by no means alone in opposing the new match. Those who didn't approve of Lan Ping, or of Mao's treatment of He Zizhen, or both, included most of Mao's senior colleagues.

China is not a puritanical society, as is sometimes supposed, but it is a very *ordered* one, in which everyone has a defined function. Fulfillment of that function is always more important than the "in-

trinsic morality" of the acts done in the process. So it was that Lan
Ping, throughout her adult life, was a controversial woman less for
her promiscuity than for rebelling against the categories, for "not
knowing her place." And so it was with sex in Yanan.

The Communists liked to spread the idea that "no one had time
for love," yet the sex issue was a pervasive, extremely important part
of the cadre's relationship to the Party.

The nightly scenes of couples making love in the bushes by the
Yan River—"undisciplined guerrilla warfare," Ding Ling called
it—were not the whole story. There was also a terrible bondage
about sex in Yanan. As in Shanghai, Lan seemed to be in an advan-
tageous place. If Shanghai had a "liberated" atmosphere, Yanan
had such a preponderance of men over women (the ratio was about
five to one among professionals) that a woman would surely be able
to pick and choose. Yet the Communists were developing their own
model of a "Nora"—a Nora whose *political duty* was to be an obedient wife.

The two basic principles of sex in Yanan were that the Party
rules the bedroom, and men rule women. If a person's sex life was
judged to be affecting his or a partner's political duties, the Party
took action "for the sake of the revolution"—as when Li Fuchun,
husband of Cai Chang, slept with a woman colleague of his wife's
and was reprimanded. The Party began to play a role reminiscent
of that of a family head in feudal China—as Lan Ping was soon to
find out.

A man could get a divorce easily; a woman who asked for one
was suspect. Girls were pressured to marry a particular man "to help
his work"; but men were never forced to the marriage bed by an
equivalent argument. A wife whose presence was inconvenient to a
husband with eyes for another woman was sent, as a tiresome child
is sent early to bed, to Moscow "for treatment"; but an undesired
husband never found himself in a Russian hospital simply because
his wife had found a more interesting man. At times, women in
Yanan were treated by the senior men as one of the privileges of
power.*

The sexual world that Lan Ping was entering was reflected by

---

* A Long March veteran, Huang Kegong, fell in love with a sixteen-year-old student. When
she refused to marry him, he shot her dead, in fury that she had "mocked the sincere love of a
revolutionary soldier." A tribunal that punished Huang also *criticized the girl* for "flirting
without the intention of marrying . . . as in the bourgeois White Areas." Another girl, refusing
to marry a brigade chief, rejected his appeal to Party discipline. "What the Party expects of
me," she said, "is that I work." The military man retorted: "No, it wants you to marry me."

the case of He Long, the famous Red Army general. During the Long March, General He married the nineteen-year-old Qian Xianren. Given the exigencies of the time, they had to live in different places, and when General He rejoined Qian in Yanan he found her installed as the mistress of a young Party official. He Long said he would accept a *ménage à trois,* but Qian wanted to divorce He and marry her lover. General He said no to a divorce. The Party intervened. With the "health and morale" of one of its most illustrious commanders uppermost in its mind, the Central Committee sent Qian to Moscow "for treatment."

The remedy seemed to work. Qian was separated from the young man, and soon she declared her wish to leave the Soviet Union and come back to live with He Long. But then she received the divorce certificate she had begged for in vain the previous year. He Long had met a lovely young woman, head of the Women's Association in a nearby village. He had already married her. Qian received a letter from He, dated the day of the wedding, saying that the distinguished soldier had changed his mind about the divorce.

Lan, as a twenty-four-year-old actress from Shanghai, was especially vulnerable. Mao told friends that "Shanghai corrupts people sexually." Yet wasn't this same Mao lassoing one of these "corrupt" beauties?

The Party felt that for Mao to choose a woman to "support" him was in the interests of the revolution, but it reserved the right to enforce certain rules about treatment of the previous "supporter" and to share in defining the "support" the chairman really needed.*

The first problem, in the view of Zhu De, Zhou Enlai, Liu Shaoqi, and others who opposed Mao, was that Lan had moved in with a man who remained married to He Zizhen (whom they all knew well and generally admired). This was against Party rules as well as against widespread opinion in Yanan's best caves. Second, Lan did not quite seem the right type to "support" their chairman. The very senior figure Bo Gu spoke for many when he questioned Lan's "colorful past, her unclear connections with certain Nationalist circles, and her vague relationship with the Party."

"The leader of the revolution," observed Wang Ming, Mao's eclipsed rival, "had better watch his private life and behave himself

---

* Thirteen hundred years ago, a similar problem had arisen at the Chinese Court. When Emperor Gao Zong began plans to replace his existing empress with another woman, many of his ministers wrote him memos saying the result would be the fall of the Tang dynasty. Furious, he replied that only his private life was in question. The new empress was the famous and brilliant Wu Zetian, whom Lan idolized.

better." (All the internationally minded Communists, for whom Wang Ming was a spokesman, tended to see both Mao and Lan as country bumpkins in their private lives.)

So the situation of late 1938, when Lan was living with Mao as his mistress—while working as an archivist in the Military Commission—was not fully resolved. Almost everyone wanted some adjustment.

Lan Ping did. Twenty-one years older than she, Mao was almost a father to her at first, and she was at times unsure that she had captured his affection beyond retreat. Naturally, it was desirable to be Mrs. Mao Zedong rather than just the pretty girl always working late at his office.

In the Central Committee of the Party, some were adamant for a regularization of the situation, out of respect for He Zizhen. A few probably hoped that the result of a confrontation on the issue would be the removal of Lan Ping, like Lily Wu and others before her, from Yanan and proximity to the "leading comrades."

Mao, though less inclined to an adjustment than anyone else, had to face the fact of He Zizhen's complaint, lodged with the Party, against Lily Wu for "alienating" his affections, with its intimate connection to the case of the woman who had now taken Wu's and He's place. When in the summer of 1939 it became known, through one or two physicians whose high connections ensured their stray remarks a wide circulation, that Lan was pregnant, it was inevitable, even in the eyes of Mao, who was benign toward ambiguity and looseness of structure, that the Party would have to take up the question of "the chairman and the movie star."

In China loyalty means everything—more than talent—and especially in that delicate territory where politics and passion intersect. It was now that Kang Sheng, the political operative from Lan's native Shandong, performed his greatest service for her.

A clever, thin-faced, nervous, scheming man, Kang looked like a crook even before he became one. At forty-one years of age, a specialist in secret police work, from his vantage point as head of the Party's organization department he was fast becoming a member of Mao Zedong's inner political circle.

From the summer of 1938, Kang encouraged the Mao-Lan liaison, and in the autumn he led the move to overcome Party resistance to a divorce between Mao and He Zizhen, and to a formal (that is, Party-approved) marriage of Mao and Lan.

Kang, seeing a potential benefit to his own career in smoothing out the situation, vouched for Lan's past, which again became an issue. He spoke of her record in Shandong, on which no one was in a position to challenge him. As for her extraordinary "noncontact" with the Party in Shanghai, he felt it was perhaps simply a result of the confusion of the times. Kang pointed to the support from Sister Xu, whose selective testimony on Lan's behalf was already in the files. Incriminating documents he destroyed; better versions he simply forged. He induced lackeys to report on the high quality of Lan's recent work as an archivist at the Mao court.

Kang came forward as a great admirer of Lan's wisdom and skill in the performing arts. On one occasion at a theatrical evening, this cunning fox was seen eagerly playing the drums as accompaniment to Lan's rendition of an aria from the Peking opera *Fishermen's Tragedy*—an extraordinary act of subservience-*cum*-flattery toward a controversial young woman of the arts on the part of a senior Party figure.

Like a chess player who neglects no piece on the board, Kang made good use of Mao Anying, the seventeen-year-old son of Mao and Yang Kaihui, before Anying left for Russia. Under Kang Sheng's orchestration, Anying spoke up as a critic of He Zizhen and a champion of Lan Ping.

With Kang Sheng banging drums at a concert and children's emotions being distilled into political evidence, there was also, in incongruous mix with the other ingredients, an appeal by Mao to Stalin! This presumed master of Communist morality and human psychology was asked by his embattled disciple in dictatorship, a continent and a culture away, to adjudicate a dispute about the bedroom arrangements of the leader of the Chinese Revolution.

It was not an easy battle. Even Zhou and Liu, who were not among the hard-core anti-Maoists in the Party, found it necessary, given the degree of feeling against Lan, to send a telegram to Shanghai, asking Liu Xiao, a Communist agent there, later ambassador to Moscow, for the facts on Lan Ping's background. Liu replied that she was "suspected" of being a "secret agent"* of the Nationalists.

Eight months pregnant, Lan strolled uninvited into a high Party meeting and found a chance to say loudly: "Chairman Mao and I have started living together." Less cool, Mao late at night went to the caves of his senior colleagues in great agitation. "Without Lan Ping's love," he told them one by one, "I can't go on with the revolution."

---

* When Communists fight each other, the term "secret agent" peppers the exchanges as unthinkingly as "bastard" might pepper an American barroom argument; Lan's link with Cui Wanqiu (to name nothing more politically conspiratorial) would have been enough to put "secret agent" on the lips of her enemies.

During one Party meeting on the issue, he threatened to "go back to my native village with Lan Ping and become a farmer" if Zhu, Zhou, Liu, and the others did not get off his back and let him have the "supporter" of his choice. Lan's own references years later to the storm confirm that her opponents were strong and numerous; there were threats to kill her, she claimed.

A compromise was worked out—some sources say the formula was Stalin's; at any rate, Zhu, Liu, and Zhou, the three senior leaders after Mao, fashioned the agreement. It gave something to everybody. Mao and He Zizhen were divorced. Lan insisted years later that the divorce was at He's request; other sources say it was at Mao's. The point is academic, in the circumstances, since the divorce came in a package with the Party's grudging acquiescence to Mao's new marriage. But it was Mao who *needed* the divorce.

Lan became Mao's regular wife, and the pressure on Mao over his private life was lifted, but at a price. Lan was required to devote all her energies to looking after Mao, and to refrain from any political activity for thirty years. Perhaps she would not become First Lady after all?

Not being an Amazon, Lan Ping could not receive the Party's approval for a political role.

A cable went to every Communist District office: Mao's divorce and remarriage "is verified as legal according to the marriage regulations of the Provisional Central Government, and also according to those of [Chiang Kai-shek's] National Government. Moreover, it follows the principle of freedom of divorce and marriage, and of monogamy. Therefore, there should not be any misunderstanding. . . ."

Although Lan had won a victory, and in less than eighteen months in the Northwest had made a staggering advance in her position, a combination of factors seemed to have made a Nora of her: Mao's own traditionalist attitude to women; the Party's assertion of its right to tell her and Mao how to conduct their marriage; and the clear implication of the Party's two stipulations *that she should have no career.* The two basic principles of sex in Yanan—the Party rules the bedroom, and men rule women—had found their most sacred crystallization.

If there was a clear loser, as the compromise emerged from a long night session in the Garden of Date Trees, it was the Chinese people. For the two stipulations were to lie like a time bomb within the Chinese body politic; and because of Lan's smoldering resentment at them, and her determination at once to escape from the Party-barricaded doll's house and to wreak revenge on those who had sought to confine her within it, and given Mao's vanity and the political difficulties he was to encounter at the start of the 1960s, the time bomb was to explode, just as the thirty years expired, in the terrible Cultural Revolution—Lan Ping's political show, Lan Ping's second career, Lan Ping's revenge.*

"They oppressed the old empress for more than twenty years!" Lan Ping was to cry in looking back on the restrictions placed upon her in Yanan.

And what was Kang Sheng up to? Twenty-two hundred years ago, a minister called Lü Buwei cunningly propelled his favorite girlfriend, already pregnant, onto the path of his boss, the emperor. As Lü hoped, the emperor liked the girl and married her. A son of the marriage was to be the famous Emperor Qin Shihuang. Meanwhile, Minister Lü accreted power as the thoughtful matchmaker; he even sent virile young men to please the empress as the emperor's sexual powers declined.

Kang Sheng was a Lü Buwei of the Communist era. While helping Lan into the inner chamber of the court, he was at the same time guaranteeing his own influence upon Mao. Peking today says Kang and Lan had a sexual relationship, and perhaps they did, briefly, during the four months Lan was at the Party School, of which Kang was deputy head. Kang's important help to Lan in gaining a position at Lu Xun College came just afterward, and some two months before Lan, Kang's "favorite girlfriend," found herself the object of Mao's passion.

Eventually Lü Buwei was executed; eventually Kang Sheng was disgraced.

For the moment, Kang and Lan had formed a fruitful link. A genius at amoral maneuver joined hands with a brilliant student, a perfect ally. Lan would become fascinated with Kang's sinister statecraft, and Kang would find in Lan a tool to help him carve out ever more power for himself. Handsomely they used each other.

One day at the Yanan airport, the American military attaché, Col. David Barrett, watched Zhou Enlai depart for the South. Deng

---

* Even today, Peking remains guarded and defensive about the Party decision on the Mao-Lan marriage. "At the time," said Hu Yaobang in the nearest to a frank summing-up that has been officially made, "Jiang Qing took care of Chairman Mao, on certain political conditions which the Party Central Committee approved and thought necessary under the special circumstances, though it is possible they were not entirely correct."

Yingchao was there to see him off, and before Zhou stepped into the plane the couple kissed good-bye. No one ever saw Mao kiss Lan Ping like that.

"As for women," said Wang Ming, "Mao has always despised them," and although Wang was biased against his great rival, there is a bit of truth in his judgment. Women were there, like a book or a wine flask, and it was excellent to have them available, but for one who liked to play around with them, Mao didn't seem to *like* women much.

Zhou Enlai, who was strictly faithful to Deng Yingchao, did seem to like the colleagueship of women. Unlike Zhou, Mao—the older Mao—did not respect women in professional situations. Zhou was solicitous, courtly, direct in his approach to women; throughout his life, no matter where he was traveling, he tried to speak with Deng on the phone each day. Mao, a bright, vain, elemental man, would neglect his wife for long periods, and he could be crude and devious, as well as exceedingly charming when he wished, toward the many women he drew close.

Mao was drawn to actresses. Like some other men of power, he found a woman from the entertainment world a perfect diversion from politics. He did not *despise* his women—Wang Ming went too far—but he could not think of them as his equals. As Lan knew all too well from Shanghai days, an actress was presumed to be light and frothy, a flexible, excitable, accommodating creature, perhaps with a temper and flaws of character, but great fun at her best.

Yet Mao did like his wife to be a strong personality. He wanted a spirited woman as long as her spirit was channeled toward his ends. In Lan Ping he had found a strong-willed young woman. He expected that her will would run in the direction of his will; she was to be strong for her husband and his interests, not independent in an open-ended quest for her own self-fulfillment.

Mao, whose life was in a number of ways a marking rod of China's protracted revolution, took, in Lan, a new wife entirely different from his previous three; the differences reflect Mao's, and China's, evolution over twenty years. The first marriage, in 1908, was an arranged one, cooked up by the parents, when the last emperor of the Qing dynasty still ruled. The girl Luo was brought along to the ceremony like a package to be presented to the boy Mao.

The second marriage, to Yang Kaihui, in 1920, was one of romantic love, in the ardent years of the May Fourth Movement, when men and women students were truly equal and believed that with their bare hands they could reshape the world.

Mao's third marriage, to He Zizhen, in 1928, was a union of two political militants; a lovematch, certainly, but also an unequal match, given the man's world of guerrilla warfare, He Zizhen's narrowness, and the billowing self-image of Mao Zedong.

The fourth marriage, to Lan Ping, for all its initial passion, was a partial return to tradition, the coupling of an emperor with an actress who was "a change" from politics and "a support" for the supreme political leader. But Mao had chosen an actress of formidable character and personality—perhaps even more than he realized at the time.

Few women have ever been less resigned to dependency than Lan Ping. Yet, because virtually all societies have forced women into lesser roles than men, perhaps *every* woman, at some moment in her adult life, experiences the temptation to sink back from the struggle to be equal—even feeling relief at giving in to the temptation—and to become dependent, as society intimates in a thousand ways a woman really should be. Half resigned, half enticed, Lan for a season accepted, if not savored, her dependence on the man who ruled ninety million people from Yanan. She "worshiped" Mao she later said, and for a time it was true.

Lan had found serenity, and because it would not last forever did not mean it wasn't real. She did not torment Mao with impossible challenges, as she did Tang Na, or lecture him on how to be worthy of being her lover, for she was genuinely bedazzled at being the philosopher-king's lover.

It was socially pleasant, after all, to be known as the chairman's "loved one." Perhaps it was a shortcut to freedom, but there was a liberty in not having to be self-protective with every other man she met, and a respite from the terrible jealousy of other women that had so often gripped her.

Marrying Mao, Lan abandoned her career in the performing arts. "We were puzzled," the American diplomat John Service recalled, "that she did not seem to be active in the Yanan theater." Mao presumed that she owed this to him, and she went along with his presumption. She kept a link with Lu Xun College, but soon it was like Lady Bird Johnson's concern for parks, or Nancy Reagan's for mental health—an interest, not a career.

Lan must have realized that she was compromising her goal of self-expression, and her cherished value of independence. She knew that, socially, wartime Yanan was light-years away from Shanghai's Bohemia. She knew that, because marriage to a Communist leader was like a priest's marriage to the Church, some outstanding women had refused offers.

Perhaps she was cynical from the beginning? It does not seem likely in a twenty-four-year-old. Perhaps, with her breathtaking ability to misjudge herself and her impact on others, she thought she would be able to tame Mao, ignore the authority of the Party, and even press on with her movie career. She never dreamed that all those terrible stories about the Party ordering people into and out of beds, about women whose charm was judged to have gone being shunted off to Moscow for medical treatment, about noble Communist leaders removing a wife from the house as one might discard a broken sofa—that any of these things ever could apply to *her*.

At any rate, in 1938 Lan Ping became Yanan's chief Cinderella. Unlike Deng Yingchao and Kang Keqing, who were Party officials in their own right as well as the wives of Zhou Enlai and Zhu De, respectively, and unlike Ding Ling (unmarried for the moment), who had a career as a writer and was also an established Communist, Lan was first and last a wife—nothing more (and nothing less) than the "loved one" (*ai ren*) of the boss.

In taking Lan as his wife, Mao did not bother with a wedding ceremony or legal marriage certificate. That was a modern touch that suited Lan; she and Tang Na also had scoffed at such wrappings.* But Mao—twenty-one years Lan's senior—seemed to regard her as a possession, to be the mother of his children and perhaps his assistant. That was a feudal touch.

In any marriage the partners' expectations of each other go through different phases; the "fit" of expectations is better at some times than at others. Didn't Lan know it from her ups and downs with Fei, Yu, and Tang? Didn't Mao know it too? Soon enough Mao's and Lan's expectations of each other would diverge, but for a few years they were congruent, because Lan asked little, kept her mouth shut about the feudal overtones of the marriage, and accepted dependence.

"Where women are rare, they wield great power," Nym Wales remarked after surveying Yanan. For Lan, the test mostly lay ahead. Her hooking of Mao illustrated a degree of truth in Mrs. Snow's maxim. But perhaps her power would turn out to have existed only

---

* "Was *his* marriage to her any more legal than *mine*?" Tang Na asked a friend spiritedly. "Did *they* have a marriage certificate?"

during the chase. Now the match was made, the doors might close behind her, and she would be nothing more than Mao's silent housewife.

Or would marriage to Mao in some way hoist her up and bring within reach the vindication, the chance to express herself, and the celebration of herself as an independent woman that were still for her the pearls of great price?

For the time being, marrying Mao was in itself a fulfillment of the expectations with which she had come to the Northwest.

Being the lover of a top leader had its nice points. Mao and Lan actually could live together, which was very rare in Yanan, where most married couples (unless they worked in the same unit) could meet only on Saturdays. There were guards and other staff to help with chores. And the food was better; the student or soldier got one pound of meat each month, whereas the high cadre got eight pounds.

When Lan Ping began to live with him in the autumn of 1938, Mao moved from Phoenix Hill to a three-room cave at Yangjialing. (At Yanan, living in caves saved on construction.) Cut into the hillside, the apartment was fifteen feet deep, backed with stone, its walls whitewashed. The front wall was of wood, broken by a latticework of paper windows, through which some light came but not very much. Outside the apartment was a leveled patch with an easy chair, stone stools, and a vegetable plot at which Mao—but not Lan—tinkered from time to time.

In all three rooms—living room, Mao's study-bedroom, and Lan's room (which she later shared with her child)—the floor covering was gray brick, with sand as mortar, and the chairs, tables, and desk were all in rough-hewn wood. There was no electricity, but tallow candles; no running water, but enamel basins that the bodyguards would fill from a nearby communal well. But the beds had mosquito nets, and a note of luxury was struck by the wooden bathtub and the ancient gramophone. A large portrait with the indentification "President Chiang Kai-shek" hung in the middle of the longest wall.

Lan brought few possessions with her, and the apartment had the stamp of Mao on it. The one bookshelf, which was in Mao's room, contained none of the foreign and current literary works that Lan used to dip into in Qingdao and Shanghai, but only Mao's books (all in Chinese) on politics and ancient Chinese history and literature. There were no photos of Lan Ping in performance, no trinkets from Bohemian days, and none of the mess and confusion of her various Shanghai residences.

Mao and Lan discussed a new name to mark the new phase of her life. Should it be completely new? Modest or bold? Should it bear a relation to Mao's name or be on a lower plane? It turned out that Lan Ping got a brilliant, daring name. "Jiang Qing" was probably at least in part Mao's idea. The words ("Jiang" means river, or waters; "Qing" means green) seem to come from a Tang dynasty couplet where the river in question is the Xiang, in Mao's province of Hunan.

The new name had a firm, clear ring to it. There was a promising fluency about a stream for a name and an uplifting connotation to Qing's secondary meaning (by virtue of its sound) of "pure." Perhaps, too, there was a whiff of ambition in the implication, from a phrase of an ancient classic, that green (Qing) comes out of blue (Lan) but is more brilliant and reaches farther than blue. To many people—perhaps including Mao, who liked a challenge if he felt he could meet it—"Green Waters" in meaning and sound alike was an apt name for a woman of purpose, allure, and enticing if also hazardous depths.

Jiang Qing's life was comfortable within the limits imposed by Yanan conditions, but it was a *housewife's* life, and this was new to her. When she later spoke of her Yanan years, three quarters of what she recounted was about Mao and his work, and most of the rest dealt with the life of an array of family members, all but one of whom were not her family.

Jiang cut a lithe figure alongside Mao, who was becoming slightly pear-shaped. Her long hair had been cut off with her Shanghai past; she now had the close-cropped Girl Scout style of a Yanan woman. Her dark, flashing eyes seemed well under control. During a conversation between Mao and a Western visitor, she would often say little or nothing, but glide in merely to be introduced ("This is Jiang Qing" was the bare, unsexist way Mao generally did it) and shake hands, as women in Yanan, under the Communists' influence, had begun to do. Or she would come in to replenish a dish of peanuts, or a tray of fried hot pepper pieces that Mao would nibble along with his endless cups of tea. She was considered very pretty—much more so than Chiang Kai-shek's wife, said Robert Payne, who met both women—and also a modest, prudent young woman.

"Jiang Qing looks after his health, daily work, clothes, and food," said a Russian official who saw a lot of the couple. At late-night meals in the Mao living room, everyone present, including Jiang, would defer to Mao if it seemed that he was about to say something. Jiang learned to cook—she had help in shopping and cleaning—and soon was "excellent" at it, according to Snow. She did not like spicy food, as Mao did, but visitors to the household found spicy dishes filling the table.

In social moments Jiang would move with alacrity to change the old 78 rpm records on the gramophone, often Peking opera excerpts, a cultural taste she and Mao had in common. Soon she was infected with the passion for bridge that most of the Chinese Communist leaders shared, and she played a shrewd hand.

Suddenly Mao sent Jiang for two or three months of manual labor in the wilderness. Nanniwan was a nonplace, an utter wasteland thirty-five miles southeast of Yanan, where teams of Communists went, with only their bare hands, to create out of nothing a productive society. Mao told none of his colleagues that Jiang, in whom a child by him was already conceived, was leaving for Nanniwan. Bidding Jiang and her workmates farewell in January 1939, Mao pointed out to them that if they failed to wrench food and clothing from the fiber of the wasteland, they would perish.

The pilgrims gouged dwellings from the hills, made garments from the hair of black mountain goats, and carried off the sacred fittings of an old temple and melted them down to fashion agricultural tools. Jiang, bundled up in padded clothes that hardly came off in the entire stay at Nanniwan, got blisters on her hands from this unaccustomed manual work. She did not like the idea of doing only the lighter tasks that women were eligible for, for it was her view that anything a man could do a woman also could do. But in fact, because she was ill, and perhaps because the nervous team leader knew who she was and wanted to be sure she returned to Yanan in good shape, she did no heavy work. She spent most of her time knitting, and when she left Nanniwan she had ten heavy sweaters to her credit.

Why did Mao send Jiang to Nanniwan? Perhaps he felt like stepping back for a while from the passionate closeness of the previous months. Perhaps it was because Jiang had contracted tuberculosis, an illness that Mao, like everyone in Yanan, was terrified of.

Jiang Qing gave birth to a daughter, her first child in four marriages, and Mao's ninth child in four marriages. This brought a timely cementing of the marriage.

For nearly all Yanan women, maternity was an unwelcome handicap, which added to the difficulty of being independent and equal with men. One simply could not have a career, in Yanan conditions, and bring up children as well. It was true that at the Saturday night dances women asked men to dance, but a woman who had to look after children wouldn't get to the Saturday night dances. Jiang was in a different position. Her career in the performing arts was over, and she wasn't qualified for a political career. A baby cost her nothing and brought benefits.

The coming of a daughter lifted away Jiang Qing's image as the pretty girl who worked late in Mao's office. The trace of fear in her attitude to Mao disappeared. He no longer seemed like her father, but, as they doted on the baby and introduced her to visitors, almost like her husband. A baby in her arms entrenched her as Mao's "supporter" the way a hundred Party resolutions could not do—or undo.

Choosing a child's name is a big issue in China. The daughter's surname, Li, was Jiang's, not Mao's, which was unusual. The given name "Na" filled more than one bill, for it is a term from the Confucian classics meaning "cautious in speech," which Mao must have chosen, and it is the same sound (though a slightly differently written character) as the given name of her ex-husband Tang Na.

In marrying Mao, Jiang had entered a merry-go-round of a family. This was due to Mao's previous marriages, to the dislocating effect of war and revolution on many people's private lives, and to the cloying power of family connections in China generally—even in Yanan, which was modern and individualistic by Chinese cultural standards. Two boys from Mao's marriage with Yang Kaihui, Mao Anying and Mao Anqing, turned up in Yanan. Mao never took them back into his household, and Anying soon went off to Russia. At first Jiang got along well with Anying—she was only seven years older than he—but Mao seemed to want him out of the way after Jiang arrived.

There were also two tiny children of He Zizhen's, a baby daughter born early in 1937, and a son of two or three.

"He is very bright," Jiang said of He Zizhen's little boy. "He can sing the 'Internationale' from start to finish." He was soon to go the way of most of the Mao-He children: "lost"; in the written gospels of Chinese Communist history, "given to a peasant family."

The baby daughter, at this time in Moscow with He Zizhen,

was to be a major figure in Jiang's domestic life. It is curious that Mao and Jiang, in naming Li Na, evidently renamed He Zizhen's baby daughter at the same time *in absentia*, for the name chosen, Li Min, is a part of the same Confucian term as Li Na's name. "A gentleman should be cautious in speech but quick in action," runs the classical maxim; Mao's last child by He was to be quick in action, his first child by Jiang was to be cautious in speech. It is also curious that "Quick in Action," who on returning from Russia in 1945 was taken away from He and made essentially Jiang's responsibility, was to grow up with a surname, Li, that was neither her mother's nor her father's, but the original name of Jiang Qing, her stepmother!

Not only the Confucian classics, but also Jiang Qing's love history offered a link between the names of the two girls. Li Min's given name was the same sound (written differently) as that of Jiang's last Shanghai boyfriend, Zhang Min, just as her own daughter's given name, Na, echoed her Shanghai husband's name.

Visitors to the Mao-Jiang home in the Garden of Date Trees (for security reasons they moved from Yangjialing in 1942) found Li Na a lively, central presence. The girl would play in Mao's study, and when he took a break to chat with a staff member or have a snack, she would go with him. A former aide of Mao's staying overnight in the household in 1942 found Mao, rather than Jiang, supervising how the child was to be treated, telling her to call the visitor "Uncle," walking with her down the hill to see the visitor off.

"She was direct and unassuming," the Briton Robert Payne said of Jiang, "and looked in every way like a sensible, fond wife and the fond mother of her children." When Payne entered the cave, Mao came forward to shake hands, but he disliked the act and performed it awkwardly, raising his shoulder high as he put out his hand. "Mrs. Mao, the former actress, shook hands far more comfortably," Payne said. Li Na and Li Min were pushed forward to shake hands, which they did with serious faces. Jiang's excellent Mandarin and "pleasantly musical voice" showed up well alongside Mao's thick Hunan accent. At the dinner table she mainly responded to the rhythms of conversation set by others. Her interventions were generally questions. She asked about everyone's health. "If things were going well her face lit up, and if badly she would commiserate with the person who was suffering."

One evening the Russian officials living in Yanan were invited to Mao's place. Mao happened to put the senior Russian in his own favorite leather armchair. This led Jiang Qing to pull out a deck chair, unfold it, and arrange it beside the Russian's chair, for Mao to sink into. A bodyguard brought him a mug of the local wine (*gan jiu*). Jiang, neat in slacks and a black sweater, hopped back and forth, dropping peanuts into Mao's outstretched hand. The Russians asked Mao what he would do if Japan attacked the Soviet Union, and the question did not please Mao. Jiang put on one gramophone record after the other, tactful and modest in the situation. After Mao had grown silent, he ordered hot peppers. These he ate, washed down with the fierce *gan jiu,* until his face became red. He yawned and stretched long and low in his chair. Jiang chose for her next record an excerpt from an old Peking opera. Mao began to clap his hands in accompaniment to the wailing sounds. As Jiang continued to perform her duties as hostess, Mao's slow, measured clapping gradually put him to sleep in his deck chair.

"Without Jiang Qing," one of the Russians, who was a physician, remarked when Mao was suffering from arrhythmia during 1942, "he becomes capricious, and sometimes even refuses to have his temperature taken, or drink his medicine."

"Both were plainly dressed," the American journalist Harrison Forman recorded of his evening with Mao and Jiang, "she in a practical pajamalike outfit belted at her slim waist, he in a rough, homespun suit with baggy, high-water pants." Forman found a tranquil scene in the gloom of the cave. "The only light was furnished by a single candle fixed on an upturned cup. For refreshments I was served with weak tea, cakes, and candy made locally, and cigarettes. Mao chain-smoked his abominable Yanan cigarettes, while youngsters ran in and out during the whole conversation."

Of Li Na and Li Min, Forman recalled: "They would stand and stare at me for a few moments, and then, seizing a piece of candy, race out again. Mao paid no attention to them."

A Chinese medical couple who often baby-sat for Li Na said that Jiang was not an attentive mother. Li Na was sent for lengthy stretches of time to stay with the physician, who was chief of pediatrics at Yanan Central Hospital, and his wife, who was chief of nursing at the same hospital. The couple, who had no particular reason to be hostile toward Jiang at the time they recalled Li Na's upbringing, felt that she neglected her daughter.

It was not the style for a mother in revolutionary Yanan to coddle her child, and Jiang by nature was less inclined to do so than most women. Charming with adults, she was not one to dote on children, her own or others. She had a sincere belief that a child was better served by having to fend for itself than by a fussing protectiveness, and this harmonized well with her self-preoccupation.

After a few years, a cocky possessiveness began to show itself in place of Jiang's shyness of 1939. She would venture opinions in Mao's presence as she had not done before. She began to bestow favor on those she liked and to single out enemies for discrimination.

Sometimes as she smoked a cigarette, or tossed back her head in an unbridled burst of laughter, or flashed a frown at conduct that annoyed her, the spirit of Lan Ping seemed to have come back—now toughened by a consciousness that she had achieved a certain status. The apartment started to look as if a woman lived in it, and Jiang showed more panache in the way she wore her simple garments.

Otto Braun watched her out riding a splendid horse, dressed with flair, attended by four helpers, and noted that she was beginning to take leave of "the simple customs of Yanan." One day Rewi Alley, a New Zealander who has lived in China more than fifty years, was kneeling to look closely at a Song dynasty inscription on a path just out of Yanan. "A girl on a white horse came up," he recalled, "rather dashing, making her presence felt in a slightly forced way. I didn't know who it was, but when I got home and mentioned the incident people drew in their breath and said, 'Ooh, it's the new Mrs. Chairman.'"

Jiang Qing took to horseriding the way an American woman might go driving in her car, as a zone of liberation from the captivity of the household. She cut a girlish, modest figure as she pushed her spirited horse through the dust, ribbons holding her braids to the back of her head, wooden sandals on her white feet. Yet it was also the spectacle of a woman with a touch of class, for horses were in short supply in Yanan, women in particular rarely rode them, and no woman rode one with Jiang's dash and verve. She found a way to express herself in the solitary habit of horseriding.

On his way to see Mao, Russian filmmaker Roman Karmen, riding across the Yan River, was overtaken by a fast-galloping horse. To his surprise the rider was a woman. "Drawing up even with us," he recalled, "she sharply reined in her horse, and with a wide gesture welcomed us gaily." It was Jiang Qing, elusive, taciturn, but with a certain vigor that seemed to come from her horse. She had come down from her retreat on the hill to welcome the

Russian visitors. "I will tell Mao that you are on the way," she said quietly. She reversed her horse abruptly. Leaning forward as it charged ahead, she gave a wave of her right hand through the cloud of dust.

Zhou Enlai lectured one afternoon at the Party School, and Jiang Qing persuaded Mao to let her go with him. She wanted to go on her horse, and perhaps as well to be seen in Zhou's company in the auditorium where, until she met Mao, she had been an unnoticed member of the rank and file. Returning on their two horses, Zhou and Jiang galloped along the banks of the river, Zhou's horse leading, Jiang's close behind. Jiang, fifteen years younger than Zhou, not weary as he was from the long session at the Party School, and savoring the freedom of horseback, insisted on pushing her steed faster than Zhou wanted to go. Suddenly Jiang's horse, under her excessive whipping, locked its front hooves with Zhou's horse's back hooves. Zhou's horse reared high, tossing the future premier of China to the hard red soil. His right arm was broken and remained disfigured for the rest of his life.

"Ever since Miss Lan Ping, the movie star, married Chairman Mao," noted a commentary on Yanan published in Chongqing in 1943, "the formerly extremely dull and monotonous" life of the Communist bastion has "changed immensely." The observer explained that "bourgeois dancing, feudalist local opera, Hollywood love songs, have all flowed into Yanan." Did such things not help the leaders "recover their revolutionary morale" after a hard day's work?

It was a fine Saturday evening, and the sky was high and dark blue above a lively scene in the Pear Garden. *Le tout Yanan* gathered for the weekly barn dance, Jiang Qing's great contribution to the society of Northwest China. Soft light from candles covered with red, green, and yellow paper came down from the fruit trees. Music, now hearty, now sentimental, soared into the night. The orchestra was like an assembly of volunteers from the music schools of a dozen nations; there was an old Chinese fiddle, an American violin, a Cantonese zither, a British mouth organ, a banjo in the style of Shaanxi villages, and a pedal organ left by a deceased missionary.

The dance floor was packed earth. "Better for the *yang ge* [a sedate folk dance] than for the waltz," recalled John Service. Jiang Qing was too good a dancer to be troubled by an undulating mud floor; most of the other dancers were too bad to find anything wrong with it. Everyone, including the bright-eyed kids who scampered among the lurching frames of the leaders of the Chinese Revolution, wore cloth slippers or rope sandals, so what was the difference?

A fox-trot to the tune of "Yankee Doodle" was in progress as Mao entered in a white shirt and dark trousers, puffing on a cigarette, looking benevolent. Jiang Qing, dressed like the other women in a pajama-type belted blouse and trousers, had already been present for an hour. Quickly she walked across to a trio of young girls leaning against a tree. She took the arm of one of them, a nurse from the International Peace Hospital, and led her across to Mao. "Chairman, please dance with me," dutifully piped the beaming girl, her pigtails gleaming in the candlelight.

As the music changed to "The Blue Danube," Mao careened off with the nurse, while Jiang, after watching for a moment, swept off to secure Zhou Enlai for her own next fling. Mao was not a good dancer. He looked as if he were doing physical exercises. But the little nurse stuck with him, even when the rag-bag orchestra switched to "Jingle Bells," doubling the speed. Greeting Zhou, Jiang glanced back over her shoulder at her husband and his partner and gave a smile of pride and relief.

Zhou was an excellent dancer, nimble and graceful, remembering steps he had picked up in France twenty years before, and when he and Jiang Qing took the floor, a rural barn dance gained a touch of the great dance evenings in Shanghai's Bubbling Well Road. (If Tang Na could have seen her, would he have felt proud of her, or furious with her?) Jiang was enjoying herself, reveling in the attention she was getting, pleased that she knew exactly how to handle Mao on such an occasion.

Agnes Smedley grabbed General Zhu De and the pair of them, like mating elephants, turned a French minuet into a tank maneuver. "I felt," Smedley said later to Edgar Snow, "as if the whole Chinese army had walked over my feet." Meanwhile, Jiang was waltzing with a young American GI, part of the visiting Dixie Mission led by Service and Col. David Barrett. A moment later she was jitterbugging with Ye Jianying, a military leader, who danced well for a man of his size. "They were the center of the party," a participant observed.

All evening Jiang Qing never danced with Mao. At intervals, weaving her way between General Lin Biao's prancing form and the mighty combination of a truck driver in locked embrace with "Backwoods Boadicea," Zhu De's wife, Jiang would dart across the garden to bring the prettiest available girl to Mao's side. He Zizhen would have taken a knife to Mao if she had seen him flirting with nurses, teachers, and serving girls as Mao did that night. But Jiang was a brilliant political wife.

Mao and He Zizhen would never have gone to a dance—had such rollicking functions existed in pre–Jiang Qing Yanan—because Zizhen would have refused. Nor did they go to the theater, as Mao and Jiang often did. If Mao went to visit a foreigner's cave, He Zizhen would ask him where he'd been. Jiang took such things in her stride; she would rather give her husband some freedom, and in return expect some for herself, than be rooted with him as two peas in a pod.

Thanks to Tang Na, Jiang knew more English than Mao did. It wasn't all that much—"not impossible" was the nicest remark any Westerner in Yanan ever made about it—but she used it when she could. She proudly taught the Western alphabet and some English phrases to Wang Dongxing, a bodyguard of Mao's who later rose to the Politburo and played a major role in Jiang's fall in 1976.

"Comrade Jiang Qing coached us," one of the three servants in the Mao-Jiang household reminisced. "As well as holding classes for us, she showed us how to keep a diary, and came and corrected the entries we made." Jiang loved to be the center of attention, bending down to instruct the humbler ones. "Not like that . . . how stupid of you . . . do it the way I show you."

Going with Mao to Yanan's makeshift theatrical performances, Jiang would carry herself like an ambassador escorting her president on terrain more hers than his. If the performance was of a modern play or a foreign play—rare in both cases—Jiang would enjoy it more than Mao and tell him what she thought it was all about.* But mostly it was Peking opera. Little Li Na became "opera crazy," a reflection of Jiang's and Mao's shared liking for this traditional form.

Jiang did not welcome interruptions, as she and Mao sat enthralled by an opera, with its heroes in gorgeous silk and its villains in horrible masks, its clanging instruments and piercing, high-pitched voices. But Liu Shaoqi, the somber organization man who was number two in the Yanan hierarchy and who didn't care for opera, sometimes would try to discuss business with Mao in mid-performance. One night Liu edged up to Mao, his horselike face in earnest concentration, a document in his fine bureaucrat's hand.

---

* Jiang would jokingly call Mao a "rural dumpling" (*tu bao zi*) and he would reply that she was a "foreign dumpling" (*yang bao zi*).

Jiang killed Liu with a glance, raised her elegant shoulders in disgust, and whispered loudly in the direction of the ceiling: "Oh, here is that lout again."

One afternoon Mao was talking in his living room with Wang Ming, his old rival, now largely defanged, but whom Mao still liked to prove wrong whenever possible. The two of them were arguing about Russia, which Wang Ming knew and esteemed more than Mao did. Jiang sat bored and quiet in a corner, wondering how much more of this well-worn duet she could stand. In came Wang Ming's wife, red and puffing. "I've been looking for you everywhere," she said to her husband, "and it turns out that you two are arguing again." Jiang advanced from her corner and took charge of the situation. "How marvelous that you've come," she pronounced. "These two old cockerels are impossible; they no sooner meet than they start to fight." She made a move to lead Mao away. "Get hold of yours and take him for his supper, and I'll take mine off for his supper."

Serving as "secretary" to a man of Mao's power and deviousness was gradually putting Jiang on Yanan's political map. It was not that she joined in political deliberations—except very rarely—but that other people viewed her as a possible influence on any decision Mao might make.

This was reasonable. Jiang would be silent when Mao talked politics with a visitor at home, but she listened carefully, and afterward she would give Mao her opinion.

When Zhang Zhizhong, the chief Nationalist negotiator, was staying in Yanan, Jiang Qing would come around to his cave early each morning. "How did you sleep?" she would ask. "Now, what should we see to for you today?" She was courteous and demure, "but one felt she was speaking for Mao."

Yuan Muzhi, who once wrote a message in lipstick on Jiang's stomach but later criticized her, suggested making a documentary movie of Mao and Jiang together in Yanan. If there was a touch of flattery behind the idea, Jiang did not notice, or did not mind. She wanted to do the movie, which Yuan would direct on behalf of the Yanan Motion Picture Organization, which he headed. Mao did not want to. Military problems were pressing him, and a campaign called the Production Drive needed constant supervision. Jiang twisted his arm. She put to him the arguments that on Yuan's lips had seemed so persuasive: The masses were *interested* in the lives of their leaders; it would be *inspiring* to the cadres to see the chairman and his wife themselves doing physical labor, setting an example that no one could fail to follow. Mao gave in.

Jiang busied herself like a debutante before a coming-out ball. She readied a variety of clothes, laid down the law to Yuan about the sequence of scenes, and rained down upon Mao tips as to how he should conduct himself before the cameras. This was not a resumption of her movie career, she told herself in moments of anxiety; this was going to be cinema to serve the chairman's political interests, and further the political education of the people.

Yanan possessed no film studio, so Yuan began to shoot his documentary at the sports field of a school just beyond the town's south gate. Each day Mao and Jiang were driven to the school, and watched by a knot of curious townsfolk, went through routines of strolling in deep thought on questions of war and revolution, digging a ditch and grinding wheat just as real workers did, and mingling with selected representatives of the people in the stylized way that became famous in the post-1949 documentaries.

Mao felt uncomfortable, but Jiang reveled in the filming. He refused to concentrate, while her smiles and gestures seemed almost too studied. He would not put on special clothes, but she was done up as if for a Shanghai production. Jiang looked like a politician running for reelection; Mao looked like the candidate's husband taking time off from his research.

The movie was never released; no one recalls having seen it; perhaps it was never fully edited and finished. "Mao never liked to appear in movies," Jiang remarked years later. "He was like that as far back as the Yanan days, when I first came to know him."

Inevitably there were clashes as Jiang Qing began to carve out patches of territory as Mao's secretarial assistant. For Mao's chief of personal staff, Li Liuru, she developed a visceral hatred, not unknown among First Ladies when confronted by one of their husband's protective confidants. For his part Li, a veteran revolutionary intellectual, felt that Jiang was throwing her weight around in Mao's office, making arbitrary judgments, nagging Mao personally, and falling into a life-style out of keeping with the austere norms of Yanan.

One day in 1942 Li, pressured, he says, by outrage among Mao's staff at Jiang Qing's behavior, went into Mao's study and directly raised the delicate matter. He catalogued the grievances against Jiang and argued to Mao that she was damaging his image and authority. Unbeknownst to the two men, Jiang was in the apartment, resting in her own room, and she caught snippets of the devastating case Li Liuru was building against her. Furious, she burst into Mao's study. Her eyebrows rising toward the ceiling, she glared at Li with enormous eyes and pounded the wooden table at which Mao and Li were sitting. She cried, and at the same time she shouted the accusation that her husband and his chief of staff were conspiring against her. Li had *no right,* she said in a fury, and *no qualifications* to blacken her in this fashion.

Mao rebuked Jiang, there and then, in front of his chief of staff. He told her to "shut up," according to a pro-Li account. He pointed out that Li had been doing revolutionary work longer than she had—a sore point with her—and apparently, after Li discreetly left the room, asked her to apologize to him, at least for the manner of her surprise intervention.* This Jiang refused to do. Henceforth she treated Li icily and got away with it. (Years later, when she had outright power, she helped destroy his career.†)

That Mao and Jiang quarreled in the presence of others—it was to happen many times—was extremely unusual among the Chinese Communist leadership. There is no record of Zhou Enlai and Deng Yingchao doing so, or Zhu De and Kang Keqing, whatever may have gone on in a more restricted environment. Mao and Jiang were strong-willed individuals; the spiritedness of each stimulated, but at times also infuriated, the other. And Mao and Jiang stood out among the Chinese Communist leadership for their blunt, crude ways; Jiang, the refined actress, also could be a vixen when roused; Mao, half peasant and half intellectual, never lost the earthiness and fire of his native Hunan.

---

* Mao's reaction reminds us of an emperor of the early Chu state who put the interests of his realm above the feelings of his lover. A banquet was in progress, attended by all the emperor's commanders, as well as his wife and concubines. Suddenly a breeze blew out the flames of the wax candles on the tables. One young commander took the opportunity to embrace the emperor's favorite concubine feverishly. The candles were relit, the commander retreated, but the concubine was left holding a tassel from the officer's headdress. She held it up in accusation. But the emperor did not agree with his concubine's idea of checking all the headdresses to see who had taken advantage of her. It would be a terrible humiliation for the guilty man, the ruler felt, and the whole purpose of the banquet was to heighten morale in the kingdom. The emperor ordered the candles extinguished once more and each commander to tear the tassel from his headdress. From then on, no one would know who had jumped upon his favorite concubine. Later, in battle, the reprieved, grateful young commander, fighting heroically, saved the life of the emperor.

† What Li Liuru did falls to a degree into the tradition of the courageous official criticizing a female regent. One such was Du Gen, who in the year 107 criticized Empress Dowager Deng and petitioned that her power should go back to the emperor. Infuriated, the empress dowager ordered Du Gen to be put in a heavy silk bag and beaten to death at court—but Du survived, after staying in the silk bag, pretending to be dead, for three days. After the empress dowager died, Du Gen became a hero.

"Jiang Qing has an air of independence about her," Vladimirov, a Russian official, observed. "She is quick to find her way to unfamiliar questions. She is inquisitive and ambitious but ably conceals it." Vladimirov, catching the flash of steel that had pushed through Jiang's discreet, housewifely charm, saw her exercising an influence that she had not tried to exert in the first few years of the marriage: "Jiang Qing dexterously and unobtrusively pushes on her husband to solving the most diverse questions, which are far from being family matters."

On her secretarial work, and her relation with the political operator who had helped put her where she was, Vladimirov's diary for December 1942 is eloquent: "Her husband's whole secret correspondence is in her hands now. She knows all his plans, and she is worshiped by Kang Sheng."

The Russian put his finger on the core of this woman who still, as in Shanghai, knew how to deploy her various talents, "now one and now the other," like a pianist using all ten fingers, but not at once: "Extreme purposefulness is her outstanding quality."

Jiang made a return visit to Lu Xun College in her new capacity as Mao's wife and secretary. The occasion was a series of lectures by Mao on the relation of politics to the arts, later famous as *Talks at the Yanan Forum on Literature and Art.* Everyone in Yanan who had anything to do with the arts was there, pencils at the ready, as Mao began to talk in his quiet, intense, immensely effective way, coughing repeatedly from his chain-smoking, on the first of several electric evenings in the spring of 1942. Jiang sat proudly near the front, her proprietorial air deeply ironical in view of what Mao said to the nervous literati of the Northwest. Years later she said she had influenced the *Talks.*

Mao had come to Lu Xun College to declare that "art for art's sake" was wrong. He derided the "clamor for independence" of the writers, as Ding Ling and the other finest writers in the Northwest, many of them directly influenced by Lu Xun's spirit of independence, winced at the assault on the central value of their craft. Showing the universal politician's bias toward the notion that dissent from intellectuals undermines national security, intensified a hundredfold by the Marxist view that truth is a destination rather than a quality that gives meaning to the journey, Mao insisted that every piece of creative work must serve the purpose of hastening the liberation of China from Japan and for communism.

"Opinions should not be allowed to become conclusions," he ground on. The packed benches of intellectual talent were being warned that they only had the freedom to be correct; an incorrect opinion was *not allowed* to become an openly stated conclusion.

Jiang sat half smiling as her husband snapped the writers and performing artists of tomorrow's China into the straitjacket of Leninism. As if her Shanghai years had been all dross, she was embracing, with how much comprehension we do not know, the cold, bare skeleton of Yanan communism. Such worthy principles as existed in Lan Ping's artistic world view died as Jiang Qing maintained a wife's supportive silence at this terrible defeat for the arts.

The boldest of the dissenting writers in Yanan, Wang Shiwei, wrote an angry essay in defiance of Mao, decrying political paternalism toward the arts and the Communist leaders' loss of ideals. Wang called his piece "The Wild Lily." The choice of the flower's name did not follow from the essay's contents. It was surely a slap at Mao's treating women as one of the privileges of power, for everyone knew Lily Wu (Wu Guangwei) by the first name she had acquired in Shanghai. Someone at least had a dagger out for the outspoken Wang, for he was executed with a scandalous lack of justification not long afterward.

"Jiang Qing battles against illness," one of her later political associates noted, "as staunchly as she fights politically." It was true; she came to dramatize her physical ups and downs to the point of hypochondria. But in Yanan, where she contracted tuberculosis soon after marrying Mao, Jiang said little about her health. It was the Party guardians who spoke of her ailments, for their own purposes.

"At the time the Dixie Mission left for Yanan," Colonel Barrett recalled, "we had been informed [Jiang Qing] was suffering from tuberculosis and seldom if ever appeared in public." The Americans took at face value the link between Jiang's poor health and her exclusion from any public role. On the trip from Chongqing, Barrett and his colleague John Service took canned milk and cocoa for Jiang Qing to help "build up her strength."

Yet when Mao introduced his wife to the American ("Colonel Barrett, this is Jiang Qing"), Barrett was struck that she "did not appear to be in bad health at all." In fact, Jiang rather swept the colonel off his feet with her "grace and polish." Dr. Orlov, Jiang's Russian physician, said of Jiang and Mao about this time: "Both of them are healthy—I wish I was as healthy as they." Service, who lunched long and alone with Mao and Jiang in their home, recalls that "Jiang Qing looked fit and healthy."

In Communist politics illness, or alleged illness, including mental illness, can become the coin of political struggle. Jiang was later both a sad victim and a fierce practitioner of this horrible tactic. In Yanan she got her first taste of it.

In 1945 her Shanghai acquaintance Zuo Shunsheng, a leader of the China Youth Party and a colleague of Cui Wanqiu, arrived in Yanan for a visit. It was natural for Zuo to see Jiang, but Mao told Zuo that "Jiang Qing is ill." He had to make do with seeing Jiang's daughter (whom he found a "small model" of her mother). Either Mao felt Jiang's period in Shanghai was a phase best forgotten, or he feared—with one eye on Party reaction—the consequences of Jiang "appearing in public" too much.

Later Jiang would speak about her illness in Yanan, but at the time she kept her "struggle" against it very private. It was left to others, who wished to keep her pinned down as an inactive housewife, to publicize the health problems that limited her "appearances in public."

In the summer of 1945 Mao went to the Nationalists' capital, Chongqing, to talk with Chiang Kai-shek in the hope of staving off renewed civil war between the two parties. Patrick Hurley, the U.S. emissary, and Zhang Zhizhong, the Nationalist representative, flew to Yanan to fetch Mao, Zhou, and other members of the Communist delegation. A couple of weeks later, as the difficult talks droned on, Jiang Qing appeared, with her daughter, Li Na, in the steambath city of Chongqing.

"I am here for dental treatment," she said sweetly to a number of people who met her at the house of Zhang Zhizhong, a graceful two-storied mansion called "Cassia Garden," where she and Mao were staying.

On this trip—the only occasion she ever appeared with Mao on a diplomatic mission—Jiang was the private helpmate, observing the Party requirement that she play no (obvious) role in public affairs. The hungry newspapers hardly mentioned her presence—though Mao was big news, and he even leaked his self-aggrandizing poem "Snow" to *New China Daily.* No foreigner observed her, and until now no Western account has spoken of her presence at the Chongqing summit. Chinese who saw her recall a "fresh-looking young woman" who did not look at all like the other leaders' wives. At a reception in the home of General Zhang she wore a "simple short-sleeved blouse and skirt, a bit like a high school girl's uniform, her short hair not done with a permanent wave, and coming down in a fringe over much of her forehead."

Said another guest: "She did not look like a person just out of a cave."

During the reception she was called upon by General Zhang and his wife to make a short speech, which she did with quiet grace. One listener seated in the tenth row found her Mandarin exccllent, with hardly a trace of Shandong accent. She made a point of mentioning, no doubt conscious of the danger of seeming prominent, that the sole purpose of coming to Chongqing was to see a dentist. It seemed an odd, unnecessary remark to some listeners.

Nationalist sources later avowed that she came because of a scandal that erupted beneath the elegant black wooden beams of General Zhang's house. During the early part of his stay in Chongqing, these sources say, Mao and Zhang's eldest daughter drew close, no doubt at Mao's initiative. General Zhang and his wife wished to avoid a public explosion, but equally they had to put an end to this apparent affair between their young daughter and the leader of the Communist challenge to Nationalist rule. The solution was to send a plane to Yanan for Jiang Qing, on the assumption that the arrival of Mao's wife would divert Mao's lust from the delicate Zhang daughter.

(A variant of the story has Zhang Zhizhong encouraging his daughter to cross Mao's path, as part of his larger design to abandon the Nationalists when the time was ripe; upon joining the Communist camp—which he did in 1949—he would enter with a splendid feather in his cap.)

It does not seem likely that much transpired in Chongqing between Mao and Ms. Zhang—the fourth daughter, Zhang Suchu, has vigorously denied that anything transpired, as has her brother, Zhang Yizhen. Probably Jiang followed Mao to Chongqing simply because Mao wanted her nearby, as the talks dragged on for some weeks, or because Jiang twisted his arm to permit it, as she was starting to do on issues that mattered to her—and because she had to go to the dentist.

Jiang paced the rooms of "Cassia Garden" in the Red Cliff district of Chongqing. She played with Li Na in the salon with its silk screens and its smell of wealth. She bounced on her lap General Zhang's daughter, Suchu (who recalled the experience pleasurably thirty-six years later). With a strange sense of imprisonment, Jiang gazed out over the tiled roofs of the hilly city. In her dreams of herself as she would like to be, she seemed torn between the pleasures of being First Lady of Chinese communism (which, given her husband's rising fortunes, was getting close to being First Lady of

China) and the insistent tug of another China that the sight
of Chongqing set in motion in her mind—for Chongqing was full of
refugees from Shanghai's Bohemia, driven west under the Japanese
sword and trying to make movies, produce plays, and write stories
for a new era.

Jiang Qing decided to telephone Tang Na! According to a
source very close to the scene, she wanted to have one more talk
with Tang, now a Chongqing journalist and an adviser to the British
Embassy, from her new, secure vantage point as Mao's wife.

Jiang Qing tracked down Tang, as she tracked down Yu Qiwei
in Peking in 1933 and in Yanan in 1937; she would never cut off all
connection with a former lover unless he severed the link irrevoca-
bly himself. But she did not meet with Tang Na. Either she did not
succeed in contacting him, as Tang says, or he did not want to meet
her again.

One night as the political talks drew to a close, the reception
hall of the Nationalist Government mansion was jammed. Mao and
Chiang were both present, nodding, smiling, as Chongqing society
sipped drinks, ate from dishes of pastries and peanuts, and craned
for a glimpse of the president and his opponent. Ministers, businessmen, and leading journalists shuffled in a line, waiting to shake
hands with China's two rival leaders. Smart in a light suit, hair
slicked down, a cigarette held in a hand never still, Tang Na waited
his turn. Mao greeted each guest slowly, as was his habit, bending
slightly, holding the person's hand in his soft grip as he asked a
question or made a quip. Tang reached the third spot from Mao. He
looked at Mao's broad, calm face and listened to the quiet, almost
feminine Hunanese voice. Suddenly Tang Na swung around and
walked in the opposite direction, past the tables of pastries and peanuts, out of the mansion and into the steamy evening. Jiang Qing's
third and fourth husbands were never to shake hands.*

One day in March 1947 a Nationalist bomb fell close to the
Mao cave in Yanan, violently shaking the furniture. Mao went on
reading a document, but Jiang, who had seen little of war, was
frightened. The next day she spent huddled with Li Na in an air-
raid shelter, singing songs to keep spirits up, as the Nationalists, all
efforts at reconciliation between the two warring parties having
failed, pounded the once-tranquil Communist outpost, making an
evacuation unavoidable.

* Tang Na did meet Zhou Enlai, and he admired him. Often he would compare Zhou favorably with Mao.

Mao waited as long as possible, wanting to choose his own moment to begin a new phase of mobile warfare, and some of his colleagues grew nervous at the danger. "You're a coward," he snapped at Jiang when she mentioned to him the widespread view that the evacuation should begin at once. "And if you're going to be a coward, why not join forces with them?"

Within a week, Mao, Jiang in "colorful clothes," Li Na, and two guards packed themselves into a jeep and drove slowly out of the snow-covered, deserted, half-destroyed streets of the town that had been home for ten years. The Yanan era was over. For the next two years, because of the exigencies of the last fight against Chiang Kai-shek, Jiang, unexpectedly, took leave from household routine and played a modest role in war and politics.

She was appointed a political assistant in the Third Detachment of the Communist forces, and in the fluid conditions of fighting while moving found herself in close proximity to Mao and Zhou Enlai as they ran their half of the North Shaanxi campaign. (Zhu De and Liu Shaoqi ran the other half.)

The job was a violation of the Party-mandated marriage agreement, but no one raised their voice about that, for the time being.

It was a life on the road, traveling on horseback by night, staying in farmers' cave-homes, a week in this village, a month in that, as Communists and Nationalists grabbed bits of China from each other. There were frequent air assaults. To cross one river Jiang's unit had to pull down a temple on the bank and construct a bridge out of the pieces. Often she was ill with gastrointestinal problems, as for days on end she ate only string beans.

She and Mao sometimes rode the same horse, and it greatly satisfied her to be thus physically coupled with "the chairman" in the midst of dramatic struggle. It was almost like being before the footlights again, with a public to play up to.

For a while she kept Li Na with her, but after a scare, when it seemed the eight-year-old was lost, she was put in Deng Yingchao's care in a safe village. Li Min and the other child relatives had earlier been farmed out to friendly households in a more stable state than Jiang's.

Looking back, Jiang saw 1947–48 as exciting, eye-opening, and a time of great pride at being "a soldier." She agreed with the point of view that full women's liberation involves gaining "the means of coercion—armed force," and with the peasant women who said to Smedley, "We are strong as the men! Give us guns!"

At her trial decades later, Jiang shouted passionately: "I am the one, the *only* woman comrade, who was each step of the way at the side of the chairman during the North Shaanxi campaign!"

Yet her work as a political assistant was wispy in character, and her performance of it was bizarre.

Lecturing to villagers on the bounties of communism, she was almost a spectator of her own emotions as a performer, stirring the masses, telling them with unshakable fervor, just like any politician's wife, that her husband's cause was just. Asked to focus a meeting on the recall of past suffering (to heighten the appetite for the socialism about to arrive) she recalled *her own* past sufferings "as a model for others." This reduced everyone to tears.

Tears, indeed, were the hallmark of her efforts, for she was on an emotional ego trip, free from the bondage of the household, and given her dramatic gifts, any emotion she felt was soon communicated effectively to her audiences. When she flayed Nationalist POWs with her whip of moral indignation, she brought them to the point of bursting into tears and had them begging to join the Red Army on the spot—she claims.

Yet when she tried to trace the North Shaanxi campaign years later, she floundered. She required maps and briefing papers provided by others to reconstruct the events, and handling these, she seemed like a monkey faced with a papyrus of hieroglyphics. Only when she spoke of human drama or aesthetic detail did she flash with conviction. At Tianziwan she went "among the people," and finding a sick woman, "combed her long, tangled hair." When the Red Army encountered the Moslem tribes, who loved clothes, the local women's faces lit up with delight on seeing the quality of the cloth of Jiang's own garments.

One day as they were camped at the Huaizhu River, she saw a soldier wearing a Nationalist cap. Since the collapse of the United Front he should have switched back to the Communist cap with its red star. In fury she yelled at him to take it off. Trying to make vivid to the soldier his mistake, she rammed the Nationalist cap on her own head, thrust her face into his and glared at him.

There must have been something manic about her intervention—or perhaps it wasn't easy for a soldier to take a rebuke from a woman—for those watching the incident turned upon her angrily, and she ended up shouting to everyone a brittle reminder that she *must* be obeyed for she was the unit's *"political instructor"* (in fact, assistant, not instructor).

Mao did not include Jiang in meetings of the leadership. When at Wangjiawan a dispute arose in the Central Committee over which direction to march in, she learned of the issues "only indirectly." At Jiaxian she found herself "excluded" from an emergency meeting to revise strategy. None of this was surprising, but it annoyed Jiang.

During one stop she had to move out of her cave when the four top leaders (Mao, Zhou, Lu Dingyi, and Ren Bishi) decided to hold a meeting, and Mao's cave was the best place to hold it. Relegated to a donkey shed, she lived with asses for several days, lost weight, became infested with lice and fleas, and developed a lump on her neck. Perhaps illness followed anger. Toward the end of the war, Mao one evening sent out an important telegram, which Jiang felt she ought to have been shown but was not, and she went on a rampage to make her point that women comrades must be *respected*.

Mao often became annoyed with her impulsive, egocentric ways during the North Shaanxi campaign.

Jiang and Zhou Enlai deepened their association in 1947–48. She talked with Zhou more than with the other male leaders on the campaign. Noticing her downcast mood, Zhou would come up to chat and inquire how she was feeling, and whether perhaps she was afraid.

Jiang Qing felt, as did many Chinese women, from Song Qingling down, an attraction toward Zhou that may not have been strictly physical but did stem from his masculine charm. He danced well (unlike Mao), and Jiang liked that. And Zhou, for his part, treated Jiang not only graciously but even fondly. He was solicitous toward virtually all women, and with Jiang Qing there seemed to be the extra dimension that she offered a total, enticing contrast to his own beloved wife. "Zhou loved Deng Yingchao morally," said an observer of that marriage, which had always been a union of co-workers. "But he did seem to find an excitement, missing in Deng, in his association, platonic as it was, with Jiang Qing."

"Vice-Chairman, your socks are showing through the soles of your shoes," she said to him one day as they paused for lunch in the midst of a grueling march. Zhou was exhausted, but he turned to smile at Jiang. "No wonder my feet are feeling the bumps on the road as I walk," he quipped. This kind of banter did not come easily between men and women in the Chinese Communist leadership.

Into 1948, Mao, power now dangling before him like a ripe peach, seemed less preoccupied with Jiang than she had to be with him. Settled in the city of Shijiazhuang, where the Communist elite gathered prior to the final triumph of taking Peking, some three

hundred kilometers to the northeast, his eye wandered, in a fresh
discovery of sex as a privilege of power. Who should arrive in Shijiazhuang, as an actress taking part in a theatrical performance, but
Yu Shan. Now divorced from Zhao Taimou, Yu Shan had come to
Zhangjiakou, a city a little to the north, because her brother, Yu
Qiwei, Jiang Qing's husband of Qingdao days, had become its
mayor. While Yu Shan was in performance at Shijiazhuang, it
seems that Mao had a furtive affair with her.

What Jiang said about this when she saw Yu Qiwei, also in
Shijiazhuang, we do not know. But she was a political wife, after all,
and she did not deliver an ultimatum to Mao, as He Zizhen would
have done. Still, Jiang later denigrated Yu Shan as a "reactionary"
who had "bullied" her "endlessly."

A Western woman would have blamed the man. He Zizhen
would have assailed both the woman *and* her man. But Jiang, on
this occasion as on others still to come, blamed only the *woman*
whom her husband had dallied with. (The rising Empress Wu had
been the same thirteen hundred years before; when the emperor
went to bed with Empress Wu's niece, Helan Guochu, she did not
take direct issue with him but chose instead to kill Helan by mixing
clay with her food at a banquet.)

By this time, in another realm, Tang Na had left Chongqing
and was working on the left-wing Hong Kong newspaper *Da gongbao*. A colleague watched him sitting late in the paper's offices writing a love letter "in his neat, square characters." He had met an attractive Shanghai journalist, Chen Renqiong, and was on the brink
of marrying her. He would never live in mainland China again.

If Jiang Qing was out of her element, in terms of the day-to-day
tasks of the North Shaanxi campaign, she was also caught in the
damaging contradictions involved in being Mao's wife. Her job as a
political assistant was widely seen as a fig leaf for her presence as
Mao's comforter. It wasn't possible to assign her an independent political job. Tasks were invented for her from week to week, as she
followed Mao around. Few took her seriously as a professional.

She gathered crab apples for Mao as a treat in the midst of a
tense engagement. She took dictation from him when his Parkinson's disease prevented him writing his essay "The Present Situation
and Our Tasks" in his own hand. She left her political duties,
toward the end of the campaign, for the family duty of going to retrieve Li Na (who was being cared for by Deng Yingchao at
Shuangtu) and bring her back to her father at Shenchuanbao.

That she was not a success as a political assistant—and perhaps never could have been, given the pervasive perception of her as first and foremost Mao's wife—was a black mark against her. As the ripe peach fell into Communist hands and Chiang Kai-shek's China became Mao Zedong's China, Jiang felt the thrill of victory, yet with it a shaft of anxiety about her future role.

5

Letdown (1950s)

*We live together, but he is the silent type; he does
not talk much.*
                              —*Jiang Qing of Mao.*

Mao's triumph was Jiang Qing's eclipse. With the Communist victory in 1949, there began for her a decade of illness and depression, with some promising but in the end false starts at this or that public activity, and through it all a vexing ambiguity as to her status. The revolution settled down, but she could not settle down.

The proud residents of Peking were wondering what the new dynasty would be like when on March 25 a rumor flew through the alleys that Mao's plane had arrived from Shijiazhuang. Jiang Qing sat beside her husband for the short flight from the anteroom of power, where they had spent ten months as the Communist armies mopped up North China, to the city of emperors. By the time the plane landed, *People's Daily* had an extra on the dusty sidewalks, its four-inch headline in red ink shouting, "CHAIRMAN MAO HAS ARRIVED IN PEIPING."* In streets hungry for clues to the future, the one-page issue sold out in forty-five minutes.

Mao looked well and confident, Jiang Qing thin and weak. "You've put on weight," a friend who hadn't seen Mao for four years said to him. "The reactionaries caused me to get thin," Mao rejoined with good humor but a touch of smugness. "Now that they've been chased away I am filling out." Jiang Qing, her face pale, her eyes darting nervously, weighed less than a hundred pounds; she realized, amid the bewildering swirl and bureaucratic complications of the capital, what a toll the two years of the North Shaanxi campaign had taken on her health.

Nor were the clouds that hung over the Mao-Jiang relationship helpful to her condition. Was Yu Shan really out of the picture, or

* Mao soon restored the name Peking (northern capital), Peiping (northern peace) being the name the Nationalists gave the city in 1928.

might she reappear in Peking, with the same gall that had led her to throw herself at Mao in Shijiazhuang? Now that the fluid days of civil war were over, would Jiang's enemies in the Communist Party, abetted perhaps by Mao, box her in again?

"Will the tattered clothes change Peiping," Mao mused as his peasant movement stretched its arms around the city, "or will the change run in the opposite direction?" Jiang Qing, too, wondered about the direction of influence. Perhaps she would be able to deploy her talents, "now one and now the other," to make her mark in Peking. Or perhaps the post-revolutionary Peking establishment would stymie her—making a tame creature of her as surely as it threatened to co-opt the militants in their tattered clothes.

In the first days of April 1949, Jiang Qing found herself on a train, headed far from Peking, her husband, and the excitement of new China's birth. With nurses and bodyguards in tow, she was bound for a Russian hospital. Six months later, as Mao in a new suit mounted the Gate of Heavenly Peace to proclaim the People's Republic of China and headed a festive parade of the entire Communist elite along the Boulevard of Eternal Peace, Jiang Qing was still in Moscow, alone, unwell, wondering if she was to become the He Zizhen of the 1950s.

Years later Jiang spoke enigmatically about this first foreign trip of her life. She felt desperately ill, she said, and years of strife had "destroyed most Chinese hospitals." Yet only one hospital was required, and none of Peking's major hospitals had been destroyed. Would a desperately ill woman want to travel miles by train, moreover, to a country utterly alien to her, which neither she nor her husband had ever visited?

Jiang Qing was indeed ill, with tonsillitis, and generally run down as well. But she was not desperately ill. The reasons for her being treated in Russia, rather than within China, were personal and political rather than physical, and they reflected her complex personality and the awkwardness of being Mao's wife in Mao's China.

The vivacious Yu Shan, well known in artistic circles for her vivid performance as Salome in a bizarre Chinese adaptation of the Richard Strauss opera, had indeed found her way to Peking, and it is possible that one reason Jiang Qing was lying in a Russian hospital bed was that Mao wished to see "Salome" again.

Mao cabled the poet Liu Yazu in Hong Kong on February 28, urging him to return to China and play a role in building socialism.

On March 25, the day of his own arrival from Shijiazhuang, Mao received poet Liu at Peking's airport. When, the next day, the Communists decided on "peace talks" with the Nationalists, Liu wrote a poem to celebrate this and also the liberation of his own hometown. A month later, on April 30, Mao replied. By this time, as we know from Jiang Qing's reaction to the *Amethyst* Incident, involving a British-Chinese clash on the Yangzi River, Jiang had already been in Russia long enough to make a trip south to Yalta. The next day, May 1, Liu was taking a nap when a knock on the door announced Mao and "Jiang Qing." Mao, the woman, and Liu went off to visit the Summer Palace, where they ran into Lin Biao and his wife and later dined with them.

It seems that Mao's companion was Yu Shan, in such intimacy with Mao that Liu took her to be Jiang Qing (whom he had never met).

In Chinese history, most peasant rebellion leaders had strong sex drives. Mao was in this tradition. At Yanan he had told Party colleagues he needed Jiang Qing "for the sake of the revolution." In Peking he was even more conscious of his own importance than before, and with Jiang Qing looking poorly, and probably depressed, it would not have been out of character for Mao to declare that he needed a little flutter with Yu Shan "for the sake of the dictatorship of the proletariat."* And given the Communist principle that Party interests outweigh individual feelings, Liu Shaoqi, Zhou Enlai, and the others certainly were not going to spring to the defense of Jiang Qing or of "bourgeois morality."

It is possible that Jiang Qing, suspecting an affair between Mao and Yu Shan, flounced out of Peking of her own accord, given her strong-willed nature, Mao's tendency to let people who were in his way twist slowly in the wind until they gave up in disgust, and her own desire to see a foreign country. If so, she later preferred to present her departure as a *fait accompli* handed her by others.

Some people who knew Jiang well suspected that she preferred to go to Russia rather than stay in Peking. "The Yanan years were austere and tough," Su Fei, who saw much of Jiang there, recalled. "It was very much the 'in' thing to go to Russia in the early fifties— like going to America in the early 1980s—and I think she wanted to go. She thought the Russians would treat her marvelously, that she'd be hobnobbing with Stalin the day after she arrived." Tang

---

* Mao's deputy for many years, Liu Shaoqi, may have been swiping at Mao's philandering, which was never criticized in more than a whisper, when he burst out during a Red Guard interrogation on the subject of his own six marriages: "Look, *I* acted publicly, instead of having secret immoral liaisons."

Na had a similar view. "She wasn't really sick," her former husband felt. "She just wanted to go abroad and have a look. She'd never had that chance. In the fifties the logical place to go was Russia."

Jiang Qing was met at Moscow station by an ambulance. Yet the most serious medical treatment she underwent in Russia was the removal of her tonsils. Mostly she rested, trying to put on weight, in the Black Sea resort of Yalta, and in the heavy mansions of old Moscow. If she was less than desperately ill, she was certainly brittle emotionally. Small incidents made her break down and cry. Her memory of a visit to the Kremlin is so bizarre that it seems she was either in a psychotic condition at the time, or she later fabricated her account to reduce the impression of her stay in Russia as one of isolated misery.

Stalin invited her to visit, she said, but when she arrived at the Kremlin the Soviet leader's staff members were surprised that *Mao was not with her.* It is beyond belief that the Soviet government did not know whether Mao Zedong, leader of the newly triumphant Chinese Revolution, which Stalin had been nurturing for a quarter of a century, was in the Soviet Union (it would have been his first visit there). Perhaps Stalin did not invite her at all. Or perhaps she was in such a poor state on arrival at the Kremlin that the Soviet aides felt it inappropriate to take her in to see Stalin.

It is clear that in 1949 depression and illness gripped Jiang Qing and that her first stay in Russia disappointed her.

Back in Peking, on a crisp November morning, Jiang Qing rode in Mao's car to the main railroad station. He had sent her to say farewell to an important visitor. Song Qingling, widow of Sun Yat-sen, was returning with her entourage to Shanghai after a stay in the capital to attend the inaugural festivities of the People's Republic of China. Jiang Qing wore blue woolen trousers, a blue and white striped blouse, and the blue peaked cap of new China's professional class, the cadre. She looked thin but not sick. Announcing herself as "Mao's representative," she chatted with the PRC's number one non-Communist female dignitary in the velvet-and-lace compartment of the special train. She treated the older woman, whose husband had died when Jiang was eleven years old, with great respect. "Jiang Qing is courteous and charming," Song Qingling said to her staff as the train sped toward Shanghai.

Jiang always impressed people in such brief social situations. She was good at a play of a couple of hours.

The Mao-Jiang house was splendid. Mao pronounced death

upon all old things but kept one or two for himself. As walls and gates were pulled down and foreign missions were ordered out to a sterile suburb, Mao, far from erecting a Stalinist bungalow, moved himself and Jiang Qing into the western flank of the Imperial Palace. At the edge of the porcelain-blue waters of South and Central Lakes, a private delight of the palace, their Ming dynasty pavilion, with red pillars, golden tiles curving up to an apex brushed by the elegant branches of gnarled old plane trees, and white marble steps with bronze dragons to each side, reeked of history and the self-importance of a ruling class.

The "authorities" had selected "separate but connected" apartments for the chairman and his wife in a building once called Small Palace of the Fragrant Concubine. Each was double the size of their Yanan cave, with tall ceilings, carved wooden screens, silk hangings, and tall windows curtained to befit the discretions of power. It was all very grand after the garrets of Shanghai, the caves of Yanan, and the farmhouses of the North Shaanxi campaign period, but it was not easy for Jiang to relax in such a place.

"Separate but connected" described not only the apartments but also the marriage. "You don't seem to have an ounce of affection for Daddy," the eldest son of Mao's marriage with Yang Kaihui blazed at Jiang during an evening of argument. "All you do is nag at him." At least in the judgment of Mao Anying, who was now working at Party headquarters as a translator of Russian, the marriage in romantic terms was at an end. "If you don't love Daddy," the twenty-eight-year-old declared to her after another bout of domestic strife, "why don't you clear out?"

Mao Anying must have known that his father, given his position, the fuss he had made in Yanan about securing Jiang, and the hold she had over him by virtue of having lived with him prior to marrying him, hardly had the option of driving Jiang out. Perhaps he hoped that Jiang would leave. But Jiang was not so foolish. She was not like He Zizhen. She would not leave Mao Zedong on the trivial ground that the romance was dead.

Jiang could see in the attention Mao was paying to the family of Yang Kaihui a sign that he had pulled back emotionally from her. It was natural enough that the brother of Mao's first chosen wife should send a telegram of congratulation to Mao when Changsha, the Yangs' home city in Hunan Province, fell to the Communists. But it seemed extraordinary that Mao responded as he did. Within five days he replied at length to brother Yang, writing fondly, giving detailed news of his two sons by Yang Kaihui. Soon he sent both youths, on separate trips, to the Yang relatives, bearing his greetings. He invited brother Yang and his wife, Li Zongde, to South and Central Lakes for a long, nostalgic afternoon of conversation. In general he paid an attention to the Yangs (including poems a little later to Kaihui's memory) that seemed more appropriate for a widower of Yang Kaihui than for the current husband of Jiang Qing.

The distance that had entered the marriage was not really Mao's fault or Jiang's but the result of a change of circumstances, and perhaps a ransom exacted by monotony. Mao's dalliance with Yu Shan in Shijiazhuang was less a cause than a consequence of the marriage's staleness. Mao's life was becoming highly structured, with a large staff, constant appointments, and long hours in the office. Gone was the Mao-Jiang marriage as a companionship of a leader and his helpmate, as at Yanan, where a visit to Mao was often a visit to Jiang as well, and on the road during the civil war, when they rode the same horse and their bedroom sometimes had to double as the Politburo's meeting room.

When the Long March ended, Mao sent his bodyguard and man Friday, Chen Changfeng, off to school. The personal bond between the two was over in the new circumstances of Yanan. Chen wept for the broken spell of the Long March months as he tried to set his mind to books. To a degree—for in Mao's eyes a wife was "his" almost as a bodyguard was "his"—Jiang Qing felt the same sting of change after the end of the civil war that Chen Changfeng felt after the end of the Long March. She would be needed less now.

Jiang was not content to be purely a housewife, no matter how well Mao might happen to treat her. She wanted a job. Everyone had been assigned work, it seemed, except her. Her old theatrical colleagues hummed with the busyness of new tasks, as did the wives of the other top leaders. But she was supposed to be a high-status but impotent Nora.

Her position in the People's Liberation Army had been terminated, which seemed natural, but it disappointed her. While she was in Russia an All China Federation of Literary and Artistic Circles was founded. Almost every cultural figure of note became a member, including Tian Han and Zhou Yang, figures from her Shanghai years, and the beautiful Sun Weishi, who had taken Jiang's place in the affections of Xu Yixin at Lu Xun College in Yanan. But Jiang Qing's name was not on the list.

Every position Jiang occupied during the 1950s she had to wrench from extremely reluctant hands. The bureaucracy, or Mao, or both, tried to hold her down to private life. Only Zhou Enlai encouraged her, and later she thanked him publicly for it.

Jiang had not struggled all these years, left Tang Na, and made her way alone to Yanan to be a nonfunctioning decoration in Communist Peking. She was still the Lan Ping who wanted to express herself, which meant both to promote herself and to do real work; still the Lan Ping who felt that if anything important and exciting were going on, she wanted to be in it.

Jiang was not content, as some wives might be, to remain a ladylike consumer of the amenities of South and Central Lakes. She liked the luxuries and took them as her natural entitlement. But she also felt an itch to push aside the elegant tables, put on a hat and a pair of strong shoes, and get out and be at the center of things. Was not the redistribution of the land from rich to poor—land reform—in which she had gained some useful experience during the civil war the very heart of socialist revolution?

Mao did not want her to make a land reform trip. No one else wanted her to. She simply insisted until the opposition gave way.

She chose the tea and silk districts around Wuxi. Bureaucrats arranged for her to go first to Shanghai, where the Party chief, Rao Shushi, sincere as he probably was in trying to make the best of a dubious experiment, infuriated Jiang by "controlling" her. When she sought to go shopping in her old haunts on Nanjing Road, Rao insisted on going with her. When she pressed to leave immediately for the tea and silk villages, Rao recounted all the difficulties and warned that her "personal safety could not be guaranteed."

Rao faced a problem common to many officials who found Jiang Qing on their hands: He thought her plans were bizarre, but he had to show her respect and see she came to no harm, because she was Mao's wife. Perhaps he suspected she might contact former boyfriends—a habit of hers—and was terrified of having to report such events to Mao.

One moment she complained that Rao was keeping her from mixing with the masses by bottling her up in Shanghai. The next she complained that the Party chief allotted her a hotel room (in Victory Mansion) that was too cold and lacked a southern exposure. The thread running through the whole trip, which was supposed to be for the purpose of rural investigation, was that bureaucrats were seeking to rein her in, to prevent her from expressing herself.

Jiang took for granted that anything she was moved to do was important for socialist revolution, and so she depicted those who frustrated her (like Rao and others in Shanghai) not as mere personal enemies but as renegades from socialism. That she could say Rao's supervision of her gave her the nasty sensation of always being "on the verge of being kidnaped," just as in the Nationalist-ruled Shanghai of the 1930s, showed that in Jiang Qing's moral universe political systems meant nothing and her own self-assertion meant everything.

Jiang Qing did spend a few days looking at mulberry trees and tea plantations near the lakeside town of Wuxi, and for years she was able to toss off such remarks as, "My role in land reform has never been presented correctly to the public."

Jiang *was* a problem for the bureaucrats. The era of "marital politics" had not yet arrived; wives were not given jobs just because they were wives. Deng Yingchao, Zhou Enlai's wife, received posts because she had long been a career politician in her own right. Yet when Jiang Qing showed dissatisfaction at being on the sidelines, the bureaucrats could not simply put her down, for she was not just a leader's wife, but *the* leader's wife.

Many women were happy to put their heads down at "women's work." But Jiang Qing was not. All her life she despised such activity. Although she had been discriminated against as a woman, Jiang was not willing to embrace the assumption of women's separateness that, she felt, underlay "women's work." She did not want to think she was any different from men. A humiliation was involved in women's organizations that she never was able to endure.

The flashing colored lights of Jiang's personality added to the bureaucrats' problem. She did not have the background to do high-level political work, yet she was not prepared to do low-level political work. And her attention span was short. She loved to start new things, but she quickly became bored. The impulses of work on the stage were not easy to transfer to the work of bureaucratic bricklaying.

As the Peking winter set in—the apartments in South and Central Lakes were nicely heated, unlike the average home in frigid North China—Jiang Qing could boast two very modest posts. Being an alumnus of the Soviet experience, she was made a member of the China-Russia Friendship Association; as one among scores of members, she was not going to cut much ice in that choirlike group. More to her tastes, she was appointed to a Film Guidance Committee set up within the Ministry of Culture to evaluate all movie projects. (The committee was apparently in principle under the Film Bureau, which was headed by none other than "Lipstick" Yuan Muzhi, who had pursued Jiang in Shanghai, spoken icily of her acting ability in Wuhan, and made a documentary about her and Mao in Yanan.) Mao did not obtain these posts for Jiang Qing—indeed, he seemed to want her to be even more publicly invisible than she was. Zhou Enlai wangled them.

Culture was Jiang Qing's specialty, and when the Communist regime, Russian-influenced and very proud of itself, began to re-shape China's cultural life, it was natural that she, a former practi-tioner in that realm, wanted to put her oar in. It was also inevitable that her relations with Mao, chief architect of the reshaping, tainted her efforts.

Jiang approached the films and plays of 1949–51 as a French chef with one star in the Michelin guide might approach the kitchens of chefs newly blessed with three stars. The *pâté* had too much liver, the rack of lamb was dry, the chocolate mousse was bit-ter—of course. In her part-time advisory capacity with the film committee, and on any cultural terrain where she could get a foot-hold, she wielded the broom of iconoclasm.*

To Jiang, denunciation of the artistic accomplishments of nearly everyone around her as "bourgeois" or even "feudal" was a logical way to try to assert herself in a realm she felt largely shut out of. Censorship? The more the merrier, for each kick in the shins she aimed at a movie of the late 1940s or very early 1950s was a step up the ladder of her own power over the arts.

It was also true, as Jiang had written to Tang Na in the 1930s, that she sincerely despised Bohemian circles. Having wanted to get into the arts, she nevertheless did not want her life in Shanghai to be defined by the arts. By the 1950s that feeling of distance had grown. She felt superior to the Bohemians—as a man of power feels he is nearer to the heart of things than a man of ideas.

One afternoon in Shanghai, when Jiang was on her way back from land reform at Wuxi, she slipped out of Rao Shushi's control

---

* Witke refers to Jiang Qing as having been "the chief censor," and the director of the Film Bureau of the Party's propaganda section, but she was not such. She ranked twenty-nine in the thirty-two-member Film Guidance Committee. Her official rank in the complex hierarchy of the Party was a very low "12," the lowest niche of a "senior cadre." By comparison, Zhou Yang and Deng Yingchao were in the "4–6" range, Yuan Muzhi and Ding Ling were in the "7–9" range. Mao was "1"—alone in that niche—so in bureaucratic terms there was a yawning gap, difficult for the bureaucrats to cope with, between Jiang's rank and her husband's.

to visit Wu Mei, the actress who had resented her flirting with Zhang Min when Jiang played the lead in Zhang's production of *A Doll's House* and Wu Mei smoldered in fury at her small supporting role. Her black limousine crept along Nanchang Street to Lane 136. Jiang, in a *qipao* and black-rimmed sunglasses, hopped out and went to Wu's door at number 23. Wu Mei received her cordially. She was awed that Jiang was now the chairman's wife, and it was a pleasant relief to find the First Lady in a friendly, charming mood. The two had fourteen years of news to catch up on.

Jiang made two requests of Wu Mei. Could Sister Wu, who lived in Shanghai and was well connected with businessmen in the city, find a really good dentist for her, to do a complicated job on the problem of her once-broken, "yellow" tooth? And would her fellow actress buy for her some cosmetics, the top-quality kind that did not exist in Peking but could still be found in Shanghai stores that carried Western imported stock from the previous year? Jiang asked Wu to be discreet in these two tasks. Wu Mei used her aunt, an employee in the telephone company, to fulfill Jiang's requests.

From her new vantage point of high status, Jiang was showing off a bit in front of her old rival, just as she did by trying to contact Tang Na on her visit to Chongqing as Mao's wife in 1945. But she probably envied the freedom that Wu Mei and other artist friends from the 1930s enjoyed, compared with her captivity as Mao's political Nora.

Jiang also went to see Zhao Dan, who had played opposite her in *A Doll's House* and whom she had known well enough to flee to his apartment in the middle of one of her quarrels with Tang Na, and Zheng Junli, who had been best man at her wedding in Hangzhou. She asked them both to dinner at the Jinjiang Club. At this old haunt of hers in the French Concession, once a haven for the French elite and now for the Chinese Communist elite, she treated them both with warmth and respect. "We can all make a new beginning," she said. "I think we can work together, in the new era, to achieve new heights in the performing arts."

But Jiang never followed up. On later trips to Shanghai she asked these senior men of the theater to small parties. Again she charmed them, again she spoke earnestly of how they could all cooperate. But it was only a performance to show Zhao Dan and Zheng Junli who she was now; at the same time it betrayed a wild hope that she still could be Lan Ping, creating and expressing herself as these two actor-directors were able to do.

If she had anything concrete in mind by talking of "working together," she was thinking of making these former Shanghai colleagues serve her. "She merely wanted lackeys," said one who knew the contents of her talks with Zhao and Zheng. The only way Jiang could deal with her aching envy of these beautiful birds of the theater was to cage them under her control!

But Zhao and Zheng knew her too well to accept her vague offer to "cooperate." And when they had meetings with Zhou Enlai on cultural matters and joined committees on the arts that were under Zhou's supervision, Jiang Qing was furious. The subtle mix of emotions in her spirit turned into pure hatred. If these old colleagues of hers would not look up to her and would not help her ease the ache of her envy of them by flattering her, then she would turn against them.

On the alleged need to reform Peking opera, Jiang already fired a few shots at the end of 1949. In Yanan, Ding Ling and others had talked about the need to give modern settings to the stylized old librettos, but the task was not easy and the war effort diverted them. After the People's Republic of China was founded there was an inclination, as the new leaders filed into the great auditoriums for festive theatrical events, to *enjoy* the established glories of Chinese tradition and to believe they were rendered valid for the new era simply by being executed, and watched, by Communist figures. So it was that Mei Lanfang, the greatest Peking opera actor of his day, found himself busily engaged in planning traditional performances, to nearly everyone's satisfaction.

But not to Jiang Qing's. She saw an opportunity to brand Mei as "attached to the old," in the name of a new order she felt able to represent because her husband was its chief powerholder. Using a classic technique of the Chinese Communist court, she invited pliant intellectuals to write memos critical of Mei's "feudalism," which she then tried to coordinate and deploy. Mei was especially furious at Jiang's crusade against him because in the 1920s he had himself tried to modernize Peking opera, updating the stories and using contemporary costumes, but had come to the conclusion that one could not fiddle with the ancient and produce something modern, that an opera about kings had to *be* an opera about kings, and that history and current themes would never be married in the Chinese theater.

Jiang Qing did not yet have enough influence to discredit Mei Lanfang, much less to topple him. Two of his operas she managed to have banned, but Mei sailed on with little damage into the patriotism-minded decade of the 1950s, much to Jiang's disgust.

Along came a wonderful movie, *Inside Story of the Qing Dynasty Court,* full of color and action and passion, set in the era of the Empress Dowager and the Boxer Rebellion. Audiences in Shanghai and Nanjing greeted it with enthusiasm in the spring of 1949. *Inside Story* was made in Hong Kong by Kunlun Studios, from a 1943 play by Yao Xinnong. The Communists held full political power, but not the power to make an overnight transformation in Chinese culture. Pre-Communist and imported films and books and products of all kinds simply could not be dispensed with. .

Still, for Jiang Qing, "foreign things" and the fruits of the "capitalist era" were luscious targets. A movie made in decadent Hong Kong! A movie that prettified the intrigues of dynastic China, treated the foreign intervention in China in 1900 as a reasonable act, and cast a slur on the militant young Boxer resisters! A movie that utterly failed to engage in class analysis! In her bid to get attention by carving out irresistible territory she was like a junior delegate at a John Birch Society meeting who wildly bangs the drum about Communists in Central America and in the high schools, sure that the standpoint will be judged correct, hopeful that the net effect will be admiration for the drumbeater.

Jiang Qing had not always felt that class analysis should underlie all works of art; nor was the Shanghai she had reveled in during the 1930s less decadent than Hong Kong. But the words she spat out against *Inside Story* were not the point. One can understand the "leftism" of Jiang Qing only by translating two key political concepts into the meaning they had within her personal universe: communism meant power; class struggle meant revenge. Here was the point of Jiang Qing's iconoclasm in the years 1949–51.

Didn't she think about the effect of her behavior on the ordinary men and women who *liked* the color and action and passion of *Inside Story*? Her priority did not lie in such considerations. One might as well ask how Prince Charles of Britain and his bride, Lady Diana Spencer, reconciled in their own minds the glitter and expense of their wedding with the economic tribulations of millions of Britons. From the pinnacle of power, as Jiang Qing was starting to find out, the lives of ordinary people are not a vivid reality, and the purpose of the moment, which is lent excitement by the high stakes of power, is very easily seen as its own justification.

Using persuasion and her status as Mao's wife, Jiang Qing succeeded during 1950 in convening a meeting of cultural figures, chaired by Lu Dingyi, head of the propaganda department of the Party, to "discuss" *Inside Story of the Qing Dynasty Court.* Writers, historians, and arts administrators gathered apprehensively in Jiang's own apartment at South and Central Lakes. Everyone in the room knew she was bent on banning *Inside Story*.

One after the other the cultural figures spoke up for the historical and entertainment merit of the movie. No less a force than Liu Shaoqi, second to Mao in the hierarchy, was quoted as approving the "patriotic" thrust of the plot. Furious, Jiang Qing at first lapsed into total silence and later shouted that *Inside Story* was in no sense patriotic but actually "traitorous."

This being Communist China, there was no question of taking a vote, or even trying to pluck a formal decision out of a delicate political minefield. Jiang "instructed" two historians to write an attack on the movie, but they dragged their feet in time-honored Chinese style and never really came up with a finished, satisfactory document. Probably Jiang Qing converted no one to the view that *Inside Story of the Qing Dynasty Court* was a poisonous weed. Yet by denouncing it and instilling a certain amount of fear in all minor officials who had anything to do with it or its distribution, Jiang Qing managed to hang a question mark over the movie's future. For a time it was largely withdrawn, though it later reappeared, and an opera version became popular in 1954, as did a revival of the original play in 1957.

Jiang Qing's drive against *Inside Story* was a performance by a cast of one, and in the face of Mao's indifference it had very limited success. So little was Mao involved that in 1954 he was able to say, "We haven't criticized *Inside Story* yet"—a stinging remark in Jiang Qing's ears. But during 1951 Jiang hurled herself against another movie, *The Story of Wu Xun,* and this time, with Mao's backing, she won a major victory.

Wu Xun was a famous beggar from Jiang Qing's own province of Shandong who rose to become a philanthropist by proxy and establish a network of schools. Like a Chinese Vinobe Bhave, the Indian moralist who persuaded the rich to donate land to the poor, Wu Xun sought contributions from the well-off for education. The pleasant, slightly treacly movie about his success story came out of a pre-1949 Hong Kong studio. Edited under the supervision of Zhou Yang and Xia Yan, Jiang's senior colleagues from the Shanghai arts world of the 1930s, now cultural decision-makers, it was screened to huge appreciative audiences in Shanghai, Peking, and Tianjin during the first months of 1951, and forty to fifty articles praising it appeared in the media of these three cities. On seeing it, Jiang Qing was "disturbed."

Her passion against Wu Xun was genuine in part; she hated paternalism and the softness of spirit that it both built upon and evoked. She called the movie a trash can full of "bourgeois reformism" (in Communist parlance that means it exalted a do-gooder instead of exalting class struggle aimed at structural change).*

Though it seemed that "no one listened" to her in those days, Jiang Qing resolved to try to blacken the name of Wu Xun, and the movie about him, learning some lessons from her difficult experience with *Inside Story of the Qing Dynasty Court.*

Her first efforts were not encouraging, perhaps because her methods were angular, perhaps because some Party leaders had put out the word—once more—that she should be kept totally out of public life. When she went to see Zhou Yang, second in command at the Culture Ministry, and told him she felt *The Story of Wu Xun* was reformist, he did not take her seriously. "I can put up with a little reformism," he drawled, as if to a tedious child. Later, aroused, he spoke sharply: "Who are you [to make such an attack]?" Jiang lost her temper. "Go ahead with your reformism!" she shouted as she slammed the door in his face.

In Jiang Qing's own account, Mao at first did not support her either, and she had to walk out on him too when he said he disapproved of her crusade. But Jiang, speaking in 1972, was exaggerating her own efforts and understating the importance of Mao's eventual support.

She says she wrote an article denouncing the movie, which, when published, "disarmed the enemy" and essentially put an end to the movie's run. There is no record of an article by Jiang Qing being published, but she did inspire critical articles by others in April 1951. Then she indeed disarmed the enemy by persuading Mao, in May 1951, to pen a scoffing editorial in *People's Daily.* Jiang appealed to Mao's pride in his own principles: Were not Zhou Yang and Xia Yan slipping back from the standards of Mao's *Talks at the Yanan Forum on Literature and Art?* Was not this Confucian do-gooder, Wu Xun, the very antithesis of the Maoist man of the coming collectivist age?

The chairman, who in this period rarely stepped down from Olympian generality to comment on a particular current work of art, panned the movie, complained of "ideological confusion" in "our country's cultural circles," and ominously demanded to know

* Yet wasn't Wu Xun the same kind of man as Professor Tao Xingzhi, leader of a "going to the peasants" movement that Jiang had been keen about in the 1930s in Shanghai? (see page 55).

"Where on earth is the Marxism that *certain Communists* claim to have grasped?" Zhou Yang retreated; Jiang Qing was on the offensive.

It is not difficult to understand why many cultural decision-makers came to resent Jiang Qing: Herself without senior office, she was using Mao to influence events in accordance with her taste and ambition. At Yanan and during the civil war, Jiang had quietly stepped into an issue in order to please Mao. Now, for the first time, on a public issue she had used Mao to satisfy her own wishes.

The quest for power and place, as imperious in China as elsewhere, eclipsed the issue of content in these amazing capers over movies, plays, and books. Jiang Qing's call for a new approach to *Inside Story* and *The Story of Wu Xun* was like the decision of a First Lady, on moving into the mansion of office, to shift every piece of furniture to a new position, or the impulse of a freshly elected mayor to name a bridge or park in the city after himself—the point was largely to flaunt, or consolidate, power.

For centuries Chinese politics knew recurrent tension between the court and the bureaucracy (not dissimilar to that between the White House staff and the executive departments in Washington). Especially was this true under the founding emperor of a dynasty, whose court tended to be personal. Thanks to Jiang Qing's restlessness, talent, and ambition, the Wu Xun affair was re-creating the pattern in Communist China. A "bureaucratic group" found itself pitted against the "emperor's group." Zhou Yang was perfectly justified in thinking that even in consenting to talk with Jiang Qing about the movie he was making a concession to her; but structural rectitude could at times be overcome by household talk at South and Central Lakes.

As the 1950s led on to the 1960s and 1970s, the court-bureaucracy tension would rise. Perhaps it was inevitable, given China's traditions, sprawling size, and cultural disposition to factionalism. At any rate, the key figure in the evolution of the pattern was Jiang Qing, and the campaign against *The Story of Wu Xun* was the first jewel in her crown.

It was characteristic of Jiang that she rammed home her victory with excessive jabs. Once Mao had committed himself—to the principle of the matter, not to support of Jiang's every sally—she decided to form an investigation team and go to Wu Xun's home county to pin down in vivid detail the man's evil record. Mao objected, she said, but she went ahead regardless, her only concession to him being to travel under a false name so that any mistake she made would not make him look like a fool. All the cultural administrators could do was add two representatives to the investigation team to keep an eye on Jiang and in desperate circumstances to rein her in.

But it was Jiang Qing's show. The results were no more in doubt than is applause at the end of a stirring aria. Her first act was to fall ill, and then spurning assistance, to treat herself with an assortment of drugs, as if her dizzy spells and dripping eyes were personal enemies that only she could vanquish.

The situation lent itself to fantasy, and Jiang Qing, who hadn't really changed since her girlhood days of rage and dreams, and her Shanghai days of finding personal reality within a theatrical plot, felt the thrill of having hit upon a new vocation—the woman leader who braves any storm to save her people.

Meeting the local boss of Wu Xun's home county, in territory close to her own birthplace, where she knew the choppy dialect and seemed to gain confidence from each point of association with her upbringing, she grandly declared of the local hero: "Continued veneration of such a man will ultimately destroy our Party and our nation."

In China, local power—and truth—are helpless before a *démarche* from Peking. The cards were stacked against Wu Xun; soon Jiang Qing's notebook recorded firsthand testimony from some terrified old farmer that "Wu Xun's lips dripped with saliva, a symbol of his greed," and other such newly minted truths.

In her account of the Wu Xun affair, Jiang never mentioned Mao's pivotal article in *People's Daily*. She spoke of her husband mainly as an obstacle, though his basic agreement with the attack on Wu Xun was the chief reason for the drive's success, as his silence on *Inside Story of the Qing Dynasty Court* had been Jiang's gravest handicap.*

Jiang Qing was a unique character, in world history as in Chinese history, and yet there are moments when she reminds us of Eva Perón. If it is the former Argentine First Lady, a political prima donna and folk hero, who more than any other woman in the political life of our times resembles Jiang Qing, it is perhaps because a courtesan's and an actress's bent lay behind the almost unstoppable

* Jiang exaggerated the time she spent in Shandong; her claim of eight months conflicts with clear evidence of her appearance in Peking during that period and with the fact that the results of her investigation, which were quite rich, were substantially published in the last week of July 1951, at most three months after she went to Shandong.

willfulness of both women. Jiang, on her tour of Shandong in search of Wu Xun's scalp, and of a leg up for her own political career, showed the same traits of self-dramatization, extreme subjectivity, and a shuttling back and forth between reality and the script that made Eva Perón (and would make Jiang) passionately followed, deeply reviled, and always the focus of attention.

Jiang Qing was not needed—or did not want to be—at Mao's side. Soon after shooting a final arrow into Wu Xun's corpse, she began a new enterprise away from Peking. For three months toward the end of 1951 she joined in a further bout of land reform, near Wuhan in Hubei Province, at the belly button of China.

This time Mao did not oppose Jiang's trip, either because he felt she had done well in Shandong, or because he was content to see her far away. But others did. So she had to use her pseudonym, Li Jin, and when she got to the villages she found herself hamstrung.

It was not her own land reform team, but a large one led by Li Xiannian, a senior economic official. When the team was subdivided, Jiang was weighed down by so much supervision that her group consisted entirely of her array of bodyguards and herself. "You divorce me from the masses!" she shouted at an interfering bodyguard when she was not allowed to stride out alone to confront a landlord and hear the tale of woe of his poor peasants. Yet the next moment she tossed off an elitist remark about the "greasy food" favored by this same bodyguard, fare that Jiang herself "would not have served at my own table."

If the farmers cried, the lady from Peking sat down and cried with them, her tears falling like an imperial blessing on the soil of the Hubei villages. An attack of bronchitis notwithstanding, she threw herself into identifying the tyrants, then distributing their land, furniture, and garments to people who had seldom possessed anything in their lives. She was shocked at rural backwardness and at times condescending toward the peasants; she must teach them "broadness of mind," she said. Yet she was not squeamish, and her analysis of the women's issue was trenchant and enlightened.

At the same time Jiang should hardly have wondered that people found her an enigma. She was never without one of her fur coats, though the people around her, except for the silk-clad landlords, whom it was her purpose to have murdered, were dressed in dull rags. She carried a camera; as lives were snuffed out and others were set afire with hope, she clicked away to get some unusual shots for her album. She could report without shame that some of the peasants, seeing her unfamiliarity with rural life, bluntly said, "Who do you think you are?" because, as well as being a participant in land reform she seemed also to be a bemused, delighted *spectator* of herself in that role.

Tigers, like wolves, often figure in the fantasies of Chinese, and Jiang Qing's self-image in Hubei included standing up to a tiger. A rumor went around the area that a tiger was on the loose. Jiang took it upon herself to go out and raise morale, and mobilize people to arm themselves with sticks. Lying on her bed in the moonlight, she heard a terrible roar. Her bodyguard was afraid, but Jiang calmed him. "You've nothing to worry about," she managed to say with *noblesse oblige*'s false but necessary confidence.

When Jiang's three months among the farmers drew to an end, she "dared not attend" the final celebratory land reform meeting, evidently feeling that since the people were "nearly beside themselves with excitement" they would *drown* her with gratitude. As she left for Peking, the peasants, she recalled, thronged around beating gongs and drums. Some of them were crying, and Jiang cried too.

Jiang said she was seeking to get "close to the masses," but it seemed that what she wanted from the masses was adulation. Try as she did to execute land reform seriously, she managed to seem only like a leading actress out in the paddy fields rehearsing a *drama* about land reform.

During the winter of 1951–52 Jiang rose one big step higher and then was rudely pushed down. Despite its bland name, the General Office of the Party's Central Committee is a powerhouse, and soon after her return from Hubei Province Jiang was named head of its secretariat. It was easily the most important Communist Party post she had ever held, or would hold until the quite new circumstances of the mid-1960s. The secretariat of the General Office controls the flow of secret papers in which all key decisions in the governance of China are refracted. Being head of the secretariat as well as Mao's wife, Jiang was not only the watchdog over documents but also the potentially crucial link between the General Office and Mao's personal office. Questions about the transmission of Mao's instructions, the materials to be sent to him, his schedule of meetings with visitors, the destination of the handwritten notes gathered up at the end of each night from his desk—all were in Jiang Qing's province.

But she held the job only a few weeks. She later said that the work was "more grueling and pressured" than she expected and that she began to suffer from a high fever and a pain in the liver. But a crisis had arisen that was more than medical. Jiang was forced out of the job on the "recommendation" of her superior, the head of the General Office, Yang Shangkun, an able Sichuanese who was to clash with her more than once. That Jiang was relieved of her other posts at the same time—on the Film Guidance Committee and in the China-Russia Friendship Association—shows that she had struck trouble. Indeed, Mao did not feel able to back her. He went along with Yang's "recommendation" and merely smoothed the path to a face-saving solution to the crisis: Jiang would do important work but henceforth she would do it "on her own."

The problem was twofold. "When Jiang Qing is present," murmured Zhou Yang, "work is difficult." Many people in the bureaucracy agreed with him. (Famous for years, Zhou's remark was used as a sword to impale him during the Cultural Revolution.) Jiang was difficult when working in a team because of her subjectivism, theatrical ways, and sensitive ego.

She was not the kind of person who could sit at a desk for four hours and do paperwork step by step. She was not able even to read a document for more than ten or fifteen minutes on end. She needed drama, excitement, and intrigue to keep her spirit alive. Otherwise she became bored, depressed, and ill.

But it was also because she was Mao's wife that she was difficult as a co-worker. Many people still resented her, not for what she was in herself but simply because she radiated some of Mao's reflected glory and so was difficult for the bureaucrats to categorize and handle.

Zhou Yang went to see Liu Shaoqi about the problem of Jiang. Zhou did not dislike Jiang. He had not really "persecuted and suppressed" her in Shanghai, as she insisted on believing. That claim was like the complaint of a seed seeking to sprout that the earth is "persecuting and suppressing it." The seed struggles to go beyond the earth. The earth is surprised that the seed is not satisfied with the status quo.

But Zhou Yang was perplexed about how to handle Jiang's "suggestions" or "requests" in the cultural realm. "She sends in dozens of opinions on scripts," Zhou explained to the head of state, "and it's confusing, because no one knows if it's her opinion or Chairman Mao's opinion." Liu listened carefully, as was his habit. At length he told the Vice-Minister of Culture to try to raise the issue with Mao himself. Zhou Yang did, no doubt very delicately, and it seems that Jiang's loss of her posts was strongly determined by the Mao–Zhou Yang conversation.

Probably Jiang Qing's appointment to the General Office was a mistake from the start. She was pushing too far in her desire for "real work," the kind that men did. The Party guardians felt she was violating the Yanan marriage agreement. And by 1952 Mao, his honeymoon with the nation and the Party largely over, no longer could stick his neck out on her behalf, assuming he wanted to. Even Jiang's presence at Mao's side during receptions, not so unusual in 1950 and 1951—if less common than the presence of Liu Shaoqi's and Zhou Enlai's wives with their husbands—seemed to be a thing of the past by 1952.

It was a sign that Jiang's health was not impossibly bad—and that her will was as relentless as ever—that sometime in early 1952, even though the crisis over her role had hardly simmered down, she asked the Party for an assignment in the "Resist America and Aid Korea" campaign. On the surface it appeared to be a reasonable request; the cause was impeccable, and all available energy was needed to turn back "the imperialists."

But Jiang Qing was such a hot potato that the issue spiraled up to the Politburo. "Comrade Jiang Qing's present task is extremely important," purred Liu Shaoqi, the number two figure in the regime. "She is, on the Party's behalf, taking care of our great leader's personal and nutritional and household needs." Liu, whose own wife, Wang Guangmei, a strong and vivacious woman of whom we will hear more, held posts beyond the home, killed Jiang's request. "What work could possibly be more important than that? Under no circumstances should Comrade Jiang Qing be deflected from her highest task entrusted by the Party." In twice mentioning that Jiang's duty to Mao was a duty *to the Party,* Liu had effectively reminded everyone of the Yanan marriage agreement.

The year 1952 was a difficult one for Jiang Qing, and it was a harbinger of even tougher ones to follow. The work "on her own" became work as "Mao's secretary." This was a vague category, but it was often employed because Jiang hated to see herself as merely a housewife and because in a society that lionized the proletariat and was bent on socialist construction, everyone had to be *said* to have a job. Mao never publicly referred to any help received from Jiang in this period, but Jiang claimed she did research assistance. She scoured the newspapers and magazines and passed on items she thought he should be alert to. While she was resting she read aloud to him, as he sat on her bed, from a pile of telegrams and background papers.

Mao would send her to visit someone he wanted to keep in touch with but didn't have time to see. In the summer of 1952 she went to the home of Zhang Zhizhong, the former Nationalist leader who had come over to the Communist side, to bring Mao's greetings and a gift.

"Oh, you are twins," Jiang said sweetly to the two daughters of General Zhang.

"No, Auntie Mao," young Suchu replied. "It's just that we are wearing identical dresses." Jiang Qing did not seem surprised at the form of address, though "Auntie Mao" (*Mao bo mu*) was a very traditional term that denied individual identity to a woman.*

"I very much regret," Jiang Qing said, "that I do not have two children—only one, a daughter."

The Zhangs, in whose house Mao and Jiang stayed during Mao's historic visit to Chongqing, found Jiang's manner unassuming and respectful of their seniority, as they had in 1945. She looked thin but not emaciated.

Visitors to the private quarters in South and Central Lakes saw a quiet and domesticated Jiang Qing. It was a Saturday in the spring of 1952 when Zhai Zuojun, a former aide-de-camp to Mao, called on his old boss. Jiang was in the middle of a game of bridge with Mao Yuanxin, the son of Mao's deceased brother, whom she and Mao had assumed responsibility for since Yanan days. She welcomed Zhai warmly and without airs and brought the two girls, her own Li Na, aged thirteen, and He Zizhen's Li Min, aged fifteen, to say hello to the overawed soldier. The family were all dressed in plain cotton garments and cloth shoes. As the preparations for dinner went ahead, Mao came in from his rooms on the northern side of the compound. At the table the children ate ravenously of eggs, meat, and vegetables, as Mao, his meal as usual bolted down quickly, chatted with Zhai, and Jiang played the role of an attentive wife and mother.

Jiang pinned high hopes on Li Na, but the thirteen-year-old was not very attractive. Square-faced and solid, she looked more like her father than her mother. Jiang was not yet able to discern where Li Na's talents and enthusiasms lay. She wondered at times if

---

* *Mao bo mu* could be rendered "Auntie of the Mao family."

her daughter would grow up to possess the drive that she, Jiang Qing, expected of her. (As for Mao, he was markedly less concerned with his daughters than with his sons—which meant unconcerned.) During the years on the road prior to 1949 Jiang was more often than not separated from Li Na. And now Jiang's illnesses and absence in Russia made it difficult for mother and daughter to draw closer to each other.

One day when Jiang Qing accompanied Mao to a large reception, who should be there on the balcony of the Gate of Heavenly Peace but Li Liuru, Mao's chief of staff from Yanan days. Jiang hated the very sight of Li, after their terrible clash of 1942. She didn't have the heavyweight status to flounce out in protest at Li's presence; yet she did not feel she had to be civil to him either. She and Mao noticed Li Liuru as they sat watching a parade below and listening to the regimented cries of joy that wafted up to the verandas of power. Later, when the mandarins rose from their armchairs and began to circulate, Li drew near and said pleasantly: "And how is Comrade Jiang Qing?" Jiang stiffened, glared at him, and kept her mouth closed. Mao came over to rescue the occasion with a few lofty remarks.

The storm of the winter of 1951–52 was not over. Jiang's work at home for Mao was "taken away from her" in 1952, she claimed, as "certain leaders" decided she should go to Moscow for another medical cure.

Something else happened, we find, to precipitate Jiang Qing's transfer to Russia for what turned out to be a year of unhappy exile. During 1952 she again tried some feats of cultural iconoclasm, hoping to repeat her success in squelching *The Story of Wu Xun*. She set in motion the devising of a modern Peking opera on the life of Song Jingshi, a bandit in Shandong who had rebelled as Wu Xun failed to rebel, and whom she had come to admire during her investigation of Wu Xun. But Zhou Yang felt it was substandard and would not permit its completion (later a film was made about Song Jingshi, but no mention of Jiang occurs in the credits).

She helped with the production in a Shanghai movie studio of another military extravaganza, *A Thousand Battles* (*Nan zheng bei zhan*), but it ran into severe controversy. Two other theatrical brainwaves of hers, *The Liaoshen Campaign* and *The Huaihai Campaign*, also were aborted by Zhou Yang and his cohorts. "Too broad and simply inappropriate," said Zhou Yang crisply of these efforts to make operas out of famous civil war military battles.

In none of these ventures did Jiang Qing enjoy Mao's backing, and in all of them she ran into political and artistic opposition. With no card left to play, she found the forces pushing her to leave Peking and be "cured" irresistible.

The pressure on Jiang Qing to stay out of public life was to a degree part of the pressure on all Chinese women in the 1950s to disappear into the home and raise babies. Gone were the fluid days on the road of revolution when men and women knew a certain equality. A stress on social issues, including the women's issue, gave way to a stress on organizational stability, of which a conservative conception of the family was the keystone.*

Perhaps it was a question of the iron laws of a revolution's growth into middle age, for a similar subsidence of feminism occurred in Russia in the 1920s. Alexandra Kollontai's avant-garde spirit of independence, and her view that having sex should be as casual as drinking a glass of water, gave way to the family-minded values of the Stalin era, and it turned out that Kollontai herself was not only the Soviet Union's first female ambassador but also, to date, its last. Jiang Qing was never much of a feminist—certainly not a Kollontai—but she was affected by the changed mood of the 1950s.

If a Chinese woman was to rise to prominence, it could not be as a private individual with a distinguished career of her own. The Communist system centralized power to such a degree that a private career was a virtual impossibility. And whatever the political system, in Chinese culture there is no sharp division between the private sphere and the public sphere. Those professionals who naïvely felt they could pursue a private career after 1949 either sank into obscurity because they were not trusted by the powerholders, or were struck down as "capitalists" because their boss lost out in a power struggle to someone else's boss.

So culture and the Communist system conspired to make politics the only route to prominence for a woman who was to be other than a housewife. And such political women were always one of three types: figureheads (such as Song Qingling, the widow of Sun Yat-sen); chieftains of women's organizations (such as Deng Ying-chao); or women whose grasp on political power was due to their

* The widely read magazine *Women of China* eulogized the housewife during the 1950s, educating its readers on fashion and beauty, and venerating childbearing. "The housewife was shown as contributing to society through her husband and family," Delia Davin sums up, "by acting as a sort of (unpaid) service worker for those who participated in production."

husband's power (such as Ye Chun, the wife of Lin Biao, of whom we will hear more).

What was Jiang Qing to do? A private career as an actress was out of the question. Indeed, even the evidence of her past career had to be destroyed to establish a suitable image for the Madame Mao of the 1950s. Prints of her movies, reviews of her performances, articles about her life as an actress—all were gradually tracked down and burned.

The role of figurehead was out of the question for Jiang. Figureheads were few and far between, they were born and not made, and Jiang was in any case poles apart from a figurehead's temperament—she would rather have been a struggling prostitute with work on her hands than a lofty figurehead pouring tea.

A political role in association with her husband (the third type) was also difficult for Jiang Qing. There were three problems. The Party was constantly trying to keep her from any highly visible or powerful public position. Jiang herself was too proud openly to seek a post that came only through her husband's position. And Mao during the 1950s gave very little encouragement to her hopes for a public career. Liu Shaoqi did not seem discomforted by Wang Guangmei's public activities, nor Zhou Enlai by Deng Yingchao's, but at this time Mao, for reasons that included but also transcended the Party's views on the matter, did not want Jiang to have a real job.

Zhou Enlai, chatting with a daughter of General Zhang Zhizhong about her career plans, suggested she talk to his wife, Deng Yingchao, about the possibility of a job at the Federation of Women. Zhang Suchu turned up her nose and said she didn't care for women's work. "You're a woman, and you don't like women's work?" the premier exclaimed. "So the sexes are not equal in your mind!" Deng Yingchao from an early age not only claimed equality with men but even felt she had attained it. As her husband's remark to Zhang Suchu suggests, this freed her to work in the Federation of Women without a sense of humiliation; equality between men and women was believed to be an unquestioned fact, and the work of women's organizations was simply to tidy up a few loose ends.

Jiang Qing, who had a tougher upbringing than Deng Yingchao, felt she could not take equality between men and women as an established fact. Lacking such a serene confidence, she wanted far more than to tidy up an existing edifice. Feeling she had *not* enjoyed equality, Jiang had a goal that reached beyond the attainment of a theoretical equality for her gender. She burned with an *individual* ambition; for such a turbulent spirit the lack of equality could be redressed only by an assertive, vengeful vindication.*

Sometimes it has seemed that in China there are two types of women: the amah type, the vast majority, meek and submissive; and the empress type, that rare spirit, domineering and full of infinite yearning, who seems to be trying in one lifespan to avenge the fate of every amah down the centuries. Jiang Qing was the empress type.

Clothes told the story. Jiang Qing looked different from the war horses of the "women's movement." These worthies wore baggy trousers or a dark skirt that could have come from a charity bazaar, a pale polyester blouse that hid any shapes underneath it, and plastic sandals over pastel socks that did nothing to enhance any color combination. Their clothing style, like their short, straight haircuts and their unadorned complexions, seemed a mere copy of how the men looked.

Jiang Qing, on the other hand, within the limits of Communist Chinese regimented culture, always found a way to assert her individuality by her appearance. She would appear in shoes with a modified high heel, Western frocks in an array of colors, and nicely tied scarves. She made careful use of good-quality cosmetics, and her hair was always brilliantly groomed. Her spirit being inclined toward struggle as an individual, rather than toward participation in collective feminism, Jiang dressed not to merge with the crowd but to stand out from it.

"I did not even have any underclothes," Jiang recalled of her first trip as a nervous teenager to Peking. Having been deprived, which marked her off from most of the Women's Federation elite, she had a kind of weakness for luxury that girls from rich families did not have. In the Jiang Qing who was so proud of her appearance, the little girl Yunhe emerged, happy and vindicated.

Jiang was responding to her situation as Mao's wife, just as Deng Yingchao's sentiments were influenced by the kind of man Zhou Enlai happened to be. As Mao was a more brooding, devious, and ambitious man than Zhou, so Jiang was cast on far stormier seas than Deng was. Jiang was propelled into the sex-and-power game because that was the game Mao, in his own way, had long played. If Mao took women to be one of the privileges of power, it seemed inevitable that his wife would develop the idea of getting out of her domestic box by the route of political power.

---

* Zhang has a point of view different again from Zhou's, Jiang's, and Deng's. "If men and women are truly equal," she said to me, "women's organizations make no sense."

Playing the sex-and-power game meant, indeed, turning one's back on women's solidarity. In Jiang's autobiography as told to Roxane Witke, there is not a single word about Empress Wu, the Empress Dowager, or other famous female Chinese rulers; nor of Nym Wales, Agnes Smedley, and other such foreign women who were involved in the Chinese Revolution and were known to Jiang. The game Jiang Qing was playing could be played only on her own behalf, not for the cause of women in general. She would use her feminine skills to get where men were, to attain the posts that men attained, almost to be like a man.*

In her own eyes, Jiang was "Mao's secretary"; in Mao's eyes she was really just "Mao's woman." For the moment she was a person in a vacuum, a thoroughbred in search of her species, a Gertrude Stein of the netherworld to which Chinese culture and Communist politics consigned such a woman.

Given Jiang's personality, Mao's enormous power, and the churning cesspool of politics in Communist China, it was an unstable situation, making for recurring tensions, so long as she was not in bed or in Russia or both.

The problem facing Liu Shaoqi and Zhou Enlai, who were the prime movers in arranging Jiang's second transfer to Russia, arose, in their opinion, from Jiang's personality, her performance during the civil war, and the objective dilemma of what to do with the supreme leader's wife.

It would have made things much easier for Liu and Zhou if Jiang Qing had a taste for women's work. It probably would have made things easier if Jiang possessed independent political stature. It would have been best if Jiang were content to be Mao's domestic helpmate, but Liu and Zhou knew their prickly friend too well to hope for that. Jiang Qing was Jiang Qing. She was a lurking unit of one whose charm did not conceal a metallic core of purposefulness. Mao's colleagues needed a box to fit Jiang into, and there seemed to be none until they hit upon the respectful, horrible box of "invalid." She must stay as long as possible in Russian hospitals.

With a pain in the liver and a high fever, Jiang Qing went to Moscow in the early autumn of 1952. Few Chinese enjoy living in Russia, especially in the cold seasons, and Jiang had extra reasons to

---

* The Federation of Women was not a women's movement; the life and career of the White-Boned Demon would be inconceivable in a land which *did* have a strong women's movement, dedicated to an open-ended pursuit of more power for women.

be miserable. She was weak and terribly isolated. The entire stay of eleven months was little more than a slice of her medical and psychiatric history. Her diseases rolled by like tramcars at rush hour; her mental condition also was shaky.

For her fever the Russian physicians prescribed penicillin, and for her liver trouble a preparation was injected that allowed the extraction of the poisonous matter that had made her bile turn black. She went to Yalta again, and on her return to Moscow divided her time among the superior Palace Hospital within the Kremlin walls; a rambling sanatorium in the suburbs; and a country cottage with a tennis court, a nearby pine forest, and a projection room for the movies she loved to watch.

Ill as she was, Jiang's life never was in danger, and her complaints were mainly about homesickness, being kept in the dark as to what was going to happen to her next, and the refusal of her requests to go back to Peking—a step she would not have contemplated if the help of the Russian doctors was a matter of life and death to her.

Jiang was in an almost exclusively women's world, and this did not bring out the best in her. Except when being seen by one of her male physicians, she was always in the company of her Russian interpreter, a battleship whom Jiang said looked exactly like Stalin apart from her yellow hair; a polite but apparently dull Chinese assistant-interpreter in her thirties; a middle-aged Chinese doctor whose relations with Jiang were at times tense; and other female staff who came and went according to the grinding of the bureaucracy at Peking's embassy in Moscow and the ebb and flow of Chinese delegations visiting the Soviet Union.

The entire entourage was bound tightly together in an existence whose sole purpose was the nurturing of Jiang's body and spirit. A doctor's visit would be followed by a game of bridge, a languid dinner, a walk in the pine forest around the country *dacha,* followed by a privately screened movie. Always it was the same little cluster of women, reading each other's minds, trying to think of something fresh and safe to talk about, each one wondering if the others were as bored as she was.

In such a hothouse, it was easy for Jiang to find fault with people. She felt this person was whispering a criticism of her behind her back, or that one was lazy, or another one was cheating at bridge by glancing over her shoulder to see what cards she held.

Jiang was cut off from Soviet society, and she was hopelessly far away from Chinese society.* The maneuvers, the intrigue, the struggles that she loved were all denied to her in the white vacuum of the Palace Hospital and the stuffed, dark splendor of Stalin's *dacha.* Not even her fiercest critics—some of her staff members later spoke very poorly of her—ever claimed that she developed any amorous attachments during her total of some two years in the Soviet Union. Her only child, Li Na, did not accompany her to Russia; and when Li Na briefly visited during a school vacation, the situation did not permit an easy communication between mother and daughter.

Being an avid reader would have helped, but Jiang liked to learn from experience rather than from the printed page. There were Chinese translations of Stendhal's *The Red and the Black* and Tolstoy's *Anna Karenina* on her table, but she did not seem able to concentrate on any book for long. She received briefing packets from the Chinese Embassy, but much of the material was about foreign policy, which then as later failed to grip her.

She could not speak Russian, and relying on interpretation for every word became tedious and claustrophobic. She complained that she had been reduced to the status of a deaf-mute. If her Russian and Chinese interpreters chatted together, Jiang Qing would grow uneasy and start coughing, or ask in a steely voice what topic so absorbed them. Perhaps they were conspiring against her! There is a long tradition of insular members of the Chinese court suspecting that a foreign tongue was a tool being used to undermine them. So it was that Jiang Qing, like the Empress Dowager Ci Xi a half century before, convinced herself that staff members uttering strange phrases were talking about her, isolating her, making a target of her.

During the long winter months Jiang became nostalgic for the days of her acting career in Shanghai. She would tell the younger people around her about the movies of the 1930s, which they had never seen. To the older ones, such as her Chinese physician, who had lived in Shanghai, she would insist that regardless of appearances the *purpose* of her films always had been revolution, not merely art. And she would reminisce about the actors and directors she had worked with. She was contrasting her Shanghai years of activism, gregariousness, and success with her present stagnation,

* For whatever reason, she almost never visited the Chinese Embassy, the old mansion that had been Chiang Kai-shek's embassy, adorned with Russian handicrafts and ancient Chinese *objets d'art*—both of which Jiang then admired. (Later Peking built a new embassy, a functional box in the Lenin Hills.)

forced upon her by illness and her clashes with Yang Shangkun and other colleagues of Mao.

Jiang Qing watched scores of movies while in Russia, most of them European, and she lapped up their romanticism and their display of bold, individual character. (Chinese films, being tales of social morality, did not offer these.) Forgetting her illness, she would get quite carried away by the adventures of the strong, passionate Western women she saw on the screen. Jiang Qing wanted to be that kind of woman.

One day a box arrived from the Chinese Embassy, with items from Peking requested by Jiang Qing, including dress material she had asked Wang Guangmei to choose. At this time Jiang's relations with Wang, the elegant and assured wife of the head of state, Liu Shaoqi, were cordial (and their two husbands were close colleagues as China's top two). Jiang's assistant-interpreter opened the box, pulled out the packages, and unrolled the first length of material. Jiang let out a cry of scorn. "Duck egg yellow! Entirely unwearable." Tossing it aside, she rummaged for the other pieces. The next was candy pink. "My God, so unsophisticated." Jiang also denounced the third piece of material, though its shade, apple green, was one she often favored. In high dudgeon she declared that Wang Guangmei "doesn't know the world" and sniped, in one of her classic *non sequiturs,* that Wang had been a member of the Communist Party for less than five years and got in only because of her marriage to Liu.

Jiang Qing loved to make a show of magnanimity—when it did not interfere with her line of purpose—and as the women sat among the harvest of items from Peking she announced with a winning smile that she was making a gift of the pink material to her assistant-interpreter, and of the other fabrics to her Russian servants.

When Stalin died in March 1953, Jiang Qing heard the news on the radio in her room at the sanatorium, and fellow patients and medical staff were the only people she discussed it with. Doctors and nurses kept telling her that Chairman Mao *must* attend the funeral. The advice irritated her, for she was quite out of touch with developments in Peking, and no one informed her whether her husband was going to come. She could only reply lamely that such a matter would be solemnly decided by the Chinese Communist Party.

And if Mao came, would he bother to see her? Perhaps he would scoop her up and take her back to Peking. Perhaps he might order her to stay for another season of this dubious convalescence in a world of white silence.

Mao did not come, as Jiang learned by listening to the mournful radio coverage. Her distant husband wrote a tribute calling Stalin "the greatest genius of the present age," but he was the only Communist leader in the Soviet bloc who did not attend the rites. Zhou Enlai led the Chinese mourners, and served as the only non-Soviet pallbearer. It seems that the premier did not see Jiang while he was in Moscow (on this matter he would surely be following Mao's instructions). Jiang spent the freezing day of the funeral at the windowsill, marveling at how readily the Russians show their feelings, by comparison with the emotionally shuttered Chinese, and chatting idly with the other invalids about the hole in the world left by the "genius's" death.

Jiang's mind took strange leaps, and her emotions were as brittle as the twigs on the snow-clad trees outside her sanatorium window. In her complex efforts to cope with her predicament upon Stalin's death, she convinced herself that many of the world Communist leaders who came to Moscow for the funeral *died from the cold* soon after. This was not the case, however much the notion may have helped Jiang feel less embarrassed at Mao's absence and her separation from him.

At the *dacha* she would grow hysterical, or silently furious, at the slightest incidence of noise, wind, or glaring light. A massive search would have to be made for the cause of a faint rattle, or for an insect rustling in some corner of the dwelling. However benign a breeze, it could put an end to her stroll in the forest, or require the immediate addition of extra headgear, and a parasol held by a staff member against the offending zephyr.

Too much light always seemed to pose a challenge to Jiang's dominance over her own environment. Only in a dim room did she feel in control. Outdoors, a pair of sunglasses gave her better possession of herself. At Yalta, the infinity of the beach was especially bothersome. She would cover herself with a large straw hat and an engulfing shawl, and surround herself with umbrellas. She never went into the water; it was as if the open-endedness of nature constituted a threat to her soul.

It is easy for staff members in daily proximity to an invalid to see that person's weak points, as some of Jiang's assistants with hindsight did. Yet it is probably true that Jiang, unhappy with herself, was also so unhappy with everything around her that she was difficult to cope with.

Jiang Qing never took solace in religion. She scoffed at China's religious traditions, and in Moscow she chuckled with incredulity as she gazed up at the onion-shaped spires of the Eastern Orthodox churches. Unlike many of the women of great influence down the centuries—the biblical figures, Joan of Arc, Catherine the Great, Eva Perón—Jiang Qing was utterly secular. Mao in his later years talked about God, but Jiang thought it silly even to *talk* about God, an afterlife, ultimate mysteries, or forgiveness.*

That religion was nonexistent in Jiang Qing's mind meant that naked will held center stage. She acknowledged no supernatural reference, and she made no supernatural appeal. The categories of meaning stopped at the doorstep of her own will; her life meant what she defined it to mean.

Jiang felt Russia was corrupt. Hospital staff had their hands out for tips. Her nurses wore jewelry. There were aristocrats hanging around who liked to talk in French and actually looked up to the West. Yet Jiang's own instincts seemed at least as vain and bourgeois. She was pleased that the Palace Hospital had been chosen as her medical base, for that was where the Soviet elite were treated, and she liked to say that the *dacha* where she stayed was Stalin's own. She bandied it about that Stalin personally ordered for her a tailor-made nightgown in her favorite shade of green, adding that the patients around her, all attired in regulation white, envied the lovely color and envied too her slimness.

She went shopping at GUM department store with her entourage, having promised each person a length of dress material at her expense (at least not at *their* expense). Her mood turned to thunder when she discovered, on paying the bill, that the cost of the piece chosen by her assistant-interpreter was a few rubles above the cost of her own selection. "My God, Shao Ren," she rasped, "the material you got today will do you for a lifetime." A little later, when a tailor arrived to discuss styles with the various women, she murmured that, alas, she feared the cloth chosen by Shao Ren would make her "look like a bear."

In her heart Jiang Qing liked much of what she glimpsed in Russian culture—the affluence; the romantic music; the variety in clothes, especially the flowing gowns and high-heeled shoes; the stress upon the individual in European tradition. But she felt cut off from it, she knew she could not partake of it, so she condemned it. (It is the same mental process that allows young Chinese of the

---

* However, when swearing she used expressions such as *tian ya!* or *tian na!*, which can be translated "God!" or "My God!" as well as "Heavens!"

1980s to envy the West and yet shout anti-Western epithets at su-
perpatriotic demonstrations.)

Jiang showed disgust at the activities of the Soviet secret police,
as if in her own mind the Chinese equivalent was no more than a
cheery Scout troop or a cloud of handsome young men who fixed
the air conditioners at South and Central Lakes and carried her
suitcases at Peking Station.

One day she found herself on a crowded street when, from
somewhere above her, "March of the Volunteers," the Chinese national anthem at that time, blared out its jerky phrases of optimism
and defiance. A Soviet passerby stopped, walked up to her, and in a
friendly way asked her to convey his greetings to Chairman Mao
and his colleagues. As he finished, a security agent grabbed him
from behind and pulled him to a car.

The irony of Jiang's reaction to Russia was that she learned her
anti-Westernism there.

Many of Jiang's political enemies of the 1960s were people of
some international experience. They had lived in France (as Deng
Xiaoping); they spoke English (as Wang Guangmei); they had been
educated in Japan (as Xia Yan). One may speculate that Jiang Qing
in her heart would have enjoyed much of the music, fashion, and
theater of the West and Japan if she had seen it on its own terms.
Instead, her only experience of the non-Chinese world, her only
taste of Europe, was in the capital of world communism, soon to become "revisionist" and "anti-China." In Moscow, alas, she learned
just enough about Western culture to know how to attack Deng for
bourgeois thoughts, Wang for love of European clothes, and Xia
Yan for his defense of art for art's sake.

The statesman, a Chinese tradition warns, in order to run the
country well, must first run his household well. But Mao was too
strong-willed to have a tranquil home; and Jiang Qing, no less
strong-willed, was in addition too ambitious to make the necessary
sacrifices for a tranquil home. A great deal of Jiang's limited supply
of energy, after her return to Peking in the autumn of 1953, was
spent on family maneuvers and quarrels.

Mao's approach to family members was to treat them with a
certain detachment. He could toy with them, instruct them, abandon
them, lavish time on them—always he dealt with them as if they
were self-reliant individuals. Jiang was different. Family members,
to her, were not discrete individuals but troops with a specific alle-

giance. They had to be for her or against her. If Mao didn't care much about relatives, Jiang cared all too much—and made herself the eye of the eternal domestic storm that hovered over South and Central Lakes.

She was in a difficult position, as the fourth wife of one of the world's most powerful men, surrounded by remnants of previous marriages and still regarded by many of the political guardians as a semiprostitute who was seeking power through sex. An inner coil of resentment added to her difficulties.

So many of Mao's relatives spent lengthy periods in the Soviet Union—Mao himself did not—that it was almost as if the Mao family had two bases, Peking and Moscow. Like Jiang, He Zizhen had been there for "treatment." How ill He had been we do not know, but in 1948, a decade after the end of her life with Mao and her departure from Yanan to Russia, she was judged fit enough to come back to China; wife number three left Russia for home just a few months before wife number four left for her first stay in Russia.*

Her hair now white, her face more serene, no longer in charge of the Mao child who had accompanied her when she left Yanan, He Zizhen made a lonely train trip home to face life as the ex-wife of China's leader. In the past she has been judged a total absentee from the story of the Mao-Jiang marriage in the 1950s, but this was not quite the case. Where she would reside and what she would do were thorny issues in which Jiang took a quiet interest.

He Zizhen wished to live in Peking, but Jiang objected. With Mao no doubt the arbiter, it was decided that He would go to Shanghai, where she was put in a sanatorium for the mentally ill. The mayor of Shanghai, Chen Yi, later China's foreign minister, intervened to ensure she was given good care and to provide her with some financial security (as he did to help He Zizhen's sister, He Yi, and her husband, the pair who had suffered for making a fuss in Yanan about Mao's treatment of Zizhen).

For the moment He Zizhen at least was six hundred miles away. But Jiang, in her own household at South and Central Lakes, had to reckon with the increasingly assertive presence of He Zizhen's daughter. Li Min, now at high school, had since Yanan days been brought up alongside Li Na, Jiang's own daughter, who was

---

* Zhu Zhongli says that in 1947 she and her husband, Wang Jiaxiang, arranged for He Zizhen to leave the asylum in Russia and go to Harbin. He Zizhen was grateful for this; Jiang Qing was annoyed with Wang and Zhu when she heard of the matter.

two years younger and also at high school. But Jiang and Li Min were not getting along well. Jiang discriminated against Li Min— she was made to wash her own clothes (even her own sheets, one relative says), while Li Na was allowed to pass hers to the servants—whether as a unilateral act of spite, or because Li Min was starting to show a teenager's dislike for her stepmother. Jiang felt that Li Min, despite her name (Quick in Action), was not the brightest of girls.

The legacy of Mao's second wife bedeviled Jiang Qing even more than that of the third. Yang Kaihui was a "Party favorite" of whom everyone spoke well. Mao had grown extremely solicitous of her surviving relatives in his home province of Hunan. And the two sons of the Mao-Yang union were an intermittent presence at the Mao court.

Neither Mao Anying nor Mao Anqing had been closely brought up by their father. In the decade away from him following the Communist disasters of 1927, they drifted, at one point selling newspapers in Shanghai, at another living in a deserted temple outside which they posted the sign "WE TELL STORIES—ONE PENNY." For some years they had been in Russia with their ex-stepmother, He Zizhen, enrolled as students. Anying did well; Anqing, a troubled boy, mostly played chess and pursued a Russian blonde. When the sons returned in the mid-1940s Mao sent them to a remote village to look after pigs and train donkeys to carry bags of manure.

But the pair were after all the only sons of Chairman Mao, which meant a great deal to the Chinese establishment, so much in awe of status and prey to family connections. At the Party offices where Anying worked, bureaucrats would invite him to join them in the dining room reserved for high officials. This infuriated Mao, who ordered Anying to eat his lunch in the cafeteria for clerical workers.

Tall and refined, Anying was a young man of spirit, as his readiness to tell Jiang Qing she might like to leave Mao suggests, and it happened that, perhaps under Russian influence, he quietly criticized the "cult of the leader" that was rising around his father. Jiang Qing reported his murmurings to Mao, which led to an inquiry in which Premier Zhou Enlai took part, and a written self-criticism from Anying.

Perhaps it was not surprising that Jiang began to take a dislike to Anying. As the eldest son, he was in Chinese cultural terms Mao's "successor," and Jiang felt that her position "next to Mao" was threatened by an Anying now an adult, only seven years younger than she.

Mao Anying married a bright girl called Liu Songlin, who soon got a job doing sensitive research work in the army. "For a woman to please a man is a noble effort," Lin Yutang wrote in his commentary on Chinese family *moeurs,* "but for her to please another woman is heroic, and many of them fail." Jiang Qing and Songlin were not heroic, and they failed spectacularly to please each other. From the beginning, according to Songlin, Jiang treated her with "scorn, sarcasm, and insult."

When China entered the Korean War in 1950, Mao Anying was sent to the battlefield. Within weeks an American air raid killed him. Anying's death brought "immense ecstasy" to Jiang, said Songlin. Be that as it may, Jiang failed to attend Anying's funeral. And apparently Mao said to Songlin: "Anying is dead. I'm afraid that for Jiang Qing it amounts to less than if it were the death of a dog."

Although it was absurd for Songlin to claim that Jiang had conspired to have Anying sent to the perilous Korean front—this must have been Mao's decision—it is true that in discussing the tragedy Jiang expressed no feelings of sadness or sympathy. Perhaps there is some truth in Songlin's claim that Jiang was quite "airy" about the loss; and in the claim of Li Min, He Zizhen's daughter, that her stepmother refused to join in any discussion of the fact and circumstances of Anying's death, or in any conversation about his life and character.

Jiang brought in her half sister to live at South and Central Lakes and serve her as a supplementary force. Li Yunxia, considerably older than Jiang, resembled Jiang to a degree. She was tall, with good bearing and a strong face, though she did not wear spectacles, as Jiang did, and she lacked Jiang's interest in the arts. Her husband had died before Liberation, leaving her with two sons, one of whom subsequently died in a swimming accident in Shandong. The other son, Wang Bowen, she brought with her into Mao's household. Li Yunxia was given a nice apartment, though Mao grumbled about her arrival, announcing tersely to Songlin that "Jiang Qing has arranged for Li Yunxia to come and settle at my place."

Jiang Qing dominated her half sister, who lacked Jiang's flair and status, and deployed her to watch out for Jiang's domestic interests. It was natural enough for Li Yunxia to pay more attention to Li

Na, Jiang's daughter, than to Li Min, the daughter of the Mao–He Zizhen union, with whom she had no blood relation. Yet given the tense and complex situation in the compound, Li Yunxia's presence was oil on the flames.

Polarization grew. Jiang and Li Yunxia coddled Li Na. Li Yunxia, following Jiang's cue, fell into a bad relation with Li Min. Mao, while fairly neutral in the tug-of-war over his two daughters, became especially fond of Songlin, Anying's widow, whom Jiang and her half sister could not stand. Gradually Songlin and Li Min drew closer, in Mao's corner, distant from Jiang Qing.

One morning Mao, after working most of the night, came out of his study and suggested that the whole family have lunch together. This seldom occurred, given Mao's work habits and the lines of division, but when Mao proposed it, his word was law. It was a lovely day. The autumn sun glistened on the orange tiles of the palaces and on the shimmering waters of the lakes. Songlin recalls that everyone was "extremely happy" as the time for the meal drew near. But in *whose apartment* should lunch be served? Mao tipped the scales by strolling over to the rooms that Songlin and Li Min shared and sitting down to chat.

The food followed the chairman, and soon everyone was seated at a large round table in an apartment that Jiang regarded almost as enemy territory. Present were Mao and Jiang, the two daughters, Songlin, Li Yunxia, and Mao Yuanxin (Mao's nephew).* Something was wrong with the atmosphere as the spicy chicken and steamed fish arrived. Mao was chatty, Jiang Qing was silent. It fell to Jiang's half sister to be the hit-woman. Her mood ever more thunderous, she disagreed with each remark made by Li Min or Songlin. Suddenly Li Yunxia pushed back her chair, threw her chopsticks in the air toward Mao, and flounced out of the room. Mao, furious, said nothing, but later, when Songlin asked him why Li Yunxia had become so angry, he replied: "Simply because I went to the apartment of you and Li Min."

That Jiang was a strong-willed person, confined by poor health and Party pressures to a domestic realm, set the stage for trouble. At South and Central Lakes she had to deal with people from Mao's previous marriages, and it was a cardinal problem for her, given Chinese cultural norms and her own ambition, that whereas Mao had sons, she did not.

* Yuanxin's father, Mao's younger brother, was murdered by the Nationalists in western China in 1943, and since then Jiang Qing and Mao had largely brought him up.

Jiang was combative, to be sure; but she saw her struggle as a defensive operation—to avoid becoming a helpless appendage to Mao, or worse, his reject, as He Zizhen in her asylum was a previous reject.

In China a smooth exterior in family, social, or political relations often masks an interior of intense passion. Factionalism is as Chinese as apple pie is American, because in China it is essential for everyone to belong to a group, connections and background and loyalty are of enormous importance, and grudges are harbored with the tenacity of the ages. Mao held immense power, around which passion always swirls, and in China more than most places it is impossible for the top leader's family to remain outside the vortex of power.

In America a family is a few individuals who live together; in China a family is a social entity whose lines run out to society. *Gongjia* is a common word for "public" or "state"; *gong* means public and *jia* means family. As with the word, so with reality: Family abuts into the public realm. The networks, unspoken obligations, and little corruptions that stem from the *jia* were all fuel to the fire of Jiang Qing's determination to make her mark in the wider realm of *gongjia.*

If the Communist Party were going to confine her at home, Jiang would use her household power, as Chinese women always did to compensate for their exclusion from politics. And since it was *Mao's* household, the realm of the *jia* was almost by definition the realm of the *gongjia*—a great pasture of possibility where Mao's Nora might no longer be a Nora, and no longer be merely Mao's.

So lines of allegiance, balances of power, and conspiracy became facts of life in the home of which Jiang Qing was mistress, just as they were in the Chinese power structure which Mao headed.

Whatever Jiang's inner feelings about Mao Anying's death, her household power did increase after he was gone. She took the view that Songlin, the widow, was no longer a Mao-Jiang responsibility. Week by week Jiang put pressure on the young woman to move out of South and Central Lakes. Later Jiang tried to confiscate Songlin's pass to enter the compound.

Songlin overheard Mao and Jiang arguing over her future. Jiang insisted that Songlin's allowance be phased out. Mao angrily announced, "As long as there's a breath in my body, I'm going to take care of her." Chatting with Songlin in his study, Mao complained about Jiang's "nagging" and her lack of reverence for Anying's memory. Pacing the mellow old room in agitation, he stopped at a bookshelf of classics and pulled down a volume. As Songlin listened, he read a romantic verse about a tree and a river. The tree, growing old, lost its leaves, declined, and fell; the river beside which it grew, for long its companion, was so sad at the loss that it, too, lost its strength and ran dry of water. Mao appeared to be telling Songlin that even trees and rivers have more feeling for each other than Jiang had for his family members.

Songlin eventually married again—persuaded by Mao, she says, who felt this would solve the problem of her bad relation with Jiang—but Songlin and her new husband, though living away from South and Central Lakes, were to clash even more severely with Jiang during the Cultural Revolution, as we shall see.

Jiang made a rare foray into public life to reevaluate China's most famous novel, *Dream of the Red Chamber*. It was the fall of 1954; her health had picked up, and Mao, harassed by critics within the Party, was taking more notice of her than usual.

Lying on a sofa in her apartment, she came upon an article in a university journal from her own province of Shandong that said *Dream of the Red Chamber,* revered by generations of Chinese as a harmless tale of intrigue and lust, was an evil gust of incorrect political ideas. It should be analyzed politically, not simply read as a novel. Jiang Qing agreed. And she saw the possibility of a wonderful fight with Zhou Yang and her other enemies in the cultural establishment.

She got hold of the novel and read it as an evangelist might read Harold Robbins in quest of dirty passages. In its pages she saw revealed the dagger of iniquity and the scepter of righteousness. It was wrong to read the book as entertainment, she felt; it should be read as a manual on class struggle.

The next day she gingerly approached Mao, passing on the article by the unknowns from Shandong, together with her own apocalyptic commentary. Mao was at that time not pleased with the Peking establishment, and he was in the mood to listen to an outside voice. He said the article on how to approach *Dream* had a point; he told Jiang to ask *People's Daily* to reprint it.

Jiang Qing, playing the sick heroine roused from her bed by a great cause, drove to Wang Fujing Street to the *People's Daily* offices. The editors said they had received but turned down the attack on *Dream* eventually published in Shandong. Jiang said that she and Chairman Mao felt that more "lively, critical articles by un-known writers" such as this one ought to be seen in Peking's premier newspaper. The editors grumbled but said they would run the piece.

Jiang could not resist taking the article, still in its Shandong form, to Zhou Yang, to see if she could lasso him in the act of taking a "wrong" position on *Dream*. Without telling him of Mao's views and the pressure on *People's Daily*, she asked him to read it. Zhou and his associates at the Party's propaganda department made their judgment: "That's written by such small people. How can such small people dare to criticize [the established view of the novel]?"

Mao himself—pushed by Jiang, she claims—then wrote a memo to members of the government about the evils of *Dream*, the way its uncritical supporters were "poisoning the minds of the young," and the "great bourgeois oppression of small people." Mao's words were tough, and it was striking that he linked the case of *Dream of the Red Chamber* with that of *Inside Story of the Qing Court* and *The Story of Wu Xun*, two earlier crusades of Jiang's. Yet the outcome of this "literary" fight was a compromise; in part be-cause of the widespread dislike for Jiang, in part because Mao did not pull out all the stops against *Dream*, a book that he basically admired.*

People's Daily did not after all publish the critical article; it was left to *Literary Gazette*, an important organ but less prominent than *People's Daily*, to reprint it. Readers were warned about the novel, but it was not swept from China's literary canon.

Jiang had shown her will to dabble in cultural policy when she had the strength to do so. Zhou Yang had expressed—and he spoke for many—the bureaucrats' irritation with Jiang. And Mao had re-vealed that, although he could show Jiang the cold shoulder of ne-glect, he also had it in him to champion her.

Mao was gaining some satisfaction from Jiang's cultural icono-clasm. He disliked most of the intellectuals and wanted to see them

---

* That Mao was more subtle than Jiang in his approach to *Dream*, or more cynical in using literary ammunition for a political purpose, is suggested by an exchange with his young rela-tive Wang Hairong in 1964. Wang happened to complain to Mao about a classmate who was always reading *Dream of the Red Chamber* instead of his English grammar. Mao seemed to stiffen:

MAO: Have you ever read *Dream of the Red Chamber*?
WANG: Yes, I have.
MAO: Which character do you like in this novel?
WANG: None.
MAO: *Dream of the Red Chamber* is worth reading. It is a good book.

While his niece was busy educating herself to be a cosmopolitan, modern woman, Mao had just read *Dream* for the fifth time.

discomforted. Mao's attitude toward intellectuals was like Jiang's attitude toward actors. In both cases a colossal ego was bent on arranging toys for its own satisfaction. Mao had not been a top scholar, but perhaps he would like to have been one. Jiang had not been a top actress, but she would like to have been one. Each of them—Mao effortlessly, Jiang when she battled fiercely—now turned the impulses of personality into political campaigns.

In the midst of the *Dream of the Red Chamber* affair, a newly buoyant Jiang Qing made a surprise appearance on top of the Gate of Heavenly Peace for the National Day parade, with its floats, balloons, acrobats, and fireworks. It was the fifth anniversary of the founding of Mao's regime, and Nikita Khrushchev was the special guest.

The leaders mingled stiffly on the purple balcony high above the Boulevard of Eternal Peace. Khrushchev looked like a farmer eyeing the crops. Mao, frowning slightly, seemed to have six things on his mind. Jiang stood modestly to one side.

Zhou Enlai, spotting Jiang by herself, made a move to introduce her to Khrushchev. But Mao snapped back to attention. With the swiftness of a waiter intercepting a falling plate, he glided to his wife's side and steered her away. In a remote corner of the festooned balcony, far from the First Secretary of the Soviet Communist Party, and from a Zhou Enlai who tried to look as if he had not made a mistake, Mao and Jiang silently watched the colorful wonders of the parade.

It is not likely that Mao feared Jiang would divulge state secrets to Khrushchev; or that Khrushchev, through Jiang, would try to bend China nearer to the Soviet position on the Manchurian problem and U.S. policy. Perhaps he was still sensitive to the Party's rule about Jiang's role laid down at the time of his marriage (observed in the foreign-policy realm so far). At any rate, Mao simply did not like Khrushchev, and he found distasteful the idea of the Soviet leader chuckling in a corner with his wife. He may have heard that at a Kremlin party Khrushchev called Jiang "Mao's nice mattress."

Jiang, prim and quiet beside her husband on the ramp leading down from the balcony of the Gate of Heavenly Peace, was not yet a full-fledged "Madame Mao," a First Lady allowed to play a prominent, natural role among the leaders of China on a state occasion.

If persecution of Mao had really been Jiang's motive, the chairman's nephew, Mao Yuanxin, would have felt some of Jiang's blows. But Yuanxin, a solid and handsome boy, got along well with

Jiang. During the 1950s Jiang often took Li Na and Yuanxin boat-ing at the Summer Palace and to children's entertainments. In the household Jiang singled Yuanxin out for praise and encouraged Li Na to think of him as her own brother.

The reason for the close Jiang-Yuanxin bond was simple. In balance of power terms, Yuanxin was her natural ally. His father wasn't Mao, and his mother wasn't one of Jiang's predecessors. In-deed, Jiang, in the measure that she came to think of her position as independent from Mao's, saw Yuanxin as her "crown prince." She had no son, alas, but here was the one man in the Mao family who was not really someone else's and who perhaps could be cultivated into *hers.*

For now it was the warm tie of "Young Auntie," as Yuanxin called Jiang, and "Little Pea," as Jiang liked to call him; one day it would be a political bond that nearly lassoed the Chinese state.

Mao received a visitor who made Jiang nervous. It was He Yi, the sister of He Zizhen; she and her husband had made a fuss in Yanan about the Mao-Jiang marriage. He Yi, in thrall to the prom-ise of serpentine family links, proposed to Mao that a search be made in Jiangxi Province for the lost son and daughter of the Mao–He Zizhen union!

He Yi no doubt had a mixture of motives for this idea, but in Jiang's mind it was simply a scheme to undermine *her* position. This buzzing insect from a past era was reasoning that, since Jiang had no son, and, of the two sons of Mao and Yang Kaihui, one was dead and the other mentally troubled, to find a son of He Zizhen would be to introduce into the power games of Mao's household the trump card of a "successor" to Mao. Moreover, to find and bring to the Mao court *any* of the Mao-He children who were unaccounted for (one boy apparently died in Russia, and Li Min was in Peking) would do no harm to He Yi and her relatives, all of whom were waiting in the wings for crumbs from the table of the Mao dynasty.

How enthusiastic Mao was about He Yi's suggestion is not clear, but he did not discourage her. After many interviews in Jiangxi, where during the Long March Mao and He Zizhen had left two or three of their children with peasant families, a teenage boy was found. He was brought to Peking to be inspected and quizzed. But he turned out not to be one of the missing children. "Today you bring one son," Jiang Qing blazed at He Yi. "Tomorrow, another. God knows how many you'll scrape up." In the end, for whatever blend of reasons, no further children of the Mao-He marriage ar-

rived at South and Central Lakes. The array of young pawns remained the same as before.

Jiang Qing did have feelings of affection for people she liked; it
was just that at South and Central Lakes there were a number of
people she didn't like—given her sensitivity to being opposed by
others and to having her right to direct the household undermined.

Songlin eventually did move out, to go to Russia to study in
1955. The son of Jiang's half sister, Wang Bowen, happened to be
setting off for Moscow at the same time. Mao, hearing from Songlin
that the standard issue of clothes for those going abroad (*chu guo fu
zhuang*) did not include a heavy coat, which was essential in Russia,
gave both Songlin and Wang Bowen some money to buy one. When
she heard about this from her half sister, Jiang flew into a rage.
"She's *his* family, Bowen is *my* family!" the staff heard her shout.
"It's *I* who'll give him the money for his coat!"

With no family member did Jiang Qing have more difficulty
than Anqing. Aged twenty-six at the time of his brother Anying's
death in Korea, Anqing, already a troubled personality, went
through a major crisis in the autumn of 1951. Fluent in Russian, he
worked as a translator in the Marxism-Leninism Institute under the
Party Central Committee. A dispute occurred in the office; tempers
were lost, blows exchanged, and Anqing made repercussions inevitable by delivering hair-raisingly obscene insults to the face of his
boss.

Mao and Jiang stepped in to bring Anqing to South and Central Lakes (Anqing, like Anying, had never lived at home) and supervise his self-criticism. Whether Jiang kept him confined to a
"cell" normally used to house one of her monkeys, as alleged by
Anqing's future wife, is not certain. She did quarrel with him a good
deal until Mao, who seemed noncommittal toward his son, decided
Anqing should be sent to another city for psychiatric treatment. For
a blend of reasons, including an almost complete lack of parental
love in his upbringing, the recent death of his brother, the impossible strain and intrigue that engulfed everyone in the Mao family,
and Mao's coldness and Jiang's hostility, Anqing from the age of
twenty-seven was seriously ill mentally.

At his hospital in Dalian, the Manchurian port city, Anqing
was not cured of his mental disorders, but he did fall in love with a
pretty nurse called Xu. It annoyed Jiang that Anqing was promiscuous with women, and she opposed the affair between Anqing and
Nurse Xu. Jiang's particular point—from the larder of her home-

style medical and psychological lore—was that a retarded person could not make a valid choice of partner.

Anqing suffered from the disadvantage that his Chinese was less than fluent because of his long period in Russia. To Jiang's shrill attacks, he would respond only with a shrug or a smile, hoping that whatever she had said was not too important—and this made Jiang furious.

Anqing was transferred from Dalian to a hospital in Russia that offered an alternative treatment. Jiang's detractors claim she sent Anqing "to Moscow for treatment" against his will, to get him out of the way, just as Jiang says *her* enemies sent her "to Moscow for treatment" against her will. Probably the decision to transfer Anqing, as with two or three of Jiang's own journeys to Russia, was a combination of bureaucratic process, medical opinion, and Mao's blessing. But Jiang did struggle—successfully—against the plan for Nurse Xu to accompany Anqing to Moscow.

From Moscow, Anqing wrote letters to Nurse Xu, but Jiang managed to intercept many of them. During 1954 the bureaucratic wheels once more were geared up to send Xu to join Anqing, but again Jiang managed to frustrate the plan, and the next year the poor nurse, her own health now impaired, gave up on Mao's son and married a Dalian man. Meanwhile, Anqing, fluent in Russian and in lovemaking if not in all of his mental processes, had grown passionately fond of a Moscow nurse.

If a Chinese goes with a foreigner, even from a friendly country, there is opposition to the match from the Chinese side. (Liu Shaoqi's eldest son had recently fallen in love with a Russian girl but had not been permitted by his father and the Party to marry her; we shall hear more of this.) But Jiang became a loud champion of the idea that Anqing *should* marry the Russian nurse!

Hoping the young man might settle in Russia and be forever out of her hair, she sent jewelry and dress material to Moscow as early gifts for the bride-to-be. Unfortunately for Jiang, the marriage did not occur; the Party frowned on the idea, and Anqing was ogling so many other girls that the Russian nurse spurned him.

Mao, as usual, left much of the handling of this family issue to Jiang, but he was ultimately responsible for the decisions made about Anqing. Certainly Jiang criticized her stepson excessively and became obsessed with his sexual promiscuity. Her enemies later said her "persecution" caused Anqing's mental illness; Mao's political enemies later said *he* "drove his son mad." Anqing's troubled history prior to the crisis of 1951 suggests that these explanations are too simple; yet the young man had little to thank either Mao or Jiang for.

It was a warm evening, tempered by a breeze off the sea, as Mao, Jiang, Li Na, and Li Min greeted their dinner guests. The family's faces looked healthy and relaxed from the sunshine and the salty air, and all were comfortably dressed in light cottons and sandals. It was the summer of 1954, and the site was the Mao villa in Beidaihe, the beach resort east of Peking. Zhang Zhizhong, his wife, and their four children came inside and immediately felt at ease. Mao and Jiang had seldom been so cordial, nor Mao in such good form.

At the dinner table, Mao held court. He asked each of the former Nationalist leader's children what their work or study was. Jiang looked well but said little. Her main activity was to pass around the plentiful supply of dishes. She kept an eagle eye on Mao's plate, and whenever it grew low, as Mao pressed on with a line of inquiry, she silently replenished it with the spiciest items from the table. Zhang Zhizhong's eldest son told Mao he had just joined the Communist Party. Mao beamed and expressed his pleasure. Jiang leaned across as he spoke and added spoonfuls of double-cooked pork and cabbage to his plate.

"Jiang Qing was modest and attentive," one of the Zhang daughters recalled. "Mao's two daughters said more during the meal than she did."

After dinner, Mao showed the Zhang family around the villa. "This is my room," he announced as the party came upon a large room with a wide wooden bed, one side of which was covered with papers and books. Jiang Qing had her own room down the corridor.

This was a year of improved health for Jiang Qing, but within twelve months, by mid-1955, she felt very poorly again. A fever soared, and her weight plummeted. From the villa by West Lake at Hangzhou, where she was staying alone to escape the heat, she flew to Peking for a medical examination. A gynecologist diagnosed cervical cancer.

Jiang's mood became deeply nostalgic and pessimistic; she recalled to a woman physician, a family friend, her leading role in Tian Han's play *Tragedy on a Lake* when she was a drama student at Jinan, and gloomily mused that real-life tragedy was going to snuff her out.

Jiang was not anxious to go back to Russia, but the collective decision was predictable; in July 1955, with a new eighteen-year-old nurse on her staff, she returned, more or less willingly, to the hands of her Moscow doctors. Once more she was separated from her daughter, Li Na.

Perhaps Jiang was really as ill as Mao and the bureaucrats felt when they decided again on Moscow. Yet an account by a visitor to the household on June 17, just prior to her departure for Moscow, conveys no mood of crisis. Lin Jinlai, a former bodyguard of Mao's, arrived at South and Central Lakes at 3:00 P.M. and stayed for dinner. He and Mao went swimming, then came into the living room, where Mao introduced the young man to Jiang. She shook hands with Lin, brought in Li Na ("Give a salute to Uncle, Na") and sat down with Mao and bodyguard Lin for a hearty dinner with a celebratory wine.

In the Soviet capital, Jiang mustered the strength to exert her will again over Anqing, who was in a Russian sanitorium, and over Songlin, who along with Bowen, Jiang's half sister's son, was a student at Moscow University.

She told Songlin, who had remarried, that Anqing's mental health was too fragile to permit Songlin to see him. On the other hand, apparently she gave Mao a too-optimistic report on Anqing's condition—an extraordinarily callous piece of deception in light of her own bitter experience of how awful it was for a Chinese to be ill, and trapped against his or her will, in a Russian hospital.

Four months later, Songlin, after running into Wang Hongbin, a former physician to the Mao family who was then at Moscow University, heard from this firsthand source that Anqing's condition had worsened. She wrote an alarmed letter, and made the complicated arrangements needed to get it into Mao's hands. Her ex-father-in-law, inclined to trust her, was shocked. He set aside Jiang's sanguine report and ordered Anqing back to the Dalian hospital.

Jiang, back in Peking, heard upsetting news from Dalian. Anqing, whom she'd once hoped would marry a Russian nurse and gravitate toward the Soviet Union, was deep into a courtship with Songlin's sister, Shaohua!* No scheme hatched in the depths of hell could have tormented Jiang more than this news did. Such a fresh marriage bond would strengthen Songlin's hand and add to the "Yang Kaihui forces" at South and Central Lakes.

* Shaohua used the family name Zhang at this time, evidently taking her mother's name, while Songlin took her father's name, Liu; later, Shaohua was known as Liu Shaohua, or simply as Shaohua.

Jiang began to monitor Anqing's letters to South and Central Lakes, delaying many, destroying some. But Mao, now too aroused to let the question of Anqing slip by him, got wind of the interference. He wrote to Anqing: "When you write to me, don't entrust your letters to others." Apparently he meant Jiang, for he went on: "It's better to ask Songlin, Shaohua, or Li Min to pass your letters to me." The Anqing-Shaohua marriage went ahead. But in the many years since the crisis at Dalian over Shaohua, Jiang Qing has never once talked to Anqing.

Jiang did face a real problem with Anqing. The young man was mentally ill, and Mao tended to wash his hands of the situation, with all its complications. Jiang filled the breach, but clumsily. Her opinion that Shaohua, who was fifteen years younger than Anqing, married Mao's son partly to get a footing in the Mao household probably was correct; but again, Jiang's passion on the issue turned suspicion and tension into open warfare.

At the height of Jiang's family maneuvers, Mao wrote a letter to the collective organs of Shichengxiang, a town where there lived many relatives of Mao, the Wens from his mother's side of the family. Each year some of the Wen cousins had been in the habit of coming to see Mao in Peking, and he'd heard that on their return they would swagger, and drop heavy hints that the folk of Shichengxiang had better treat them well because they were related to Chairman Mao.

"Please don't give the Wen family any special consideration just because they are my relatives," Mao asked the county officials. "My attitude," his letter went on, referring to the Wens, "is that I love them because they are part of the ranks of the workers, and in addition because they are my relatives."

No doubt Jiang saw the letter—she may have been the first to do so—but to her its sentiments were ultrapurist. Unlike Mao, she came from a struggling, chaotic family. It was all very well for Mao to be Olympian about his relatives, but she was so much more vulnerable. She felt that if she didn't put together some forces to counterattack those who tried to hold her down, she would never get even but just go under. She also felt that if Mao abdicated his family responsibilities, she had to do *something* about the issues that arose.

During June 1956, Jiang and Mao spent a few quiet days at Wuhan in central China. Mao swam in the Yangzi River while Jiang sat on the deck of a boat in midstream, a bit bored, but happy to replenish her husband with *man tou* between his swimming bouts. Mao would emerge dripping in the fierce heat, ask Jiang how she felt, eat a steamed bun, then dive back into the muddy torrent. They were close on this trip, and Mao wrote a poem, "Swimming," which some Chinese believe contains erotic references to Jiang Qing.

It was a lovely autumn evening in Shanghai, and Song Qingling's mansion was brilliantly lit for the reception. President Sukarno of Indonesia had left Shanghai's airport for Jakarta that afternoon after his state visit. Sun Yat-sen's widow, a prestigious figurehead who had to space her political dinner parties carefully, had invited the Chinese leadership to a party. Her many servants prepared the heavy old rooms for the cigarette-puffing members of China's dictatorship of the proletariat.

Ke Qingshi, the mayor of Shanghai, arrived. Soon after, Mao strolled in, as calm as a professor entering a library, and Jiang Qing was at his side. Song Qingling greeted them simply, and soon turned to receive Liu Shaoqi and Wang Guangmei. Song liked Wang and felt at home with her cosmopolitan ways but she also thought well of Jiang, and as the evening progressed she chatted with her several times. Jiang, slender and neat in a Sun Yat-sen jacket, was quiet to the point of being retiring. She indulged in any conversation that was begun in her presence. She did not move about the house with Mao, but she kept an eye on him, and throughout the reception she was the dutiful wife.

Jiang Qing did not feel well in Wuhan and Shanghai, and soon after she and Mao returned to Peking, her cervical cancer flared up. She was unwilling to be operated on. Yet she declared that she could not stand the radiation implants and cobalt 60 that her Chinese doctors saw as the only alternatives. Within a few weeks she was back in a Russian hospital.

Jiang had been too unwell to join in the decision-making about arrangements for her trip—during which an advance party went to Moscow, and three days of telephone conferences ensued between Peking and Moscow—and she said she was unhappy with the decision others made for her. Once again Li Na faced a period of many months without seeing her mother.

Traveling with a Chinese woman gynecologist, Jiang arrived in Moscow so weak, ill, and distressed that the Soviet medical authorities, apparently fearing she might die on their hands, were hesitant to treat her. They shifted her from one hospital to another, either because no one was willing to accept responsibility for her, or because her mental state set up a barrier to each successive attempt at treatment. Her white blood cell count went down to three thousand, leaving her vulnerable to the slightest infection. She had to be given blood transfusions, and, as the cobalt treatment assaulted her system, an oxygen mask.

Was Jiang Qing the victim of medical politics? Soviet hospitals were at times arenas for political punishment and vendettas, and as Soviet-Chinese relations were deteriorating, one cannot exclude that Jiang's health had become a card in some game between the Kremlin and Peking. Certainly it is extraordinary that even when she begged to be allowed to go home to China, as she says she did, Moscow, or Peking, or some combination of the two would not hear of it.

Yet on balance the evidence suggests that Jiang's own mental state and her inability to adapt to foreign life accounted for a good part of the desperation she felt. When Zhou Enlai, who had a soft spot for Jiang, visited her during his trip to consult with Khrushchev in January 1957, Zhou concluded, after exhaustive study of the medical reports, that what she needed most was humor, good company, and diversion. He brought her a string of visitors, joked with her, and took her out of the hospital for dinner (so engaged with her did Zhou become that he forgot to hand over a letter to her from his wife, Deng Yingchao, and ended up taking it back to Peking).*

Out of any danger to her life by the spring of 1957, Jiang ordered her staff to phone to Peking for food more appetizing than the underprepared slabs that the Russians considered meals. A plane arrived with live fish, bananas, apples, eggplant, tomatoes, and other fresh vegetables, all chosen from the larders of South and Central Lakes by Li Yunxia, Jiang's half sister. At the *dacha,* Jiang's eyes gleamed. Striding around the kitchen while her staff did the work, she offered her theories on slicing a carp and scolded a terrified interpreter who had dared to judge the timing of a steamed dish without using her watch. Jiang ate heartily of the resulting meal, explaining between mouthfuls the mistakes that had been made—a lack of seasoning here, a coarseness of texture there.

An invitation arrived for dinner with the wives of Russia's top four leaders, and Jiang felt well enough to accept without hesitation.

---

* It seems to have been a sign that Jiang was afflicted with a touch of persecution mania, as well as diseases, that apparently she told Witke an entirely false story about Mao failing to visit her in Moscow. The marriage was in such a bad state, Witke noted, no doubt reflecting what Jiang said to her, that on Mao's second trip to Moscow in 1957, he did not see her or phone her. This is an amazing tale, for when Mao went to Moscow in November 1957, Jiang was back in China. Investigation reveals that Jiang was in Qingdao in July 1957, months before Mao left on his trip.

Dressed in a rice-colored suit of Western style and a fur overcoat and hat, she drove, with her interpreter beside her in one car and her Chinese woman physician following in a second car, to the heavy gates of the Kremlin. A dark, long table covered with crisp, white napery was laden with Russian fare. In an anteroom furnished with sofas in a floral pattern, the four formidable Soviet ladies greeted Jiang and her two attendants. On one vast sofa, Madame Khrushchev sat at Jiang's left, Madame Malenkov at her right; Madame Molotov, Madame Kaganovich, the Chinese woman physician, and other ladies sank into flanking sofas. Jiang smiled, fidgeted, and could find little to say. Everyone discussed Jiang's health with desperate concentration, eyes glazed, handkerchiefs twisted in sweating hands.

As the meal unfolded, Madame Malenkov remarked to Jiang that, although the Russian and Chinese cultures differed, perhaps she would appreciate the opportunity, when her recovery was complete, of becoming a student for a while at the Soviet Film Academy. Jiang looked the color of the smoked sturgeon she was pretending to eat. Stiffly she said the rigors of student life would be too much for her. The knives and forks clattered on. For a moment it looked as if Madame Molotov, wife of the foreign minister, might have thought of something to say. But it was Madame Malenkov who found her tongue. How old was Madame Mao Zedong? Jiang almost choked as she grated, after a long pause: "Not so old and not so young . . ."

Home at her *dacha*, Jiang threw off her coat, began to patrol the living room, and, her face thunderous, declared that she had been "slighted" by the suggestion that she become a student and "insulted" by being asked her age, "in a Western country where that is just not done."

Knowing how much Jiang craved approval, the Chinese woman physician, a fluent speaker of Russian, reported that after the dinner group had broken up the Soviet ladies remarked among themselves that Jiang Qing was a "cultured" and "stylish" Chinese lady. Jiang cheered up. She had not felt like eating much in the Kremlin banquet room. Now, after a game of cards to help calm her nerves, she sat down with her entourage to a hearty Chinese dinner.

After she came back from her fourth Russian stay, Jiang Qing said she thought death might be near, and her spirit was hardly healthier than her body. Mao seemed to take little notice of her. Li

Na, now eighteen, at times treated her almost as a stranger. And in terms of employment she was a dropout from the Chinese Revolution.

Mao himself struck political trouble, as his Great Leap Forward turned into a nasty lurch sideways, other policies failed, and longtime colleagues began to criticize him. But he did not confide much in Jiang. Mao's and Jiang's expectations of their marriage, which were congruent in the 1940s, when Jiang was prepared to defer to Mao and be his Party-mandated helper, were no longer so. Jiang wanted more than she was getting. To the stalemate, a mutual distance was the only possible response.

Mao in his introspective mood tied himself closer to the legacy of Yang Kaihui, his early wife. He sent Anqing (now out of the mental hospital) and his wife, Shaohua, on missions to Changsha to keep in touch with Yang Kaihui's relatives. Four times beginning in the summer of 1957 he received the nursemaid, Chen Yuying, who had served him and Kaihui in the 1920s, to reminisce. "Seeing you today," Mao said to the elderly Chen with tears in his eyes, "it seems as if I have seen Kaihui again." And he wrote a beautiful and astonishing poem, "The Immortals," about Yang Kaihui.

Jiang Qing spent much time away from Peking in the late 1950s, alone with her staff of nurses and helpers, out of touch with public events and equally so with her husband and daughter (soon to enroll at Peking University). It seemed typical of Jiang's absentee marriage that after the terrible Lushan meeting of 1959, at which Mao clashed with his defense minister, Peng Dehuai, and gave a maudlin, King Lear–type speech in which he speculated that he was under some curse ("Of my two sons, one is dead and the other has gone mad"), Mao went to rest in Changsha, his old base, while Jiang, who was seldom in Peking when Mao was there, flew to Peking. She took with her, to Mao's irritation, Mao's personal physician, seeking from him remedies that probably were in no physician's power to provide.

One place Jiang did not go was Hunan. She disliked Mao's home province and avoided going there. Mao's birthplace, Shaoshan, to which tens of millions of Chinese have gone as pilgrims at some stage in their lives, she "hated." Never in her life, not even in the 1960s when it was virtually obligatory to pay homage there, would she ever set foot in the village.

When Mao and Jiang did meet, a gulf opened between their ways and tastes. Mao liked to travel by train; Jiang favored planes.

In literature and the theater, Mao liked the traditional, Jiang liked the modern. Mao would work half the night and rise late; Jiang rose comparatively early. Mao bolted down his food and cared little what was on the plate; Jiang liked fancy or unusual preparations, and she would hardly have started her meal when Mao would throw down his chopsticks to signal the end of his. Mao could not stand flowers, ornaments, or pets in his place; Jiang had a passion for orchids and kept pet monkeys. Mao wore the nearest garment at hand; Jiang spent many hours a week on her wardrobe—certain colors (coffee was one) she adored; other colors (as yellow) she could not abide; and sometimes she wore three different outfits in a day.*

Mao did not like seeing doctors and seldom listened to them, whereas medical personnel were often the chief human presence in Jiang's life, and she counted up her diseases like a list of personal enemies. "I have never heard of so much high blood pressure and liver infection," Mao remarked in a swipe at Jiang and people like her. "If a person doesn't exercise but only eats well, dresses well, lives comfortably, and drives wherever he goes, he will be beset by a lot of illnesses."

One morning in Peking, Mao was finishing a piece of writing that had kept him up all night, and Jiang Qing was at the house of Li Lisan, a Party figure whose Russian wife was a close friend of hers. Mao sent a message saying he'd like to lunch with her. Jiang was in the middle of a gripping game of poker, and she waited until it was over before returning. When she reached South and Central Lakes, Mao had finished his lunch and gone to bed, annoyed with her. She in turn was annoyed with him, for she had to lunch alone, and she would have liked to have stayed on at the Li Lisans' for another round of poker.

It was a fierce summer day in 1958. Mao was on a rural tour in Henan Province, and Jiang Qing was with him. She rarely traveled on these trips, but Mao wanted to take his two daughters and his nephew Mao Yuanxin, so Jiang went too. After a late-afternoon discussion with some farmers' spokesmen, Mao suddenly waved them into the dining room of the guest house where he and his family

* "He just wears the same old black or green Lenin suits," Jiang once complained of Mao to Song Qingling. "A foreigner once gave him a tie, but he hung it up and he has never worn it." Jiang went on to Sun Yat-sen's widow: "I've seen photos of Sun Yat-sen in a Western dress suit and a bow tie, and you in a *qipao* with a colorful fringe—how beautiful! These days, foreigners come to China and laugh at us for all wearing the same type of clothes. They think we don't have the freedom to wear what we like."

were staying. Jiang and the three children were waiting at a round table. "These are my daughters," Mao said, pointing to Li Na and Li Min, "both are students." After introducing Yuanxin, Mao turned to Jiang Qing, smiled, and said to the Henan farmers: "This one's my wife" (*Ta jiu shi wo de ai ren*).*

The locals took only boiled rice; they were too scared to take a portion of the fish and pork. Mao and Jiang both put portions of fish and pork on top of each bowl of rice, but at this the Henan folk were so moved they could eat nothing at all. It was the same when apples were brought to the table. Their guests paralyzed, Mao and Jiang and the children ate the apples themselves. At the end of the meal all five of the Mao family stepped outside to bid farewell to the farmers' spokesmen. Jiang said good-bye modestly, playing the role of a quiet and polite housewife as she had done throughout the dinner.

The news came late at night. Yu Qiwei was dead of heart disease at forty-six. Jiang did not attend the funeral. Mao sent a wreath, in his own name alone. Later Jiang read the obituary in the newspaper, which didn't mention her, and described Yu (by then called Huang Jing) as "an outstanding revolutionary fighter." Jiang Qing had scarcely seen him since Yanan days. Did she allow herself to think back on how he had taught her in Qingdao and helped her get started in Shanghai? Or was her mind swamped by thoughts of Yu's subsequent wife, the journalist Fan Jin, and fears as to what stories Yu Qiwei might have told Fan?

During her nadir Jiang often was in Canton. She stayed in a government guest house with her large orchids and her small monkeys. She was ill and difficult. Surrounded by staff, she seldom dealt with equals who had a claim on her mind or attention, and she became self-centered.

Her voice had shrunk to a whisper, and she would allow no one in the house to speak louder than she did. She changed her mind about arrangements, in the morning deciding to fly to Jinan, after lunch switching to Beidaihe, and then in the evening upbraiding her staff for not having divined that she really wanted to stay in Canton after all. She summoned a doctor for an urgent medical test, and when he arrived she postponed it indefinitely.

Bored and willful, she coaxed one of her monkeys to spring out

---

* In Yanan, he had generally introduced her with "This is Jiang Qing," or "This is Comrade Jiang Qing," rather than with the label "wife."

at an old servant, terrifying him, amusing her. She summoned staff members at all hours of the day and night to play bridge or poker with her. When she was feeling fresh, she gave a running commentary on how each player ought to play his or her hand. When she was tired, the staff members eagerly waited for her to nod off so that they could be released. But she would snap back and cry, "I'm not asleep!" just as they were smiling with pleasure at the prospect of going to bed.

Her conversation turned often to life in the Shanghai theater during the 1930s. She was "really Red" then, she stressed to her staff; in her own spirit what she seemed to be nostalgic for was that period of being her own woman, buoyant, fluent, building her own life by the free actions of each day.

Khrushchev came two more times to Peking, in 1958 and 1959, and asked after Jiang Qing, but she was too ill, or judged too ill to see him, or to meet any other foreign dignitaries. Meanwhile, Wang Guangmei, wife of Liu Shaoqi, and Zhang Jian, wife of the foreign minister, Chen Yi, were reveling in the roles of Wives of the Important—gracing receptions, meeting interesting foreigners, traveling in Asia on diplomatic missions with their husbands.

A work conference was about to begin in Shanghai with Mao presiding, and it was arranged that Jiang would join him there. The two of them would later go off to their lakeside villa at Hangzhou. When Jiang arrived from Canton, an unpleasant surprise awaited her. Mao had met with He Zizhen, his previous wife. Furious, Jiang could talk and think about nothing else. Mao stubbornly defended his action on the ground that He was an "old fighter-in-arms" (she was that, and Jiang was not).

At a dance for the Party elite in the Jinjiang Hotel, formerly the French Club, Jiang arrived with a nurse in tow at 9:00 P.M. She chose a table far from those of the senior leaders and sat grim-faced, whether out of illness or anger. Mao came in at 10:30 P.M., but he did not join her. The military leader Zhu De walked over beaming to her table and asked if she would like to dance.

She declined, saying she was too tired, only to step onto the dance floor a few moments later with a dashing young man from the Culture Ministry, the pair of them executing a fancy step that few people knew how to do. Mao chatted here and there, now with a Politburo member, now with one of the pretty girls from the bureaucracy. Jiang's dancing with young men was revenge for Mao's neglect of her. Both went their own way. "You have your girls, and I'll have my men" was one of the unspoken rules that allowed the marriage to survive.

At 11:00 P.M. Jiang suddenly left. She upbraided the nurse, as they drove back to her quarters, for encouraging her to dance when she was really not up to it and for allowing her to stay so late at the function!

Mao decided against a Hangzhou stay. The next day Jiang went alone to the secluded villa at West Lake that was to have been the soothing setting for Mao and Jiang to spend an autumn break together. It was a pagodalike home with a red tile roof brushed by languid branches at the edge of the beautiful lake, where the only sounds were the distant cry of geese and the lapping of the water against the shore.

Jiang decided to have it redecorated. She laid down a number of rules and requirements: double-glass doors and windows to keep out dust; apple-green paint throughout; toilets, phones, and other fittings adapted to reduce their noise; a movie screen in the living room, to be discreetly covered with an ancient silk scroll; completely self-contained quarters for Mao and herself, the two apartments to be linked by a reception room, washroom, and dining room. She was pleased with the results, and the villa became a favorite base for her for some time.

"Because I lived so long in China," Pearl Buck, who knew Chinese life as well as any American has ever known it, remarked to me, "marriage was but an incidental thing in my life; that is the Chinese way." So it was with Jiang Qing. In Shandong, she rejected a husband as one sends back a hardly worn shoe to a store. In Shanghai, she earned the reputation of one who used men. In Yanan, during the "era of love," she had married for reasons more complex than love. It was hardly surprising that in the 1950s, the decade of machine tools and regulations in triplicate and labor camps, she would discount romance; many others, including Mao, also did so.

"Sex is engaging in the first rounds," Jiang once remarked, "but what sustains interest in the long run is power." By the late 1950s she had neither. Mao was no longer interested in her as a companion. Being Mao's wife had opened some doors, but not always the doors she really wanted to go through. A dull, passive life amid external splendor did not seem a stable resting point for a woman who believed in nothing but her own will.

She seemed a finished woman. All one could say of her as the

1960s began was that she believed, if no one else did, in a high destiny for Jiang Qing. There was an intriguing straw in the wind: Mao had run into political trouble; would he (like Franklin Roosevelt, who, after being afflicted by polio, turned to Eleanor for support as he had never done before) begin to take fresh notice of his quiet wife out of a need to use her bottled-up talent?

6

Recovery and Revenge: Politics as Theater (1960s)

I'm a doctor, not a nurse.
—Jiang Qing

We dragged them out and hung them up.
—Jiang Qing (of her activities during the Cultural Revolution)

Zhou Enlai, desperate, had a bright idea. He left Jiang Qing's room at the Moscow hospital on a freezing day in 1957, and after a round of talks with Khrushchev, came back to the ward with a famous opera singer, Cheng Yanqiu, who happened to be on a cultural mission to the Soviet Union. If the physicians were at their wits' end, the prime minister of China, for whom any problem had a solution if one remained calm, and who once had played female roles in an amateur dramatic society in Tianjin, would bring culture to Jiang's sickroom to divert her from her diseases! As Jiang lay back in her green pajamas, the brilliant Cheng did mimes and sang arias, and Zhou cracked jokes until late into the evening. Jiang's spirits rose.

Two years later, as if the gods were all united in a desire to make mischief, Jiang's doctors in Shanghai, "to get her mind off her physical ailments . . . recommended that she go to see some shows." She did. In addition to acupuncture, *tai ji quan* exercises, billiards, twenty minutes of table tennis and 150 meters of swimming daily, all of which were meant to further her recovery from a battery of illnesses, Jiang began to monitor plays and operas and films.

Jiang Qing's recovery also was triggered by the altered feelings of a man in his sixties toward a wife in her forties whom he had recently taken for granted. Jiang entered the 1960s with a cherished photograph at her bedside; it was her own shot of the Fairy Cave at Mount Lu, in Jiangxi Province, and scrawled on the back of it was an ardent poem by Mao. She took the picture in 1959 when she rushed, unwelcomed, to Mao's side at Mount Lu during his fight

with Defense Minister Peng Dehuai over Mao's unsuccessful Great
Leap Forward. One evening in 1961, when Mao and Jiang were
close again, Mao took a brush and wrote a poem that was less about
Mount Lu, far away at the time, than about the very near Jiang
Qing:

> Amid the growing shades of dusk stand sturdy pines,
> Riotous clouds sweep past, the scene is swift and tranquil.
> Nature has excelled herself in the Fairy Cave,
> On perilous peaks dwells beauty in her infinite variety.

Mao copied this verse in his own hand on the back of Jiang's
photo, inscribing it to "Li Jin," a pen name she sometimes used. It
hardly matters that a close inspection reveals that Jiang's photo is
not of the Fairy Cave but of Brocade Embroidered Peak, with its
elegant Imperial Tablets Pavilion, taken *from* the Fairy Cave. The
important thing was the resurgence of Mao's affection for Jiang—
many Chinese believe the reference to the cave is an erotic image
inspired by Jiang—after more than a decade of seeming indifference.

Underlying Jiang Qing's astonishing recovery at the start of the
1960s was a third point: her own will to climb out of the pit of illness
and depression. To be sure, her willpower cannot be separated entirely from her ambition to make her mark on China's cultural policies, or from Mao's encouragement. Yet it took great determination
for a woman in her late forties to spring back from cervical cancer,
liver disease, and other ailments to start a fresh career.

"I'm a doctor, not a nurse," she announced to a theatrical
group as she prescribed for them a regimen of harsh drugs for their
artistic illnesses. This was the same Jiang Qing! The same one who
as a student in Shandong insisted that anything men could do,
women could do too; who laid down for Tang Na the improvements
he must undergo to be worthy to say he had once been her lover;
who wrote in "Our Life" that the actress was no "doll" but a full
equal of the playwright and the director; and who in Yanan decided
that she was up to Mao's level and that she could get him (or "trick
him," as Ding Ling put it to me).

Without that spirit, that shameless belief in herself, that tough
and quite unself-pitying character, Jiang never could have picked
herself up after the letdown of the 1950s.

*   *   *

In beautiful autumn weather, the wife of President Sukarno of Indonesia came to Peking in September 1962. Her visit was part of China's attempt to draw Sukarno's Indonesia close, as a young brother of Maoist revolution. The Chinese Communist hospitality machine turned on dinners, tea parties, and expeditions, all ritually reported in the official press. Liu Shaoqi, as a virtual coequal of Mao at this time, was naturally to the fore, but what set tongues wagging was that his wife, the glamorous Wang Guangmei, also was prominent. In *People's Daily,* where every paragraph and every photo reeks of policy, and news is secondary, a photo of Liu, Wang, and the beautiful Madame Hartini Sukarno chatting together appeared on September 24. The next day Wang and Madame Sukarno appeared alone on *People's Daily's* front page; on subsequent days these two ladies were often photographed together.

All this was too much for Jiang Qing. A Chinese word for enemy is *chou jia,* which means "hated household" or "hated family," and in Chinese politics few enmities cause greater fury than that between rival families. Jiang's jealousy of Wang—who was everything she was not—harmonized sufficiently with Mao's disesteem for Liu that Jiang was able to enlist his help to put Wang in her place. Five days later, *People's Daily* carried on its front page a huge photo of Mao, Jiang, and Madame Sukarno. On the second page, clearly subordinate, sat a small picture of Liu, Wang, and Madame Sukarno.

If Madame Sukarno wondered why she was one of the most photographed foreign women in Chinese newspaper history, readers of *People's Daily,* merely bemused by foreign women but passionately interested in the rivalries of highly placed Chinese women, knew at once that they held an unusually significant issue of the paper in their hands. Jiang Qing's photo had never before appeared in *People's Daily.* For seven years even her name had hardly appeared in any Chinese newspaper. In the entire history of the People's Republic of China, a photo of her and Mao together had never before been officially released.

Liu and Wang had produced a sharp response from Mao, which launched Jiang to a new level of public visibility.

In the West it is rare for a leader's spouse to be a major factor in the configuration of state power, as happened in Mao's China. Because a Western leader is elected, what his unelected wife (or her unelected husband) does or fails to do never can matter much compared with the leader's acts. Perhaps it is only when a U.S. president is stricken that his marriage arrangements can become a potent ingredient in the configuration of power—as readily happens, whatever the health of the leader, in a China still flavored by feudal ways. Had President Carter become gravely ill, but not been judged unable to remain in office, it is possible to imagine Rosalynn Carter wielding major power. And when Franklin Roosevelt was struck by polio, a subtle change occurred in his marriage that led Eleanor Roosevelt from passivity and obscurity, if not to the direct wielding of power, then to a position of substantial influence in politics and in society at large.

For Jiang, as for Eleanor Roosevelt, her husband's setback provided an opportunity for her to flower. Long years of being taken for granted ended as the politician—in Mao's case more for political than for physical reasons—suddenly needed his capable but underutilized wife. Like Eleanor Roosevelt, Jiang had her share of tribulations, so a strong drive for vindication was ready to rush into any vacuum of opportunity that opened up.

To be the wife of Mao in a polity where politics is 80 percent secret intrigue (the other 20 percent is propaganda) and to be newly needed by a Mao in trouble was inevitably to become a politician. Jiang, who wanted to be a hero and who loved to worship and be worshiped, soon found herself *condemned* to be either a hero or a villain.

This is not to say that any wife of the supreme leader of China would have done what Jiang did in the 1960s; she was a woman of singular talents, possessed by her own special demons. Quiet, she was also willful. Rustic, she was also shrewd. A husband or a visitor who raised an idea with Deng Yingchao, the wife of Zhou Enlai, may or may not have gotten a clear-cut response. With Jiang it was guaranteed; she would embrace the idea, or denounce it; her opinion would be laid on the table, she *would know.* A visitor coming out of Deng's place might well murmur, "She's a good woman." This was not a common response to Jiang Qing. But she did seem a woman who "had something." She could battle; she was bound to write a bold message of her own in the sky above her.

After the failure of his Great Leap Forward, Mao in the early 1960s had to share power with Liu Shaoqi, Deng Xiaoping, and others who believed in the politics of order and the economics of results. "They treated me like a dead ancestor," Mao complained of these believers in the rule book.

A balance of forces existed in the early 1960s. Mao, using Jiang and some new faces who began to coalesce into a "Court Faction," developed a set of leftist ideas—an assertion that class struggle was getting sharper, a demand for reform of the arts to make them sparkle with ideology, a revulsion against bureaucrats for whom the Communist regime was an end in itself—to challenge the rising power of the Liu-Deng bureaucratic establishment. Members of the Court Faction did not hold commanding positions in the ship of state, but they were active below decks, especially with their pens.

Mao's leftist ideas puzzled Liu and Deng, but insofar as they remained ideas, these two pragmatists could live with them. The same ideas electrified Jiang Qing. They contained iconoclastic possibilities, and iconoclasm was nectar to this woman who knew she had to knock Zhou Yang and other bureaucrats down if she was to climb to power over cultural policy.

Mao, sixty-six years old as the decade began, also was hemmed in by Parkinson's disease. "Our doctors cannot guarantee how many more years I can live," he remarked to Algerian visitors. "Each person must be ready with successors," he said to a gathering of military officers, launching a theme that soon obsessed him. This sense of his own mortality made Mao more open than before to traditional things, including Buddhism and the feudal ruler's impulse to prompt his wife to shore up, and perpetuate, his sagging authority.

In *Romance of the Three Kingdoms,* a favorite novel of Mao's, the formidable Cao Cao, half hero and half villain, cries out to his associate: "The only heroes in the world are you and I!" An embattled Mao, who for fifty years had thought of life in terms of a hero's will battling against large odds, saw in his wife, whose strong will often had irritated him, almost the only available cohero for his next campaign.

Mao knew Jiang's limitations. She was good at lighting fires but not at managing a conflagration or putting one out. She could fire shots from a parapet, but she did not know how to handle troops on a battlefield. It didn't matter; the Cultural Revolution was to be mainly lighting fires and firing shots.

In Mao's mind, and so in Jiang's, the army was a key ally in the coming fight to topple Liu and Deng and to purify Communist values. The defense minister, Lin Biao, a frail man with a high-pitched voice who always kept his cap on to hide a balding head, was prepared for his own reasons to be utterly loyal to Mao. He had learned the lesson of his outspoken predecessor as defense minister, Peng Dehuai. Mao began to see Lin, not Liu, as his real number two and successor. While the Party and state bureaucracy treated Mao like a "dead ancestor," the army treated him as its living Caesar. Lin ordered the military to become a "great school of Mao Zedong's thought." Mao in turn launched a drive for all of China to "learn from the People's Liberation Army."

One summer day in 1961, Jiang made an inspection visit to a military unit in Canton that had a tradition of close service to Mao and Lin Biao. Jiang noted that the Number One Guards Company grew its own vegetables to save money, that its soldiers kept their beds tidy and their mosquito nets neatly folded, and cut each other's hair even though there was a barber shop two hundred meters away with electric driers.

Because they follow the "teachings of Chairman Mao," Jiang Qing's report published in *China Youth Daily* summed up, the members of Number One Guards Company are real "children of the people." That the soldiers' frugal ways—which in any case were more the result of necessity than of the inspiration of Mao's thoughts—were poles apart from her own extravagant ways did not seem to occur to Jiang. Her concern was self-expression through wielding power. Trumpeting Mao and his loyal servant Lin was the means to it.

Jiang Qing's method of seizing her opportunity was threefold. She buoyed Mao, at times flattering him. As her health improved, she sifted through documents and publications for items to pass on to him, pinpointing the pro- or anti-Mao aspect of an incident or an idea. She wanted Mao to become outraged at the situation he saw around him, and she wanted his outrage to be personal, not merely philosophic.

"I am fond of firing cannon shots," Jiang once remarked, no doubt with a smile. "If only I had a butcher's knife in my hand!" she loved to cry, borrowing a line from a Peking opera. It was this combative streak that issued in her second tactic: She sought to polarize all situations. Reinforced by Mao's similar bent—enshrined in his famous theory of contradictions—she rushed around like an usher in a theater dividing everyone into left and right. She saw the masses of alienated youth as a shock force to create polarization.

The stage set for disagreement, or better still a fight, Jiang's third tactic was to wrap herself in the banner of "Mao Zedong's thought," assert that half the politicians and cultural figures of China were agents of darkness because they were "anti-Mao," and fight for their destruction, in the name of Mao, revolution, Chinese nationalism, women's rights, or any other yardstick at hand. For this task she needed the help of a coterie of young, ambitious, fawning intellectuals.

As her public role grew, Jiang often asked herself what she should wear.

A figurehead of middle age like Song Qingling, widow of Sun Yat-sen, could wear the grand silk gowns of pre-1949 days, but Jiang did not want to look like a museum piece. "Backwoods Boadicea" Kang Keqing, wife of military leader Zhu De, could wear boots and a mannish cap, but Jiang's idea of independence did not include *looking* just like a man. Yes, she was bent on entering the male sphere of political life, but she would enter it without compromising her femininity. The model woman revolutionary Deng Yingchao, wife of Premier Zhou, could wear tunics that took nondescriptness to a new height, but Jiang was not content to be one in the crowd—she wanted to be noticed. Women of the arts who had lived in the United States could go in for frilly dresses and hats, but Jiang did not want to look *too* feminine; the image of a plaything was out of line with her ambition to wield power.

The best outfit, she felt, was a high-authority suit with a touch of color at the throat, and maximum possible beauty for her hair.

Chinese opera, telling moral tales from the past, its heroes gorgeous and its villains grotesque, is a potential tool of ideological dictatorship. Jiang Qing saw a Maoist opera as a tool for her climb to power. Like many previous Chinese leaders, including the Empress Dowager of a hundred years ago, she would patronize the arts to express her authority. Opera reform became the launching pad for her political career, as World War II did for Winston Churchill's prime ministership, and strong defense did for Ronald Reagan's presidency.

Jiang's starting point was Mao's 1962 call to revivify class struggle (to Jiang this meant polarize, then fight) and his assertion, nearer to Confucianism than to Marxism, that the ideas in the heads of the public are the keys to political power. It satisfied Jiang's didacticism to take scripts and scores and make them "brighter." It suited her hectoring personality to order theater people around like so many pupils. And she sincerely believed that the performing arts should be reshaped to fit the socialist world view.

"Make it revolutionary or ban it" was a slogan that Jiang enjoyed psychologically. And by embodying a politicization of the arts in the name of returning to the simple virtues of the road, the slogan helped Mao politically. Chinese tend to think that everything that can happen has once happened, and that moral conduct consists of repeating the correct performances of the past. Jiang and Mao were going to insist that henceforth the past on which the Chinese theater drew was to be *their* past, the few short heroic decades since the 1920s. The rest was "kings, emperors, and nobles," of no interest to the people of new China—at least of no political value to the Mao dynasty.

Jiang began by watching or leafing through more than a thousand theater pieces during 1962 and 1963, mostly in Shanghai, where she established a close link with the mayor. Ke Qingshi was a sincere left-winger of working-class origin with no particular flair for the arts. But he was in awe of Mao, and he was one of the very few leaders who had supported the Mao-Jiang marriage.* He was doggedly loyal to Jiang.

There opened in Shanghai a theatrical sketch based on Mao's poem of 1957 in memory of his former wife Yang Kaihui ("I lost my proud poplar . . ."). The show closed after a few performances, to the puzzlement of the port city's theatergoers. Mayor Ke had banned it. Jiang Qing had asked him to, saying that the tribute to Yang was an unacceptable insult to herself.

In Shanghai, where the mayor made sure "our lady guest" had every comfort at the former French Club, Jiang Qing enjoyed the freedom of a base removed from the Peking bureaucrats, in an atmosphere of leftism. This curious Shanghai leftism, a by-product of the city's rivalry with Peking, was in part a result of Shanghai's efforts in the Communist era to compensate for its past as the bastion of imperialist presence in China ("city of sin," "Paris of the East").

With two left-wing Shanghai polemicists, Jiang Qing in the early 1960s forged a "hen and two chickens" alliance that was to shape Chinese politics for a decade. Zhang Chunqiao, like Jiang a native of Shandong and an associate for a while in the 1930s of Cui Wanqiu, the editor of *Da wanbao,* in whose circle she first met him, was an able man who had risen to be head of Shanghai's Communist Party. Yao Wenyuan, whose businessman-author father Jiang had met in the 1930s, was a younger and lesser figure, a fluent writer who soon treated Jiang as a page boy treats an empress. The loyalty

---

* Ke told Shanghai officials they ought to possess three copies of Mao's writings, one by the bedside, one in the office, and one carried in their pocket—all this before the Cultural Revolution!

This did not stop Ke from making furtive trips to Hangzhou with Jiang Qing for dancing parties at a lakeside hideout.

of Zhang and Yao to Jiang Qing was due to her charm, her left-wing views on the arts, and the appeal of her proximity to Mao.

Jiang's technique in making use of Yao and other young writers who joined her stable as her star rose had its precedent in the history of the Chinese court, and some similarity to the chain of fear of a McCarthyist witch-hunt. It went this way. A journalist or a scholar, often obscure, wrote an article that departed from the usual interpretation of a book or historical event. Its readers, knowing that in Chinese public life there is no smoke without fire, realized that the writer was not acting alone but as the hired pen of some heavy political cannon. But who? What was his or her aim? Fear soared. The search to understand the writer's "background" began. Eventually the whole affair turned into the political dogfight it was meant to be from the start. Jiang was skilled at this technique, and being the wife of Mao helped her recruit talent and added to her capacity to intimidate adversaries.

One day in May 1963 readers of the Shanghai paper *Wen hui bao* found a scathing attack on a play by Tian Han, until then a popular and much-praised work. It was Jiang Qing's doing, a first shot in her campaign of revenge against the man she felt had slighted her in Shanghai thirty years previously. The writer of the attack on Tian Han's play was an unknown. Jiang and Mayor Ke had selected him for the task. Zhang Chunqiao, as Party chief and boss of *Wen hui bao,* had ordered the intemperate piece's publication.

In Peking, Jiang dropped in uninvited on the Number One Opera Troupe to try her pressure tactics. They were devoting themselves to rubbish, she told the artists. Why not serve the future instead of rummaging in the ashes of the past? She instructed them to produce a new opera she had been working on. *Spark Among the Reeds* (later called *Shajiabang*) was about the exploits of the New Fourth Army during the war against Japan.

The troupe was confused. Here was Mao's wife telling them to curse what they had adored and to pin themselves to untested experimental pieces. Meanwhile, the mayor of Peking, the urbane Peng Zhen, who felt Jiang had no right to make destabilizing forays into the theater of "his" city, told the troupe to go on performing the traditional repertoire. If Mayor Peng heard that Jiang needed a certain auditorium for a rehearsal, he would make certain it was already booked. If he knew she was going to try to put on a colorful publicity stunt, he would instruct the city's news media not to report it.

Mayor Peng did not take Jiang seriously; he saw her efforts to reform Peking opera as the hobby of a bored wife. "It's like pure boiled water," he said when *Shajiabang* was staged.

"Only when you have pure boiled water," Jiang came back, in a mindless riposte which showed how little she now cared about the theater as entertainment, "can you make tea and wine. No one can live without pure boiled water."

But Jiang knew what she was doing politically, if perhaps not artistically. She arrived at the troupe's studios with boxes of books. For each artist there was a copy of Mao's *Selected Works,* autographed by its author; she handed them out like a gang leader giving pistols to his men. "Don't think I'm here just peddling new pieces of theater," she rasped, addressing Mayor Peng as much as the artists. "I am here to do battle against feudalism, capitalism, and revisionism."*

Suddenly Mao praised *Shajiabang;* boiled water artistically, the opera became a potent wine politically. The mayor's mistake was to think an opera was merely an opera. He also seemed to forget, as Zhou Enlai never did, that Jiang, however trying she became, remained Chairman Mao's wife.

In Shanghai, where her remark that Peng Zhen was guilty of "Peking chauvinism" (*da Beijing zhu yi*) went down well, Jiang decided to reform an opera called *Taking Tiger Mountain by Strategy,* a story of Communist armies fighting bandits in Manchuria in 1946. Seeing the original version, she strode backstage and told the cast the show was "mostly rubbish." Taking it under her wing, on terrain less inhospitable than Mayor Peng's Peking, she set about to sharpen the moral message of *Tiger Mountain.*

In her apartment, over meals, she listened to tapes of rehearsals, then rushed to the theater with fresh ideas. "Hate" was a key word in the script, she decided; it should be shouted as if it were a grenade being hurled at the enemy. Don't round off a musical phrase with a falling tone, she admonished the cast, even if that *has* been the custom for a thousand years; "resolve to act" was best expressed by a rising tone. She demonstrated how the word "spring" should be enunciated—screeched—to convey its "political content" (a harbinger of victory for the righteous forces).

"Never forget," she entreated the heroine as she taught her how to bristle with class hatred, "that beauty is less important than will and power."

* "Revisionism" was Mao's swear word for the Soviet Union's backsliding socialism.

She made the hero more heroic, taking bad language off his lips and putting a fur-lined coat on his back. The bandit villains she dressed in rags and kept away from center stage! A hero should not "mumble" or "dodder," she told the lead actor, Tong Xiangling. Mounting the stage, she ran her fingers up the handsome actor's spine and exhorted him: "Subdue those old ways! Stand tall and sing powerfully!" How should a hero get off a horse? "Don't simply slide off his back," Jiang said to Tong; "that looks weak," added the woman who never could abide her men to be weak. "Spring over the horse's head," she commanded.

In the unreformed version, Tong had worn his pistol suspended from the front of his belt. "Carry it to the side," Jiang said solicitously. Why, Tong wondered. Because Jiang felt Mr. Tong's genitals might suffer if he wore his pistol "in front for a long time."

Jiang did not direct "her" theatrical pieces; she hovered over them. Like a headmistress visiting the class of a junior teacher, she inspected, rebuked, dismantled, all without assuming operational responsibility. Knowing enough from her own experience in films and plays to command authority, she would twist her hips to show a sluggish actress how a saucy siren really moves, or explain to an actor that working-class people don't cry sitting down, with their head buried in their hands, but standing up in defiance.

Some artists thought she was crazy. Others were swept up by the excitement of making the theater a political force, and by Jiang's dramatic personality and her aura of having just come from Mao's side, and were honored to say, "We became her instruments."

Beginning work on *The Red Lantern,* one of her favorite operas, she laid down a maxim for the cast: "To act is to fight." But the members of the Peking Opera Institute dragged their feet over her demand to remove from the script the hero's occasional bouts of drinking; to "improve upon reality" by putting jazzy clothes on working-class people; and to bring military precision and healthiness to the actors' movements ("When you sit, sit well. When you stand, stand well").

Zhou Enlai phoned regularly to see how the reform was going. Jiang was thrilled with his "encouragement"; yet it seems likely that the wily premier's purpose was to check that relations between the self-appointed Maid Marian of the arts and the institute's professionals were not getting out of hand. They didn't; Jiang succeeded; and *The Red Lantern* sprang forth to bore a generation of theater-goers.

"I have seen Western operas," Jiang remarked. In them the artists "sing anything, like: 'Do you want some tea?' 'Yes, I'll have some tea. It is very good tea.' " Her mind now was shut against cosmopolitanism. "Our Chinese opera concentrates on expressing only positive emotions, important ones. . . ."

During the summer of 1964, in a sullen political atmosphere, a Peking Opera Festival unfolded. Jiang Qing received an invitation to give a speech, and some of her reformed works were staged as part of the month-long program. But also present in substantial numbers were officials from the Ministry of Culture and theatrical professionals who opposed her activities.

Jiang's speech, the first major public speech of her life, repaid a debt to Mayor Ke of Shanghai. She praised him for encouraging "three-way combinations of leadership, playwrights, and masses" in his city's theaters. It was an echo of her old theme, expressed in "Our Life," that directors are suspect and that the views of actors and audiences should be permitted to modify directors' professional prejudices.

"Do you eat?" she cried to the theater people. "That food came from the farmers! So *serve* the farmers in your plays and operas!"

One afternoon during an intermission, Jiang found herself within striking distance of an extraordinary cluster of her past colleagues and present foes, standing together in quiet conversation. There in the lobby were Xia Yan, author of the play *Sai Jinhua*, which she would love to have played in; Zhang Geng, who once officiously demanded to marry her; Tian Han, who had taken insufficient notice of her in the early Shanghai years; and Zhou Yang, who had murmured one torrid evening, "When Jiang Qing is present, work is difficult."

With a smile she joined the group. These four men of the arts had to be wary of Jiang, but they did not feel they needed to heed her opinions. They greeted her, shifted from foot to foot, and said nothing. Jiang Qing, still gauche in judging her impact on others, cried out to them: "Make revolution for a change!" The distinguished men of the theater stood dumbly.

Jiang's speech to the festival was not published, though some other leaders' speeches were. Mao was her great rock. He had just declared that his own government's Ministry of Culture, manned by Zhou Yang, Xia Yan, and the rest, was a "ministry of emperors and princes, generals and ministers, scholars and beauties." Jiang gave a foretaste of how she was going to make use of her rock. She slipped away from the festival one day and went to the Capital Hospital, where a young actor lay recuperating from an operation. One of "her" actors, left-wing, loyal, and handsome, Song Yuqing was to have played the lead in her *Raid on the White Tiger Regiment*, to be performed that day at the festival. Carefully ensuring that a journalist was present to catch her words, Jiang strode into Song's ward, greeted the medical personnel, and asked earnestly about the prognosis for the young pawn's recovery. "Little Song," she said as she held his hand, "Chairman Mao expects you to go on being a real crusader, both red and expert, for revolutionary art and literature."

Jiang's foes were not silenced. She is "picking melons before they are ripe," Liu Shaoqi said of Jiang's new pieces. "Still at the stage," Mayor Peng Zhen snapped of them, "of wearing trousers with a slit in the seat" (a reference to the open seam in a Chinese child's pants).

When eight of the new pieces were canonized by a portion of the press as "revolutionary model pieces"—five of them Jiang had developed in Shanghai—Mayor Peng said: "What the hell are these models? I'm head of the arts in this place, and I know nothing of models. Whether her pieces are models or not, one just doesn't know." Observed the testy Deng Xiaoping: "You just see a bunch of people running to and fro on the stage. Not a trace of art."

One evening in 1965, Jiang found herself at a banquet at which Peng Zhen was also present. She went over to the mayor's table and asked if they might have a word in private. He agreed to join her in a side room. She asked Peng to allocate a theater troupe in Peking as a base for her work. Holding out a new opera score for him to see, she reinforced her case by mentioning that Zhang Chunqiao, the Shanghai Party chief, was giving her this kind of help with the ballet *White-Haired Girl* and other works. The mayor of Peking, hardly more impressed with the mention of Zhang's name than with Jiang's artistic conceptions, refused, angrily snatched the score from her hand, and strode bristling back to the banquet room.

"She wants this, she wants that," Peng complained to a friend. "Doesn't she realize the mayor of Peking has other things to do besides help her with her games?"

In a calmer era Liu Shaoqi's remark about Jiang's revolutionary models should have carried the day. "Nowadays," he said, objecting to the ramming home of a political message through models, "audiences have the ability to judge things themselves." But it was not a calm era.

Moving from opera to dance, Jiang oversaw the production of

Red Detachment of Women, a feminist military saga set in tropical Hainan Island, and *White-Haired Girl,* a harrowing tale about an evil landlord and a persecuted maiden. These dance-dramas were an amalgam of Chinese ritual and Western romanticism. Jiang hated existing ballets, such as *Swan Lake,* full of birds and beasts; ballets should be full of *human will,* she said. She made her dancers live with army units so they would better portray war and struggle in their movements and facial expressions. After removing scenes of childbirth and sex from the original version of *Red Detachment,* Jiang added a nearly religious finale, glorifying Mao, on the theme of resurrection.

Red Detachment inspired Deng Xiaoping's imprudent remark: "After a week's work, people want to go to the theater to relax. Instead, with this thing, you go to the theater and find yourself on a battlefield." Liu Shaoqi said it was "a forced reflection of contemporary life." As for Zhou Yang, in the midst of rehearsals for *Red Detachment,* he ordered the artists involved in it to go to Hong Kong to perform *Swan Lake!*

But Mao saved the day. "The orientation is right," he pronounced. "It has been successfully revolutionized, and artistically it is also good." The ballet soon joined the pantheon of models, as did *White-Haired Girl,* after Jiang had emptied it of sex and filled it with class hatred.

One day in the winter of 1965 Jiang dropped in on the Central Philharmonic Society. "The capitalist symphony is dead," she announced. The musicians politely objected that she knew little about music; she retorted that she was bringing them the higher grace of revolutionary fervor. "You're attacking me with a hammer," the conductor of the orchestra complained. But nothing pleased Jiang more than to be thought of as a fearsome attacker. She later took up the conductor's remark as a boast: "With hammer in hand, I set out to attack all the old conventions."

She pounced on "unhealthy passages" in the existing repertoire. She sent a pianist south to retrace the route of one of Mao's military campaigns so that he could more movingly play the fierce "Yellow River Concerto." By sheer force of will, unencumbered by detailed knowledge of the subject, she threw together a model symphony adapted from the opera *Shajiabang.* One shocked violinist could not help murmuring: "I honestly can't regard *Shajiabang* as a symphony." Zhou Yang on behalf of the orchestra objected: "We already have a very tight schedule without adding this thing."

Jiang swept all objections aside. What counted was that *Shajia-bang* was *hers,* her child just as Li Na was her child, and when she adorned it with a flourish here and an accent there, it was just as if she were dressing little Li Na in a fresh outfit, hoping to color the girl in her own image. Eventually she surfaced with two musical models, "Yellow River Concerto" and "Shajiabang Symphony." Music was to serve "revolution"; music was to serve the career of Jiang Qing.*

Jiang Qing believed in her own will, but not in the Chinese public's. She did not blush to say the Central Committee of the Communist Party should become the "processing plant" for reform of the theater (as if the White House were to select the shows for Broadway based on the needs of the next election!). She could not applaud the performance of a villain. In a politicized theater, the villain was an enemy of Maoism, and in a personalized theatrical domain he was virtually an enemy of Jiang Qing. She could only applaud a hero, of sunny temperament, dressed gorgeously, hand-some beyond description, ready to lick the boots of Chairman Mao and huddle in the skirts of Auntie Jiang. It was a schoolchild's idea of light and darkness, of loyalty and abandonment, of joy and sad-ness.

By the time she had finished, the minds of Chinese theatergoers were reduced to mashed potatoes. Jiang didn't care about that; Mao may have welcomed it. Broadcasts had become so boring that you could not resell a good radio set for a quarter of its original price. Jiang's retained scribes in the press had a different verdict on the new operas, ballets and symphonies: "They are *shining pearls* of pro-letarian literature and art, fostered *personally* by Comrade Jiang Qing. They *sparkle* with the thought of Mao Zedong."

By the mid-1960s Jiang had Mao's support. His public praise for her theatrical pieces was the equivalent of receiving rave reviews in every major newspaper in the country. Everything she touched, Mao liked (or was it the other way around?).

She began to attend important meetings, even those of the Central Committee, at Mao's invitation. She sat in a corner and took

---

* Jiang tried to put spoken drama into the same straitjacket, but without success; she was out of her depth, and Mao gave her no encouragement. Movies, likewise, were not susceptible to her method of raid and assault, of adding a flourish here and a patch there. Moreover, the leading movie stars all *knew* Jiang; how could she stride in and order Zhao Dan around? Mr. Zhao would laugh at her, whether openly or inwardly, and tell her, or feel like telling her, that she ought to acquire a new boyfriend to ease her tensions.

notes, like Rosalynn Carter at Jimmy Carter's White House, a silent figure whose power and its source were known to all. She found herself a member of China's parliament (National People's Congress), representing her home province of Shandong, which didn't happen through election but because some shaker and mover, no doubt after checking with Mao, thought it would be timely to give Jiang more visibility. She and Mao were seen together again at public functions, including the National Day festivities atop the Gate of Heavenly Peace, which Jiang had attended only once or twice since 1949.

Jiang echoed Mao's ideas and adopted Mao's postures. "Study to be a doctor of men," she exhorted a student of veterinary science, in a phrase Mao was fond of using of Sun Yat-sen, who had studied medicine. "A bit of fighting is all right, at least for practice," she declared on hearing a report of violence in Sichuan Province, again paraphrasing Mao.

Mao's sense of his own destiny seemed to have sparked in her a lofty sense of her own destiny; "For truly great men/Look to this age alone," Mao wrote in a poem. "Nor should we portray a hero only after he is dead," Jiang remarked. "In fact, there are many more living heroes than dead ones."

There was something touching in the way Jiang, who respected very little outside the boundaries of her own ego, bowed a knee, perhaps subconsciously, to Mao's intellect. When she told stories of her early life, it seemed that she was arranging her experience on platters from Mao's cupboard. She borrowed an overcoat from a friend in Shanghai (as Mao had done). She worked in a library (as Mao once did).

Jiang Qing's handwriting, too, changed from an unremarkable woman's handwriting in the 1930s to a bold, more masculine hand in the 1960s that embodied Mao's influence. When Mao died, Jiang would characterize herself as his "student" (rather than wife, or coworker), and this indeed was one aspect of their relationship.

Mao's and Jiang's expectations of each other were once again congruent, as they had been at Yanan. But this time less unequally so, for Mao needed Jiang and she did not always have to give in to him.

In the 1940s the Mao-Jiang marriage was an affair of sexual passion. After Liberation the physical relationship declined, and the 1950s was a transitional decade, a period of detachment, for Jiang almost of emotional limbo. In the 1960s the marriage revived, not perhaps as an affair of sexual passion, but as the partnership of a mature couple, their children now off their hands, who felt their lot was cast together. Jiang filled Mao in on the disloyal situation that prevailed in the arts; Mao gave Jiang the political guidelines for her attacks on the cultural status quo.

This is not to say the marriage became all sweetness and light. Mao was attracted by Jiang's strong will, but his own strong will was such that he by no means always agreed with her notions. It was Zhou Enlai and Lin Biao who at least gave Jiang the impression of agreeing with her nearly all the time. When she made a proposal to Zhou or Lin, they would murmur that it was excellent. When she made one to Mao, he would often dispute it, and deflate and quiz her; yet in the end he would quite often endorse her proposal.

Mao and Jiang left Peking in the autumn of 1965 for a long stay in Shanghai and Hangzhou. The trip was a symbol of Jiang's growing influence upon Mao. For years she had made long trips to the provinces, while he mostly remained in Peking. Shanghai, a city Mao didn't care for, had been since 1962 an important arena for her theatrical reforms. The villa at Hangzhou, decorated according to Jiang's wishes, was a special bastion of hers, which Mao had not used for years.

In Shanghai, where they lived in an apartment at the former French Club, with a movie projection room for Jiang and a swimming pool for Mao, Jiang was a major participant in the literary, and to a lesser extent the political planning for the Cultural Revolution. In the political and military realms, where she had no constituency and meager knowledge, Mao was preparing a nationwide deployment of his twin forces, Lin Biao's politicized military establishment and the leftist Court Faction. Lin was present with Mao and Jiang in Shanghai for part of that autumn. The leftist Court Faction boasted several Shanghai figures (though Mayor Ke had just died).

At the cultural level, the plans for the coming storm looked very much like a continuation of Jiang's drive to topple bureaucrats, sweep away old modes and themes, and produce a new, politicized culture of Boy Scout naïveté—under Jiang Qing's control. It was a piece of theatrical criticism, rewritten by Jiang, appearing in the Shanghai paper *Wen hui bao* on November 10, that began the visible steps toward a chaos and ideological self-flagellation as devastating as any government of a major nation has ever set in motion.

Hai Rui Dismissed from Office was a play written in 1961 by Wu

Han, vice-mayor of Peking, about a worthy minister in the Ming dynasty who was fired by the emperor for being too critical. Mao had declared the play politically mischievous at a meeting in Peking two months before; the *Wen hui bao* review, written by Jiang Qing's protégé Yao Wenyuan, echoed that view. The Peking press ignored Yao's article, and the cultural denizens of the capital still insisted that Wu Han's play was fine.

Later it became known why Mao and Jiang felt the play raised political—not merely artistic—issues: the playwright, by analogy, seemed to be sniping at Mao's dismissal of a worthy minister, his defense minister Peng Dehuai, for being too critical in the wake of the failure of the Great Leap Forward. But the whole affair was a storm in the teacup of Jiang's maneuvering. Mao *praised* Hai Rui in 1959! And Wu Han's first piece of writing on the subject was directly inspired by Mao's singling out Hai Rui for emulation!

Yet by 1965 there was a new situation, not least in the influence Jiang wielded upon Mao.

"One day," Jiang remarked, "a comrade gave the chairman a copy of Wu Han's *Biography of Zhu Yuanzhang* for him to read." But Jiang, for reasons of her own, had already formed a negative opinion of Wu Han and all his writings, including this biography of a Ming dynasty emperor. "I said, 'Don't,'" she went on, "'the chairman is very tired. The author only wants a fee for the manuscript, or to make a name for himself. Just let him publish it. We'll then review and criticize it after publication. I also want to criticize his other work, *Hai Rui Dismissed from Office*.'" Jiang was planning to ambush Wu Han.

She saw Vice-Mayor Wu Han (and his protector, Mayor Peng Zhen) as a symbol of the Peking cultural establishment that had treated her as a buzzing mosquito in the early 1950s and as an obstacle on her path to power in the Party propaganda department and the Ministry of Culture. The analogy between Hai Rui and General Peng Dehuai (which may never have existed in the playwright's mind) provided an appeal to Mao's vanity and to his feeling of being hemmed in by grumblers and foot-draggers.

The later official description of how the article on *Hai Rui* came into being was enough to chill the spine of any Chinese intellectual. Yao wrote the piece at the "request" of Mao, said *People's Daily*, under the "direct guidance" of Jiang Qing, with the "concrete assistance" of Zhang Chunqiao, Shanghai Party chief and friend of Jiang.

In the 1960s Jiang Qing picked up from where she had left off

in the 1930s. It was as if the years between were lost, because her independence had been compromised and her body had been a hos-
tage to illness. She was back in the arts again! And this time not as a
doll, but as one of the bosses, doing what the men did! She had always hated the Confucian tradition whereby "women rule in the
family, while men rule outside it," and now, with the single stone of
power, she could knock down that philosophic bird as well as the
particular crows and hawks that had pecked at her flesh in the past.

In the Shanghai of the 1930s, Jiang was battling to preserve her
independence; the goal was the negative one of avoiding being
pushed around by others more powerful than she. Moving toward
the center of power in the winter of 1965–66, Jiang had passed beyond her negative goal and was poised for self-expression.

In Peking, Mayor Peng tried to limit the significance of Yao's
article on *Hai Rui* to the realm of academic debate. But Mao and
Jiang were in the mood for linkage; they tied literary, political, and
foreign-policy issues into one apocalyptic package. Anyone who
opposed them, on the merits of a play, on their newly vitriolic view
of the Soviet Union, even on a matter as small as an attempt to bor-
row a forbidden book from a library, was given horns and a tail as a
"class enemy." "Look, the world is being turned upside down," Mao
wrote in an amazing poem in the form of a conversation between
two birds, and that was what Mao and Jiang wanted.

It was a military man, Luo Ruiqing, chief of the army's General
Staff, who was the first top victim of the Cultural Revolution. A foe
of Defense Minister Lin Biao, who was now in constant contact with
Mao and Jiang in Shanghai, General Luo was insufficiently anti-
Soviet for Mao's taste. Not less important, Jiang Qing felt Luo had
opposed her, and she did not like Luo's wife. After a series of sharp
maneuvers, Luo lost his job. Jiang Qing was delighted.

Had General Luo not placed spies in her theater-reform entourage to report back on her every move? Had he not tipped off a
newspaper to report on her growing political role, when her plan,
based on the wishes of Mao and the advice of Mayor Ke, was to op-
erate incognito for the time being? Annoyed with him, she had
phoned him, but he did not seem to respect her, he felt the office of
the General Staff could do anything it liked, and she had hung up
on him. Now the man was paid off.*

"Comrade Jiang Qing talked with me yesterday," Lin Biao said

---

* Soon Luo jumped (or was he pushed?) out of a sixth-floor window. He survived.

to a meeting of the leathery toughs of the Chinese military. "She is very sharp politically on issues of art and literature." Sounding as Ronald Reagan might sound on announcing the appointment of Rita Hayworth to the Joint Chiefs of Staff, the defense minister went on: "She has many opinions that are valuable. You should pay good attention to them. . . . From now on all army documents on the arts will cross her desk."

The year 1966, perhaps the most exciting of Jiang Qing's life, had begun with an appointment in the army that was a sweet vindication of her self-image as a fighter. She was to be chief adviser to an army of three million on opera, dance, music, and novels. She was to wear khaki fatigues as the male officers did. The job put Jiang into the mainstream of political power.

In addition, Jiang's presence in the leadership of his army helped Lin Biao's bid to be Mao's deputy and successor. And the Lin-Jiang bargain strengthened Mao's hand against Liu, Deng, and the bureaucratic establishment.

Mao began to force out his foes, including Peng Zhen. He swam in the Yangzi to suggest that anyone hungry to succeed him would have to bide his time. He wrote a wall poster saying that everything in China was rotten and asking the masses to echo him in posters of their own. Finally he came back to Peking to anoint at ten vast rallies eleven million Red Guards for their task of "rebelling" against the bureaucracy. Jiang Qing was with him each step of the way and seemingly involved in every decision. She was a force at Central Committee and other meetings during the summer, proudly introducing herself as "a soldier." As Mao turned to youth—"they have less learning but more truth"—she helped prepare the ground by a month-long survey of trends on the leading Chinese campuses.

Much less of a traditionalist than Mao, Jiang reveled in the new lust to combat old things; she fueled the drive to smash temples, ransack the homes of intellectuals for ancient books, and in general to ban everything not born since Jiang Qing's phoenixlike rise from the ashes.

She loved it all. The breaking down of formal procedures in favor of a personal style of operation. The idea that the pen and the gun were the two tools for making a fresh and better world. The new stress on the theater as politics, and on politics as theater, as in the dawn rallies where, standing beside Mao, she languidly raised an arm to acknowledge the applause of the millions, who were "masses" to Mao, "an audience" to her. A British resident of Peking recalled a political rally at the airport. "Jiang Qing was waving her red book to the crowd, and Red Guards were shouting and clapping; her eyes were shining and bolting out from her head in an almost indecent lapping up of the adulation."

Jiang Qing loved that spectacle, from the purple balcony at the Gate of Heavenly Peace, of the two crisp characters of her name, written on banners praising her achievements in opera reform; it was even more exciting than the sight of her name on the billboards in Shanghai had been when she played Nora. Not least she loved the awareness, as the rays from the "Red Sun of Our Hearts" (Mao) gave her more vigor than all the chemical rays in Moscow's hospitals could do, that she now had the power to *get even* with all those reptiles who had made her past unhappy.

There was a psychological "fit" between Jiang and the Cultural Revolution. A nation in awe of authority and obsessed by the need to maintain harmony was throwing both to the winds. For someone of traditional upper-class background, like Deng Yingchao, it was appalling. But for a rootless one, always aspiring but often slighted, like Jiang, it was exciting. Authority had always been wielded *against* her. The appeal to harmony often had seemed an excuse to stifle her self-expression. The girl who had summed up her youth with the cold remark, "As a matter of fact, I was insulted everywhere in Jinan," welcomed any sign that heaven and earth were to change places.

For many people, the psychological "fit" between Jiang and the Cultural Revolution was ominous, proof of the madness of the mid-1960s. Socially conservative families felt that she lacked taste and restraint. "The peasants," reported one Red Guard who went to the villages, "were certain the nation would collapse if put into the hands of a woman."

Jiang's championing of the piano was a symbol of her untraditionalism. A natural candidate to be condemned as "bourgeois" during the Cultural Revolution—along with jeans, Beethoven, sunglasses, and many other things that failed to qualify as both Chinese and dull—this un-Chinese instrument came through the Cultural Revolution unscathed! This was because the Western-type individualism of it had liberated Jiang as a girl. Sitting down and playing the piano had opened new windows of the imagination for the young girl at the Arts Academy in Jinan. A Western and individualistic instrument as it is, *precisely because it is that,* the piano was permitted a role in Jiang's revolutionary theater pieces.

Jiang helped Mao by personally building up three connections of great political importance; with Lin Biao, whom Mao had not always found it easy to relate to at a man-to-man level; with the "armed intellectuals" of the Shanghai left, who were not by background or temperament part of Mao's own sphere; and, during 1966, with her old collaborator and coprovincial, Kang Sheng, whose command of dirty tricks became indispensable to Mao as the Cultural Revolution itself became one big dirty trick.

Mao, in turn, in mid-1966 gave Jiang an even more important job than the one Lin Biao had given her a few months before. She was made deputy head (Chen Boda, scribe of the Court Faction, was head) of the Cultural Revolution Group, which was the steering committee of the Cultural Revolution, and, as Mao forced Liu Shaoqi and Deng Xiaoping out of effective power in the long, hot summer of 1966, essentially the government of China under Emperor Mao.

The Cultural Revolution Group was a kitchen cabinet of the Mao-Jiang court. Jiang's Shanghai friend Zhang Chunqiao was a second deputy chairman, and the other two members were Kang Sheng, back at the center of things after relative eclipse in the 1950s, and Yao Wenyuan, whom Jiang had introduced to Mao when they came to Shanghai the previous year. It was an amazing elevation for Jiang Qing. Not even a member of the Central Committee, she was put into a Politburo-type position, alongside other Politburo members, to help Mao run the country.

To conceive how prejudiced and unrepresentative of the nation the Cultural Revolution Group was, one might imagine this parallel in the United States: President Reagan fires his cabinet and all but a handful of old loyalists from the White House staff, and appoints the leaders of the Moral Majority, under the supervision of Nancy Reagan, as an emergency government of the United States, to be chaired in part-time fashion by himself.

Liu and Deng tried to limit the scope of the Cultural Revolution, and belatedly they tried to save themselves. But probably there was nothing they could have done that would have satisfied Mao's and Jiang's demands upon them. "My mistake is that I'm the president," Liu exclaimed in mixed exasperation and bewilderment at Jiang's catalogue of charges against him, and he was correct to think that her concern was simply to get rid of him.* Mao wanted to es-

---

* The first emperor of the Song dynasty, who, when asked by the fearful king of the Southern Tang state, "What is wrong with us, that you plan to destroy us?" replied: "Your guilt is your existence; I cannot sleep peacefully with somebody standing by my bed."

tablish more deeply the values of his revolution, to solve the problem of bureaucracy and to get rid of people who consistently disagreed with him. But to a degree he was fighting two phantoms: socialism's failure to achieve what he thought it would, and his own mortality. These problems could have no answer, no political answer.

If everything that Mao had grown in his socialist garden turned out to be weeds, perhaps the soil simply could not produce the gorgeous blooms Marx had promised. If Mao was wrestling with the affront of his own mortality, *no* colleague who reached the number two position could ever meet with his approval. So it was that the Cultural Revolution had no political program; nor did it produce a new type of rule, only a new set of assistants for the ruler, chief among them the most unlikely candidate, the one from outside politics, with no merit in the revolution but only a readiness to be ferociously loyal—his own wife.

The real issue was Mao's evolution from optimistic Marxist to quizzical monkey-king as he faced his declining years and tried to fly from a recent past—the post–Great Leap Forward consolidation—that he did not like. Because Mao's personal predicament and vision were the keys to the upheaval that began at the end of 1965, Jiang Qing's role as his newly needed wife was second in importance only to Mao's.

"I was a circulating sentry," Jiang said of herself; the key to her effectiveness was that everyone knew *whose* sentry she was. Throughout the 1960s, the fluctuations in Jiang's fortunes, and in her formal ranking within the leadership, corresponded to the ebb and flow of Mao's own colossal power. When air force chief Wu Faxian knelt by her chair to take dictation, and when Zhou Enlai shouted "Ten Thousand Years to Jiang Qing!" Jiang knew that in flattering her, these colleagues had an eye on their standing with Mao. She knew it, and at times she resented it. Even the heroic youth were lauding her as a great disciple of Mao's, she realized, not as a leader in her own right.

But for the moment, the half loaf she had was a million times better than the crumbs she existed on in the 1950s.

The persona of the questing youth Yunhe, the actress Lan Ping, and the frustrated housewife of the mid-1950s all came to the surface in the public activity of the mature Jiang Qing.

The reformer of dance, who instructed ballerinas to perform men's steps, breaking down the long-standing division in Chinese dance between steps men did and steps women did, and who arrived for a rehearsal wearing military fatigues, was the young Yunhe who felt that "men's work" was a nonexistent category. The speech-maker, fixing her hair as she prepared to face a rally of five thousand Red Guards, was Lan Ping putting on her makeup before striding out to move an audience in the Golden City Theater. The Cultural Revolution politician who insisted that when an official was purged *his wife* also be struck down ("Liao Zhigao's wife is very bad" . . . "Wang Guangmei is a spy" . . .) was the housewife who at South and Central Lakes during the 1950s quarreled with the wives of Mao's two sons by Yang Kaihui.

The didactic mistress of the arts was the Yunhe who told the Fei household how to run its affairs, the Lan Ping who catalogued for Tang Na his weaknesses of character and the ways to overcome them, and the Jiang of the 1950s who told her nurse what color dresses to wear and her interpreter how to slice a carp.

But the didacticist was now instructing, not a few servants, but hundreds of millions of citizens, and banning films and books and plays as a janitor turns out lights. The specialist in family feuds was now throwing pots and pans in the inner chambers of the highest organs of the Chinese state, bringing not just tears to the eyes of rel-atives, but ruined careers to thousands of officials and performing artists all over the nation. The stylish performer was now not merely the object of applause from a theaterful of admirers, but a model whose styles became law because they were backed by the authority of a police state.

Zhang Zhaomei, a high official of the Ministry of Petroleum, remarked at a meeting held to discuss Jiang's latest bright idea: "Jiang Qing is a female comrade and she loves self-adulation." He was purged for saying out loud what scores of Peking's male politi-cal leaders were whispering behind closed doors.

Jiang Qing saw the Red Guards as *hers.* In Yanan, the Chinese Revolution had been Mao's, but in the Cultural Revolution period Jiang began to see it as hers as much as Mao's. Her revolutionary idealism had always been an aspect of her drive for self-expression. Paradoxically, since joining the revolution in Yanan, she had felt little sense of self-expression, but rather a nagging feeling of sup-pression. All the passion that she once put into her physical rela-tionship with Mao, and into her hopes for the young Li Na, she now poured into Mao's *and her* Cultural Revolution.

At her mansion in Shanghai, Song Qingling awaited Jiang

Qing's arrival. It was the height of Red Guard turmoil in the city. Some militants wanted to storm Sun Yat-sen's widow's house, cut off her long hair, and take away her books. Zhou Enlai intervened to prevent this, and as a result of the incident Mao asked Jiang to visit Song and personally explain to her the meaning of the Cultural Revolution.

Jiang strode in like a commander-in-chief. She was unrecognizable as the modest young wife whom Song Qingling had entertained during the 1950s. The non-Communist Song sat like a sphinx as Jiang discoursed on how evil Mao's enemies were and how she loved the youth who were unencumbered by past traditions. "But there should be more control," Song objected. "Harming innocent people is wrong." Jiang froze up. It was as if a mask had been placed over her features, as she stared in silent hostility at this gentlewoman of the older generation. "Jiang Qing was personally affronted," said an aide of Song who was present. "The Red Guards mattered tremendously to her ego. She simply could not imagine that anyone could see the whole movement as mistaken." Song, who had liked Jiang in the 1950s, found her manifest drive to power distasteful. "Song Qingling, like many other people, liked Jiang Qing only when she was on the sidelines of politics," the aide commented. "When she saw Jiang's love of power, she detested her."

"Tao Zhu *oppressed* me!" Jiang cried, back in Peking, to a vast crowd of sweating Red Guards in the Great Hall of the People. "And also our Cultural Revolution Group," she added as an afterthought. Speaking slowly in her sensual voice, she explained to the young zealots how she had gone the second mile in an effort to save Tao, a Politburo member from South China. "I was patient with him. How *much* I tried to help him—but he simply *wouldn't* change." She sounded like Lan Ping ticking off Tang Na. But her listeners, moved by the excitement of political turmoil and of their trip to Peking to rub shoulders with the leaders of their nation, could not be expected to know that Jiang's passions were as much personal as political.

A woman with the look of an intellectual was pushed onto the stage of the Workers' Stadium, eyes staring defiantly, hair disheveled, arms twisted high by a soldier. Jiang Qing watched the scene with an impassive expression. A number of her foes were to get their due on this frigid evening in December 1966, but no case was more piquant to her than that of the struggling woman with her arms held back at a grotesque angle. Her name was Fan Jin. She was editor of

Peking Evening News, and along with Wu Han, the playwright, one of Peng Zhen's deputy mayors.

One of Fan's crimes was to have published, during the un-Maoist season of the early 1960s, satirical essays by Deng Tuo that hinted Mao was a megalomaniac and to have sponsored a poem of Deng's that, in a complicated reference to "clouds and rain" (which can mean sexual intercourse in Chinese literature) implied that Jiang was a semiprostitute who was trying to spring to power from Mao's bed. Fan Jin's other crime, known to fewer but unforgettable and unforgivable for Jiang, was that she had succeeded Jiang as the lover of Yu Qiwei, living with him as his legal wife until his death in 1958.

A deep regret had always smoldered in Jiang Qing's heart about the personal aspect of her relationship with Yu Qiwei. Perhaps she felt that the real reason for his departure for Peking in 1933 was that he didn't want to live with her anymore after she had taken up with a boyfriend during his time in prison. It may have rankled her that the affair with Yu Qiwei did not resume when she visited him in Peking in 1934. There could even have been an aching wish—now that the Mao-Jiang household had taken on the political significance of a dynastic court—that she had borne a son by Yu Qiwei, as she had not done by Mao. For whatever reason, something in Jiang made her wish to see Fan brought low.

Following the trial at the Workers' Stadium, Jiang closed in on Fan Jin with a long list of charges and a furtive campaign within the air force, organized by Wu Faxian, its chief, to have Fan's current husband, an air force officer named Zhao Yutong, divorce her.

Fan Jin confessed to little, but her career and marriage were ended. She was arrested in the spring of 1968 and died not long afterward—not before Li Min wrote on June 24, 1968, a wall poster attack on Marshal Nie Rongzhen, a former associate of Yu Qiwei, for trying to "protect" Fan by "covering up" some of her allegedly unsavory deeds within the bureaucracy.

During the forced remembrances of past "oppression" by Liu and Deng, which were a specialty of the Cultural Revolution, Jiang coined a unique slogan. "We must take into account not only the fifty days and the seventeen years," she said in reference to an anti-Maoist period in 1966 and the entire stretch of bureaucratic rule since 1949, "but also the 1930s." Jiang wanted to drag the "wrong line on art and literature" of the 1930s into the firing line of the Cultural Revolution. Why? Because such a framework allowed her to get even with those who had taken a "wrong line on Lan Ping" in Shanghai during the 1930s.

During the 1950s, Jiang had been quite relaxed about her theatrical past. True, because she was Mao's wife, she was never identified as an actress, and there was a ban on screening *Old Bachelor Wang, Blood on Wolf Mountain,* and her other movies. Yet to her own staff Jiang talked nostalgically about her stage and screen days. In Peking as late as 1962 there were private screenings of *Old Bachelor Wang.* And in Shanghai she sometimes asked actor-directors such as Zheng Junli and Zhao Dan to a quiet party at the former French Club.

But in the 1960s a fire that seemed to have been out turned into a roaring conflagration. Jiang became obsessed with the evils of 1930s culture and with the still-living perpetrators of those evils. Each molehill of a setback she had ever experienced in the 1930s was now blown up into a mountain of revenge.

During the Cultural Revolution, Jiang was able to pick up some of the themes she had dealt with in her article "Our Life" in 1937: the social role of art; anti-imperialism; the importance of will. In the tough world of prewar Shanghai, these themes meant something to her as an actress and as a struggling young woman. Now she crudely dressed them up with a larger political meaning.

The husk was politics, the kernel was a personal drive. In Shanghai, Zhang Geng had tried to pressure her to a marriage bed, Tian Han had taken insufficient notice of her, Xia Yan had given the lead in *Sai Jinhua* not to her but to Wang Ying, and Zhou Yang had failed to help her. In the 1960s, Jiang's method of turning the tables was to declare that the Communist Party in Shanghai during the 1930s had been dominated by a wrong political line, "only recently revealed." All four men were now, at Jiang's instigation, hounded into the streets, arrayed in dunce caps, by crowds of young zealots who had not even been born in the 1930s. They lost their jobs, their families suffered terribly, and the nation was told they were "ghosts," "monsters," and "clumsy cows." Jiang remarked gaily to an audience of film workers that Xia Yan "has nothing to do but lie around in bed all day."

With Zhou Yang she had an exchange that showed how keenly she resented the allegation that in Shanghai her interests had drifted away from Communist politics. "Did you know," she said to Zhou, "that I was in Shanghai then [the mid-1930s] and what I sought?" Zhou Yang, who realized he was already bested, replied: "I knew."

Jiang rammed home the point that was now important to her career prospects: "I was trying to make contact with the Communist Party." Zhou Yang lowered his head in silence.

It was as if Jiang had kept a list over the years of all those who had opposed her, and now pulled it out and tracked down each one of them. Yang Shangkun, the former head of the General Office of the Party Central Committee, who in 1952 had helped persuade Mao to send Jiang away to Russia when she did not want to go, was grabbed from his home and marched off, bent and gasping, a huge wooden placard around his neck, his name inscribed on it, with X's slashed across each of the three characters, a sign that he had been canceled as an item in Chinese history. At the Workers' Stadium, ten thousand Red Guards, who knew nothing of capitalism, denounced Yang as a capitalist, while a soldier twisted his arm to keep him in a bowing position, and Jiang smiled tautly from a balcony above the stage of retribution.

Forgetting her own principle that a woman should be granted her autonomy, she acquiesced in the denunciation of Kang Keqing, wife of the Red Army hero Zhu De, and Zhang Qian, wife of the foreign minister Chen Yi, following their husbands' "exposure" as "capitalist-roaders." She amended a document calling for struggle against Tao Zhu and Deng Xiaoping to include both men's wives as well. When two senior generals, Xu Xiangqian and Nie Rongzhen, became victims of the Cultural Revolution, Jiang jumped in to denounce Xu's wife, Huang Jie, as a "renegade" and Nie's wife, Zhang Ruihua, as an "enemy agent."

One day she might rue all this careless revenge, for its underlying rationale—"What your husband does rubs off on you"—carried great danger for her own case.

Even Wang Guanlan was on her list of "bad men"; had Sister Xu, his wife and Jiang's longtime friend and political mentor, after all not helped her as forthrightly as she wished in settling at Yanan in 1937? So many people perished—many driven by despair to suicide—as the wind of self-righteousness and revenge blew to gale proportions, fanned by Jiang Qing more vigorously than by anyone, that in August 1966 the crematoria of Peking could not cope, and one year later, after a long winter of fighting, anguish, and suspicion, August 1967 was known in the city as "a month of death."

Jiang did not effect these purges single-handedly; some of them would have occurred without her. But she pushed hard for many of them, she shaped the crusade to her own ends, and she spiced it with passion and drama.

From Hong Kong, the football player of the 1930s who had slept with Lan Ping in a room of the Hui Zhong Hotel, after the young pair had watched the romantic movie *A Beauty's Heart,* followed in wonder the rise of Jiang's political career. "The vigor and valor of mine that you liked have gone," he wrote in an open letter, "but I am not unmoved by you, even thirty-five years later, and still have some feeling toward you." The ex-football star who had found Lan a risk-taker now observed from afar the same personality, still taking risks, on a broad new stage.

"I just hope," he concluded, "that your hunger for power does not turn your mind and that you will take into account the common people of China."

The phone rang at the Shanghai apartment of Zheng Junli, the movie director who had been best man at Jiang's marriage with Tang Na. It was the office of Zhang Chunqiao; the Shanghai Party boss wanted to see Mr. Zheng immediately. Zhang Chunqiao explained to Zheng Junli that Jiang needed to trace "certain materials" from the 1930s that concerned her "personal life." The movie director was asked to hand over to the city's Party office all letters, photos, clippings, and manuscripts in his possession that touched on Jiang's history. This he sought to do; he and his wife, Huang Chen, also a movie director, made a package of precious memorabilia and sent it down to the Party offices on the Bund. But Zheng was worried, at once by the breadth and vagueness of the request, in a season when intellectuals were being faulted politically for deeds and words from years previously, and by the repeated mention of "a letter, or letters" of Jiang's, or to Jiang. What could these be?

"Who knows?" he said to Huang Chen after his second conversation with Zhang Chunqiao. "Any day now I may go out and not return."

Up in Peking, Jiang was not satisfied with Zhang Chunqiao's haul. Did she think that Zheng Junli had kept a copy of her incandescent letter to Tang Na of June 1936? Was she worried about records of her dealings with Cui Wanqiu and other non-Communist or Nationalist figures?

She worked through an extraordinary network of soldiers and VIP wives that had come into existence as a result of her bargain a few months before with Defense Minister Lin Biao. She talked with Ye Chun, Lin's fast-rising second wife, who looked up to her, knowing how important she was to Lin's hopes of succeeding Mao, about the new situation she found herself in; if one was a leader of

China, did one not have to take images into account and correct any wrong impressions?

The next day Jiang Tengjiao, a military officer in Shanghai, received a phone call from Wu Faxian, the fat, accommodating head of China's air force who had become part of the intimate Jiang–Lin Biao circle. Ye Chun needed him in Peking for an urgent "political task," General Wu told Jiang Tengjiao. Ye explained, on Jiang Qing's behalf, the need to retrieve memorabilia, especially "a letter or letters" from the homes of Zheng Junli, Gu Eryi (married in the same ceremony as Jiang and Tang), and other survivors of Shanghai's left-wing Bohemia of the 1930s. Jiang Tengjiao flew back to Shanghai to make plans.

Meanwhile, Zheng Junli wrote directly to Jiang Qing on October 7, 1966. "I don't remember having kept any of your letters," he explained courteously, "either those you wrote to us or those to Zhao Dan and his wife." But the movie director had searched his files for photos. "Here are a few old pictures of the 1930s; dispose of them as you wish."

Zheng Junli and Huang Chen were at home at 7:00 P.M. on October 9 when in burst a band of men wearing masks that left only their eyes visible. They were not really Red Guards, as they claimed, for Jiang Tengjiao had selected the sons of some "reliable" cadres and officers for a climactic search, at the Zheng-Huang home and four others, for the evidence whose existence, or possible existence, bothered Jiang Qing.*

All night these temporary Red Guards, uttering pious political phrases, went through every inch of the Zheng-Huang apartment, turning the pages of each book for any loose pieces of paper, shouting as they made a great mess that everything to do with the "chief" (*shou zhang*), Jiang Qing, had to be retrieved. Zheng and Huang said they had nothing more, but the intruders took virtually all movable papers, including Zheng's draft manuscripts, a diary, some scripts of Huang's, and the school notes of a son. "If you were in Peking," they declared as they left at 5:00 A.M. the next day, "you'd have been shot to death long before this."

---

* The five points of "army discipline" that Jiang Tengjiao laid down for his men that night are not without interest: "(1) only letters, notebooks, photos, and other written materials are needed, no other things should be searched for; (2) when asked just answer: 'From Shanghai Red Guards headquarters'; (3) team leaders should carry pistols in a concealed manner but are not allowed to fire without authorization; (4) the military trucks' license plates must be removed or covered by paper; and (5) only tell the fighters of the garrison platoon and the selected sons and daughters: 'We are searching for a blueprint or a confidential air force document which has been lost in the homes of these people.'"

Jiang Qing is "very satisfied," Ye Chun reported to Jiang Tengjiao on the phone the next morning. "The letter, or letters," and much else, apparently had been found.

Jiang was concerned not only with the records of her romantic affairs but also with her political record in the 1930s. Wang Jipo, an official in the police department of the city of Shanghai, was summoned to see her in the spring of 1966. Apparently there were some misleading records of her arrest and imprisonment, and subsequent release, by the Nationalists in 1934, she explained to Wang, and she really felt it would be best if all material on that matter still in Shanghai files were taken out and given to her.* Wang dragged his feet on the request, according to his wife's story.

"Why hasn't Wang Jipo sent that material I asked him for?" Jiang asked a staff member in irritation late in 1966. She escalated the pressure for the recovery of documents (which may not have existed in Shanghai; the Nationalists took many files with them to Taiwan) using Wu Faxian, who was pliable and able to supply a plane at the drop of a chopstick. General Wu, perhaps assisted by Kang Sheng, arrested key members of the Shanghai city government and police department; more than twenty officials, including the unfortunate Wang Jipo, were flown to Peking and imprisoned. The same night a new search was made for documents about Jiang Qing's brush with the Nationalist government in 1934. But the results were not fully satisfactory. It was as difficult to ascertain that there were *no* papers as it was to retrieve papers and photos that did exist.

On a cold winter evening in January 1967, Jiang, Ye Chun, and the police minister, Xie Fuzhi, who was almost as obsequious toward Jiang as Wu Faxian was, dined together at Fishing Terrace Guesthouse to discuss what to do with the haul of material. "Solve the problem forever in one act" (*yi lao yong yi*) was the decision that emerged. Ye Chun phoned air force headquarters, where she virtually ruled the roost, being Wu Faxian's intimate and the wife of the head of China's military, Mao's deputy and heir, and ordered the precious boxes to be sent at once to Maojiawan, the Lin Biao residence.

The three leaders drove in a black "Red Flag" sedan to Maojiawan. Gates clinked, passes were shown, registration numbers were noted. Jiang, Ye, and Xie got out of the car and gathered in a

---

* Jiang Qing called her arrest a case of "mistaken arrest," a curious statement unless her purpose was to undermine the credibility of the accusation that she wrote a confession to win her release.

small courtyard at the rear of the mansion. The secretary of Lin Biao's office arrived to assist, just as the boxes of documents and photos were carried in by bright-eyed boys from air force headquarters. Staff in military uniform lit a fire in a briquette stove in a servants' kitchen in a corner of the courtyard. Jiang folded her arms, as was her habit when she was slightly nervous. The flames rose high and lit up the faces, Ye's tight and mousy, Jiang's expressionless, Xie's showing great pleasure. The police minister turned to the boxes, unsealed them, and began feeding the pieces into the stove. Ye moved across to help him. Jiang paced slowly up and down one wing of the courtyard, ten feet from the stove, glancing from the corners of her eyes. Now and then she paused to gaze intently at the fumbling hands of Ye and Xie as they pushed a page or a photo at the red briquettes. No one spoke.

A few months later Zheng Junli was put into prison, where he died in 1969. Wang Jipo of the Shanghai police department remained in prison until his death five years later. Gu Eryi, the actor, and Zhao Dan, the foremost actor of the era, both wed in the same ceremony as Jiang and Tang Na in 1936, soon were in prison; Gu died there.* (In China, imprisonment for political reasons often is a lifetime fate, for rehabilitation is unlikely unless the political pendulum swings.)

Had she not been Mao's wife, Jiang would have been a perfect target of the Cultural Revolution. With her bourgeois tastes and having been released from a Nationalist prison after writing a confession, she would have struck trouble in the "antirightist" campaign of 1956–57, and even more a decade later, when the Red Guards rampaged. "In 1956–57," Tang Na observed from his exile in France, "I would have been arrested, and in 1966 I would have been killed." In Paris, the worst he suffered from the Cultural Revolution was a gnawing regret that his former wife should be causing so much damage to their old Bohemian circle, and so many sightseers flocking to the restaurant he owned to gape at the man Jiang Qing once loved that he had to sell the place. "Some Chinese newspapers said I kept a special room at the restaurant full of

---

* Jiang Qing's effort to purify her past continued into 1968 and beyond. On February 23, 1968, she handed Wu Faxian a dossier about Sun Junqing, a Shanghai official, and said she "wanted to see him"; on March 1, after Wu had brought Sun to Peking in a special plane, Jiang signed a document that led to his arrest. The next day, March 2, 1968, Jiang asked General Wu to bring a former servant woman from Shanghai, whom Jiang suspected may have observed incidents between herself and Tang Na; eventually Wu wrote a report about this woman's "black ties" with Jiang's enemies in Shanghai and with "Hong Kong circles" (an easy cancellation of anyone's reputation); Jiang signed it, and the woman went to prison, where she died.

photos of Jiang Qing," Tang recalled with a bitter laugh. "Many people believed this funny idea and came to the Fontaine de Jade to see which photos I had chosen for my special room."

"You must all want to know how Chairman Mao is," Jiang Qing cried as she swept in to address a mass meeting. The throng, bent on destruction and yet blown up with a religious-type conviction that they were doing good, shouted back that, yes, they certainly wanted to know. "Let me tell you," Jiang said in the tone of one who has just arisen from the marriage bed, "he is in robust health!"

"We always thought she looked very well groomed," a former Red Guard recalled. "And her voice was memorable; a deep but very feminine voice." Another Red Guard, who eventually suffered from Jiang's fury, could not help but admire her performances. "What she must have been like when she was still young and beautiful!"

Jiang loved the cry "Auntie Jiang, we love you!" (*Jiang ah yi, wo men ai ni!*) that often went up, from men and women alike. A rip-roaring fight pleased her almost as much, as long as she could shine at its epicenter. It did not seem to matter that she often spoke nonsense (Capitalism has produced only "rotten" culture, which does not "appeal to the people," just a flood of "strip-tease, impressionism, Fauvism—there's no end to the obscenity. . . .").

At Peking University she came upon hostile students who shouted, "We'll hang you!" and "We'll fry you!" More excited by the drama than afraid of the danger, she showed a rare flash of humor in her reply. "I am terribly busy," she declared, "but I'll invite you to come and hang me, and fry me, just as soon as I find the time."

"I am an ordinary Communist Party member," she began a speech to a meeting of the Military Commission. "For a long period all I did was act as the Chairman's secretary." It was a way of sounding modest and important at the same time. Disarming the officers by saying she was sure they knew more of Mao's ways than she did ("I have enormous respect for you Red Army veterans"), she then talked intimately of Mao, greatly impressing an audience that held him in awe. (He loved "alley news," which Jiang did not; he liked his children to "talk back" to him.) She was just a pupil, she said, yet in the next breath she claimed she had educated Mao on art and literature.

"You know, maybe I'm too self-confident," she purred, confessing that she simply could not bear to see evil triumph, and had to fight back. "If only you all knew the story," she said in discussing how Peng Zhen had frustrated her theatrical reforms, "how angry you would be." Should there not be more portrayal on China's stage and screen of military heroes? "Of course there should." But there were people who stood in the way, who "wouldn't listen to the chairman, *nor would they listen to me.*" After a long speech about cultural matters that the military men knew little of, she ended by telling them to be sure to "set her right" on points where she might have "gone astray."

In this revealing speech Jiang said something of herself which, though ridiculed in China in recent years, was true. She had many weaknesses, she said, sighing, and though she tried to study, her studies had not been systematic. "Yet if I have a strong point," she came back, her head tilted to one side in the way she employed for emphasis, "it is that when I get my teeth into something, I persist, I follow through, I get the damn thing done."

And Jiang showed how resentful she was at having been hamstrung in the past. "You know in Yanan," she told her audience of soldiers, "I got into trouble for wearing a military cap. I was *ordered* not to wear it." Now, wearing a People's Liberation Army cap as she spoke, she was enjoying a vindication. Wasn't she a real soldier after all!

On a winter evening at the height of her power, Jiang appeared before a rally of high school students. The agenda was a talk by her on how dictatorship and democracy "relate to each other," and a "struggle" against a selected covey of "wrongdoers" to make an example of them.

Jiang was in wonderful form, tossing her voice to the far ends of the stadium, dropping it to a whisper to gather the students' attention into her palm. She said that youthful wrongdoers should be handled according to the policy, "Cure the disease, save the patient," but that middle-aged and old wrongdoers should be "struggled against till they fall, struggled against till they stink, struggled against till their prestige has gone." In the wings she had waiting some plump candidates—a secretary of the State Council, and a leading Peking city politician.

Like one of the directors who used to order her around onstage in Shanghai, Jiang raised an arm toward the two distinguished officials, at this moment her marionettes, and cried out to the frenzied youths: "Would you like me to bring out Zhou Rongxin and Yong

Wentao for you to see?" The crowd hoarsely shouted, "Yes, yes, we would!" Jiang swung around to face her drooping victims. "Come onto the stage," she ordered with a smile of triumph. The crowd called out, "Bow your heads!" Zhou and Yong emerged, half crawling, half pushed, to face a verdict from seven thousand children of revolution.

Jiang, with superb timing, allowed a few moments of delectation and then signaled a fresh scene: "Fine! A moment of calm, now. Young commanders, young soldiers of the rank and file! You have all recognized this pair for what they are. We shall permit them to retreat."

"Have them go back!" shouted the crowd, as obediently as they had demanded the victims come out. Then Jiang spoke about the wrongdoings the two men were responsible for (in effect, encouraging an "alternative" Red Guard group composed of offspring of the elite to oppose the more leftist, pro-Jiang Red Guards). She knew the technique of Camus' executioner: "I alternate kindness and violence. Psychologically, it's a good thing."

Many young people, reared in the routinized, unadventurous period after 1949, looked up to Jiang, because, in addition to the pleasure they took in loyalty, they were enticed by her spiritedness and her glamor. Who else would cry in front of one public, shout at another, refer to herself as *lao niang* (an earthy expression meaning something like "tough old granny"), and explain that she, Jiang Qing, had a *right* to be inconsistent?

Those of the generation of the 1960s were in a technical sense emancipated from the burdens—poverty, inequality of men and women, foreign exploitation—that had weighed down those of Jiang's generation. Yet a special woman from that earlier epoch, like Jiang, perhaps because she had had to battle to survive, impressed the young people; her flash of style from the past stood out handsomely on a plateau of conformity.

"It was as if Mao were speaking," a Shanghai actor recalled of a talk Jiang gave to a theatrical company when she arrived from Peking to help them with the reform of the opera *White-Haired Girl.* She swept into a meeting room at the city's Exhibition Hall, dressed in a grand cape, her eyes shining with excitement. "She was forceful, certain of herself. And how moved we actors were when she said she was bringing greetings from Chairman Mao and that he had asked her to wish us good luck in our performances!"

"We all believed she was speaking for Chairman Mao," a Peking cultural worker named Tan reminisced. "And she was a charming and persuasive person—except occasionally when she became hysterical and started screaming." Tan recalled Jiang's visit to the broadcasting station where he worked. "In the midst of great arguments between radicals and moderates, a girl named Li Zhuan came up to Jiang Qing. She felt she'd been wronged in the factional struggle. 'I'm not really bad,' she whimpered." Tan was amazed at Li's appeal, because her views were really on the moderate side. "But the girl's appeal struck a chord in Jiang. She took Li Zhuan's side. She put her arm around her, strode into the public meeting, and told the audience that, whatever the importance of the struggle, in the future 'her' Li Zhuan should be treated better." Tan summed up: "We liked Jiang Qing's impulsive, unbureaucratic ways."

The young ones did not know Jiang personally; had they done so, they might have become aware of an insecurity within her. But to see her in action was to be impressed and excited.

A Peking University student sat down to write a letter to Mao. It was the summer of 1967, and young Chen, embroiled in the struggles on campus between rebels and the Party establishment, had some suggestions for the supreme leader. Chen and his older sister took a bus to the reception office of the Central Committee in South and Central Lakes. Their plan was to ask an official there if Jiang Qing might be willing to pass the six-page letter on to Mao.

"I didn't have a lot of respect for Jiang Qing as a politician," Chen recalled, "but she was tremendously prominent and famous then—it seemed the best route to Mao." Just the day before at Peking University, Jiang had said to a small group of which Chen was a part: "Look, if you have something to say, to the chairman or to me, let me know—I'll arrange it."

At the reception office Chen's sister asked to see a minor official who was a neighbor of herself and her husband. Soon Qi Benyu, a very senior aide to Jiang Qing, came out to greet the young pair. "Comrade Jiang Qing would like to see you. We are driving out to Fishing Terrace."

Jiang strode out from her private office, her face tired but excited. Qi Benyu made a move to take Chen's sister, the senior of the two visitors, in to talk with Jiang Qing. Chen took a risk and said to Qi: "Comrade Jiang Qing is here; she can decide if I can join or not."

"*Both* come in," said Jiang grandly as she took Chen's arm and led him to the front of the group.

Jiang read the first few pages of Chen's letter and gave a grim smile. Chen squirmed in his wicker chair. He had written to Mao that Jiang Qing was throwing her weight around too much at Peking University. "I hadn't asked to see Jiang Qing," he explained later, "I just wanted my letter to reach Mao's hands." But Jiang responded to Chen as an eager, handsome student more than she responded to the written appeal to Mao that soon lay neglected in her lap.

Three hours later Jiang Qing ended the conversation. She had discussed family, psychology, health, and in a peck-and-swallow way the situation at Peking University. The formidable Qi had sat silent throughout, a page in the presence of his queen. Chen's sister had been largely neglected by Jiang. "Come again," Jiang said to the amazed Chen, "I'll see that you get to see the chairman. You know, I can see that you are braver and more intelligent than your sister."

"Only Jiang Qing would have received us on the spur of the moment like that," said Chen. "Zhou Enlai or Kang Sheng never would have done it. I still think she was unreliable and misguided as a politician. But she was really inspiring and energetic. She loved to reach down and embrace a young person from the ranks. She had a tendency to go against the tide—Qi Benyu thought only my sister should enter the private office; Jiang overturned him."

Chen went on: "When a person said to Jiang Qing, 'I want to be your follower,' she just couldn't resist that. If anyone said to her, 'Auntie Jiang, could we have a picture taken of you beside me?' she would be not angry but *happy*—and she'd scurry around and get a photographer right away."

It was a sultry July evening on the campus of Peking University. Their classes forgotten, students were writing wall posters, trading the latest gossip, and arguing about the merits of "work teams" sent by the government to supervise the school's participation in the Cultural Revolution. Adding to the excitement was the presence of Jiang Qing, striding from one center of activity to the next, smiling, frowning, waving a finger, tossing out greetings from Mao.

It was a high point of the Cultural Revolution. Jiang had been back in Peking only eight days, and Mao ten days, following their long stay in Shanghai and Hangzhou. There was an apocalyptic sense of expectancy in the capital city; the supreme leader and his exciting wife seemed to be promising a new world.

Jiang climbed to a dais set amid Ming-style pavilions at the eastern side of the campus, a row of lights hung in the graceful trees catching her radiant face. With her were Chen Boda, her senior colleague in the Cultural Revolution Group, and Kang Sheng, the old fox from Shandong who was evolving from Jiang's patron into her courtier. "Chairman Mao sends you his regards," she cried. After some political remarks she announced, her face growing taut, that this actually was to be an "argument meeting" (*bian lun hui*). The students could hardly believe their ears when they learned the topic.

"She has never been a true daughter-in-law!" The very trees shook with amazement: Jiang had come to this bastion of higher learning to "argue" against Zhang Shaohua, the young wife of Anqing, second son of Mao and Yang Kaihui, one of the hated beasts in her domestic jungle. "Her mother is a political swindler!" Putting bits of political icing on the cake of her personal grudge, she coupled Shaohua with capitalism, the "black line in art and literature," and the anti-China forces of the world. Again she screamed: "I have never acknowledged her as Chairman Mao's daughter-in-law! NOR HAS CHAIRMAN MAO HIMSELF!" The one thin reed that linked Shaohua to the occasion was that she had been a student in the school's literature department.

Jiang's speech seemed to go on forever. "Shaohua took advantage of Mao Anqing's mental illness to have sex with him—and so snare him into marriage." Soon Chen Boda rose from his chair on the dais and approached Jiang from behind. He leaned close to her, but she swept on. There were barbs against Liu Songlin, Shaohua's sister, the former wife of Mao Anying, who had died in Korea, as Jiang tied family politics and Cultural Revolution politics together into a riotous bundle. Chen touched Jiang's shoulder. She interrupted her flow of venom. Those near the front heard Chen whisper, "I think you should stop now." Jiang gave him a wild, stunned stare; one could have heard a pin drop among the ten thousand sitting on the ground as far as the eye could see.

"It's true, I *am* upset." She tossed her head up as if she were about to number even the faithful Chen Boda among her enemies. "For *ten years* I have suffered from this woman and her family. That is *why* I am upset!" Her voice was getting loud enough for the microphone to pick up. "Thanks to her, my heart problem has flared up again. . . ." Most of the students were silent. A few murmured against her. "You are not taking a revolutionary position," one girl, daughter of a cadre under attack, said loudly.

Mao took no action to stop Jiang exhibiting family feuds at political forums; perhaps no one dared tell him what Jiang said that night at Peking University.

Jiang was waging battles on other domestic fronts. She argued to Mao that Liu Songlin, who had married again, should no longer be allowed to come and go as she pleased at South and Central Lakes. And in a telephone campaign directed at the family of Mao's former wife in Changsha, she brought about disgrace, and loss of job, for the brother of Yang Kaihui and his wife after she discovered that this couple was trying to make use of the disorder of the Cultural Revolution to mount a revival of Yang Kaihui's memory and reputation.

When Li Min, the daughter of Mao and He Zizhen, took a husband, Jiang argued, as she had in the case of Songlin, that "when a daughter marries it's a case of water poured away" and that Li Min now should make her own living and financial arrangements. "She gets one quilt," Jiang said to her personal staff when the question of wedding gifts for Li Min came up, causing a furor, since they anticipated, and Li Min expected, a set of two quilts, two pillows, and one queen-sized cover.

Jiang drew closer still to Mao Yuanxin, Mao's nephew, who had graduated from Harbin Military Engineering Institute and was becoming a young politician to reckon with in the Northeast.

Jiang's relationship with Li Na was insecure, yet she pushed her daughter forward. During Li Na's years in the literature department of Peking University, from which she graduated in 1964 or 1965, she lived not at home but in a dormitory. But if mother and daughter seemed wary of each other, Jiang regaled Li Na with favors, including foreign movies, that were denied to Li Min.

One sweltering afternoon in August 1967 General Wu Faxian received a phone call from Ye Chun. Would he come at once to see Jiang Qing? The head of the air force sped to Fishing Terrace Guesthouse where Jiang and Ye, together with Li Na, were putting the finishing touches on a huge wall poster. Apparently its theme was an attack on wrongdoers at the military newspaper *Liberation Army Daily*.

The poster done, Jiang turned to Wu with a tired smile and began to put the case for the appointment of her only child as a senior editor of *Liberation Army Daily*. Wu's help was required on three matters. Jiang wanted the facilities of the air force made available to have the freshly done poster displayed around Peking that very afternoon. From the navy, the air force, and the Second Artillery Regiment, she wanted thirty men experienced in journalism to be ready to go that evening to the offices of *Liberation Army Daily*. And she asked Wu's "100 percent support" for the installation of her daughter in a leading post at the military publishing company.

"I completely accommodated her on all three points," Wu Faxian later recalled. The next day Li Na took over as a senior editor of China's military organ. Li Min attained no such post. Whether Li Na appreciated being pushed into high office by her mother is not known. Certainly the experience brought strains that contributed to Li Na's coming crisis.

In Shandong, with a phone call here and a private letter there, Jiang took care of a half brother. Li Ganqing once had chased away two girl bullies who attacked young Jiang in a field near Zhucheng. Now Jiang declared war against Li Ganqing's many enemies.

An investigation had begun as early as 1959, at the police headquarters of Shandong Province, to ascertain if it was true, as widely believed, that Li had collaborated with the Japanese and once been in the pay of the Nationalists. "You'd better watch out," Jiang wrote to him on May 12, 1960, in a letter of advice on how to conduct his defense. "Don't forfeit the big because of the small." She advised her half brother to keep calm and not to rock the boat in a display of outrage. "And don't be afraid," she ended. "You always have someone above to fall back on." The investigation of Li Ganqing smoldered on without a clear result.

In the new political atmosphere of April 1968, a Shandong official, Wang Xiaoyu, no doubt with an eye on Jiang's rise to fame and power, began a crusade against those in his own province who had begun the investigation of Li Ganqing. Wang approached Chen Boda. Soon six Shandong officials who had dared to question the background of Jiang's half brother found themselves in prison.

Wang Guangmei and Jiang Qing had gotten along cordially in the 1950s. Jiang would walk over to the spacious courtyard where Wang lived with Liu Shaoqi, whom she married in 1948 after he had divorced his fourth wife. Generally the talk was about family, clothes, and the problems of being the head of a political leader's household.

Wang's family was rich, well educated, and cosmopolitan. She spoke English well—in the 1940s she had worked with the Marshall mission and dealt with many Americans—and held a degree from a missionary university in Peking. Perhaps Wang was not more attractive than Jiang, yet her stylishness was more upper-class than Jiang's; she looked good without having to try. Among the Peking political elite, Wang, though she had joined the Party fifteen years after Jiang, was more popular and considered more socially desirable than Jiang.*

Yet the two women had more to unite than to divide them. Apart from her outburst to her staff about Wang's poor choice of dress material while she was ill in Russia, Jiang kept any negative feelings she may have had about Wang to herself.

The atmosphere changed in the 1960s as both women felt the mid-forties itch to do fresh and bigger things, their husbands marched toward a split, and Chinese politics became dirtier. In Jiang's crusade against Wang, which began with the battle of the photographs at the time of Madame Sukarno's visit, she showed what she would *do* with political power.†

One day in 1963, when relations between Wang and Jiang were less cozy than before but still fully civil, Wang phoned to ask Jiang's advice on clothes. She and Liu were going off on a Southeast Asian trip, and she wondered about dresses and jewelry. She knew Jiang, who loved reading novels and remembered in detail everything she ever read about clothes, would have some good ideas.

Jiang suggested that a simple black velvet dress, "like that worn by the heroine in *Anna Karenina*," would look both "elegant" and "beyond the ordinary." Since Jiang had never visited Southeast Asia, perhaps she did not realize that Wang would stifle in velvet. "On the whole I'd avoid jewelry," Jiang added.

Wang weighed Jiang's views, but the state trip with Liu was a long and exciting one, and she ended up wearing a variety of outfits. In Rangoon, Burmese President Ne Win presented her with a pearl necklace, and one evening in Jakarta Wang wore it at a gala dinner offered by President and Madame Sukarno. The atmosphere was full of Chinese-Indonesian friendship, and there was a certain amount of hilarity and high jinks. A TV film of the occasion showed

* Madame Hartini Sukarno had found Wang smarter in appearance than Jiang. "Wang Guangmei's hair was nicely waved; Jiang Qing's was straight." Added the very feminine Indonesian: "From the back, Jiang Qing looked like a man."

† One is reminded of Wu Zetian. "Her first taste of power," a historian writes of Empress Wu's career thirteen hundred years ago, "was marked by an act of ruthless savagery." It was the torture of women who had slighted and opposed her. "It was an extreme realization of malignant spite," the historian continues, "characteristic of the sudden lifting of all restraint from a hard, ambitious character." Wu ordered her women enemies to have their feet and hands cut off, then be thrown into a brewing vat. "Now these two witches can get drunk to their bones," the empress chortled. After days of agony the women died in the vat.

Wang leaning forward to light Sukarno's cigarette, and walking arm-in-arm with him from the banquet hall to another room to hear musical items.

In Peking, Jiang saw the newsreel and noted that Wang Guangmei was wearing a necklace.*

Jiang and Wang found themselves seeing less of each other, and soon their relationship turned to ice, as during the winter of 1963–64 Wang made a spectacular entry into the realm, new for her, of agricultural policy. It was a match for Jiang's new activism in theatrical reform during the same period, and perhaps a response to it. Wang took up residence in the Peach Garden brigade of a commune in Hebei Province, working on the "Four Cleanups" movement that was becoming a political football between Mao and Liu.

In Shanghai, Wang Guangmei gave a seventy-thousand-word speech on her accomplishments, which her husband passed on to the Central Committee the same week that Jiang gave her speech at the Peking Opera Festival. As Wang told agricultural officials what kind of fertilizer she thought best for Hebei's difficult conditions, Jiang was telling actors how to wear a pistol in such a way as to avoid damage to the penis.

No sooner had Mao told Jiang that she was to become a member of parliament, representing Shandong, than she read in a memo from the State Council that Wang, until then no more interested in the rubber-stamp parliament than Jiang had been, was to be appointed a member of parliament representing her home province of Hebei, site of her triumphs in farm policy at Peach Garden. It was all a far cry from sitting at South and Central Lakes talking about offspring who would not see reason, husbands who would never come home from the office, and servants who could not dust a Ming dynasty vase without catastrophe.

It was one of Jiang's ugliest ideas that in political struggle family links can and should be exploited. If she was having trouble unhorsing a particular leader, she would sniff out the possibility of having his children denounce him. When a husband fell, she would see to it that the wife was crushed as well.

"Wang Guangmei should be grabbed back to Qinghua University [where she led the moderate work teams that tried to regulate the school] to make a confession!" Jiang shouted to a mass meeting late in 1966 after Liu had been attacked as a "capitalist-roader" and "China's Khrushchev."

---

* Madame Sukarno recalled: "It was normal for Wang Guangmei to light my husband's cigarette. I also lit President Liu's cigarette. As for the necklace, it was mediocre."

"Wang Guangmei is a dishonest person," Jiang told a Red Guards rally. "Before she went to Indonesia, she came to see me. At that time I was in Shanghai, ill. She said she wanted to wear a necklace and flowered dresses on the trip." The audience was agog as Jiang, in the first of several addresses devoted to Wang's conduct in Jakarta three years before, appealed to youth's anti-elitist sentiments. "I said to her that it was right to take several dresses, and I urged black, but that as a member of the Communist Party of China, she should avoid necklaces.

"Though Wang Guangmei didn't sleep well for several nights after I gave her my advice on dress," Jiang went on, "in the end she agreed with me and said she would not wear a necklace in Southeast Asia."

Jiang had arranged to have a copy of the TV newsreel of Wang's trip made available for her series of assaults. "This film," she announced, pleased to be able to attack the Ministry of Culture and her old foe Xia Yan, the playwright (under whose aegis the film was produced) as well as Liu and Wang, *publicizes the court life of capitalism.*" What the film undoubtedly did show was that one night in Jakarta the wife of the Chinese head of state wore a necklace.

"So the film came out." Jiang's tone of regret gave way to raw anger. "By God, the woman *did* wear a necklace! She cheated me!" The crowd roared its support.

The phone rang at the besieged residence of Liu and Wang in the South and Central Lakes compound. Wang answered. Her sobbing daughter, Liu Tingting, recounted the horrible news that her sister Pingping had been in an accident. Liu and Wang both rushed to the hospital. It was a plot. Tingting probably had spoken under duress. The leftist Red Guards of Qinghua University took Wang into "revolutionary custody," and from ten that night until five the next morning, her crimes as a capitalist-roader were read out like a catechism at a struggle meeting.

Jiang Qing received hour-by-hour reports of Wang's ordeal. After a ferocious struggle in a seventh-floor room of the main hall at Qinghua, during which Wang and her Red Guard captors traded quotations from Mao, and Wang at one point lay on the floor in silent protest, three female Red Guards forced the First Lady (Liu still was head of state) into a silk gown, spike-heeled shoes, and a British aristocrat's wide-brimmed straw hat—the outfit in which she had "flirted with Sukarno." The silk gown was too small for her, and one Red Guard made a tear in each side to cope with Wang's additional flesh.

Grinning like schoolboys with a caged canary, the Red Guard leaders confronted Wang with the *pièce de résistance* among the costumes and props for the Jiang Qing-production on which the curtain was about to go up: a grotesquely clumsy necklace of gilded Ping-Pong balls with skulls painted on them. Around Wang's neck it was draped, a lasso of Jiang's revenge. Photos were taken for Jiang and posterity; a day and a night of taunts began.

Wang kept saying vehemently, "You don't have the authority to do this!" as if authority in China were any less phony than her tumbling necklace. On the dais behind Wang were a number of Jiang Qing's victims, there to listen, learn, and try to save their own skins by denouncing the newest victim (among them, Peng Zhen; the former mayor stepped forward as midday approached to tell the crowd of half a million what a bourgeois bitch Wang really was).*

---

* Here, verbatim, is part of the exchange between Wang and the prosecutor:

PROSECUTOR: You must put on that dress!
WANG: I will not!
PROSECUTOR: You have no choice in this matter!
WANG (of the dress she is wearing): This is good enough for receiving guests.
PROSECUTOR: Receiving guests? You are under attack here today!
WANG: I am not going to put on that dress. It is not presentable.
PROSECUTOR: Then why did you wear it in Indonesia?
WANG: It was summer at that time. . . .
PROSECUTOR: Why did you wear it in Lahore?
WANG: I am not going to put it on, whatever you may say.
PROSECUTOR: Let me repeat. You are under attack here today. If you are not honest with us, take care!
WANG: Even if I must die, it does not matter.
PROSECUTOR: Death? We want to keep you alive. Put on the dress!
WANG: Shouldn't we be discussing serious subjects?
PROSECUTOR: Who wants to discuss things with you? Let me tell you again that you are under attack!
WANG (angrily): On no account can you encroach upon my personal freedom.
PROSECUTOR (amid the sound of laughter): You are a member of the reactionary bourgeoisie and a class dissident. You will not be given an iota of minimum democracy, let alone extensive democracy! Dictatorship is being exercised over you today, and you are not free.
WANG: I will not put on that dress, come what may. If I have committed mistakes, I am open to criticism.
PROSECUTOR: You are guilty! You are under attack today, and you will face further attacks in the future. Put on the dress!
WANG (evasively, pointing to the fur coat she was wearing): This was a gift from Afghanistan.
PROSECUTOR: We want you to put on that dress you wore in Indonesia.
WANG: That was summer. There is winter clothing for winter, summer clothing for summer, and spring clothing for spring. I cannot put on a summer dress now.
PROSECUTOR: Skip that nonsense. We know nothing about such bourgeois stuff as what is good for summer, winter, or spring or for receiving guests or for travel.
WANG: Chairman Mao has said that we must pay attention to climate, and change our clothing accordingly.
PROSECUTOR (amid laughter): What Chairman Mao said refers to the political climate. And the way you stand in that respect, you will freeze to death even though you're wearing a fur coat. Now, are you going to put on that dress?
WANG: No.
PROSECUTOR: All right! We'll give you ten minutes. See what will happen at a quarter to

At another session within the grounds of South and Central Lakes, Li Na was on hand to supervise personally two hours of "jet plane" treatment for Wang. Her arms were wrenched behind her back, and her head was bent low before the cheering crowd. It seemed a clue to Jiang's priorities that Liu, who also was present and the prime target of the meeting, was given a mere twenty minutes of the terribly painful torment. Jiang was positioned at one of the compound's five gates, encouraging more and more people to attend her daughter's "show," and at another gate Zhou Enlai, constantly on the telephone, was trying to limit the scope and damage of the meeting.

During early 1967 Jiang hit away at Wang Guangmei. "Her father was involved with the Nationalists, you know," Jiang remarked during a political discussion when the topic of the Liu family came up. "And she herself is a big capitalist." Jiang began to work on Wang's stepdaughter, Liu Tao, whose mother, Wang Qian, Liu had divorced in 1947. "I am of the opinion," Liu Tao declared at a public meeting after fantastic inducements had been offered to her, "that my father really is the number one Party person walking on the capitalist road."

Jiang felt Liu Tao's speech against her father was too soft. Revenge gnawing at her vitals, she arranged a meeting between Liu Tao and Wang Qian, whose hatred of the man who had divorced her was exceeded only by her hatred of Wang Guangmei. A second version of Liu Tao's denunciation of her father was more to Jiang's liking; it added spice to the hair-raising portrait of Wang Guangmei that was fast becoming the talk of a hundred million Chinese households.

In conformist China, where real news is scarce, one ounce of truth (or falsehood) is packaged, repeated, and embroidered until it becomes a thousand tons of truth (or falsehood). Wall posters and

---

seven. Try to defy us by not wearing that dress. We mean what we say. (Changing subject.) What do you think of the unhorsing of Liu Shaoqi?

WANG: That is fine. Then there will be no revisionism in China. . . . I can ring someone up and ask for a spring dress.

PROSECUTOR: That won't do!

WANG: This dress is made of silk. It's too cold.

PROSECUTOR: Put it on and wear your fur coat over it.

WANG: If I were really opposed to Chairman Mao, I would deserve to freeze to death.

PROSECUTOR: You are opposed to Chairman Mao.

WANG: I am not against him now, and I will not oppose him in the future.

PROSECUTOR: No more nonsense with her. Well, there are seven minutes left.

WANG (after a pause, pointing to the pair of high-heeled shoes they had brought): How about my just putting on the shoes?

PROSECUTOR: That isn't enough. You must wear everything.

cartoons of Wang Guangmei covered the land. She had been a spy for America almost from the cradle. In Peach Garden she had lived like an empress. She had failed to care for her four children, and she had persecuted her four stepchildren. The drawings of her cuddling up to Sukarno, with lips that suggested fellatio, clad in dresses that turned her breasts into Guilin mountains, wearing necklaces of gaudy beads the size of balloons, and shoes with heels a foot high, put her into the one mold that Chinese culture reserves for the woman in public life who falls foul of today's authority—the prostitute.

One evening in September 1967, as Jiang dined with Kang Sheng at Fishing Terrace Guesthouse, the talk turned to Wang. Jiang wondered if it wasn't time to secure the case against her with the finality of a key turned in a prison door. Kang reached for the phone and ordered the presence of Shao Meng, executive secretary of the "Liu Shaoqi–Wang Guangmei Special Project Group," a commission set up under Jiang and Kang in May 1967 to draw up formal charges against the couple.

"Tonight you must have the arrest warrant for Wang Guangmei finalized," Jiang said sharply to Shao Meng as she rose from a couch. "I want it early tomorrow morning." Kang, the boss of all police matters, looked heavily at Shao Meng and said with an attempt at casualness: "The question of Wang Guangmei's spying is really now established."

Shao Meng came back to Jiang next morning with a document that declared: "Fundamentally it can be stated that Wang Guangmei has been a spy for the American OSS." Jiang scribbled at the top: "Badly done—send back to the Special Project Group." She knew all too well that in the lexicon of Chinese Communist theory, the term "fundamentally" is a time-tested escape hatch. Shao Meng went to see Kang Sheng, who, reading Jiang's notation, told the executive secretary he would write the arrest warrant himself. In Kang's draft there were no qualifications, and Wang Guangmei had become a "spy for Japan" and a "Nationalist spy" as well as a spy for the United States. Jiang signed the indictment.

Wang Guangmei would have been executed, according to the testimony of her children, had not Mao scrawled on the sentencing document that crossed his desk for approval: "Spare her from the knife" (*dao xia liu ren*). Wang remained in prison for twelve years. Shao Meng got five years.

Why did Mao allow Jiang to hound Wang Guangmei so, intervening only to save Wang's life? Because it served his own political purpose of getting rid of and discrediting Liu Shaoqi; and because Mao (unlike Zhou Enlai) thought a period of political turmoil was good for China.

A car drew up at the back door of the Liu-Wang apartment, and two police working under the Special Project Group stepped out. Most of the house's staff had left, but Hao Miao, in his white cap and apron, still was there. An hour later he was under arrest. "I'm only a cook," he said as the agents quizzed him on details of Wang Guangmei's spying for the United States. "Tell us what you remember of her activities before Liberation." Hao Miao mumbled that he was in school at that time and remembered nothing. The police made the argument that Hao Miao's cooking had been too lavish, that he had over the years corrupted Wang and Liu, preparing them for the capitalist road, robbing the people to make for them that extra-rich sauce and procure for their table that out-of-season Shanghai crab. . . .

Hao Miao got six years; he was one of sixty-four people in Peking alone who were arrested for association with Liu and Wang as a result of the work of the Special Project Group.

On a November evening, two Red Guard factions were arguing with each other. The issues were arcane, but people spoke passionately, as if the future of China depended on whether the "September 15" group or the "September 16" group was right. Jiang Qing was there. Her military fatigues were rumpled but her face shone with the excitement of battle. She listened to the arguments. Silent as she was, her presence lit up the meeting as tangibly as a spotlight. At length she arose to deliver her judgment.

"Both of you are revolutionary organizations," she declared grandly, "and you really should be uniting against the common enemy. *Nevertheless,* both organizations are harboring some bad elements. In particular, in 'September 16' there lurks a *foreign spy!*"

Jiang Qing often spat out such accusations without fully realizing the likely political consequences. But on this chilly evening in late 1966, Jiang had a target in mind and wanted total victory.

In his room at the Aeronautics Institute, a young man sat quiet and tense. He was a member of "September 16," but he had not thought it appropriate to attend this evening's meeting. The young man was neat and long-faced, like his father. His name was Liu Yunruo, son of China's embattled head of state, stepson of Wang Guangmei. He was Jiang's "foreign spy."

Jiang Qing left the hall for her waiting car, and "September 15" began its triumphant mopping-up operation against stricken "September 16." "With a foreign spy in your midst, of course your organization is antirevolutionary!" For some weeks it had been realized that Liu Yunruo was vulnerable, because his famous parents were now in disgrace, and the flick of Jiang's little finger gave "September 15" the green light to crowd in for the kill.

Jiang did have a shred of evidence for her accusation, and in a country as xenophobic as China, a shred was enough. Liu Yunruo was in love with a Russian girl. He had met her in Moscow, where he went to study in the late 1950s. Unfortunately for Yunruo, his parents were opposed to him marrying the Russian girl, and in 1960 they summoned him home to China for a "holiday," splitting the young pair up.

Crazily in love, Yunruo begged Liu Shaoqi and Wang Guangmei to relent. "Relations between China and Russia are going to get bad," Liu confided to his son. "It is not wise to marry a Russian." Yunruo begged his parents to accept that the Russian girl wasn't interested in politics, that the two of them would live a quiet private life devoted to science and literature. "I'm a political leader," replied the ever-correct Liu Shaoqi. "Once she enters my house, she has entered politics."

Yunruo and his girlfriend could only correspond. For his birthday in 1961 the girl sent Yunruo a wristwatch and a box of candies. In each candy she had put a piece of paper, the pieces together making up a love letter. For his part, Yunruo, a Communist Party member and as exact in observing Party discipline as his father, sent each of his many letters to the Russian girl to the Party Secretary of his unit to be cleared.

Liu Shaoqi and Wang Guangmei conferred with officials of the Ministry of Aviation, the supervising organization of Yunruo's unit, about the "problem" of their son. Soon Yunruo found himself surrounded with gorgeous secretaries from the ministry, and film stars who turned up "by chance" at the Liu residence. While the family was watching the movie *Five Golden Flowers,* Wang heard Yunruo murmur of the heroine, "She's beautiful; my, she is beautiful!" The next morning Wang flew to Kunming, went to the home of the female lead in *Five Golden Flowers,* who belonged to a non-Han minority race, and announced that an important interview awaited her in Peking. Soon the actress and Yunruo found themselves at dinner together in the Liu home. But the meeting was awkward, and not

only because the girl spoke little Chinese; she was as much in love
with another boy as Yunruo was with his Russian girl! In the years
until 1966, Liu and Wang were unable to tempt Yunruo with a substitute, and his affair with his Russian love went on by letter.

With the letters, Jiang Qing felled Yunruo. His very exactness
in clearing his letters with the Party, and his parents' care in keeping
the Central Committee of the Party abreast of the whole affair, had
provided Jiang with a record of Yunruo's "illicit relations with a foreign country." In the witch-hunting atmosphere of 1966, with Jiang
as the oracle of the hour, who could question her pronouncement
that Yunruo was a foreign spy? Liu Shaoqi's caution had been
proved right, but only because the oracle of the hour had none of
the Lius' procedural rectitude.

Naïvely, Yunruo moved out of the Liu home in South and
Central Lakes the night after Jiang's accusation and went to the
Public Security office to "clear his name." But no one dared to investigate the matter because Jiang had pronounced upon it. "He was
silly to move out of South and Central Lakes," a friend recalled. "If
he'd stayed there he might have been safe—at least for a while."

Shamefacedly, the Public Security officials shuffled off Yunruo
to a "place of protection" (a nice phrase for a prison in which one is
held without charges having been made). Yunruo was like a man
transfixed, the only prisoner in his block who didn't complain. He
was unwilling even to speak to most other inmates, silent in his
amazement at his fate. No one interrogated him, because it was beyond any official's power to touch a "Liu Shaoqi case."

When he was released eight years later, in 1974, Yunruo was
mentally ill. He learned that his father was dead and that his stepmother had been in prison for years. In 1977 he died of lung disease
at the age of forty-four, still unmarried. "He would have gotten into
political trouble eventually," his friend said, "but what sealed his
fate was Jiang Qing's statement that he was a 'foreign spy.' "

During 1967 an agent of Jiang Qing's flew to Kunming to seek
out the actress who played the lead in *Five Golden Flowers*. The girl
was summoned before a pack of Red Guards. "But I tell you, I *refused* their request to marry Liu Yunruo!" Her plea was in vain.
"Why did the Lius turn to you?" the Red Guard interrogator
snapped. "There must have been some reason why you were suitable for the capitalist-roaders." The actress was beaten. To this day
she is paralyzed from the blows.

During 1968 Jiang still was peppering her speeches with angry remarks about Wang, who now was in one of China's most unpleasant prisons. When Liu's name came up at a meeting in March 1968, Jiang observed: "That monstrous wife of his, Wang Guangmei, is a U.S. enemy agent!" During the same month, in an amazing conversation among a small group of China's remaining leaders, she revealed just how long-standing and personal her feelings against Wang and Liu were.

"When Liu Shaoqi was opposed to me in Yanan," she said as Zhou Enlai and Kang Sheng sat beside her, supposedly in a discussion of the parlous situation in Sichuan Province, "he was actually pointing his spearhead at Chairman Mao. Old Ke [the former mayor of Shanghai] told us about it before he died."* On what issue had Liu opposed Jiang in Yanan, where she had played no policy role? There was only one answer.

Beyond the necklace, the work teams at Qinghua University, the rivalry between Wang's work at Peach Garden and her own in opera reform, beyond all the chatter about "the court life of capitalism," it rankled Jiang that Liu, a decade before he met Wang Guangmei, had opposed her marriage to Mao and taken the lead in having the Party impose its hated restrictions on her public activity after the marriage. "This big traitor," she said in a speech of September 1968, "should die the death of a thousand, even ten thousand cuts."

And Wang, as the official First Lady, had been a very personal rival to Jiang, who had not been allowed to perform like a First Lady, with or without a necklace.

Because of chaos brought about by leftism, Mao retreated from his Cultural Revolution. But Jiang Qing could not do this as invisibly as Mao could. As the mood soured, Jiang became intermittently ill, and petulant in public performances. She still remembered to begin with her pregnant greeting: "Chairman Mao's health is good," or "I have been asked by Chairman Mao to send you his regards." Flashes of theater still were there, as when she denounced some of her multiplying enemies as "clowns," and Yao Wenyuan, who was sitting beside her, echoed her with his high-pitched cry, "Clowns! Clowns!" as he clapped his hands and a slight smile came to Jiang's ravaged face. But the buoyancy of 1966 gave way in early 1967 to anxiety that she might be blamed for the Cultural Revolution's manifest evils.

* Ke Qingshi died, in uncertain circumstances, just before the start of the Cultural Revolution.

Gatherings of dirty, babbling youths irritated her. "Time is up, I have another appointment," she said to one group that was asking her to adjudicate an impossible feud between rival factions. "I've come in a hurry and have no idea what's going on here," she began a bad-tempered speech to a delegation from Anhui Province. "Old Kang [Sheng] simply dragged me here. God knows what I'm going to say to you, without any preparation." The problem, apart from her shaky physical condition, was that the eclipse of part of the leftist Court Faction, and the growing role of the army, theatened to leave the Maid Marion of rebellion out on a limb.

At a huge mass meeting, the issue was whether guns should ever be used in a political fight, and Jiang dropped her guard for a moment. Mao's view at that time was that guns never should be used. But Jiang, like the Lan Ping for whom her own persona would eclipse the role she was meant to be playing, strayed from her script during this torrid evening. "Me, I'd certainly fight back if someone seized *my* gun." Pausing, she seemed aware that she was going against the new policy. "Of course, shooting is not good." Then she was off again: "But I've got my own ideas about it anyway." When the strain was on, Jiang Qing's will still mattered more than external arrangements decided by others, whether directors, playwrights, "capitalists," or her changeable husband.

Her nerves were frayed from the deceit that had become a way of life among warring factions. Tape recorders were found secreted in sofas and potted plants (was this why Mao came to hate plants?) at the Mao-Jiang apartments. At one meeting, shooting broke out and Jiang took cover only just in time. Wandering rebels broke through the heavy guard at South and Central Lakes, giving her a terrible scare.

Zhou Enlai, who did not split with Jiang despite their political and temperamental differences, told a meeting at the end of 1967 that "arduous struggle has impaired Comrade Jiang Qing's health" and that she had left the capital to rest at her Hangzhou residence. "Spiritual consolation and inspiration," the premier felt, "will certainly make up for her physical losses."

Why was Zhou so patient and correct toward Jiang? Why did he never blow up at her? Why did he not try to put a stop to the Cultural Revolution? Because Mao's will was unchallengeable, and Zhou had for decades accepted that fact. And because Zhou Enlai was a man who put up with many things to reach desired goals. "Comrade Yang," he once said to a colleague, Yang Ning, during a break in a meeting at Wuhan, "for the sake of the revolution one has to have one's own teeth broken and swallow blood. For that same cause, we even have to become prostitutes." Given that Jiang was Mao's wife, Zhou had to put up with her excesses. The Cultural Revolution would pass; for the moment a confrontation with Jiang had to be avoided.

As for Mao, he was very good at unleashing chaos and then, withdrawing to his mountain, disclaiming responsibility for it. This often left Jiang Qing exposed, carrying the can for Mao's leftism, unable to appear above the battle, as Mao could.

By 1968 the Cultural Revolution became a rescue operation. At first a drive against rightist bureaucrats, the Cultural Revolution later became a drive against "ultraleftists," who had proved, in Mao's eyes, good at smashing but not at building. The Red Guards were sent back to classes; a call to unite replaced that to rebel. Mao poured cold water on the scheme (originally hatched for him by Zhang Chunqiao and Yao Wenyuan) for a commune-type leap to communism in Shanghai. Several senior members of the Court Faction, close to Jiang, were arrested for "ultraleftist crimes." Most momentous, the army was called into offices, schools, and factories to restore the "order" that Mao and Jiang had so recently undermined. All this carved territory from under Jiang's feet.

She had made mistakes. She had ignored the necessity of getting some important bureaucrats on her side.* Revenge had carried her to dangerous extremes in the cultural sphere. She had been indiscriminate in embracing Red Guard groups, many of which were now unpopular.

Even her very prominence, in a society that still widely believed in the old saw, "When the hen crows at dawn, the nation is in peril," began to work against her. Jiang had not been content to stay home and knit; *ipso facto* her activism outside the household had to be put down to a shrew's machinations. She now felt the icy wind of the antiwoman tradition, reinforced by Communist self-righteousness and by the need to protect the infallibility of Mao at all costs.

That Mao's and Jiang's Cultural Revolution had turned into a mess was Jiang's biggest problem, though not separable from her own mistakes or from the bias against her as a prominent woman. Even at its peak, her power in the 1960s was only that of a copilot. She handed out Mao's *Selected Works;* no one handed out *her* se-

---

* That Zhou and his bureaucrats united with Lin Biao in resisting her over the issue of the leftist "May 16" group was a bad sign. Perhaps Zhou grew tired of being called (in the words of one Red Guard group) "the rotten boss of the bourgeoisie, toying ambidexterously with counterrevolution."

▲ Backstage with the Vietnamese leader Le Duan, whom she had entertained at a performance of *Red Detachment of Women*, 1971.

Jiang Qing listens to the remarks of a foreign leader in 1974. ▶

Poul Hartling

▲ Enjoying *Red Detachment of Women* with Richard Nixon in 1972.

▲ Jiang Qing entertains Danish Prime Minister Poul Hartling and Mrs. Beth Hartling at a Peking theatrical performance in October 1974. This was a year of great prominence for Jiang Qing, in domestic and foreign affairs alike.

▲ Jiang Qing hosts Imelda Marcos at the theater in 1974.

The political leader at the ▶
height of her power, February
1976.

At the funeral of her hus- ▼
band, Mao Zedong, Septem-
ber 1976; from left: Hua
Guofeng (reading speech),
Wang Hongwen (chairman
of the funeral), Zhang
Chunqiao, and Jiang Qing.

◀A cartoon of the Gang of Four is borne aloft in the streets of Canton after Jiang Qing's fall in October 1976.

◀A cartoon depicts Jiang Qing lusting for power. "A woman can also be emperor" reads the scroll in her hand; the figure in her mind's eye is evidently Wu Zetian. Jiang is mocked as having a "wig from the West" and "false teeth from Japan." She holds to the idea that "foreign moons are rounder than the Chinese moon," and that "foreign farts are more fragrant than Chinese farts." She puts on "crazy costumes" to emulate Empress Wu and "talks weirdly" to emulate Empress Lü. Her head is full of "imperial dreams."

A cartoon shows Jiang Qing▶ boasting of her high position in the Cultural Revolution and harboring violent, extremist elements within her skirts, while disclaiming responsibility for errors.

▶ Jiang's rival, Deng Xiaoping, victorious at the Eleventh Party Congress in 1977.

Jiang Qing, brought low, ▶ listens as the Special Court accuses her in November 1980.

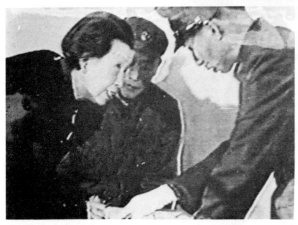

◀ Jiang Qing signs the indictment of her "crimes" in November 1980.

▲ At the Ceremonial Hall in the Street of Righteousness, Wang Hongwen testifies against Jiang Qing, as she listens from her cage, behind the label "The Accused."

At her trial Jiang Qing is defiant, shouting at ▶ judges, prosecutors, and other witnesses. ▼

▲ In January 1981 Jiang Qing listens to the sentence decided upon for her: death, suspended for two years "to see how she behaves."

lected works. "Remember," they had always harped at her, "what you do reflects on the chairman." She was starting to find out that what the chairman did reflected on her.

It was past midnight. At South and Central Lakes, in a reception room attached to their own apartments, Mao and Jiang met for an urgent strategy session on the bleak political situation with two groups, two generations, two segments of the Cultural Revolution leadership. The key Red Guard leaders were there, tired, puzzled, subdued compared with before, and yet still arrogant. So was the knot of leftists and loyalists to Mao who in midsummer 1968 helped Mao and Jiang rule China: Lin Biao and his wife, Zhou Enlai, Kang Sheng, Yao Wenyuan, Chen Boda, and the police minister, Xie Fuzhi. Until dawn they talked in tones of nostalgia, gloom, and recrimination about the situation of chaos, violence, and dissension brought on by the Cultural Revolution.

It was a night for Jiang to try to nail her colors to the pillars of law and order. It was also a night that suggested that Jiang's views, however tailored to new realities, might not be the keys to her future—for Mao went out of his way to express irritation with her.

Fighting with guns and spears is a "disgrace to the family," Jiang remarked. Mao perversely chipped in to put his wife down: "I'm not afraid of fighting; I'm glad as soon as I hear about fighting." A few moments later Jiang again condemned the armed struggles on the campuses, and Mao again chose (against the grain of his own presentation that evening) to break in and discourse on the "advantages of armed struggle!"

It was true that Mao was a little ill-tempered with everyone, but Jiang received more than her share of his barbs. She tried to back up Mao when he assured the Red Guards that he saw nothing wrong with youthful leadership: "We took part in the revolution when we were only teenagers." Mao cut in rather superfluously: "Don't feel elated; to fill your body with elation is just like one of your diseases."

As Mao discoursed on the futility of schools and colleges, he mentioned that "Gorky had only two years of formal education . . . even less than Jiang Qing." We do not know Jiang's expression at that moment. Lin Biao's wife broke the silence: "Well, Jiang Qing studied very diligently on her own. . . ." Mao stopped Ye Chun in her tracks: "Don't brag for her," he said, and swept on with an account of his own youth as an illustration of universal truths.

At this meeting Jiang never could please Mao, who often interrupted her. Even when she quoted a maxim of his that she thought suitable for the situation, he snapped, "Don't mention that."

As dawn drew near and the old and young elites of China slumped lower in their chairs, fanning themselves against the heat, Jiang several times criticized a young Red Guard leader whom she disliked. "Han Aiqing, I've pointed out your mistakes several times. What have you got to say to this?" Mao sprang to the defense of Han. "Don't criticize him," he said in a rebuke that was extremely rude for such a public occasion. "You're always blaming others; you never blame yourself." Just before the meeting broke up, Jiang again criticized young Han. He thinks only about the distant future, never about the pressing moment, she complained. "It is good to think far ahead," Mao broke in. "He is good! He is good!"

Mao suggested that the Red Guards must be all very sleepy and that they should go off to Han's room for the rest of a difficult night. There was nothing more for Jiang to say.

The Cultural Revolution had more than one cause. And what happened was not the same as what the original architects, Mao and Jiang, intended. It went on far longer than planned; its later stages were desperate responses to unforeseen events rather than part of the original vision. Still, without Jiang Qing there may not have been a Cultural Revolution, and certainly Mao would not have called it a *Cultural* Revolution.

It came about when Mao, in a slump, turned to her as a co-worker and was mentally influenced by her as never before. Its content—taking ideas and the arts as the keys to China's problems—reflected her special interest. The theatricality of its modes bore her touch. The sickening cult of personality, which turned Mao from a politician into a near-god, was due in heavy part to Jiang's pushing Mao to "be a King, George"; the higher Mao was elevated, she felt, the more glory would rub off on her. The Cultural Revolution's theme of condemning and dismantling much of the Communist Party itself cannot be separated from Jiang's burning desire to get even for the marriage agreement at Yanan.

No one understood the Cultural Revolution,* perhaps because there was nothing to understand; nothing rational beneath the vanity, frustration, and thirst for revenge that triggered it. At the same

---

* Liu Shaoqi himself said he simply did not understand the Cultural Revolution; the foreign minister, Chen Yi, said, "... if I were to lead the Cultural Revolution, there would be no Cultural Revolution."

time, many people did sincerely care about the causes they espoused. But Jiang, who knew there was no deep meaning to the Cultural Revolution, cared little about the issues (the theater apart) that were fed like manna to the people. Her undoubted political ignorance was not the point; what counted were her connections (*guan xi*), especially that with Mao; the pent-up demons within her personality; and her natural political skills—charm, a sense of drama, boundless energy when inspired, and an instinct for the balance of forces.

The Cultural Revolution had a *personal* meaning for Jiang Qing. Her independence of spirit, her will to struggle, and her inclination to seek revenge—traits that go back to her girlhood—all came together.

There were moments when Jiang called for extremism; there were others, as early as the autumn of 1966, when she urged moderation. Neither stance had a philosophic root within Jiang's mind. When she became moody because of Mao's retreat from the principles of the Cultural Revolution, from late 1967, it was less because a political vision of hers had been dashed than because the entry of the military into the centers of power was bound to weaken her grip on power.

If Jiang in her army fatigues was less like a real People's Liberation Army general than a model of one dressed up for display in a boutique window, it was not that Jiang was a "rightist" bureaucrat at heart rather than one of Lin Biao's "leftist" warriors. She was neither. The garments she put on for that crazy show, the Cultural Revolution, may have been absurd; she did not care, for she more than anyone knew they were only garments. The lights would go off, the greasepaint would be wiped off, and what mattered then was not Jiang Qing's art but her life.*

---

* The reader who hesitates in amazement before the conclusion that Jiang Qing's personal drama was the key to the Cultural Revolution should confront four large points. Peking said the Cultural Revolution aimed to stamp out the bourgeoisie and its ideas, but Jiang Qing could scarcely have been taking a stand at that level (assuming it had any meaning at all) because of the poverty of her prior knowledge of political ideas. Second, the charges of evil conduct and wrong political ideas that she made against most of the Cultural Revolution enemies were false; Western sinological scholarship established this well before Jiang's fall (and Peking now asserts, for what it is worth, that her charges were *totally* false). Third, the entire story of Jiang's adult life is one of a subjective outlook, a drive for personal vindication, and an appetite for revenge. Finally, Jiang's own account of her life, in her rambling Cultural Revolution speeches, the remarks she made informally over the years that have been discovered since her fall, and in the story she told to Witke, is replete with a stress on her personal enemies, on private concerns—illness, clothes, family, photography—rather than public policy. (No wonder Witke, as she tells us, had to write the Cultural Revolution portion of Jiang's story mainly from the "documentary record," for Jiang's own preoccupations simply did not add up to a coherent account of Chinese politics in this period.)

For all the shadows that fell upon Jiang as the Cultural Revolution misfired, she ended the decade with the formal power of a top leader, as prominent in the nation as she had been obscure in the 1950s.

Mao drove to the Great Hall of the People to bang the gavel for the start of the Ninth Party Congress in April 1969. It was hardly the "unity" congress that Mao proclaimed, crystallizing the "gains" of the Cultural Revolution, for beneath the surface the newly powerful military were in tension with the still-powerful leftists. In the struggle between "khaki" and the "helicopters,"* Mao seemed to vacillate. But his own personal "helicopter," the bitch-goddess of his life, Jiang Qing, was made a member, the first-ever woman member, of the twenty-one-person Politburo, China's ruling group.

The Cultural Revolution had established the agenda, the cast of characters, and the Orwellian concepts for the maneuvers that would keep China obsessed by political struggle well into the 1970s. Jiang Qing, star of the theatrical politics of the Cultural Revolution, was the 1960s' most potent legacy to the 1970s.

"Don't get giddy with success," Mao had written to Jiang, and it was true that he often was outraged at her ways. In one corner of his mind he felt it was a mistake to have his wife installed in formal high office. "I never approved of one's wife becoming the office manager in one's own organization," Mao was soon to remark at an informal meeting. He was referring to Lin Biao's wife, Ye Chun (also appointed to the Politburo). He may have had Jiang in mind as well.

Jiang made an expedition to Xiang Shan ("Fragrant Hills") Park to look for some seedlings of rare, exotic plants that she felt would look nice in her own garden at South and Central Lakes. The afternoon illustrated the corruption, theatricality, and medieval paternalism of Jiang Qing's political style and that of Peking politics in general as the 1960s ended.

Jiang as a Politburo member required a high local official to escort her, as well as the usual cloud of bodyguards and service personnel; for this purely personal trip to the park the high local official was Wang Li, a city leader later purged as an ultraleftist. When the group arrived, Wang said he wanted to show Jiang some Buddhas. She had come to find plants to enrich her garden, she reminded her fellow revolutionary sternly, but Wang said the five hundred Lohan

* Deng Xiaoping's derisory term for Cultural Revolution leftists who in his view rose too quickly to high posts beyond their capacity.

statues were marvelous, so she begrudgingly trooped over to the Temple of Azure Clouds. There Wang Li proudly showed Jiang a breathtaking combination of trophies of superstition that he and his colleagues, ever anxious to prove themselves 300 percent loyal to Mao, had assembled for the edification of strollers in Xiang Shan Park. There were the Buddhas, with fresh food laid before them as an offering; a hat and other clothes of Sun Yat-sen; and a newly installed bust of Mao!

Jiang was furious to see an image of Mao in a religious shrine (and irritated at being diverted from her seedlings). She immediately ordered the park authorities to remove all the Mao items from the temple. Then she dramatically announced, her face radiant but its strains suggesting her fifty-six years, that she was going to *purchase* the array of fresh food—herself taking on the aura of a messiah—and give it away to the people in the park. "Eat! Eat!" she cried as her staff scrambled to foist rice and fish and sweet cakes on the startled bystanders.

Bid to Be Empress (1970s)

I want to maintain my political youth forever.
—Jiang Qing

Man's contribution to human history is nothing
more than a drop of sperm. *—Jiang Qing*

Few people suit her taste. Only one—she herself.
—Mao of Jiang Qing, 1974

One evening early in 1971 Jiang Qing dined with a few trusted followers at the Pavilion for Listening to the Orioles, a theater-restaurant at the Summer Palace much favored by the Empress Dowager a century earlier. Jiang loved the historical associations; the musty old dining chamber, its heavy tables laid with golden cloths facing the open-air platform where Peking opera was performed for Ci Xi; and the specialties of fragrant chicken and a small froglike fish from the lake that the chefs prepared for her.

After dinner, strolling along a path that curled upward from the smoky blue expanse of Kunming Lake, she suddenly stopped before an inscription on the wall of the Hall of Dispelling the Clouds (*Pai yun dian*). "READ CHAIRMAN MAO'S BOOK, LISTEN TO HIS INSTRUCTIONS," ran the six-feet-high characters. It seemed harmless, quite usual at this time, the red and white ideological rash that lay all over the body of China. But Jiang was rooted to the spot in angry surprise, because although the words were those of Lei Feng, a famous young martyr, the calligraphy was Lin Biao's! Jiang was outraged that Lin should try to give the public the impression that he was the slogan's author. The bounder was using the cult of Mao—as Mao had several times tried to convince her Lin was seeking to do—to hoist himself up to fame. "The chairman's power is literary," she muttered to her entourage, apparently implying that for Lin to flaunt his calligraphy was an act of political rebellion.

Jiang Qing returned to her car in an evil mood. She began to realize why Lin was obsessively substituting "thought of Mao Zedong" for the simple "Mao Zedong" when bowing a knee to the fount of truth. The bastard was suggesting to the Chinese people, she thought darkly as her limousine tooted everyone off the road leading back to South and Central Lakes, that Mao's magic could outlive him and be mediated by a fresh hand. *Lin*'s hand! By the time she reached her apartment, Jiang had appalling visions of the entire population of China gazing spellbound at billboards of Mao's sayings written in the calligraphy of her sly rival. What was wrong with *her* calligraphy, for God's sake!*

During Mao's last years Jiang Qing, feared, fawned upon, and hated in proportions she found hard to assess, lived in the shadow of two alternate futures: to replace Mao as China's supreme leader, and so win a final victory in her lifelong battle to avoid being a man's possession and to express herself free of trammels; or to be hurled down as an upstart who had risen unjustifiably high by riding on her husband's back.

Some of Mao's colleagues feared he might live forever; others were panicky that he might die too soon. Lin Biao was in the first category. Jiang Qing was in the second; she needed a living but enfeebled Mao. Lin's and Jiang's differing interests on the timing of Mao's death did nothing to modify their rivalry in bidding to be Mao's most faithful interpreter.

Although he was commander of the world's largest army, Lin was a shy, boyish figure, his face doleful and mousy except when he flashed a winsome smile. Brilliant as a military strategist, he was narrow in other realms, and his approach to politics was a cloak-and-dagger one common in traditional China.

Jiang and Lin, so different from each other, nevertheless were locked together by association with the Cultural Revolution. There were two key aspects to their relationship. Every hour of the day and every square kilometer of the nation were filled with a consciousness of the coming end of the Mao era; everything Jiang and Lin did after the Ninth Party Congress in 1969 was done out of a hope to succeed Mao. And Jiang and Lin used each other. At first they did this smoothly and with great success, under the aegis of a Mao at the height of his power. But at the start of the 1970s, their use of each other was jerky and unsure as Mao entered a King Lear phase, Chinese politics became a cesspool of distrust, and authority in Peking began to fragment.

*   *   *

---

* In China, the handwriting of the leaders, in facsimile, is easily recognized by the public; it is virtually a technique of rule.

"People like De Gaulle and myself," Mao remarked to French writer André Malraux, "we have no successors." This Olympian stance of Mao's imperiled anyone who became his deputy. In 1970 it was Lin who discovered that being number two meant living in a cell for the condemned, just as Liu Shaoqi had done in the early 1960s. As for Jiang Qing, she saw that she could benefit from the old man's doubts. Perhaps Mao's remark to Malraux portended that one day, having knocked down all possible successors, he would hand the baton to his wife as a way of avoiding a successor and opting instead for an extension of life through a surrogate?

Mao's doubts about Lin's views, character, and ability to be China's leader arose just as Jiang was cementing her alliance with Lin. "I was quite uneasy about some of his thinking," Mao remarked after a meeting in the spring of 1966, during which Lin appeared to flatter Mao, hoping to propel him above politics to the impotence of sainthood. The previous January Jiang Qing and Lin's wife, Ye Chun, a tough woman who possessed neither Jiang's flair nor Wang Guangmei's dignity, conversed in the resort town of Suzhou. Ye Chun told Jiang of Lin's frustration that his poor health had prevented his making a greater contribution to the revolution. Perhaps only Jiang, a victim of illness herself, really could understand how he felt. She knew all too well, Jiang responded, but she considered that Lin's contributions had been enormous nonetheless. And she pointed out with heavy emphasis that Lin at fifty-nine years of age still was rather young. Jiang followed this hint at Lin's good prospects for succeeding Mao with a waterfall of compliments on how valuable Lin was to Mao and how profoundly he understood Mao's thinking.

It was just a few weeks after this conversation that Lin made Jiang cultural adviser to the military. Jiang and Lin began to stroke each other's political back, and Ye Chun became a shameless booster of her newfound friend. ("Protect Jiang Qing!" she cried seventeen times during a single speech of Jiang's.)

Jiang and Lin worked together against Liu Shaoqi. Jiang's crusade against "capitalists" within the military helped Lin purge his enemies. "If there's anyone you hate," Jiang said to Ye Chun, "just let me know and I'll help you nab them."

In return, Lin would give his dry little smile and tell Jiang Qing she was "our Party's outstanding woman comrade." He ordered the promotion of Jiang from a cadre rank of Nine to Rank Five (a very high level; Mao was alone at One, Lin was alone at Two). "In the past," Lin explained in a secret memo that spelled out more perhaps than Mao would have chosen to spell out, "because Jiang Qing's health was not good, everybody failed to understand her. Now in this period of the Cultural Revolution, we see the great role she can play, we see her great creativity." On a string of documents from Jiang's office designed to redress this or initiate that, Lin's handwritten "Agree completely" was to be found.

And Ye Chun became a bridge between Jiang and the air force chief, Wu Faxian, who laid on planes and guns and men for Jiang's exercise of power. She behaved like a lapdog toward Jiang. She gave her furs brought from the far Northeast by military courier, and a supply of army, navy, and air force uniforms for Jiang to wear at heroic moments. "For Jiang Qing," said an observer of the relationship, "Ye Chun would roll on the ground eating horseshit and call it a gorgeous cream cake."*

In his candid way Lin Biao once told a colleague, Huang Yongsheng, exactly what he was up to: "Since 1965 I have followed B-52 [Lin's epithet in code for Mao] and established links with Jiang Qing, in order to wrest power once enjoyed by Luo [Ruiqing, military leader who was the first top-level victim of the Cultural Revolution] as handed to him by Liu [Shaoqi] and Deng [Xiaoping]."

Lin was growing restive as Mao's heir, foolishly unwilling to bide his time until the great man died. Mao felt Lin was trying to throw the military's weight around, maneuvering crudely to become head of state, resisting his plan to open the door to Nixon, and in general bringing Mao irritating daily reminders of his own mortality.

Jiang's closeness to Lin was reduced but not terminated as the Mao-Lin relationship went from uneasy to disastrous in 1970 and the first half of 1971. She could not yet turn against Lin. They had helped each other enormously and still were cooperating against the threat of "capitalists" returning from the ashes of the Cultural Revolution to avenge their rout. Moreover, if Lin did succeed Mao, Jiang, unlike Mao, would have to work under him. Yet the rivalry between Jiang and Lin was palpable. "The Cultural Revolution became nothing more than a struggle for power between Jiang and Lin," a shrewd Chinese intellectual remarked privately at the time. Jiang was under no illusion that if Mao and Lin did have a showdown she would have to denounce Lin. For mixed reasons, she

* Claims by some Chinese sources that Jiang had an affair with Lin seem implausible in light of Jiang's close and constant cooperation with Ye Chun.

began to share the doubts of many in China that Lin was of the mettle to succeed Mao.

By the spring of 1971, Mao and Lin were irreversibly headed for a showdown. Zhou Enlai, the stage manager always there to keep the show on track, became Mao's crucial ally in the difficult task of combating Lin's military weight, his credentials as a leader of the Cultural Revolution, and his position, written in the constitution, as Mao's choice to be the next leader of China. Yet Jiang did not abandon her link with Lin and his scheming entourage. She did not really want him to succeed Mao, but the insincere game in which the two of them used each other was not quite finished.

"Each time there is a difficult turning point," Ye Chun said to Jiang on April 29, when Mao and Lin had long since ceased to be on speaking terms, "you, Comrade Jiang Qing, give help. I'm extremely grateful for this." Jiang was keeping a line out to Mao's formal deputy. "It's a while since I've met with Vice-Chairman Lin," she said on the phone to Ye Chun on May 2. "If he has time I'd like to come and see him." Perhaps Jiang did not share Mao's conviction that Lin was finished.

Jiang went so far as to have Lin pose for a personal photo. At his home, where four years before she had burned materials about her past in a stove in the backyard, she arranged Lin in a chair reading a copy of Mao's *Selected Works.* He was bare-headed, which was extremely unusual; he normally insisted on wearing a cap to hide his bald head. Pleased with the pictures, Jiang approved their publication in the July and August issues of *People's Illustrated* and *Army Illustrated,* with a caption in her own hand: "Tireless Student."

In August, when Mao's net was closing in on his deputy, Lin sent a message to Jiang encouraging her to take over some of Mao's responsibilities, "even if this should tax your own health somewhat." That same month, she made a trip to Qingdao, the port city of her student days, and Lin provided every facility for her, including a senior officer who opened and closed the door of her car as she toured the city, taking photos of old haunts. At the Qingdao auditorium, she arranged for the hanging of a fresh portrait of Lin beside one of Mao—a duo of two men who now were virtually bent on murdering each other!

On September 8, at the eleventh hour of Lin's and Ye Chun's lives, Ye phoned Jiang from the seaside resort of Beidaihe, where the Lin entourage, on the pretext of a combined vacation and cele-

bration of Lin's daughter's imminent engagement, were preparing to
set up an alternative government in the southern bastion of Canton.
"Comrade Lin Biao sends his best regards," she said calmly, "and
says to take care of your health." The Lins were sending some excellent watermelons, Ye told Jiang, the kind she particularly liked in
the early autumn. "Tell Vice-Chairman Lin not to get worried,"
Jiang said at the end of this amazing conversation.*

In the late afternoon of September 12, Jiang passed several
hours at her villa within the Summer Palace, where the refreshments
included four watermelons from the Lins. "Vice-Chairman Lin gave
me these melons," Jiang remarked brightly as she shared portions
(at room temperature; she could not stand chilled melon) with palace staff members. "Let me pass a slice on to you people—they're a
symbol of the vice-chairman's solicitude for us."

A few hours later, after a shoot-out at Beidaihe, and perhaps an
earlier one in Peking, an air force Trident carrying Lin, Ye Chun,
and some followers took off under emergency conditions, only to
crash two and a half hours later over Mongolia. No live bodies were
found in the wreckage; Lin Biao and Ye Chun were dead. "Let him
go, he won't get far," Mao had commented that evening. "If Lin
Biao had not run," he said four years later, "we would not have
killed him." Jiang Qing knew a good deal less than her husband
about Lin's approaching demise.

In China the demands of truth are as nothing compared with
the demands of appearance, and a few months later Jiang was portraying Lin as her virtual lifelong enemy. It was a December evening at the guesthouse in Canton where she often retreated in
winter, to satisfy her constant urge for a change of environment,
drink in the lively atmosphere of the southern city (films from Hong
Kong were easier to get there), and enjoy mild nights strolling in her
orchid garden.

Her entourage included not only personal and medical staff
but, as befitted a major national leader, a portion of her political coterie, many of whom were young, leftist, and Bohemian.

After a dinner that included chicken broth and steamed fish,
which she judged essential for her health, and pigeon, which southern friends had recommended for sustaining the sex drive, she began
to talk about "the overreacher." Lin not only wanted to become em-

---

* Throughout 1970–71, Jiang's colleagues Zhang Chunqiao and Yao Wenyuan were dis-
tinctly more opposed to Lin than she; it is possible Ye Chun's flattery of Jiang had its intended
result of reducing her doubts about Lin. Perhaps, too, Mao wanted Jiang to remain close to
Lin, to lull the defense minister. Jiang was not scoring high marks as a political strategist.

peror, but he also went out of his way to persecute *her*. Did they know that he put poison in her food; that he instructed a film laboratory to ruin her amateur movies by developing them in a strange reddish hue; that she and Mao were so bedeviled by his saboteurs in the spring of 1971 that they had to move out of their apartments at South and Central Lakes and live in a hotel?

Jiang stooped to massage her ankle, as she remarked that the strain of Lin's plotting had devastated her body as well as her spirit. The sleepless nights had put an added strain upon her heart, already weak, she added almost inaudibly, her eyes gazing into a far distance. Of all those who had plotted against Chairman Mao, she ventured, Lin Biao really was the most devious and *boorish*.

It was a vintage performance, a nice blend of the actress's professionalism and the hypochondriac's pathos.

Yes, Jiang Qing faked the truth about Lin—as did everyone else. If the truth changed, what never changed was the source of truth: the Party power center. The race to grab that power was all the more shameless because so *much* power would become available when Mao went. Jiang did not yet fully realize it, but for her the weightiest consequence of Lin's fall was that Zhou Enlai, without whom Mao could not have bested his deputy, would now rise to the pinnacle of his prestige. The stage manager would move in line to become director. Another boulder in her path.

In Chinese tradition, the only person who had any business asserting his individuality was the exceptional man—virtually never a woman—with a mission to uplift society. The assertive Jiang Qing seemed to fall outside these bounds. Most people who didn't like her saw her—still—as the troublemaking wife. Only a few realized that she had in her own mind placed herself within the Confucian tradition; her self-expression was justified because she was in training to become the ruler of China! She had begun to see herself in the perspective of China's four-thousand-year history as a woman in whom personal self-fulfillment and beneficent rule over the Chinese race were fused as one goal.

After years of struggling to be her own woman, against convention, she would turn her shackles into wings. Convention could even be made to support her lonely try for heroism, for in Chinese history *there had been one woman* on whom the mantle of supreme leadership fell.

Wu Zetian's rise from toy to stateswoman thirteen hundred

years ago resembled Jiang Qing's. The tough, pretty Wu began as a concubine—the only route to power for a woman of old China—and became China's Catherine the Great.

One day during concubine Wu's service to Emperor Tai Zong, the crown prince left the emperor's presence to go to the bathroom. As he emerged into the antechamber of the washing room, concubine Wu stepped forward with a golden dish of water. Moments later, on a silken couch in the anteroom, the heir to the throne was burrowing deep between the thighs of his father's most magnetic concubine.

Emperor Tai Zong soon died, and as custom dictated, his women of the night were sent off to a convent for a change of pace as Buddhist nuns. But the crown prince, upon becoming Emperor Gao Zong, did not forget Wu. He already had an empress, Lady Wang, who had stepped up to the position from her previous post as senior concubine, first class. But he found an excuse to visit Wu's convent, and another to bring Wu back, against all the rules, to a modest post at his own court.

The historian's comment on Wu's first big step toward power applies in part to Lan Ping's arrival at Yanan in 1937: "She [Wu] had . . . made the first great move, to return to the Palace; now she had still to win the emperor's lasting favor, to give birth to a possible heir, and to achieve the downfall of the reigning empress."

Wu proved as good at imperial affairs as she had been on the silken couch. After hair-raising plots—apparently Wu framed Lady Wang by suffocating her own infant in its bed and pointing a finger (to the emperor, an irresistible finger) at the innocent empress—the concubine retrieved from the convent supplanted the worthy Lady Wang as empress, the First Lady of a promising administration in a distinguished dynasty. In a way it was the story of Lan Ping's replacement of He Zizhen.

Wu's position was buoyed by the birth of two sons and by her systematic removal of elder statesmen who objected to her rising influence. She soon eclipsed the emperor, an irresolute character who spent much of his limited physical energy upon seductions (his list included Wu's sister and niece). It was Wu who masterminded a difficult war in Korea, filled the kingdom with shrewd appointments based on merit, and eliminated all opposition to the administration.

Her influence upon Gao Zong was all the greater because she did not hesitate to cater to his prodigious and unusual sexual demands; the sober official historians observed that she "abased her

body and endured shame in order to conform to the emperor's will."
Similarly, Jiang's hold upon Mao was due in large part to her having enticed him sexually, not by any rare feats so far as is known,
but *before* he married her and while he was still He Zizhen's husband.

When the emperor gave an audience, Wu sat beside him on a
throne equally elevated but, in deference to the tradition that
women should keep out of politics, hidden by a screen. The official
histories reluctantly noted the real situation: "The whole sovereign
power of the Empire passed into her hands; life or death, reward or
punishment were decided by her word. The Son of Heaven [em-
peror] sat on his throne with folded hands, and that was all." If this
suggests Jiang Qing's role as Mao grew old and weak, the great difference lay in what happened after Emperor Gao Zong died in 683.

Wu, by then fifty-five years old, should have become empress
dowager and faded into dignified retirement. But as a result of quiet,
fierce struggle, during which Wu coolly disposed of two crown
princes (her own sons) and others who threatened her bid to be
number one in name as well as in fact, she made herself in 690 Emperor (Empress) of China—the true "Son (Daughter) of Heaven,"
the first woman ever to be such.

She gave herself the title "Holy Mother Divine Imperial One"
and founded a dynasty of her own, the Zhou, which provided a remarkable interregnum within the span of the Tang dynasty. The
Buddhist clergy, like the ideologues of the Cultural Revolution in
Jiang Qing's day, busied their pens with a lofty justification for the
rise of a woman to a position hitherto reserved for men; they produced a sutra called the Great Cloud Classic, which praised Wu as
the greatest blessing ever to fall upon China and "revealed" that she
was an incarnation of Maitreya sent by Yama to rule the earth.

Wu not only benefited from her sexual charms in her rise to
power, but (here she eclipsed Jiang) she also used the power she attained to bring an array of handsome men to her bed.

Using a lady-in-waiting as a "taster," she searched for vigorous
men. Two brothers called Zhang, carpenters whom she named court
architects for the sake of appearances, pleased her for a time, during
her seventies, but she remarked one day to the lady-in-waiting:
"Zhang Zong has a face as beautiful as a lotus flower, but what a
pity he is so much better to look at than to be used."

The staff member understood and initiated a search for men of
exceptional virility. This resulted in the arrival at the court of a ped-

dler named Xue, famous in the brothels of the capital for making women faint and bleed under his ministrations. "The whole empire," Wu said to Xue after their first night of lovemaking, "is less valuable than your extraordinary thing." Xue was appointed Imperial Buddhist Adviser to fit him without scandal into court routine, an arrangement that led Wu to refer to his organ, in her discussions with the lady-in-waiting of what she liked and disliked, as the "little monk."

Although her love life added to her difficulties in governing late in her reign, Wu seldom put sex above politics. For her there was a time to play and a time to turn to state affairs. She never put any of her lovers on an unlimited leash; when ex-peddler Xue became overbearing, through hearing so many compliments about his physical prowess, she arranged for four strong Palace women to strangle him.

Allowing for the fact that intrigue was endemic to the imperial system and that an obsession with the issues of succession affected virtually all decisions—both features of Chinese dictatorship continued undimmed in the Communist era—Wu ruled with success and a degree of enlightenment until she, and her one-woman dynasty, came to an end when she was eighty-one. She had in essence ruled China for fifty years.

Jiang Qing, who had previously taken little interest in Chinese history, became an avid student of the career of Wu and the careers of other great women near the throne. Her personal library swelled with books on the subject. Teams of writers from her fanatically loyal faction scurried to prepare articles showing that Empress Wu, until then generally regarded as a lustful, power-hungry shrew, was "anti-Confucian" and hence "progressive." "Women can become emperor," Jiang would say to her staff members. "Even under communism there can be a woman ruler."

Jiang was up against enormous odds. Two iron laws seemed to mock her: No woman was supposed to become the supreme ruler of China; no woman could play an honorable role at the forefront of politics. Every Chinese female was expected to nod her head at the unshakability of these immemorial truths.

Wu Zetian had become emperor, but it was an aberration never repeated, and she was considered to have clawed her way to the throne by violence and lust. In Chinese history books, the model emperors' wives always were those who refrained from becoming politicians in their own right; and those empresses who did wield power in one way or another were judged evil or disastrous. When Peking intellectuals in private conversation began to refer to Jiang as "Wu Zetian," this was meant to blacken Jiang.

Under the dynasties, the Palace was a self-contained world of its own, the size of a small city, with only one resident man, the emperor (eunuchs did not count). Women could be terribly important—the loins of the emperor and his line of male heirs knew it well—but only in their relation to the emperor and his heirs. Scores of empresses were praised for supporting their husbands, and thousands of concubines for their own kind of selfless assistance toward an emperor's career and China's presumed welfare.

"Women are the true revolutionaries," writes Empress Wu's modern biographer, "in that, forced by weakness to recognize the limits of physical strength, they repudiate, in their hearts, all the mental barriers men have built to restrain the use of open violence." Yet Chinese political women, however much they knew in their hearts that the laws and moral conventions were men's instruments, time and again pretended that these were eternal verities and went along with them.

There has been another kind of woman, rare but unforgettable, who becomes a true revolutionary by labeling the men's toys for what they are. Knowing the pretenses well, aware of what dictatorship means because she has felt the smack of men's authority over women—that reverberation of society's wider dictatorship—this rare spirit refuses to keep her grievances secret. It is her aim to sweep away the pretenses that prevent a woman politician from standing openly and proudly at the pinnacle of the Chinese state. With a shout she challenges the house of cards that allots to women of the Palace only the concubines' quarters. (This does not mean she is a revolutionary on behalf of women in general; her quest is for individual satisfaction.)

Wu Zetian was such a woman; Jiang Qing was another.

Yet power—leaving aside the impossible dream of praise—was available to a woman only through her husband or her son. In Chinese history, a handful of women attained effective power (Wu alone reached the throne) by this means. They were empresses dowager, permitted to rule from behind a screen when the formal emperor, either their husband or their son, was sick or mad or juvenile. This was perhaps the height of what Jiang could expect for herself as Mao's life drew to its end in the early 1970s.

Jiang began to mention favorably one of these empresses dowa-

ger, Lü Zhi. Upon the death of her husband, Liu Bang, who
founded the Han dynasty in 206 B.C., Empress Lü locked up the
proposed heir, had his mother's hands and feet cut off, and propped
up in his place her own young and malleable son, Zhao Di. She ran
the kingdom—not terribly well—for sixteen years. When Zhao Di
grew to adulthood Lü murdered him, and to replace him on the
throne reached into the ranks of Palace children for another young
boy. In his gorgeous robes he was a puppet; she was the ventrilo-
quist. As soon as Empress Lü died, the bureaucrats and generals
killed her entire family and restored orderly, acceptable male leadership.

Lü's political use of her relatives was like Jiang Qing's use of Li
Na and Mao Yuanxin in the 1960s. Lü's extreme nervousness about
two of her husband's concubines was like Jiang's defensiveness
about He Zizhen (and her daughter, Li Min), and the family of
Yang Kaihui.

Empress Lü is a villain in the stylized morality play that passes
for history in China. But Jiang Qing quietly spread the word that
Lü's career should be reassessed. In Jiang's mind—not a well-
stocked mind when it came to history—Lü's ruthlessness could be
counterbalanced by three factors, all beautifully pertinent to her
own requirements in the Communist China of the 1970s.

Lü was able and courageous enough to hold the Chinese ship of
state on a steady course after the death of her emperor-husband in
195 B.C.

Lü was not a licentious woman. The Chinese love to read about
licentious women, but they also like to keep reassuring themselves
that such women are rotten. Lü, having been the longtime wife of
Liu Bang and being quite old and not very interested in sex by the
time she grasped power, could not be written off as a whore-poli-
tician.

Third, Empress Lü had proved her mettle by sharing wartime
hardships at the side of her husband as the Han dynasty was struggling into existence.

Among other empresses dowager, the great recent example,
personally remembered by some Chinese of Jiang Qing's era, was
the formidable Ci Xi (1835–1908). An emperor's concubine, she rose
to be empress because she happened to be the mother of this emperor's only son. Her emperor-husband's death in 1861 led to nearly
fifty years of rule by Ci Xi, based upon scheming, murder, and a
good sense of the balance of forces.

Using her brother-in-law, she confounded the elder statesmen's opposition to her willful rule; it was similar to Jiang's use of her nephew Mao Yuanxin to encircle the old cadres who felt Mao's wife should take a back seat. Ci Xi put her own son on the throne under strict control as Emperor Tong Zhi. When he died an early death in 1870, she selected her nephew to replace him as Emperor Guang Xu—only to jail this interesting young man after he began to sympathize with an anti–Ci Xi reform faction. She ruled despotically but tolerably well, choosing some brilliant advisers. Her mind did not stray from state affairs to love affairs, from long memorials to long members, as Empress Wu's did. Without her, dynastic China might have come to an end well before it did in 1911.

Jiang Qing was deeply interested in the ideas and methods of Empress Dowager Ci Xi. But it was impossible for her to praise Ci Xi publicly because ultimately Empress Dowager Ci Xi failed to keep the West at bay and because she was too vivid a part of the *ancien régime* that the Communist Party had gloriously buried. One cannot choose a model from the ranks of last night's enemy.

If it was almost impossible for a woman to gain supreme political power in old China, it was totally impossible for a woman to gain favor for any political role she might play. When things went well for an empress who was calling the shots herself, she was said to have attained success by sordid methods. And when things went badly for an emperor-plus-woman team, invariably the female was blamed.

To many Chinese, the wife of Mao was playing havoc at the court like wicked concubines of the past (Da Ji in the Shang dynasty, Bao Si in the Zhou, the famous concubine Yang in the Tang). Unlike Empress Wu and Empress Lü, such favorites were not career politicians but meddling amateurs. They were linchpins of the court's emotions, but they were not part of the court's political structure. They played upon the weakness of the flesh of their emperor-lovers and defied a doubting or angry bureaucracy. They were husband-dependent, amateur, female politicians. They brought disaster to the Chinese state as well as to themselves.

In a culture where it is thought that everything capable of happening has already happened before, Jiang Qing was seen to be following in the footsteps of Da Ji, Bao Si, and concubine Yang—as surely as Mao was following in the footsteps of the great founding emperors, tirelessly dealing with affairs of state with one hand as he tried to swat off his wife's quixotic imprecations with the other.

The shoe did not really fit. Jiang was more than a meddling

amateur; hedonism did not govern her. She had a theatrical career behind her, she was in the midst of a spectacular political career, and her ambition was to be China's ruler (chairman of the Communist Party). She was more than a silk-clad playgirl, bored with life in the Palace, cooking up fantastic schemes to get her husband's attention, stretching out a milky leg to lasso him from the office to the bedroom.

Then was Jiang like Empress Lü, a *son*-dependent *professional* politician? Of course, no. For all the power and influence Jiang had built up since 1966, she lacked the one thing needful in a Communist court that increasingly functioned like a Confucian court: She had no son to be a stalking horse for her advance to power.

"By 1971, when I saw her again," said an acquaintance of Jiang Qing's who had last seen her in 1969, "something had happened to her voice." Previously it had been a beautiful, commanding voice, which she used slowly and confidently. Now "something tight and desperate lived in it." The political trials of the late 1960s had taken a toll of Jiang's equanimity. Her temper was less under control. Her sense of being boxed in by enemies was at times absurdly exaggerated. She had become more vain and egotistical.

"In came Jiang Qing like a small whirlwind, buzzing in a suit," the same visitor recalled; "her voice [was] loud and imperious. She sat down and stood up, sat down again, wiped her face, wiped her arms to the elbows, wiped her neck to the armpits with the hot towels handed to her; as if she had just come from the fields. . . ."

"You ask her about the theater, she tells you about her illnesses," this visitor found. "You ask about the concept of 'continuing the revolution' and she speaks of how badly this or that person has treated her."

Like Lyndon Johnson, Jiang was elemental enough to exhibit parts of her body as visual accompaniment to a conversation. But she exceeded LBJ—for whom a scar on the stomach was just that—in making her body the pivot of philosophic truths. She would pull apart her big mouth to show a broken tooth; a man had done that—was the suffering of the female half of mankind not appalling? She would hoist up her frock and push a finger against a tiny scar; a dog had done that—were the enemies of the revolution not omnipresent?

Jiang had become a politician in her own right, and she was a most unusual one. In China, politics is economics plus geography plus guns. But Jiang had few interest groups as her natural backers and little (except for Shanghai) in the way of a regional base. Her power was personal. She dealt in the coin not of political majorities, military divisions, and industrial output, but of personalities. She had no constituency; she had followers. No good at keeping track of who had historical associations with whom, or anticipating what the next fight over economic policy was likely to be, she was a genius at spotting a young man with ambition, or sensing which important marriage was nearing the rocks.

Of Empress Wu during the period of the decline of her emperor-husband, it was written: "The court was already beginning to understand that Wu [Zetian] as empress in the conduct of business was not merely a convenient channel for influencing the emperor, but an exacting mistress with a clear head." Jiang, too, had gone beyond the role of a channel for influencing Mao and was the exacting mistress of a burgeoning political operation. She was no longer to be seen handing out signed copies of Mao's *Selected Works*, like a combination of loyal wife and amateur publicity agent.

Like Empress Wu, Jiang counterbalanced her hostility toward senior officials with an open heart toward junior officials. This was the accidentally revolutionary nature of both women's rise to high place. The audacity of their bid for power—every fiber of Chinese culture seemed to cut against the idea—required the summoning of a new world to redress the imbalance of the old. To find an undiscovered cadre of the best and brightest was their only hope.

For years Jiang bore, as Eleanor Roosevelt did, the consequences of being the wife of an imperious powerholder. In the 1970s Jiang was in a position to even the score a little, as Mrs. Roosevelt was in the 1940s. The terrible food served in FDR's White House was one of Eleanor Roosevelt's "quiet revenges with a moral excuse," it has been recorded. "If her husband did not like eating badly, why there were passages in their joint past she had not liked either." Jiang Qing's "quiet revenges" took two forms. She made use of Mao's authority to beat down officials not well disposed toward her and to raise up those loyal to her. Half the top victims of the Cultural Revolution were Jiang's personal enemies; half the strong new faction of ultraleftists were her personal protégés.

And Jiang began to exercise her right to "equal freedom" within the marriage. It was not her style to throw herself to the wall over Mao's peccadillos, just as it was not Eleanor Roosevelt's style to storm out over FDR's affair with Lucy Mercer. He Zizhen had done that when Lily Wu came on the scene in 1937, but Jiang was a broader, shrewder woman than Mao's earlier wife. It was a political marriage that Jiang now had with Mao.

Nevertheless, in the 1970s, Jiang Qing practiced a bit of "quiet revenge" in the realm of sex. When Mao took as a lover a girl named Zhang Yufeng, whom he met on a train where she worked as a conductress,* and showed more than a passing interest in his English-language tutor, Zhang Hanzhi, wife of the foreign minister, Qiao Guanhua, Jiang became quite brazen about her intermittent bouts with Zhuang Zedong, the dashing young table tennis champion (who found himself rewarded with a meteoric rise to the post of Minister of Sports). Mao was getting old; Jiang was riding high; a bit of "quiet revenge" seemed in order.

By 1974 she grew bold about it. "Why shouldn't a woman have male concubines?" she said to a women's audience that summer in Tianjin. "Empress Wu Zetian had male concubines. . . ." (This led a woman official in the audience to start receiving boyfriends at home; her husband later said he dared not protest.)

Mao and Jiang differed in their amorous tastes. Mao in his old age didn't seek out intelligent or famous girls—just pretty and innocent girls. But Jiang liked her boyfriends to offer an excitement that went beyond the physical. She would go for a pianist, a Ping-Pong player, a rising young writer. Mao was narrowing down to basics; Jiang Qing still was trying to broaden her life.

As she rose higher and studied empresses who rose and fell by intrigue and violence, Jiang became security-mad. A rumor led her to fear assassination by a helicopter attack from above South and Central Lakes. Could an army chopper not swoop down by night before the palace guard, called Unit 8341, knew what was afoot? A bomb might be tossed into her chamber; or the helicopter crew might reach down, haul her aboard, and carry her off to a torture room as bad as any devised by Empress Wu.

Jiang felt that "special equipment" could be erected on the roofs of her Ming dynasty residence to resist a hostile helicopter. Too defensive to broach openly with her staff the vulnerability she felt, she summoned her chief bodyguard, a man supplied to her by Kang Sheng and well versed in Kang's ways, and hinted at the danger she foresaw. Pointing to the sky, then plunging a finger toward

* A child of this union, eleven years old as of this writing, lives in South and Central Lakes.

her own breast, she could have been directing an opera, but her bodyguard, who had probably heard the rumor that an "anti-Empress Dowager" group in the army had taken an oath to kill Jiang Qing in her own bed, got the message.

The elegant tile roofs were surveyed, guns on swivel bases were discreetly acquired, money was transferred from a fund for the restoration of Buddhist temples to pay the colossal bills. No helicopter attack occurred, but a machine-gun section was added to Unit 8341 (dismantled only years later, after Jiang's fall).

During a period of ill health when she became dependent on an array of medications, Jiang Qing became convinced that her medical personnel, in the long tradition of court intrigue, were giving her the wrong pills to kill her on behalf of a highly placed enemy.*

A nurse called Zhao Yisi (Melodious Thought Zhao) one evening brought in Jiang Qing's usual sleeping pill, which Jiang took in silence. Half an hour later Jiang rang the bell for Nurse Zhao: Where on earth was her sleeping pill? Zhao pointed out that she'd taken it, but Jiang said she hadn't and insisted on downing a second. The next morning she felt so poorly she could hardly move her limbs. To other staff members she conveyed her conviction that Nurse Zhao was a secret agent sent by Lin Biao's remnants to kill her with an overdose of pills. When an assistant nurse scoffed at the idea, Jiang lunged at her with a pair of scissors. Jiang ordered a long "investigation" of Nurse Zhao in Villa 17 at Fishing Terrace Guesthouse, and the girl lost her nurse's badge and certificate.

Absolute power is a magnifying glass for personality. "The absolute monarch," writes a biographer of Empress Wu, "is like an actor posturing before a gigantic distorting mirror, which projects his every movement to colossal dimensions."

For all the changes that communism brought to China, the larger-than-life shape of political leadership—now heroic, now demonic—was the same under Maoism as it had been under Confucianism. Nor was this simply a conspiracy visited upon the Chinese people by a vain and selfish elite. Chinese society was not dramatically less backward in the 1970s than it had been a century before; the readiness to see leaders as gods was by no means dead.

The point was especially true of Jiang Qing, because her participation in politics from the start was an exercise in personal self-expression. By the early 1970s, in the kingdom of Chinese com-

* Soviet sources claim that Jiang assisted Mao in efforts to kill Wang Ming with poisonous medications in Yanan.

munism, her smile was a bumper harvest, her frown was an earth-quake, her indecision was a bureaucratic logjam.

People's Daily, with its prefabricated slabs of political concep-tualization, tried to suggest that at the top of Chinese politics indi-vidual taste, lust, vision, and fear meant nothing. In truth, they meant almost everything, and even more in the case of a woman than of a man, because her position was less secure.

Empress Wu became terribly proud of having trained a cat to live in harmony with several parrots in the same cage, a feat accom-plished by keeping the cat at all times sated with food of its liking. One day she summoned the cage to be brought to the Hall of Audi-ence and had it passed around the assembly of officials for everyone to wonder at. This magnificently restrained cat had become, in Wu's mind, almost a symbol of her own brilliance and ingenuity as empress. It was important to her that the officials see and marvel at it. Unfortunately the cat, perhaps excited by the occasion, sud-denly attacked, killed, and began to eat one of the gaudy parrots. The empress almost dropped off her throne. Many a chuckle was with difficulty suppressed around the Hall of Audience. But the empress was livid; there would be hell to pay, and not only by the cat.

Jiang's monkey became as important to her as the cat to Em-press Wu. The more experience Jiang had of men, the more she liked her monkey. She dressed it in silk, fed it only the finest fare, and trained it to jump out unexpectedly and frighten people as they walked along the paths of her orchid garden in Canton. By the mid-1970s it was a litmus test of staff members' loyalty to Jiang to fawn upon her monkey. It was a necessary sign of political rectitude to accept in good grace its sudden, terrifying descent upon one's shoul-der during an evening stroll in the orchid garden.

Becoming nervous about the impact among Chinese intellec-tuals of foreign comment that she was positioning herself to try to succeed Mao, Jiang arranged with the censors to have pages carry-ing articles about her cut out of foreign magazines before they reached their destinations within China. People who sat down with an issue of *Time* or *l'Express* or *Die Zeit* that had a page or two missing appreciated Jiang Qing's ambition, sensitivity, and will-fulness.

Power that is not accountable to an electorate not only cor-rupts, it also makes a spoiled child of the absolute powerholder in allowing an individual personality to become a universe of its own without reference beyond itself, not subject to the sting of criticism, not restrained by the habit of compromise.

Jiang Qing in power talked of the world, her colleagues, and policies as if all had been cut down to the level of life in a township of which she was a leading light. The Soviets were nasty neighbors who polluted the air and couldn't be trusted not to steal chickens from her side of the fence. Zhou Enlai was a reliable uncle who always knew what to do at the right time. Lin Biao was the ex-lover from down the street whose buddies slandered her in idle gossip in the town square and undermined her work at the local dramatic society. Yao Wenyuan was an obedient valet who never raised difficult issues. Mao was the father she looked to for protection, though she didn't always understand him, and sometimes he said no to her pet projects. The "masses" in the neighboring hovels were but stage props for her performance as First Lady of the township.

However much it was the system of Chinese despotism, and her own upward struggle as a woman, that forced Jiang into a pattern of personalized, arbitrary politics, the result was appalling. A revolution was betrayed; a great people were taken for granted like a herd of tame sheep; a nation was diverted from economic development to the vain rituals of court politics.

"Even Mao does not divulge the details of his personal life to other people," Huang Hua said to his visitor in irritation as he talked about an extraordinary piece of self-revelation by Jiang Qing during 1972. Roxane Witke, a brilliant and determined scholar of Chinese history, spent days with Jiang in Peking and Canton, hearing her views on life, the Chinese Revolution, and herself. "Let me dissect myself before you," Jiang purred to the American scholar, taking an approach poles apart from Chinese tradition and Communist practice alike.*

Huang Hua was not correct about Mao; he did speak at length of his personal life to Edgar Snow in the 1930s, and somewhat less publicly on many later occasions. But the former foreign minister's

---

* Two skillful recent interviewers of Chinese women leaders gave this report on the difficulty of getting them to talk about their own lives: "In one interview we reminded the subject four times that we were more interested in her own story than a political analysis. Four times she smiled broadly, dismissed our request, and proceeded to talk about the revolution, about China, about women in general. . . . This reticence might be explained as simple politeness or political discretion. But there seems to be more to it than that. Socialist ideology reinforces elements of tradition that encourage all people, men and women, to not draw attention to themselves. Beyond that, however, women seem especially modest and comfortable with being less assertive than men."

"even Mao" was heavy with meaning; in this delicate territory Mao was alone. *"Only* Mao may divulge the details of his personal life to other people" would have been a more candid way to put the matter.

Yet Jiang did unveil herself. Once more she crossed the boundary of the permissible.

This was the "new Jiang Qing," bent on carving out a persona that defied her enemies, Chinese political conventions, and, sadly, the truth about her own past. She did not ask Mao's permission to meet with Roxane Witke; Jiang must have known he would not have approved. But now she was reaching beyond Mao, presenting herself not as his wife but as his accomplished follower. She did not talk much to Witke about Mao. Jiang talked of herself, as a different, lesser, but also parallel revolutionary figure—one who had learned much at Mao's side and was equipped to take the kingdom from his trembling hand.

This was the same *old* Jiang Qing, the Shumeng, Yunhe, and Lan Ping who wanted to express herself, to be understood her way, to be taken note of as an independent spirit who set her own rules.

Having in the Cultural Revolution removed (she hoped) the traces of her contacts with Chiang Kai-shek circles, Jiang Qing could in 1972 paint a picture of a Communist fighter who even as a teenager despised the bourgeoisie. Having torn out from the pages of history (she supposed) the evidence that Yu Qiwei gave her a start as a young political activist and that her charm and her ego drove Tang Na to several suicide attempts, she was free to thrust upon Witke the image of a one-man woman, Mao's "supporter," available to carry on his work.

If Jiang was filling up for Witke the blank page she thought she had created by destroying many records of her Shanghai years, she did not fill it with the story of her real heart and mind. Not only were her second and third husbands—leaving aside her first, the young Mr. Fei—never mentioned in the interviews, but neither did Jiang once utter the names of Empress Wu, Empress Lü, or Empress Dowager Ci Xi. The men in her life and the women in her dreams were omitted, like the steak from a steak dinner.

Of course, Mao would not have liked Jiang to speak to a foreigner of Tang Na or Empress Wu.* But he did not like the

* When this point was put to Tang Na, he responded: "That's not the only reason why she didn't mention my name; she was *ashamed* of the way she'd treated me!"

whole idea of the interview; he cursed her for having given it—emptied as it was of her private passions—because he felt that the act of giving it was a bid to be empress. That she divulged "state secrets" was not clear (in China a phone book can be a state secret). This accusation was a fig leaf to cover the real rock of offense: She had divulged the unmentionable secret of a woman's unbecoming desire to grab supreme power.

Never mind that Jiang told Witke about civil war battles; leave aside her remark that Mao had no taste in food and simply would eat the dish nearest him on the table. Her real crime was to use a *red pen* to sign the photos she gave to Witke—in old China red ink was the sign of the emperor's writing.

Were there highly placed officials in Peking who were delighted to see Jiang commit this act of self-revelation—so risky in Chinese culture—and felt she had walked into a trap? Jiang at any rate felt no qualms at the time. She did consult Premier Zhou in advance of meeting Witke. "A conversation of about an hour is good enough," Zhou wrote in reply to her query. She disregarded this advice (it was hardly an instruction). But as the Jiang-Witke meetings continued, the premier intervened to urge Jiang to "talk about art and literature only, not other issues." This made Jiang angry. Gazing at the message from Zhou Enlai, she shouted at the far-off Zhou, in the presence of the staff who brought it to her: "You just keep out of my business! You've got guts—daring to encircle *me*, to attack *me!*"

Jiang Qing showed her American visitor how she could be militant and feminine at the same time. She gave the young but experienced scholar advice on how to overcome bourgeois ideas, and how to drink a brew of lotus to enhance urination. She thought it wonderful that both of them should find in life objects of worship; when Witke confessed that she had found in this female Chinese leader a "teacher" (*lao shi*), Jiang was in the seventh heaven of ecstasy.

Silk sheets lay on the bed in the airplane that bore Witke to Jiang's presence at Canton, just as silk sheets had been a badge of power for a previous Chinese female politician, Madame Chiang Kai-shek; in both cases men critics felt the lady had gone to "extremes." One night at the dinner table, Jiang reached for a box and presented Witke with a skirt. "I like skirts," Jiang declared, "and they're comfortable in summer."

How was it possible for Jiang Qing to be at once a Communist and a self-indulgent empress? A vicious woman who helped dispose of many people and yet a charming companion, gossiping, snapping

photos, talking about clothes? Because, cushioned by the environment within a cocoon of power, she had made a series of identifica-
tions between her own personality and the Communist cause. Her
rebelliousness, born when she saw her father attack her mother, she
aligned with the class revolt of the dispossessed against "capitalists"
and "landlords." Her quest for vindication as a woman she now saw
as requiring the gathering into her hands of supreme power within
the Communist Party of China.

The Tenth Communist Party Congress late in the summer of
1973 was a standoff between Jiang Qing's radicals and Zhou Enlai's
moderates, with Mao brooding above, as if only half interested in
the struggle going on at his feet, refusing to choose yet another successor to replace Lin Biao. Jiang was not pleased when Mao, locked
into the antileft logic of his fight with Lin, brought Deng Xiaoping
back on deck. She and Deng were as far apart in temperament as it
was possible for two Chinese Communist leaders to be. "He is the
old king of counterrevolution," rasped the queen of revolution.

Yet Jiang carried herself like a woman of destiny. If history
seemed bound to knock her down, she was blissfully blind to the
odds against her.

It was an evening to remember at the Great Hall of the People
as Jiang Qing played host to the Pine Mountain Ballet Troupe from
Japan. The past decades must have rolled away before her eyes. In
Shanghai in the thirties she begged Japanese visitors to pressure
their government to stop destroying China; at the Great Hall she
grandly received on behalf of China's millions a bowing and scrap-
ing Japanese delegation that was timidly hoping Chinese audiences
might find its dances acceptable. Beaming, she gave the head of the
troupe a photo of a landscape. Peering close, the Japanese dancers
recognized a famous picture: This was "Li Jin's" shot of the Fairy
Cave at Mount Lu, on the back of which Mao had written his ardent
verse, signed "For Li Jin."

With a flourish Jiang took a pen and wrote on the back of this
print: "Taken by Jiang Qing" *(Jiang Qing she)*. It was a daring act.
For years the Chinese reading public had known of Mao's poem,
but, since it was considered an erotic poem, Li Jin's identity had
been kept a secret. On this evening filled with the good feelings of
Chinese-Japanese friendship, Jiang decided to tell the world that Li
Jin was herself; that the master photographer was none other than
the object of the emperor's passion, Jiang Qing herself.

"It's better not to see each other," Mao wrote to Jiang in the spring of 1974. "You haven't carried out many of the things I talked to you about over the years. What's the use of more meetings with you?"

The marriage had reached yet another stage. During 1973 Jiang moved out of South and Central Lakes to a grand apartment at Fishing Terrace Guesthouse. Mao, in a moment of anger at Jiang's growing willfulness, decreed that she must write him a note if she wanted to come to see him. "You're one of those people," Mao's 1974 letter went on, "who never discusses big matters but sends daily information on trivial matters." Jiang's meetings with Witke had damaged her in Mao's eyes.

Yet this marriage, whose state probably was the single most important factor in Chinese politics, was by no means over; for both partners it still carried personal and political weight.

In the 1960s the marriage had soared because the pair's expectations were congruent: Mao needed Jiang, and Jiang had everything to gain by seizing the political opportunity Mao's need gave her. In the 1970s they were no longer working together as a political team. Mao reigned but no longer ruled. "My body is riddled with diseases," he lamented to Australian Prime Minister Gough Whitlam; "I have an appointment with God." In a loosened-up situation, Jiang Qing became an independent force. She did indeed fail to "carry out" some of his advice to her; with her eyes on the post-Mao era she was no longer the loyal wife expending her own life for her husband's career. Yet Mao and Jiang were locked together, structurally and even emotionally.

Mao did not always agree with Jiang and the leftists—he did not always agree with himself—but probably he disliked the "rightists" more. The Cultural Revolution had not gone well; but Mao did not want to admit it, or forgive and rehabilitate its victims.

The claim now made in China that Mao by 1970 had "seen through" Jiang and her leftist associates and realized that they and Lin Biao's group were "in collusion" is unconvincing. After 1970, Mao had a great deal to do with Jiang and her leftist associates; if he'd wanted to get rid of them and hand the future to Zhou, Deng, and their type, the period immediately after Lin's fall was the ideal time. But he did not do so. His reliance on Zhou at that time seemed grudging; and Deng was left to feed pigs in a village.

Jiang's new independent power irritated Mao, yet it did not mortally offend him. "She's poking her nose into everything," he snapped during the summer as she rode high in Peking while he received foreign leaders at a southern resort whose name the bureaucracy kept secret. "She lectures people wherever she goes—anyway, she represents only herself."

By the end of the year he was telling associates, "Jiang Qing has wild ambitions." Yet this was hardly a fresh discovery; and still Mao was merely slapping her wrist. He declared on this same occasion, "Jiang Qing wants to become chairman of the Communist Party." It was the first time the unutterable possibility had been uttered. Yet Mao did nothing decisive to kill her ambition.

A weird campaign to "criticize Confucius and Lin Biao" (one dead two and a half millennia before, one dead two and a half years before) was going on. It was a bottle into which the struggling factions poured whatever wine served a current political purpose. Jiang Qing treated "Confucius" as a code word for any political or intellectual force that thrived before the Cultural Revolution; consolidating the "gains" of that storm was essential to building up her image as a stateswoman. Zhou (who cunningly tacked an anti–Lin Biao fringe onto an existing campaign against Confucius) stressed Lin's "leftist errors"; consolidating the anti-Lin coalition was essential to shore up his position. Mao was ambivalent. Now he supported Jiang and her ultraleftist circle; now he placated the moderates ("It's time to settle down," he declared at year's end); now he simply sat on the mountain and watched the tigers fight below.

It was crucial for Jiang to read correctly the signals coming from Mao's wavering mind. It was only after Mao became cool toward Zhou in the spring of 1974 that she felt able to make veiled public attacks on the premier (as a backward, elitist "Confucian"). At the end of the year Mao and Jiang exchanged long letters. Jiang had to retreat a bit from her anti-Zhou position; she had slightly misread Mao on that. But she also complained of "idleness," making a bold request for more political responsibilities. "Do research," he said in his reply.

Once again Jiang was finding it hard to be a success at her work and also a success as a woman. In a precarious way, in Shanghai, she had been both; then for years she was Mao's wife and nothing more. As the Cultural Revolution unfolded she again had a career and a rewarding marriage—but now she had lost the second. She must have wondered if in China it was impossible to have both kinds of success.

* * *

Not since her great year of 1966 did Jiang Qing play such a prominent public role as in the second half of 1974. She was everywhere, she saw everyone. She signed letters "Director of the Anti-Lin and Anti-Confucius Office," which meant chief of the hot political crusade of the moment. She was routinely listed first when any gathering of Chinese leaders in Peking was described. With Mao away from Peking for eight months, she seemed to be the linchpin of the government, *the* person for the ever-nervous bureaucrats to take their lead from.

The tenth anniversary of her foray into opera reform in 1964 was commemorated as if she were a sage. *People's Daily* called her an "expounder of Chairman Mao's thought"; this spine-chilling appellation was an honor until then reserved for Liu, Lin, and other putative successors. She gave out "instructions" (*zhi shi*), which in Chinese communism were what a papal pronouncement is in the Vatican. As a "national leader" of China, she received the president of Cyprus, the presidents of Togo and Mauretania, and a string of other foreign heads of government, greeting them in Mao's name, summarizing for them the glories and burdens of the realm.

Turn on the TV and there was her face, smiling as she looked upon light, stern as she beheld darkness. Open the newspaper and there was news of her activities, troubleshooting here, exhorting there, inspecting somewhere else, with photos of her in a professional-looking Sun Yat-sen jacket and trousers.

"Don't appear in public too often," Mao urged her from his mountain in South China. "Don't write pronouncements on documents all the time, or act as a string-puller for a kitchen cabinet." Content to be out of the fray, the sinking emperor nevertheless was closely observing the situation. "You have offended too many people. . . ."

Meanwhile, the various branches of the rooted tree that is China's official press burst out with articles in praise of Empress Lü. Firm of purpose, she won glory by taking over upon the death of her husband, Liu Bang, first emperor of the Han dynasty, and carrying on his policies. What was said of Jiang's other woman-ruler hero, Wu Zetian, when she reached the top, could now virtually be said of Jiang herself: "Life or death, reward or punishment, were decided by her word. The Son of Heaven [emperor] sat on his throne with folded hands, and that was all. Court and country called them the 'Two Holy Ones.' "

"That summer," a Peking resident recalled, "we saw film and TV footage of Jiang Qing greeting foreign guests, and her hair was permed. Until then it was a *crime* for any Chinese woman to have a permanent wave. After that it was permitted, and many women tried this style."

Just after Mao left Peking, when Jiang was riding high as the apparent number two in the regime, she wrote an audacious poem, matched it with one of her own photos, and took it to the editor of *China Photo*. The poem was about a mountain, and the photo was of a soaring peak, but this lofty, beautiful, modest, underrated mountain was none other than Jiang Qing! The poem would win no literary prize:

> Overlooking the river a soaring peak
> Its face obscured in mists
> Mostly it is not beheld
> Just occasionally its majesty is revealed.

The word for "river" is her own name "Jiang," and the entire quatrain is an echo of the Tang dynasty couplet that had inspired the choice of her name (replacing Lan Ping) in Yanan. Both words of her name are in the second line of the Tang couplet: *Jiang shang shu feng qing* (Overlooking the river rise a number of green peaks). Whether or not Jiang had Mao in mind when she wrote of "mists," as her critics later said, the poem conveyed Jiang's feeling that she had not yet attained the acclaim that was her due. (Jiang led Witke to believe that *Mao* had written this poem of praise *to* her!)

The poem and photo, Jiang told the editor of *China Photo,* were to appear under a pseudonym, the name of a famous ancient monument in her home county of Zhucheng. She wanted informed people to know who the author was—after groping their way through mysterious clouds—but she did not want to make an overt announcement of vanity and ambition by signing her own name.

Jiang wanted to locate her sense of herself within China's great literary and political tradition—indeed, in the illustrious Tang dynasty that Empress Wu did much to shape. And she wanted to remind the *cognoscenti,* many of whom knew that as she and Mao began their life together in Yanan her new name had been drawn from the Tang verse, of her long and intimate partnership with the great man of the Chinese Revolution, soon to die and be replaced.

After submitting the poem and photo to *China Photo,* Jiang

abruptly withdrew it. Changing her mind, she sent it in again. *Five times she sent it in and hauled it back*, like a cat unable to decide on a hiding place for a just-caught fish. At the end she stopped publication.

Perhaps Mao, returning from Changsha, criticized this project which had so excited her. More likely, Jiang herself grew nervous and changed her mind. For all her self-confidence, she was alone as a woman in the man's world of politics; and the bid to be empress was taking her into terrain new not only to her but also to Chinese Communist (and any Communist) history. Either way, the killing of the poem and photo showed that she was in a minefield—political, psychological, or both.

One day while Mao was away in South China, the leading newspaper *Brilliant Daily* came out with a long political article entitled "Solitary Anger." The piece was written twenty-two hundred years ago by Han Fei of the *Realpolitik* or Legalist school of political thinkers. But read together with a preface supplied by *Brilliant Daily*, it was all too clearly about the parlous state of Mao's court in 1974.

Han Fei described a kingdom so sunk in lies and factionalism as to be headed for destruction. The emperor is being misled by fawning courtiers and "traitorous ministers" and especially by "an important person" who has put "villains" and "incapable people" in high government posts. It was a "monstrous crime" for the emperor to be treated like this and a "great mistake" for him to permit the "important person" to make a circus of his regime.

Citizens of Peking scrambled to get copies of this July 23 issue of *Brilliant Daily*. Debate swirled as to the identity of the "important person" leading the Mao regime to ruin (in the newspaper's view). The preface, in the Chinese way, identified only "Lin Biao–type" villains; with yesterday's villain dead three years ago, readers had to infer who today's villain was. It could only be Zhou Enlai or Jiang Qing. These two, now rival number twos, were the center of sharply differing camps. Which was attacking which?

Within hours, the July 23 edition of *Brilliant Daily* was withdrawn and burned. A new edition for the same day came out, and "Solitary Anger," which had filled page two of the first edition, had been replaced by five innocuous items of local news. Perhaps Jiang was attacking Zhou? Yet the prime minister had been in the hospital since the spring; everyone knew he had cancer and was a fading force. If Zhou was the target, the anti-Jiang group showed its power by the lightning production of a new page two for the July 23 issue of *Brilliant Daily.*

Probably the article was an attack on Jiang Qing as the "important person" who was leading the Mao court to ruin as she disputed the post-Mao future with Zhou, Deng, and others of a more bureaucratic stripe than she.

One day soon after the fuss at *Brilliant Daily,* Jiang went to a meeting of her supporters from Peking and Qinghua universities. A Talmudic-style discussion raged about choosing texts for the drive against Lin and Confucius. In the middle of it, Jiang reached for a translated copy of a dispatch from Peking by a Western journalist. "The current struggle in China," she read out to the gathering, using a foreigner's words to convey an idea she approved of but was not in a position to state openly herself, "is a struggle between moderates represented by Zhou Enlai and radicals represented by Jiang Qing." As she put down the article and glanced around the room, her expression was that of a cat munching a canary. She knew she was squared off against Zhou. She relished the struggle. And she loved the label "radical."

"Zhou can hardly wait until he is able to replace the chairman," Jiang hissed to a colleague. Her remark reached Mao's ears, and one evening, after a meeting with the king of Nepal, he said in the midst of a talk with associates about the tension between Jiang and Zhou: "It's not the premier who can't wait to be chairman—it's *my lady.*"

Jiang's hostility to Zhou Enlai came to the surface in a fight over "black art." Jiang alleged that the premier had permitted the Great Hall of the People, leading hotels of Peking, and other public places to be decorated with "unhealthy" art and furniture. Helped by Yao Wenyuan, she sent teams to report on the situation. They seized seven hundred pieces of art and decor, from buildings that Zhou Enlai had sought to grace with a cosmopolitan touch. Jiang began to replace them with "revolutionary" paintings, sculptures, and rugs. Two hundred of the seized items were gathered into an "Exhibition of Black Art." Government workers and delegations from street committees were bussed into the city center to give momentum to the month-long exhibition.

Then came the movie-operetta *Song of the Gardeners,* about two wise schoolteachers who guide youth toward light and justice. A rising Hunan politician, Hua Guofeng, had encouraged the making of the film, and many audiences liked it. It made heroes of the teach-

ers; it endorsed the idea that brilliant flowers come only from pains-
taking cultivation—both sentiments have a substantial following in
China.

But one night in the summer of 1973, Jiang Qing, flanked by
Zhang Chunqiao and Yao Wenyuan, saw *Song of the Gardeners* and
erupted against it.

"The title itself is wrong," Jiang Qing declared as the three
Shanghai radicals sat down to review the film over a late-night meal.
"How on earth can you have the gardeners be schoolteachers?"
Jiang scoffed as she toyed with a steamed fish. "They should be
Communist Party figures!" There was a song in the film that particularly upset Jiang. "Without culture," it began, "how can we shoulder the great responsibilities of revolution?" She took it—and she
was correct—as a veiled attack on the Cultural Revolution, when
culture was laughed out the doorway and teachers were sent to feed
pigs.

Wasn't this a direct assault on them all, a challenge to their political power? "The whole environment of the movie is peculiar,"
Jiang Qing went on to her dinner companions. "God, the female
teacher even says good things about the male teacher!" Whatever
Zhang and Yao may have felt, to Jiang such a state of affairs was not
"typical" of what life in her kingdom was going to be like.

Letters and phone calls about *Song of the Gardeners* flew back
and forth within Jiang's circle. About a hundred articles were published in the spring of 1974 denouncing *Song of the Gardeners*, em-
broidering garishly the points Jiang had made at dinner with Zhang
and Yao. Chu Lan, pseudonym for one of Jiang's writing teams,
came out with an article that said the film "sings the praises of the
revisionist educational line."

But Jiang Qing's attack did not enjoy plain sailing. The film
had originated in Hunan, Mao's own province, where Hua Guofeng
was powerful, and a counterattack began from Changsha. One cold
evening in December 1974, during his long stay away from Peking,
Mao, at his guesthouse near Changsha, asked to see a movie. *Song
of the Gardeners*, viewed in Changsha as a triumph of local film-
making, was chosen for the chairman. Mao was tired, and sick of
reading documents, and he enjoyed the film. He applauded. Seeing
this, a shrewd Hunan staff member observed: "Chairman, this film
is being criticized." Mao looked around the room benevolently.
"Why the criticism? You tell me what's wrong with it—I think it's a
good movie."

Mao's late-night remark hit Jiang like a bombshell. She sought out the man in Hunan who had orchestrated the counterattack. "You *made* the chairman see *Song of the Gardeners,*" she blazed. "You *imposed* that appalling film on the chairman." But in the face of Mao's remark, carefully husbanded by a network of Hunan officials and anti-Jiang officials in Peking, Jiang could not press on with her attack.

"Zhang Chunqiao is in charge of these cultural matters," she drawled to the minister of culture when he phoned to ask instructions about *Song of the Gardeners.* "He has stronger feelings about the movie than I do. . . ."

Jiang's sense of herself as a majestic peak, shrouded in persistent mist, soon was displayed in the port city of Tianjin. As Empress Wu disliked her capital of Changan, and got away whenever she could, so Jiang felt a resistance to Peking and favored her various bases around the country. As well as the apple-green villa by the lake at Hangzhou, the guesthouse with its orchid garden in Canton, and the former French Club in Shanghai, she had a "model village." Xiaojinzhuang lay on the outskirts of teeming Tianjin, the first of China's very big cities that Jiang had ever visited, from Jinan in 1927.

Chinese rulers often have gone in for model communities—a sign of putting ritual and control above the concrete progress of the whole nation—and at Xiaojinzhuang Jiang intended to express herself in just such a manner. Wang Guangmei (before Jiang got rid of her) had *her* place, where everyone talked about output and incentives. Ye Chun (until she and Lin Biao died in the aftermath of the showdown with Mao in 1971) had *her* place, where soldiers were bussed in to help the farmers. Xiaojinzhuang was Jiang's own place, where she would display the glories of mass culture and demonstrate how art can shape life.

"Chairman Mao sends you his regards," she would say in a ringing voice as her car drove up to Xiaojinzhuang and the entire population of six hundred farmers and their families gathered to greet her. "I am representing Chairman Mao and the Party Central Committee"—an astonishing formulation which, by establishing *two* lines of authority, seemed to grant her a base and mandate additional to that of the Party Center. The leading farmers of Xiaojinzhuang benefited greatly from the connection with Jiang, and they loved it when she would say, over meals at the big round table in the reception quarters, "Xiaojinzhuang is my place" (*wo de dian*). Some of them also caught the significance of her adding: "It's also the Party Center's place."

Jiang lectured leathery old men on the need to allow women more power in running the village. Arias soared from the wheat fields; teenage girls wrote clumsy poems about how resisting Confucius's rotten ideas would produce a better quality of corncob. The people of Xiaojinzhuang were told that, if they lived like the heroes of the model revolutionary theater pieces, then Xiaojinzhuang, and one day all of China, would be a just and happy place.

From Peking Jiang brought gifts: a straw hat for each citizen; sample grains of wheat; a hairpin for each woman. At the same time she behaved like a prima donna. She required all nearby fowls and animals to be locked up when she was ready for bed, since the slightest noise robbed her of her sleep. She also felt it necessary to bring to Xiaojinzhuang her special padded toilet seat with its fur trimming.

Taking a turn at working in the fields, she displayed both her enthusiasm and her vanity. She threw herself into the harvesting, sleeves rolled up, hair tousled, shouting out how much she loved manual labor. Yet she never lost her old instinct for show business. She worked feverishly for a short time and then complained of total exhaustion. Had she not been up much of each night the previous week in Peking, reading documents for the chairman? "I can't take it the way you real farmers can!" But she never left the field before the village cameraman had done his work.

A producer *manquée*, Jiang Qing viewed the farmers as a cast of characters for a drama—her bid to be empress—that had little to do with their lives.

Jiang arrived expectantly at the Tianjin port. Fresh from Xiaojinzhuang, she was joined by two loyal followers for a tour of the offshore oil drilling enterprise near Dagang. Zhuang Zedong was the table tennis champion who during Jiang's rise to power became one of her boyfriends and also minister of sports. In nicely tailored gray trousers and shining black leather shoes, his hair in perfect order as usual, he did not seem to be needed in his ministerial capacity. But Jiang had asked him to come, and so he was there. Yu Huiyong, a former musician from Jiang's home province, now minister of culture and one of Jiang's left-hand fingers, was present too, despite his ignorance of oil. In China, sports and arts people always have felt a close affinity for each other, and both men were loyal to Jiang Qing.

One reason for the visit was the struggle going on between the moderates and the radicals over economic development and foreign involvement in it. Jiang, criticized by Zhou and Deng for being all ideological talk and no economic action ("She sits on the toilet but does not manage a shit" was Deng's inelegant phrase), wished to show the Chinese public that she too cared about China's balance of payments.*

A second reason was her desire to investigate the social and cultural level of this enclave of special economic activity that may, as one of her aides suggested, be drifting away from proper imperial control.

It was a sparkling summer morning as Jiang boarded the number two oil rig at Dagang. She seemed in excellent spirits, digging Zhuang in the ribs as she asked him what he'd been doing the past week, regaling Yu with the latest anti-Deng joke that she felt may not yet have reached the Ministry of Culture. But soon after this party of urban Bohemians began to interact with the oil men, the mood darkened.

"Sing a revolutionary song for me!" Jiang brightly asked a middle-aged worker. The man stood at attention before her, a wrench in his hand, a smear of oil on his impassive face. But he could not think of a song.

"Only production, no revolution," Jiang muttered to Zhuang and Yu with a frown. It turned out that no one on the entire oil rig was able and willing to sing an aria from any of the model revolutionary theater pieces!

"I wish to meet some women workers," Jiang announced. Alas, the platform was without females. When this was reported to Jiang by the chairman of the revolutionary committee of the oil company, she became thunderous, and even Zhuang and Yu lost their everlasting smiles. "Why are there no women workers?" Jiang pressed on icily. "Have you forgotten Chairman Mao's saying that women hold up half the sky?" The pragmatic oil men replied that the rig was new and the first batch of available workers happened to be all male. "Anything men can do, women can also do," she reminded the assembly.

Jiang's word was law. The next week four women were hired to start work on the rig. At the time of Jiang's visit there had been no toilets at all on the rig; during the periods away from the dock the

* A little later Jiang remarked at a closed meeting: "Deng Xiaoping sold out all our crude oil . . . at deflated prices. He is not even a low-grade patriot."

men simply used the edge of the platform. As well as sleeping quarters for the women, a toilet for the women had to be constructed, and then, because the women had one, a toilet for the men also.

The chairman of the oil company revolutionary committee quietly cursed Jiang Qing. The men workers laughed. The four women left after three months.

Few citizens of Tianjin were prepared for "the dress." Suddenly it appeared at the women's counter of clothing stores, a garment half old and half new, half Chinese and half Western, such as no one had ever seen before. Based on a dress worn during the Tang dynasty, it featured a tight bodice with an old-fashioned side zipper, a small Chinese-style collar, and a full skirt in the Western manner. The waist was tight, and there were set-in sleeves. "It's a blend of China and the West" (*Zhong xi jie he*),* said Jiang, whose brainchild it was, unperturbed that during that same period of 1974 she was busily attacking Western music as "decadent," the filmmaker Antonioni as "that clown from Rome," and American culture as "unhealthy." She wanted to add a fresh note of pride to the appearance of Chinese women.

The garment went on sale for twenty yuan (more, later, in some other cities). Few women were ready to spend what could be one or two weeks' wages on an untested dress whose future could not be vouched for any more than Jiang Qing's. In her cocoon of privilege, Jiang simply did not realize how expensive the garment was. To give the dress a boost, she ordered cultural officials to buy huge quantities for girls appearing on public occasions as government servants. In Tianjin, TV announcers, concert artists, and the staff at fancy state establishments appeared in it, replacing their trouser suits. Sportswomen traveling to Iran for the Asian Games were supplied with the dress, as were artists in theatrical troupes on tour outside China. To meet the problem of lagging sales in the stores, Jiang Qing authorized a time-payment scheme: four yuan down and the dress was yours.

Perhaps in heaven, or hell, all women will wear identical state-prescribed dresses, but not on earth; at any rate not, it seemed, on the Chinese earth. "I can't breast-feed my baby without taking the whole thing off," one woman complained when unable to follow the usual Chinese pattern of hitching up the blouse to pull out a breast. "Five meters of material—it's too much," said another. "And wearing it I can't ride my bike or play Ping-Pong." Women would tease

* The same phrase was used for the East-West blend of the curriculum at the Arts Academy in Jinan.

or outrage each other by asking, "When are you getting your Jiang Qing dress?" In the tropical southern provinces it was from the start a suffocation, with its tight top and abundant lower half.

Women who did adopt the dress began to practice variations in fabric or accessories. Rare types who always had wanted an excuse to be different came out in a black velvet version, or adorned it with a *diamanté* clip, or seized the chance to wear shoes with one-inch heels (as extraordinary in China as five-inch heels in Paris). The dress excited some women, annoyed some, puzzled many, amazed all.

"It's exhibitionist," said a Peking woman, and that was the heart of the matter. For Jiang, ever since as a child she had been forced to wear her half brother's castoff shirts and trousers, clothes were a badge of the larger issue of freedom. In her dresses and her hairdo she sought to express herself.

Chinese culture and Communist style alike rule out flamboyance, and it was flamboyance that Jiang could not resist. Over the top of a military cap she would wear a scarf tied with a flourish under her handsome chin, and a long coat (in cold weather), cinched in at her perfect waist. Did she realize what an electric shock she sent through Mao's kingdom?

Some Chinese women were thrilled to see her take her place at the top; it was the same sentiment that some British women felt at Margaret Thatcher's capture of Number 10 Downing Street. Others felt Jiang had broken ranks with ordinary women. In sponsoring the dress, didn't Jiang only draw attention to the precariousness of her position within the male-dominated Chinese political establishment?

"If only she'd had a more modest style," lamented one woman, "she would not have been attacked in such a savage and sexist way."

In her new role as the "national leader" who gives the ultimate audience to a visiting foreign dignitary, Jiang met with Imelda Marcos, the wife of the Philippine president, on September 20, 1974. (Li Xiannian, who outranked Jiang in Party and state, was present as mute accompaniment.)

Over the next two days, Jiang ebulliently escorted Señora Marcos to cultural shows and factories. The former beauty queen from Manila touched off a spark of excitement in Jiang. Both were tough women who had to fight to get where they were, yet in each other's company they found it nice to let their hair down and chat about the man's world they had pierced.

There always had been a blend of the battle-ax and the shy girl in Jiang Qing. She could be as coarse as a British fishwife, yet she would never put a cherry in her mouth and withdraw the stone later, but take a tiny knife and delicately pit the cherry before allowing it in her mouth. She was a girl from the gutter who had become a woman unable to put on her shoes without the help of a maid.

In Imelda Marcos's company she felt able to let the two sides of her character come together. She found she could relax and have a good time without ceasing to be conscious of herself as a powerful woman. That the Philippines had diplomatic relations with the Chiang Kai-shek regime on Taiwan, and none with Peking, was the last thing on Jiang's mind. In Señora Marcos she had a mirror to see herself as she wished to be seen: powerful and attractive, a success in politics without ceasing to be successful as a woman.

On the afternoon of September 23, Jiang decided to ask Marcos to extend her stay in China. After telling her guest of the plans for the theater that evening, Jiang (disregarding the fact that it had been Premier Zhou who invited Señora Marcos to China) asked her to stay on. "I have a surprise in mind for tomorrow," she said with a little laugh. Marcos agreed to prolong her visit.

At 9:00 A.M. the next morning, Jiang and Marcos arrived in Tianjin to be greeted by a crowd of one million. Vice-Foreign Minister Han Nianlong rushed like an errand boy to fulfill their every need. Wang Hairong, a relative of Mao's who was a senior foreign ministry official, went along to assist and marvel.

"I think Jiang Qing wanted to demonstrate," said a member of the Marcos party, "as one woman politician to another, what a following she had in this city." Jiang also was answering Wang Guangmei, who twelve years before had made a display in playing host to Madame Sukarno. It was the first time Jiang had accompanied the wife of a foreign chief of state on a tour of China. Jiang made the most of it by driving her guest in triumph to "her place," the village-turned-cultural festival of Xiaojinzhuang.

The farmers sang and danced and expressed their political militancy for the two lady visitors. Inspecting animal sheds, cornfields, and flour mills, Jiang recapitulated for her Filipino guest the themes of a speech she had given in Tianjin in midsummer. Did Señora Marcos know that China's Empress Wu was "stronger than the men" of her age? Had she heard of the "great feudal stateswoman," Empress Lü?

Marcos returned to Manila feeling that Jiang Qing was not a "radical ideologue" after all, but actually a "soft-spoken and very feminine" person, grappling successfully with her high responsibilities. Meanwhile, the trip to Xiaojinzhuang had given wonderful national publicity to "Jiang Qing's place." Zhou Enlai may have invited Señora Marcos to China, but Jiang Qing had taken her over.

Jiang was playing with the building blocks of power. She went among the masses as her audience; she talked about politics with the ambitious young Bohemians of her circle. But she did not know how to use power. Military affairs, administrative work, the calculation of interests—she had no head for these. If she became empress, what would she stand for? Her policy would center on Peking opera; her idea of a political journey would be a trip to Xiaojinzhuang.

The separate villas of Fishing Terrace Guesthouse dot the shores of a lake; its high walls keep out prying eyes. Since she had effectively moved out of South and Central Lakes, and had become the ringleader of a "Shanghai faction" of radicals, Jiang Qing made Fishing Terrace her personal and professional base. Villa 10 was her residence, Villa 17 her office.

In all dictatorships, and not a few democracies, there are factions with their own habits and places of meeting, their favorite restaurants and clubs, their little networks of corruption; Jiang's Fishing Terrace was not especially evil, but it did have its own style. As her power grew and her staff expanded, there were more things she could not do without, and more she could not stand.

She liked to begin the day with a report on the weather so detailed as to seem more suited to an airline pilot than to a person who intended to spend the morning in bed reading documents. Wind, noise, and light still were her chief worries. As well as the temperature in each room and at each point in the guesthouse gardens, Jiang needed to know the velocity and direction of the wind and how intense the rays of the sun were likely to be. She favored a Western breakfast, eaten in bed, of two eggs, two slices of toast, and a touch of butter. She would remain in her nightclothes, reading and jotting down notes, until the cry, "I'm getting up!" would rally her private staff to the complex tasks of washing, dressing, and making her up. Bathtub water too hot or too cold would produce an accusation that someone was trying to kill her. In her toilet she kept a supply of Hong Kong movie magazines.

Jiang did not like any interruption of her morning thoughts. "Commander, good morning," a new young guard said one day, and Jiang flew into a rage. Zhang Chunqiao came to smooth the waters. "The commander is reflecting on important affairs of state," he admonished the guard. "How could you interrupt her by saying good morning?"

Jiang avoided banquets. At those ponderous affairs in the Great Hall of the People there was too much ritual, too much noise, and too many people. She could not control the situation as she could in a smaller gathering at Fishing Terrace. Moreover, a good many of the dishes served from the factorylike kitchen of the Great Hall were a terrible threat to her health, and how the dining-room staff banged the plates as they cleared up!

When in the mood, Jiang would cite the Party's call for "frugality" and the importance of avoiding "privilege" and insist that her staff join her for lunch or dinner. Most Chinese slurp their soup, and clatter their chopsticks against the bowl when eating the last portions of a dish. Jiang could not abide these sounds. Junior members of her staff, terrified lest they exceed the low acceptable noise level, would find themselves leaving Jiang's table hungry and creep off to ask the cook if they could eat another dish amid the friendly chaos of his kitchen. The cook understood, and they would all sit down, eat like pigs, and poke fun at their amazing boss.

Jiang loved dancing, but it was not easy for her staff to organize the dance evenings, at which a prima donna and a roomful of courtiers were supposed to enjoy themselves together. Who would and should dance with the empress? How to satisfy Jiang's pride as an actress who knew how to dance, when senior colleagues turned up for a dance evening with their clumsy old wives?

When the dance was held at Fishing Terrace and Jiang was its star, her staff had to try to strike a balance between the requirements of her health and her ego. If she danced throughout the evening she would become exhausted. "You know I'm not permitted to dance as much as that," she would reproach her nurse afterward as she sprawled in an armchair and peeled off her stockings. Yet the results were worse if too few handsome men asked Jiang to dance. Since no man from her court dared to ask her to dance without a signal from the line of command, the anxious staff constantly had to read Jiang's mind and observe her body. When she looked fresh, a man would be spirited into her presence. When the staff judged that she'd had enough, women staff members would humor her, trying to take her mind off the fact that no one was asking her to dance. When she couldn't or wouldn't dance for a long period, it was terrible, because no one was bold enough to start dancing until Jiang had been once on the floor, and sometimes she forgot to announce that she wouldn't be getting up and that others should feel free to commence.

At general dances for the Peking elite, it was the custom to spread a white powder on the polished wood tiles to avoid the old and sedate coming down with sprained ankles and broken hips. This annoyed Jiang. How could she jitterbug properly on a floor slowed down with a layer of powder? Was she to be dragged down to the level of matronly Deng Yingchao and "Backwoods Boadicea," Kang Keqing? Jiang's staff would scheme and plot against the staffs of other leaders who favored the white powder. If she lost the battle, Jiang would refuse to dance, go home, and watch a movie.

One evening, after a grueling battle with Deng Xiaoping over barefoot doctors (she regarded these paramedics as brilliant flowers of the revolution; Deng felt they eventually should give way to fully trained physicians), Jiang Qing's thoughts turned to the more appetizing prospect of an evening of home movies. She had just seen *Day of the Jackal* and loved it; now a Yugoslav film, *At Sarajevo,* was on hand, and she'd heard it was a fast-paced thriller, just what she felt like after the bout with the powerful vice-premier. It might be nice, she thought, if Zhang Chunqiao and Yao Wenyuan came over to Fishing Terrace to see it with her. Phone calls were made, and the answer came back from the offices of both Shanghai colleagues that they'd seen *At Sarajevo.* Jiang watched the film alone, then played a round of poker with her nurse before retiring.

The next morning Jiang learned that Zhang and Yao had not in fact seen *At Sarajevo.* Furious, she accused the two secretaries from Zhang's and Yao's offices of having lied to her the night before. She called them "counterrevolutionaries" and apparently succeeded in persuading Wang Dongxing, the security chief and a rising Politburo member, to have them arrested. Almost certainly it was Zhang and Yao, not the secretaries, who lied.

In the political warfare of 1975 and 1976, the most prized ammunition was Mao's written approval of an idea or a plan. Much of the battle consisted of twisting Mao's words this way or that. When the phrase "Push the national economy forward" fell from Mao's lips, the Deng circle sprang into action and made of these unexceptional words an imperial edict. "Chairman Mao never said it," Jiang Qing snapped. "It's just a damned rumor, started of course by the president of the rumor mill [Deng]."

At times Chinese politicians chastise foreigners for taking note of "gossip," as for taking an interest in the nonpolitical passions of Chinese leaders, as if this were to venture into irrelevant terrain. In fact, Chinese politics works by gossip, just as the lineup of forces is heavily influenced by grudges, family links, and other nonpolitical passions.

At a "report" meeting (*da zhao hu*) or through informal networks, a case consisting of innuendo, guilt by association, and dirty bits and pieces gathered through surveillance is made against an enemy judged too weak to counterattack successfully. It is crucial to know who is loyal to your enemy, and to whom your enemy is loyal; "Before you beat a dog," runs the Chinese saying, "learn his master's name."

If the smears stick, the power play is launched, and the press goes into action (first by indirection); eventually the enemy is toppled, and it is explained that in fact he or she has been evil since childhood. For Jiang Qing, all those years as Mao's "secretary" were not wasted; she had long been in a splendid position to gather information and sow innuendo.

The air was full of cries of a "two-line struggle," as meaningful as the Latin Mass to most Chinese people. Was there an abundance of new work in art and literature? (Yes, said Jiang; no, said Deng.) Was involvement in the international economy good for China? (Yes, said Deng; no, said Jiang.) Jiang threw around the word "capitalism" as Senator Joseph McCarthy threw around the word "communism." Deng and his friends chose "dogmatism" as the swear word to apply to Jiang. It all meant very little. There was only one issue: Who would gather up Mao's power when it fell from his hands? Jiang's maneuvers during 1975 were mostly about securing, or preventing, appointments that would affect the balance of power when that moment came.

Some of the maneuvers (to try to stop Deng from becoming chief of the general staff of the military; to try to make Zhang Chunqiao premier in place of the ailing Zhou) were quite legal. Others conspiratorial and even violent. Yet in China the difference was not great. Legal methods, like the illegal, were so utterly secret, so breathtakingly free from any checks, that they were simply, like the illegal, part of the infinite available apparatus for the practice of dictatorial politics.

As five thousand people turned to watch, Jiang Qing strode into the auditorium of the Great Hall of the People, with Richard Nixon grinning from ear to ear on her right, and Pat Nixon in a two-tone lavender dress on her left. Zhou Enlai was there, but a little to the rear. For this evening's performance of *Red Detachment of Women* the host was Jiang Qing, a woman of mystery to the Americans, presumed to be hostile to the link with the United States that Mao and Zhou had begun to forge.

She chose to be charming but lofty, which suited the situation. Nixon was a squalid bourgeois, she knew that; but her husband felt his visit could serve China's interests, so she was going to do her best, while making a few points of her own and gaining international fame for *Red Detachment*. She was dressed in an austere trouser suit, like Deng Yingchao, Zhou's wife, who was sitting a few chairs away. Yet she looked different from Deng and the other Chinese women because of her exact grooming, her carriage, and the way she tossed her head when talking or acknowledging applause.

"Why did you not come to China before now?" There was metal in her voice as she threw the question at the leader of the anti-China lobby in the United States during the 1950s and 1960s. Fortunately for President Nixon, the drama of a heroic girl's struggle against rapacious landlords was just getting under way on the stage; he cloaked his silence in fierce concentration on the screech and clatter in front of him. In a quiet moment, Jiang mentioned to Nixon the names of a number of radical American writers she admired. Perhaps he did not like John Steinbeck as much as she did? Exactly why, she inquired, did Jack London commit suicide? When Nixon asked Jiang the names of the writer, composer, and director of *Red Detachment,* she gave him a benevolent look and said the dance-drama was "created by the masses." Nixon smiled weakly.

The whole Nixon visit in February 1972 was a well-planned piece of Chinese theater. Not for Jiang Qing the group appearances, the tedious negotiations, the salami-slicing sessions with the foreign press. She came out only once for the Nixons, to introduce them to one of her dance-dramas, on this evening when she could be the star. For the rest, the visit by the Americans was Zhou's affair, not hers.

Jiang Qing was "undeniably successful," Nixon said later, "in her attempt to create a consciously propagandistic theater piece that would both entertain and inspire its audience." Jiang was pleased that Nixon liked *Red Detachment.* Her art had proved its power to reach out and touch even a bourgeois.

When Jiang talked about international relations, she sounded sentimental one moment and bloodcurdling the next, magnanimous in her lofty cosmopolitanism on some occasions, a chauvinistic China-firster on others. The key to the contradiction was the thinness of her knowledge and her staggering subjectivity. A single delegation from abroad could leave an impression that filled the screen of her world view. One visitor's personal impact—Khrushchev's "arrogance" or Señora Marcos's "graciousness"—weighed more than a decade of diplomatic dispatches.

Talking of the India-China border war, she found its essence in the story of one Indian soldier. He carried his life's savings with him in battle, lost them, and sat down in the Himalayas and cried. A Chinese soldier found the purse of money and managed to have it returned to the Indian soldier, who was overjoyed. The Chinese side was generous, able to be so because convinced of the justice of its cause.

Using Marxist vocabulary, Jiang would denounce an enemy as a "spy" or "imperialist," unaware of the terrible chain reaction that would ensue. After a former Nationalist leader, Li Zongren, was welcomed back to Peking, Jiang called him a "foreign agent." She did not like Li, nor his wife, nor the way Zhou Enlai had "taken over" this senior figure returned from Taiwan and the United States. Her reckless use of a heavy epithet set in motion a train of events that led to Li Zongren's premature death.

At a dinner for Prince Sihanouk of Cambodia in the Great Hall of the People, most of the Chinese leaders were present, and Jiang Qing, unusually, was there too. Seated next to the charming prince, she decided to enjoy herself, feeling able to make her presence effective. She laughed, she told jokes, making the cheerful Cambodians even more cheerful. As dish followed dish, she rose repeatedly to toast each Cambodian at the head table in *maotai*, a fiery drink. "Toward the end," recalled an ambassador who was present, "she did not look too steady on her feet." Sihanouk was enchanted.

Jiang was not a great lover of *maotai*. But on this occasion she used her glass as a lever to rise above her colleagues and put herself personally into the center of China-Cambodia relations. "The only other Chinese woman I ever saw offer toasts in *maotai* was Nancy Tang [one of Mao's interpreters]," said the diplomatic eyewitness, "and Zhou Enlai himself criticized her for it." Jiang stepped out of line, made her mark, avoided being a passive member of the leadership pack. Perhaps, as the ambassador concluded, "she was taking the opportunity to advertise her ascendancy" in Mao's collapsing kingdom.

Corning Glass Works of New York State, having done some business in color video tubes with the Fourth Ministry of Machine Building, presented as a gift to ministry officials a collection of beautiful glass snails. "Where are those snails?" Jiang cried when she heard of the Corning gesture. "Bring them to me—we'll exhibit them." Hostile to the Zhou-Deng policy of increasing China's international economic involvement, she felt the Corning gift was a rope to strangle her opponents. "It's a humiliation to us," she explained to officials summoned to Fishing Terrace. "The plot is to depict us crawling." She vowed she would have every glass snail sent back to the American Liaison Office and kill the trade in color video tubes.

There was consternation in the bureaucracy. Jiang's leaping to conclusions over the significance of the gift of glass snails was matched by a general ignorance as to the meaning (if any) of such a gift within American culture. Perhaps the Americans *were* trying to insult the Middle Kingdom? . . .

Zhou Enlai began an investigation; memos flew back and forth; Hong Kong businessmen friendly to China were consulted. "After investigation," the final report said, "it was discovered that 'snail' in the United States is a kind of artistic craft . . . reflecting no malice."

Jiang acted out of colossal ignorance, as well as hostility to Zhou and Deng, and she now became extremely embarrassed. She furtively returned the sample glass snail she had retained for purposes of her campaign, and she tried to destroy all her correspondence on this matter.

Jiang often appeared antiforeign. She spoke of the "decadence" and "obscenity" of Western culture. She argued that to use "foreign equipment" at the Daqing oil field meant a "loss of face" for Chinese industry and she claimed that the export of China's oil "brought the international economic crisis to the Chinese people . . . [and] offended the Third World while saving the lives of the First and Second worlds."

To be sure, it is normal in China for politicians to accuse each other of "selling out the nation" and of "having illicit relations with foreign countries." Yet it is a fact that in policy disputes Jiang Qing stood on the isolationist, nationalistic side.

Jiang did not seem a likely candidate for antiforeignism. In habits—her piano playing, taste in movies and clothes, and resistance to social traditions—she was not a typical Chinese. But she was also didactic and ambitious; the combination, in the circumstances of Chinese politics as she rose to power, resulted in antiforeignism. Inclined to lay down the law to others on the basis of her own bits of knowledge about the West, and possessed of Mao's nationalism as one of her own badges of authority, she turned her back on the cosmopolitan and open-minded values she knew from Shanghai in the 1930s and became a Chinese chauvinist.

There were inconsistencies; she railed against Western "pornography" but loved the old Chinese sex novel *Jin ping mei.* But for a self-centered, ambitious person (in competition with "pro-Western" Zhou and Deng), consistency was something to laugh at. Leave consistency to the bureaucrats—they had so little else.

In a plush room of the Fragrant Hills Hotel west of Peking, a full assemblage of Chinese diplomats above the rank of consul waited expectantly. An important speech was to be given, for which they had left their desks and come with notebooks in hand. It was Jiang Qing who stepped to the podium, severe in a dark outfit, gravely placing the sheets of her text on the rostrum.

Jiang Qing on foreign policy! If there were some suppressed snickers, there also was apprehension. The drive against Lin and Confucius already had brought many bizarre acts of "interference" with the steady round of the Foreign Ministry's work. Mao had been out of Peking nearly eight months, and Jiang's was *the* voice to listen to. What was she up to?

Jiang looked across the silent mass of the cream of China's foreign service and smiled faintly as she adjusted her spectacles. She began with her favorite, brilliant maneuver of one step back and then two steps forward. "In regard to diplomacy I am a layman," she said with a candid shrug. "In many, many things I must learn from you." Then she impaled the diplomats on the sword of her authority. "I merely pass on to you what I have learned from the chairman. He is so busy, you know, and it is my *duty* as a Party member to gather up oral messages from him and lay them before you."

It was outrageous. Her Party duties did not include passing messages from Mao to the foreign service. But she had gotten hold of her audience. The word "oral" hinted to them that she was going to mention material beyond the documentary record.

Jiang Qing offered the tired clichés of Mao's former world view. The world was in flux. Only struggle would bring a final triumph of light over darkness. China didn't want "rich, white, and big friends"; it sought "poor, black, and small friends." "Hurricanes" of revolution were just around the corner. Waiting for them, the ambassadors extraordinary and plenipotentiary of the People's Republic of China should be "Red in quality as well as in name" and spice up their diplomacy with a bit more revolutionary militancy.

Jiang had read a few policy documents, and she was straining to be Mao's Mao. It was a naked effort to extend her power into the territory of foreign policy by linking the drive against Lin and Confucius, of which she was the chief, to international relations, of which she knew little.

Like a pupil in Bible class who knows it is best to stick close to Scripture, she assailed Henry Kissinger on the basis of Marxist texts. "His basic point of view is limited by the class interests of the bourgeoisie." Never mind that Mao had decided China needed the United States. It was entirely safe within Chinese domestic politics to throw around a few hand grenades of class analysis. She knew Mao had recently become irritated with Kissinger. Anyway, Kissinger was *Zhou's* friend, not hers.

"Enhance your awareness," she admonished, in the spirit of Confucian moralism. "Don't be temperamental," said the woman whose life was fueled by temperament. The point of the day-long meeting at the Fragrant Hills Hotel was Jiang Qing flexing her muscles in the new realm of international theory. She had sufficient mandate from Mao—or was perceived to have—to speak with authority.

At one moment in the speech, real fire came to Jiang's eyes. Quite out of context—she was speaking of "sugar-coated bullets" (one of Mao's terms for temptations) directed by foreigners at Chinese diplomats when abroad—she denounced an enemy of hers, the recently dismissed minister of foreign trade, for his sex life in Peking. "Bai Xiangguo failed to withstand the poisonous snake that took the form of a beautiful woman."

Mao and most of the other leaders never dwelled like this on a fallen colleague's sex life. But in the swirl of Jiang's mind there was no distinction between private misconduct and political shortcoming. (Minister Bai probably was a Lin Biao follower.) She had been a "poisonous snake" herself once or twice, but that she had put out of mind. Now robed in the mantle of statesmanship, Jiang still was playing the simple game of winners and losers. There were Good Men and Bad Men, those who were for her and those who were against her.

Jiang Qing had sounded like a traditional ruler. Foreigners were an unavoidable evil, to be used but not really respected. The world outside China was significant mainly as a place where China might pick up a few tips. All Jiang's Maoist words could not hide her paternalism, which, like her narrowness, was firmly within Chinese tradition.

Among Mao's enormous powers, there did not exist the power to stop people from concluding that he was dying. He *could* lop off fingers that reached too overtly for his crown. And he did this frequently, adding to the fear that enveloped Peking's palaces, closing tighter the small circle that hovered by the emperor. Because of his terrible physical weakness and because in his bitterness at death's approach he distrusted most of his top colleagues, Mao became subject to courtiers—personal staff, the guards of Unit 8341, and family members. Ironically, his increased dependence on his wife and other relatives came at a time when the disharmony of his household never had been greater.

After the marriage of Li Min, the daughter of Mao and He Zizhen (who still was in a mental home near Shanghai), Jiang succeeded in drawing a distinction between her and Li Na, her own daughter. As Li Na flourished in high posts, Li Min and her unwitting husband found themselves in the 1960s branded as "counterrevolutionaries" and imprisoned. Mao did not seem to oppose Jiang's trumpeting of Li Na; he did not seem to oppose her ill treatment of Li Min.

Over Mao's daughter-in-law Songlin, Jiang and Mao continued to pull in opposite directions. Songlin had remarried. She and her new husband, an air force officer named Yang, kept in touch with Mao, but Jiang was vigilant to keep them from visiting him at South and Central Lakes.

Jiang Qing suspected that Yang, who was considerably younger than Songlin, was ambitious to climb on board the imperial household as a full replacement for Mao's late son, Songlin's first husband. "The age difference between Yang and Songlin is far too great," she sniped once in Mao's presence. "If it wasn't for some political reason, there's no way they could really make a life together." Jiang may well have been right.

One day soon after the death of Lin Biao, Songlin and her husband were taken into custody at the Shanghai garrison. Held separately, they were grilled on what they knew of the Mao-Jiang relationship. The aim of this investigation, which Jiang was involved in and Songlin claims she directed, was to establish how much they knew about Mao's criticisms of Jiang.

Songlin denied she'd ever talked to her new husband about Mao's view of Jiang; he was from a simple peasant family, she said, and such high (or low) issues of imperial household diplomacy were not among his interests. For more than forty days there was a stalemate, with Yang saying nothing and Songlin murmuring generalities that did not satisfy the investigators of the Shanghai garrison. Jiang spoke to Wang Hongwen, a handsome ex-textile worker from Shanghai who rose rapidly during the Cultural Revolution. Wang dispatched a flunky to the house of detention. "Write a full confession of all you know on this matter," the flunky warned the couple, "or you'll never be released." After nearly five months, apparently they wrote something, and a date of release was announced.

Mao Anqing, the mentally troubled son of Mao and Yang Kaihui, was stably married to Shaohua, sister of Songlin. Jiang Qing would have nothing to do with them. In 1970 Shaohua gave birth to a baby at Number 301 hospital in Peking. Jiang saw in this event a danger of renewed contact between the young couple and the imperial household. Helped by Wu Faxian, the air force chief, she put a virtual quarantine around Shaohua's ward at Number 301 hospital. According to the young mother, the phone connection to the ward was cut off, and her own mother's home phone number was changed. Anqing, the infant's father, who was in the middle of one of his mental crises, came to the conclusion, after seventy days of silence from the hospital, that Shaohua and the baby must have died! Was Mao too busy or too ill to focus on these maneuvers among his own family members?

Meanwhile, Li Yunxia, Jiang's half sister, had moved out of South and Central Lakes in the early 1960s to live at Qinghua University with her son, Wang Bowen. "After Li Na and Li Min grew up," neighbors of Li Yunxia at Qinghua explained, "there was no longer the same need for her in Mao's household." In fact, tensions had swirled about her because she was so tenaciously loyal to Jiang, and Mao was glad to see her go.

At Qinghua University, Li Yunxia became a quiet liaison officer for Jiang's activities, from the house on campus that she shared with Wang Bowen, the one who had gone to study in Russia at the same time as Songlin, now a professor of Russian. In the harassment of Wang Guangmei and later in the development of an ultraleft group at Qinghua devoted to the Shanghai radicals, Li Yunxia did her part for her famous half sister.

Mao's nephew, Mao Yuanxin, was now at thirty-two a formidable political figure who looked up to "Auntie Jiang" as his leader. A graduate of the Harbin Military Engineering Institute, he had risen to be deputy head of the military region centered at Shenyang and a key ally of the Shanghai radicals in economically advanced Manchuria.

It was Yuanxin who, as chief of propaganda for the province of Liaoning, helped Jiang initiate a movement of "going against the tide" in schools in 1973. One hero of this movement—the boy refused to write exam answers, handing in instead a letter attacking the whole idea of exams and book learning—was a firebrand named Zhang Tiesheng. Jiang loved this youth's spiritedness ("My self-assertion is more vigorous than an ox's," he declared), and the youth loved Jiang's unbureaucratic leadership style. Yuanxin brought many people like Zhang Tiesheng into Jiang's circle of "armed intellectuals."

Empress Wu had an able and ambitious nephew, Wu Chengsi, who saw himself as the empress's crown prince. Aunt and nephew used each other for a time. It was the same with Jiang Qing and Yuanxin. Jiang saw him as her crown prince; Yuanxin for his part drifted away from Mao, whether because Mao was too detached toward him, or because Yuanxin saw his uncle as a sinking ship and found excitement in the leadership of his "Auntie Jiang." Regardless of what Peking says of Jiang Qing today, a man of Mao Yuanxin's ability and experience never would have paid allegiance to Jiang if she had not had some qualities of political leadership.

"In the future," Mao wrote to Li Na in a typically hair-raising dedication when she graduated from Peking University in 1964 or 1965, "sorrows will plague you and you will suffer many reverses. . . ." It was true. Despite her high positions in *Liberation Army Daily* and Peking City, Li Na had grown quiet and moody. It was difficult for any young woman who had risen quickly at work to find a suitable husband, and excruciatingly so for Mao's and Jiang's daughter. As she approached thirty, Li Na began to fear that no one would marry her—unless she reached down and took a farmer.

During the retreat from the Cultural Revolution, Li Na ran into difficulties in her high posts and she found herself at a rural camp for the revamping of officials. There she married a farmer. Mao did not mind, but Jiang Qing was displeased. Jiang felt that Li Na ought to be ambitious and independent-minded like her mother. She wanted Li Na to marry a man who could help her advance, while at the same time avoiding subservience to him. But Li Na was of another generation, and she lacked Jiang's drive. She was overweight and square-faced, and she had not distinguished herself at Peking University. Jiang's pushing of Li Na was more than the young woman was capable of dealing with. Mao's insouciance toward her perhaps was easier to bear than Jiang's zeal.

Li Na—now the mother of a baby daughter—was not well and for one reason or another she left her posts with the army paper and the city government. Jiang tried to persuade her to divorce her husband. But what seemed logical to Jiang did not appeal to Li Na; and Mao did not mind at all that his daughter was failing to advance. Four times Jiang and Li Na had long arguments over the divorce issue. Jiang had in mind for Li Na an older widower of ministerial rank. Li Na did divorce her farmer, but it seems that she did not marry the widowed minister. Meanwhile, she was diagnosed as a schizophrenic; it seemed that, like her half brother Anqing, Li Na would be on the sidelines of society for the rest of her life.

Jiang Qing used intermediaries, chief among them Wang Hairong, the daughter of Mao's cousin, who now had risen to be assistant foreign minister, to try to persuade Mao to give a fresh job to Wang Hongwen, her Shanghai colleague.

"Wang Hongwen was completely under her thumb," said a foreign Communist leader who often saw the two of them together. "Once at a banquet in my honor, when Wang was to propose a toast, Jiang Qing prompted him, digging him in the ribs in a familiar way." The visitor was left with the impression of intimacy: "I wondered if there was not a sexual relation between Wang and Jiang Qing." Jiang expected that Wang—young, loyal, and blessed with Mao's stamp of approval—would be a key minister in a future Jiang regime.

From Villa 10 of Fishing Terrace, Jiang summoned Wang Hairong and Nancy Tang, Mao's interpreter of English. This inseparable pair had become more influential with ailing Mao than formal ranking would suggest. Jiang wanted the two young women to take a message over to Mao: The estranged wife respectfully urged her infirm husband to give Wang Hongwen a vice-chairmanship in the state structure to match his vice-chairmanship of the Communist Party. Wouldn't this be a grand *encouragement* to the able young man, and a precaution against any *tricks* from Deng's people who were becoming so entrenched in Zhou Enlai's state apparatus?

Jiang's choice of intermediaries may have been unwise. The two young women doted on Mao, proximity to whom was making them political stars in the Peking firmament. For Jiang they felt less affection. She seemed a bit haughty as the "top woman" around, and they often heard their adored boss complaining about her. Mao turned down Jiang's suggestion of giving Wang Hongwen a state office. Perhaps he thought that Jiang also wanted a high state post.

Jiang Qing, agitated after a series of governmental meetings at which Zhou, stepping out from his hospital, made a large impact, sent once more for Hairong and Nancy. From her zone at Fishing Terrace, Jiang wished to convey to her husband at headquarters in South and Central Lakes her complaint that a number of colleagues were drifting to the right, as well as constantly singling her out for attack.

Wang Hairong and Nancy Tang went back to Mao with Jiang's message. "Few people suit her taste," Mao murmured to the trusted women. "Only one—she herself." The dutiful Wang Hairong tossed Mao a softball question: "What about you?" Mao continued to confide in this junior pair. "Oh, she has no respect for me." Mao seemed to share in the general obsession with the post-Mao succession: "Come the future, she'll have disputes with everyone . . . after I die, she'll make trouble."

While Mao was in Changsha, Wang Hongwen flew down to badger him about Zhou Enlai's "ambitions," the danger from Deng Xiaoping, and other grievances of Jiang Qing's circle of Shanghai radicals. He hinted—this idea was Jiang's—that the premier was not really very ill and was spending his days at the hospital plotting to advance Deng and oppose Mao's cherished policies. Didn't the chairman think it was time to make Zhang Chunqiao premier?

Mao did not. He felt that Jiang and her three chief associates, whom he began to call the "Shanghai Four," were pressuring him, and nothing makes a dying man more contrary-minded than the suspicion that he is being pressured. No wonder Mao refused to promote Wang Hongwen.

Jiang Qing, while failing to carve out any political territory of her own, independent of Mao's authority, nevertheless used high-handed methods that often put her in bad odor with the one she chose to identify with totally.

"When you go off to Fishing Terrace," Mao, ever more suspicious of the "Shanghai Four," said to Chen Yonggui, a peasant-turned-politician with radical sympathies, "take care that the Gang of Four doesn't become the Gang of Five."

Although various state and Party budgets took care of the vast majority of Jiang's expenditures—staff, trips, villas—she needed ready funds for clothes and photographic equipment. Mao gave little thought to money. He was well supplied, because the publishers of his books sent him fat royalties, but Jiang had moments of shortage. At one point Mao set up a fund of some tens of thousands of yuan for Jiang's use. She was embarrassed that in drawing from it she had to deal with a female assistant of Mao's, Zhang Yufeng, whom he had slept with more than once. Zhang missed no chance to keep herself informed of Jiang's patterns of consumption.

"Little Zhang," Jiang said defensively one evening after arranging to draw from the fund, "I know this seems a large amount to you, but in my situation it's hardly enough to keep my life in one piece."

Jiang wanted Mao Yuanxin, Mao's nephew, to do the books on her fund; he was a young man who understood his "auntie." But Mao would not let the matter slip from Zhang Yufeng's hands. He liked Yuanxin, but he knew that his nephew was at least as close to Jiang as to himself; Yufeng served him alone. In January 1975, when Jiang's distance from Mao made the money question more difficult than ever, she had to write a note to Zhang Yufeng. "Can I withdraw eight thousand yuan from that amount of money?" Apparently she had borrowed money to buy lighting equipment and other costly photographic items. Her lines to Mao's "secretary" were a blend of magnanimity and toughness that was her specialty. "I later gave the equipment to the New China News Agency as a gift without charge." Of course, she could charge the agency, but really she felt the state and Party's interests should be put first; the equipment was needed for important tasks.

"So I have to pay back a loan of eight thousand yuan." Jiang explained gently to Yufeng that she really did not *have* to pay it back (the amount was huge, more than a decade's wages for most people), "but returning the money will set my mind at rest." So she asked for an immediate transfer of eight thousand yuan from her fund. "If eight thousand yuan can't be taken out, please go to the chairman when he isn't busy and request him simply to give me eight thousand yuan."

Jiang did not get all of the eight thousand yuan, and in the spring and summer of 1975 she got little of anything from Mao, who began to think better of Deng Xiaoping than before. "I am old, already eighty-one, and in poor health," he wrote to Jiang, "and you show not a spark of consideration for me." Mao added an unusual reference to his premier's private life: "I do envy the Zhou Enlai marriage."

Jiang Qing suggested that a film be made of the story of "Iron Wang," a worker at the Daqing oil field who was strong-willed and politically militant. But when the film appeared, she didn't like it. *Pioneers* smacked of order, rational planning, and fidelity to Party procedures—not virtues in Jiang's eyes. Its few sentiments of "revolutionary optimism" (such as the cry, "Use the sky as house and the earth as bed") were uttered in sarcasm by "rightists."

Worse, the hero was made to utter a scathing remark about officials "as talkative as an old lady, yapping in your ears all day long." Yao Wenyuan gently told Jiang, in a memo of February 25, 1975, that the hero's reference seemed to be "almost a duplication of you." With ten points of criticism drawn up against the film, Jiang was able to stop it dead in its tracks that spring.

But the screenwriter hit back. Taking advantage of the tension between Mao and Jiang, Zhang Tianmin wrote a letter to Mao speaking up for his film. "This film contains no great mistakes," Mao scrawled on Zhang's letter. "Recommend it be distributed." Mao had not seen the movie, but that did not impair the infallibility of his hardly legible comment. "It's no good demanding perfection," he added, an old man's swipe at his wife's relentless vigor.

"He's laying false charges against the grandma," Jiang Qing snapped of Zhang's letter to Mao. *"But Granny is not afraid."* An amazing series of memos, phone calls, and midnight meetings ensued, involving Zhang Chunqiao, Yao Wenyuan, Minister of Culture Yu Huiyong, and scores of others. "Too much technical jargon," Jiang said of the movie, and "poorly connected scenes." Moreover, "Mao's thought is misinterpreted." But the heart of the matter was the fleeting reference to a "talkative old lady."

Despite the efforts of Jiang Qing's political team, Mao's judgment could not be bucked. Jiang retreated. "Although I made recommendations about the film," Jiang purred in a speech at the Dazhai model brigade in September, "the ten charges against it actually were not my doing."

Even in her backpedaling, Jiang Qing could not, as Kang Sheng could, hide her feelings and call a tiger a pup. "Damn it," she shouted at her vast audience, which included the movie's screenwriter, "it's a frame-up against me! This man, Zhang Tianmin, wrote a letter to the chairman." She was warming to her real concern. "There must be some supporters behind him—maybe some evildoers." With her finger she singled out screenwriter Zhang. "How old are you?" Zhang politely replied that he was forty-six. "You're still a baby. You tried to frame me, didn't you? Well, today this old granny is going to teach you a lesson.

"Who gave you the idea of criticizing me to the chairman?" she asked with a snarl, still before a crowded auditorium.

"No one," answered Zhang.

"Then write a retraction to the chairman, for God's sake! If you're bold enough to write to him, write again, tell him you lied!"

In a torrid session in Villa 17 at Fishing Terrace, Jiang continued to try to justify her role in this storm in a teacup. "Zhang Tianmin wrote *two* letters," she announced triumphantly. "One to the chairman, on which the chairman made *no* comments. Then he sent a second letter to Deng Xiaoping to pass on to the chairman." Jiang felt she had uncovered the root of the injustice done to her. "It was Deng who *forced* the chairman to make his damn comment!"

Zhang Chunqiao backed up his boss. "The chairman is careful with words," he summed up. "He said it does not contain great mistakes. But we can make it clear that it does contain *medium* mistakes and *small* mistakes."

Mao himself felt that Jiang had become too talkative. Earlier that year he scratched out a neat phrase in classical mold about Three Mores and One Less. "Zhou should rest more," ran the lines, which expressed his mood of irritation with the ultraleft. "Deng should work more, Wang [Hongwen] should study more, and Jiang Qing should talk less." To this line—of which screenwriter Zhang had surely heard—Mao apparently added: "She should take a tip from nature; the ears are made so as to remain open but the mouth may shut."

Because of her tight, difficult relationship with Mao, Jiang Qing's political situation could only be volatile at best. On the one hand, since the fall of Lin Biao she could justifiably view herself as a leading candidate to be number two in the regime—a seductive if perilous spot—and hence one day succeed Mao. On the other hand, as a woman she found herself in the maddening straitjacket of being the leader's wife—his "arm," as she put it. It is difficult enough for any number two to carve out an independent image, but far more difficult when that person-in-waiting is a Chinese wife—or any wife. Should she be assertive, in anticipation of an eventual reaction against Mao, and take her own stand on the issues? Or should she be the devoted wife, the model Maoist, on the ground that supreme power could come to her only via her husband?

Suppressing her instinct to express herself in an untrammeled way, Jiang mostly remained the model Maoist. This was probably a mistake. In part she was overconfident, failing to realize how much resistance there would be to her ambitions and how much emotional anti-Maoism there would be after Mao's death. In part she was a victim of the entrenched antifeminism of Chinese society.

Jiang remained the "arm." Had she begun to speak discreetly of Mao's shortcomings and of how difficult he was at times, especially appealing to the women of China by making a link between the patriarchalism of the Maoist Communist system and the oppression of women—themes that her own life experience could have propelled her to probe—perhaps she could have ridden the waves of revulsion against Mao that were quietly gathering momentum. It is impossible to be sure, but she did not try. She proved less calculating, farsighted, and detached from the fascinations of her own ego—and more loyal to a man—than Empress Wu had been.

No doubt there rang in her ears all those whispered, carping remarks. She ought to be content simply to look after Mao! Why did she alone among the women comrades express her opinions on every issue under the sun? The bitch should stay home and knit!

The approach of Mao's death brought out every hoary ghost from the closet of Chinese feudal tradition. Few could look at Jiang without seeing a scheming empress. In the mid-1970s she was reaching for a new independence as a person—a throwback to that which she had enjoyed as Tang Na's wife in Shanghai's theatrical world. But a savagely conservative public opinion was in no mood to grant her—in the very different realm of politics—the right to independence as a person. "Granny" declared that she was not afraid; but it was a crippling thing to have to *see* herself as "Granny."

"Don't cook up a Gang of Four," Mao told Jiang in mid-1975 in a reference to her three Shanghai colleagues. (There was a saying about the quartet: "Jiang's head, Zhang [Chunqiao]'s tricks, Wang [Hongwen]'s legs, and Yao [Wenyuan]'s mouth.") Before the whole Politburo, he criticized his wife for scheming methods and ultra-leftist views. Jiang, wounded and angry, wrote a letter of self-criticism. "Because I did not want to impair unity," she said later to a sympathetic audience, "I took all the blame."

She felt that Deng Xiaoping was taking Mao's criticism of her, blowing it up, and trying thereby to destroy the Shanghai radicals (the mirror image of what she was trying to do to Deng). "The chairman has been criticizing both sides," she pointed out, quite correctly. "But [Deng] never alludes to the criticism of him and his friends and goes on overstating the chairman's criticisms of us, particularly of me."

She simply could not resist cursing Deng. "In China," she grandly announced to one of her factional gatherings, "we have an international capitalist agent named Deng Xiaoping." Yet in the next breath she admitted: "Nevertheless, our chairman has been protecting him."

Mao was a lid holding down a cauldron of strife. He may well have hoped for a time that Deng, and later Hua, would succeed in cooperating with Jiang (and Deng and Hua may both have tried for a time to do so).

Jiang decided to go to Dazhai for a series of political meetings. At them, the top leaders were all campaigning fiercely, at once trying to satisfy Mao and to offer themselves over Mao's head to a Chinese public anxious about the post-Mao future. To the hilly township in Shaanxi Province she traveled in a special train with a retinue of more than a hundred people. At the guesthouse for visitors, she asked for black curtains to keep out every chink of light, and new fluorescent lamps, because the existing ones hummed too loudly when turned on. She asked for a ban on motor vehicles entering the brigade area for the duration of her stay.

To establish herself with the locals, Jiang hit upon the idea of building an air-raid shelter on a nearby hill called Tiger Head, and she went out accompanied by a cameraman to do the first five minutes of digging herself.

"I am denounced every day!" she shouted in her Dazhai speech. "Well, you could hardly be called a real Communist if someone wasn't denouncing you." To her well-disposed audience of film people and young intellectual leftists, brought in at great expense from various cities to hear the week's speeches, she revealed her pain and her defiance. "It's been a hell of a struggle in Peking. But, you know, I'm not afraid. This old granny simply isn't afraid of being denounced!"

Jiang gave her audience a summary of all the policies she stood for. Were the "revisionists" and some military people sniping at the art and literature that the Cultural Revolution produced? Let them snipe. "But, oh, when I see their attacks, I cannot help swearing. These snipers are *bastards* pure and simple!"

"In the Party there are moderates and leftists," Jiang Qing declared. She drew her arm up in a majestic gesture and touched an index finger to her nose. "And I, humble I, am the leader of the leftists."

From the festival of political struggle at Dazhai—officially a conference on farm issues—the speeches by Deng, Hua Guofeng, and others were published. But when Jiang Qing's speech came to his desk, Mao exploded in scornful rejection of it. "It's bullshit," he wrote in the margin. "She's barking up the wrong tree. Don't publish this talk."

It was not only his wife's speech that Mao did not like, but also the grandstanding nature of her whole trip to the model brigade of Dazhai.

Kang Sheng lay ill in a Peking hospital. His secretary sent word that he wanted to see Wang Hairong and Nancy Tang, the two young courtiers who were rising high on clouds of privileged information. The women went to the bedside of the formidable boss of security and dirty tricks (after checking with Mao, they claim). Kang explained that soon he would die and he had a final matter of some importance to raise with Mao.

"Jiang Qing and also Zhang Chunqiao have historically been traitors to the Communist Party," Kang Sheng gasped to the young pair. "Jiang has shown me the files about Zhang's betrayal," he added. As for Jiang's case, he, Kang Sheng, knew the circumstances of her collaboration with the Chiang Kai-shek forces in the 1930s very well. He wanted Hairong and Nancy, before reporting the whole matter to Mao, to visit two old cadres who could supply further details of Jiang's and Zhang's political rottenness. One was Wu Zhongzhao, a Peking museum official who had worked in the Shanghai underground during the 1930s; the second was Wang Guanlan, husband of Sister Xu Mingqing, Jiang's friend from Shanghai who accompanied her from Xian to Yanan.

Even the close, intense tie between Jiang and Kang, based on hometown links, reinforced by years of quiet mutual help, had not survived the blight of intrigue, distrust, betrayal, and decay that was dragging Chinese politics down into the sewer. Kang, believing Jiang would fail to succeed Mao, was trying to protect his reputation.

How different Kang and Jiang were from each other! Kang lied and fixed and killed; he was a cool engineer of power; he knew he was doing wrong. Jiang was too engaged in the advance of her own ego to be a cool engineer of power. She never doubted that those she struck down deserved their fate.

Jiang's quest for self-expression, vindication, and, ultimately revenge, was almost naïve compared with Kang's calculated efforts to maximize his own power. Yet it was an absolute, all-engulfing quest, no less devastating than Kang's self-conscious use of various means to one simple end. Kang used everyone, including Mao. Jiang was not politically shrewd enough to use many people; mostly she was used, by Mao and others.

Hairong and Nancy felt a pang of doubt about the appropriateness of entering such treacherous waters. Before going to see Wang and Wu, they felt they should consult with Qiao Guanhua, as foreign minister their boss in the bureaucracy, and his beautiful wife, Zhang Hanzhi, the one who was giving English lessons and female companionship to Mao. One hot summer evening in 1975 Hairong and Nancy went to the foreign minister's residence. This was a mistake, from Kang Sheng's point of view, because Qiao and his wife liked and admired Jiang Qing. They stonewalled cordially before the young emissaries. Qiao did not himself know Wang and Wu. . . . There certainly were materials from the 1930s about Jiang's colorful private life, but Qiao and Zhang Hanzhi knew nothing of her supposed political treason. . . .

It was a reasonable response by the foreign minister and his shrewd wife. "We persuaded Hairong and Nancy not to pass on Mr. Kang's words to the chairman," Zhang Hanzhi later reported. "Our view was that if Mr. Kang did indeed have something to say to the chairman, he could dictate it to his secretary. We saw no reason to encourage these two young comrades, unaware of many things, to convey his message."

Hairong and Nancy, for their part, offered their impression that the Party establishment was in no mood to "exacerbate the Jiang Qing affair" but that there still was a widespread view that she should be "kept out of the political limelight" and "live a sequestered life for her remaining years." For the moment, Hairong and Nancy kept their stick of dynamite to themselves.

A day of tears for China in January 1976: Zhou Enlai was dead of cancer at seventy-eight. Unbelievable that the man everyone always took for granted was gone. In freezing weather a million people gazed silently at the cortege with its hearse draped in black and yellow rosettes. It was bad luck for China that the premier died before Mao. Zhou's presence could have smoothed Mao's passing, but Mao took Zhou's passing as an opportunity to lurch to the left, which polarized Chinese politics.

Jiang Qing's long, close relationship with Zhou had given way after Lin Biao's death to cold rivalry. The modesty and charm that had attracted Zhou in the 1940s and 1950s seemed to have been eclipsed by an Empress Wu-type hardness and calculation. When Jiang lay in a Moscow hospital bed suffering from cancer, Zhou had gone out of his way, and beyond any mandate from Mao, to try to cheer her up. But during Zhou's battle with cancer, Jiang responded coolly.

The truth was that Zhou's death, perhaps a relief to Mao, was an immense boon for Jiang Qing. "I was a person locked up in a cage," she remarked to a gathering of trusted followers a little later. "Now I am out and can speak up!"

Hours after Zhou's death, Jiang strode into the hospital room with a self-important air that irritated some of the other leaders. "Little Chao, my dear," she said to Deng Yingchao, hardly casting a glance at the bed. Everyone, including the medical staff, was shocked, for "Little Chao" was the intimate term that only Zhou himself used for his wife.

Zhu De, now ninety, rehabilitated after his disgrace during the Cultural Revolution, could not restrain himself after he saw Jiang fail to remove her cap at the bedside. "God, haven't you done enough damage to people already?" he crackled to Jiang in the anteroom as the leaders dispersed from Zhou's bedside. "And to the Chinese Revolution!" In fury Zhu recalled an old bone of contention. "Don't you remember in Yanan, you and Mao came to me one night, begging me to approve your wish to marry, saying you would always keep out of politics?" Jiang was silent. "You are hardly a human being," the old hero raged, his body trembling.

Millions watched on TV as the leaders visited Zhou's decorated bier in an ornate pavilion west of the Forbidden City. Deng Yingchao, greeting the arriving dignitaries, received Deng Xiaoping affectionately as he drew near the bier. Toward Jiang Qing she was stiff. Jiang walked to the bier, and again she did not remove her cap, an apparent slight noted from one end of China to the other. A soldier in Shenyang threw a chair at a TV set in anger; a crowd in

Canton, watching the incident on a neighborhood TV set in Peking Road, began to chant: "Beat her up! Beat her up!"

One detail was not recorded for the huge TV audience, but an eyewitness noticed it with awe: Beneath her somber black coat Jiang was wearing a crimson blouse!

Jiang and Deng Xiaoping squared off in political struggle. During a Peking spring filled with rumor, fear, and regret, Jiang had two advantages over Deng. Zhou's death weakened the moderates. And Mao was in a wholly different frame of mind from 1975. He had his knife out for Deng and his policies, and he reverted to an indulgent view of Jiang Qing.

Jiang and her friends blocked the appointment of Deng as premier in place of Zhou. The moderates in turn blocked Jiang's move to give Zhang Chunqiao the job. A Mao protégé, Hua Guofeng, was named acting premier as a compromise choice; he had fewer enemies than the abler candidates.

Although Jiang did not quite know what to make of the amiable Hua, she felt in a stronger political position than during 1975. Her prospects of succeeding Mao were alive once more. At a meeting of her supporters she spoke of the "sally launched to struggle against me" as essentially a thing of the past. Boldly she began to call Deng a "fascist."

Visitors to South and Central Lakes found Jiang supervising access to Mao's private quarters. She seemed to be spending more time at her old apartment, adjacent to Mao's, than she had for years. Mao Yuanxin left his high post in Shenyang to become a virtual chief of staff to his uncle, who now seldom left the compound. This added to Jiang's influence. She and Yuanxin monitored the phone lines, kept an eye on the flow of documents, and replaced interpreters they did not like with others more pliant.

Jiang escorted Richard and Pat Nixon to the theater, at Mao's request, and this time Zhou Enlai was not on hand to cloud her mastery of the evening. The program of songs and dances included "People of Taiwan Are Our Brothers," with its lines about Peking's determination to "liberate" the island province. As the song finished, Jiang jumped to her feet and clapped loudly. Pat Nixon joined her and began to clap; but she noticed that her husband (who evidently heard the lyrics) made the minimum gesture of rising slightly from his seat and then subsiding. Mrs. Nixon sat down abruptly. Jiang continued to applaud and beam.

* * *

The poem, hung up on a monument at the Square of the Gate of Heavenly Peace, was elliptical yet its meaning was clear:

> Lady X, indeed you are insane
> To be empress is your ambition
> Take this mirror
> And see what you are like. . . .
> You deceive your superiors
> And delude your subordinates
> Yet, for types like you,
> Good times won't last long.

Tens of thousands of citizens milled around the Monument to the People's Heroes, reading this attack on Jiang Qing in wonder. It was a festival when the dead are remembered, and a display of wreaths and tributes to Zhou Enlai was becoming the focus of a quiet protest against the ultraleftists, so strong since Zhou's death three months earlier.

As well as swipes at Mao ("The day of Qin Shihuang [a despotic emperor] is done") and a vein of anxiety about where China was headed, there was a spectacular undercurrent of angry, narrow-minded criticism of Jiang. "As in times past," ran one poem in huge black characters, "the emperor is wrongly bewitched by beauty." Puns on her past and present names made fun of her. "Don't let the river waters wash away the memory of Zhou" (river is *jiang,* and the line also had an allusion to *huo shui,* an old Chinese term for a woman who brings disaster). As speeches were made, there were tributes to Mao's early wife, Yang Kaihui, another slap at Jiang.

Huddled at South and Central Lakes, hearing reports on the situation in the square, Jiang Qing was apprehensive, yet not as much as she ought to have been. There was little she could do about the ingrained prejudice against the very idea of a woman ruler. But she continued to underestimate the danger of her turn against Zhou Enlai.

These days of tribute to Zhou had a special quality to them. Bicycles weren't stolen, cigarettes were extinguished at the approach to the monument, people in the buses going to and from the square did not look at each other. It could be said that the episode marked the birth of public opinion as an independent factor in Chinese politics. But Jiang's political judgments were narrow.* Her understanding of public opinion, never great, had been reduced to nothing by years of intrigue within the corridors of the court, and mere manipulation of such sentiment as existed outside those corridors. Unwisely, she wanted the wreaths and tributes removed from the monument. This was done, no doubt when Mao gave his agreement.

As a result, an orderly if excited memorial turned into an ugly riot. It went on for fourteen hours and involved at least a hundred thousand people. Vehicles were burned, people were roughed up; there were many injuries and some deaths.

Although Jiang spoke often of her relation to the "masses," she seemed to think of them as toys and buffoons, to be moved this way or that on the political stage as convenience required. Now those toys and buffoons bade fair to move and speak and think like human beings.

All Jiang could think of was Deng, though the incident in the Square of the Gate of Heavenly Peace was not instigated by the semidisgraced vice-premier.

The Politburo met in panic, and Jiang was to the fore in demanding strong measures. Mao was not present—he sat at home, talking to pretty girls, seldom receiving a political colleague—but he transmitted through his nephew Mao Yuanxin a motion to dismiss Deng from all his posts. The decision was "unanimous." Yet although Deng was out as Mao's successor, Jiang was by no means in; and she did not seem to realize what a devastating portent for her own future the popular eruption had been.

Jiang's enemies were cowed, and the winds of policy blew her way, for the moment. Cultural officials were summoned to help her plan a variety of theatrical shows designed to mark the tenth anniversary of the Cultural Revolution. Acting through her group at Qinghua University, including her half sister, Jiang induced the university to announce a new history course on the careers of Empresses Wu and Lü.

Entertaining foreign leaders, Jiang behaved with a panache that recalled her great year of 1974. "She . . . lost no opportunity of laying down the law to one or other of the leaders who were among

---

* Jiang did not have Empress Wu's breadth of vision or cool restraint when confronted with a challenge. A scathing attack on Empress Wu's sex life and political leadership, brilliantly written, was on one occasion brought by nervous aides to her attention. "Who wrote this?" Wu inquired. When told it was Luo Binwang, a scholar who had joined an anti-Wu association, she responded: "The first ministers are to blame. A man of such talent—and they leave him out in the cold without a promotion." Jiang Qing did not possess such detachment from the vibrations of the ego.

the party," Prime Minister Robert Muldoon of New Zealand said after an evening with her. Having sat beside Jiang and some of her colleagues at a soccer game, Muldoon mused: "It was easy to see where Jiang Qing got the reputation as a 'nagger.' . . ."

Suddenly the report of Kang Sheng's denunciation of Jiang reached Mao's desk. "Last summer we heard a trumped-up charge against Comrades Jiang Qing and Zhang Chunqiao," Zhang Hanzhi began her belated letter to Mao. "I now think it was all stage-managed by Deng Xiaoping," the foreign minister's wife explained. She had found a safe way to package her delicate message, for in the spin-dryer of Chinese politics, Deng now was cast to the bottom layer of filth.

Zhang related the whole story, as she knew it, of Kang's death-bed decision to retrieve his place in history by stabbing Jiang Qing in the back (he had died, meanwhile, in December 1975). She ended with a crack at Wang Hairong. "The whole matter died down, but later we saw an old man walking with difficulty from a banquet at the Great Hall of the People. Hairong happened to pass, and I asked her who the old man was. 'He is Wu Zhongzhao,' she replied. I must say I wondered if she hadn't deliberately arranged for Wu to attend the banquet."

Although Zhang Hanzhi's report was presented to Mao in a twisted way, it did contain the naked, unchallenged fact that one of Mao's closest lieutenants, Jiang's oldest colleague among the Communist leaders, had said on his deathbed that Jiang was a longtime renegade. Mao didn't care. He shelved this stick of dynamite. No investigation of Kang's charge took place.

The foreign minister's wife also told Jiang herself of the whole affair. "In every way that bastard has surpassed even Lin Biao," she burst out to Zhang Hanzhi. "To be bitten by one of your own is *especially horrible.*"

Of course, the main reason why Kang Sheng's poisoned arrow did not impale Jiang was Mao's changed attitude toward her. He was in a left-wing mood on many issues, and the advance of his Parkinson's disease stirred a streak of sentiment for his wife of thirty-eight years.

With Zhou dead, Deng knocked down, and a mediocre figure, Hua, chosen to receive whatever trust he had to bestow, Mao seemed once more to be rejecting the very idea of anyone truly succeeding him and to be turning to Jiang as the one who could *perpetuate* him. Was she not controversial, even hated in many quarters?

But Mao's own mood was so quixotic, and so frequently bleak, that the monkey in him may have been delighted with the thought of cheating all his ministers and tossing the kingdom to the willful actress who (he liked to believe) owed everything to him.

Mao chose a plot at the Babaoshan cemetery for a joint grave of husband and wife; the pair of them went several times to inspect it together. During the summer of 1976 he sent her what reads like a farewell poem. "You have been wronged," the lines began. "Today we are separating into two worlds. May each keep his peace.

"In the struggle of the past ten years I have tried to reach the peak of revolution," Mao went on in a typically gloomy and self-critical reference to the Cultural Revolution period, "but I was not successful. You, though, could reach the top." Personal as his last poem to Jiang was, Mao could not neglect the political realm, nor fail to express his half hope that Jiang might mend her ways and take over the leadership, and his fear that she might not be able to do so. "If you fail, you will plunge into a fathomless abyss. Your body will shatter. Your bones will break."

The Politburo, Jiang excepted, came to Mao's bedside for a meeting in midsummer. Mao could barely speak and many present sensed it was his last session with China's ruling body. "Help Jiang Qing," he gasped as his feuding ministers bent close to catch his instructions for the future. But the words trailed off into a mumble. Zhang Chunqiao and Wang Hongwen claimed that Mao added, "to carry the Red Flag," which could well have meant to take over his work as chairman of the Communist Party. Moderates at the bedside reported that Mao uttered the words, "Help Jiang Qing to *correct her errors.*" This amounted, in the view of Ye Jianying, Li Xiannian, and others, to a repudiation of Jiang's views and ways.

It is very likely that Mao had ambiguous but not hostile feelings about Jiang's ambitions. "According to my opinion," he said during another part of the same meeting, "there should be no presidency for the country." Mao spoke of the need for a tripartite leadership of old, middle-aged, and younger officials. "It is up to the Politburo to decide whether Jiang Qing shall be included." This is the authentic Mao voice: elliptical, seemingly fence-sitting, yet really not against the idea.

But Jiang Qing did not have the skill and tact to give herself a chance. She knew how to play court politics but not how to build a national political organization.

*   *   *

Jiang planned a whirlwind day of visits to three Peking units full of her supporters, tipping off a staff member that the visits should be covered in the press. She would appear on behalf of Mao and express her solidarity with the people at this time of national anxiety. Dressed in black, looking every inch the First Lady wracked with worry yet keeping her chin up, she drove to Peking University, the printing plant of New China News Agency, and Qinghua University. She spoke of her hopes for China's future.

That afternoon a Peking journalist wrote a dispatch entitled, "Jiang Qing, as Representative of Chairman Mao and the Party Central Committee, Visits with Solicitude the People of the Capital City." But even Yao Wenyuan, who had authority over national organs, could not approve this puff piece. Jiang's staff member rushed to try to arrange its appearance in *Peking Daily*, which is under the city's authority. The editors, held back by the text's mixture of melodrama and showmanship, dragged their feet long enough for the piece to die.

"I wanted to come and see you last summer," Jiang said to her captive audience of culturally saturated peasants at Xiaojinzhuang during a trip to Tianjin, "but they wouldn't let me." Now she was free, she cried—yet she did not sound free. "I daren't send you documentary materials," she told the farmers, who may or may not have been interested in the details of Peking squabbling, "because they say I've been sending secret materials and that this is a criminal offense."

She settled down in the village for a few days, perhaps trying to rid herself of the strains of Peking. In a very choosy mood over meals, she had chefs shuttle back and forth to the capital to bring herbs and desserts not available in the Tianjin area. At night she delivered rambling speeches.

"Deng Xiaoping wants to consign me to hell!" she cried. "He's far worse than even Khrushchev ever was! The man wants to get crowned, to declare himself emperor!"

In this mirror-image battle with her rival she randomly lumped together all the units friendly to her as targets of Deng's sabotage. "The Culture Ministry [her arts projects], the Physical Education Committee [the base of her loyal young man friend, Ping-Pong champion Zhuang Zedong], and Xiaojinzhuang [it always was wise to include her current audience]—*all have suffered from Deng's oppression.*

"At the moment in the Politburo I'm a unit of one, standing

alone," she told the silent farmers. What was the meaning of this remark? "When government positions are being allocated," she went
on, "they don't know what to do with me—they just have to accept
me." Jiang's meaning was that she as a woman was an undigestible
morsel for the Politburo. "A great male chauvinism reigns there,"
she burst out.

Jumping back and forth between the situation in Peking, where
Mao was dying, and that in Xiaojinzhuang, she criticized the locals
for having a man, rather than a woman, lead off the discussion at
their political and cultural meetings.

"In the sphere of production," she declared, getting to the heart
of the matter and managing to put her point in proper Marxist dress,
"women are fundamental. For labor is the basic force of production,
and *all labor is born of women.*" She was trying to turn the facts of
reproduction into a Marxist theory of political power. It is the
woman in the hospital who gives birth to human history. *"Man's
contribution to human history is nothing more than a drop of sperm."*
She concluded: "Men should move over and in the future let women
take over the management of things."

"I've come here to fight against revisionist errors," Jiang announced as she arrived at the barren hills of Dazhai on September 2.
"I'm Chairman Mao's secretary; anything that's in his hands is also
in my hands."

To the villagers of Dazhai, bastion of leftism, where poverty
was called virtue, it seemed awesome (and, with hindsight, outrageous) that Jiang drove up in a convoy of seven vehicles, with four
horses for her riding pleasure. To those who knew her well, she was
either intoxicated with the vapors of supreme power rising before
her nostrils, or she knew she was doomed and had decided on a last
fling.

"How's my air-raid shelter?" she asked, referring to her scheme
of the previous year. Alas, the gnarled realists of Dazhai, feeling the
shelter was unnecessary since there are many gulleys and cavelets on
Tiger Head Mountain, had reconstructed it as a pigpen. "Who the
hell said you could destroy my air-raid shelter?" she yelled in a
voice loud enough to make the deer and rabbits jump. *"It's Deng*
who ordered you to fill in my shelter!"

"We've never met Deng Xiaoping," the woman who was guiding Jiang croaked fearfully.

Jiang was annoyed, and a few minutes later she got even. Having grabbed a mattock to help dig a ditch, she tired and drew back.

"I'm sweating like a pig—someone take over." The local woman leader stepped forward and took the mattock. "Not you," Jiang snapped. "You're not suitable as *my* replacement!"

At the village store, after grandly buying some things she did not need, Jiang said she would address the staff. "Take a piece of paper," she instructed, "and write down the names of your parents." When most wrote the father's name first, she told the storekeepers this was wrong. She discoursed on early Chinese matriarchal society, in which people respected their mothers but did not even know who their fathers were. "Women held the power," she said proudly. "Always think of your mother's name first—and *rebel* against domination by your father."

There was a manic touch to Jiang Qing's performance in Tianjin and Dazhai, as if the growing tension were making her brittle. She felt the strain of being on a knife edge—as Empress Wu had for a while—between moving up to be empress and moving down to the shame of prostitution (or its equivalent in Communist society: denunciation as a counterrevolutionary woman who corrupts a proletarian hero).

Like Wu, she could be seen as inordinately ambitious. Yet like Wu—and Empress Lü and other Chinese women politicians—she could also be seen as trying against great odds to save herself from the subordination—and probable infamy—that was the lot of the woman at court who had no husband or son to hold fast to. It was this sense of insecurity, as well as a lack of political *savoir faire,* that caused a desperate note to enter Jiang's activities in the late summer of 1976.

The phone rang in Jiang Qing's suite at Dazhai at 9:30 P.M. on September 5, 1976. It was Peking; Mao had lapsed into unconsciousness and Jiang should return at once. Already in bed, she arose and packed. Waiting for the train to Shijiazhuang, she played bridge and chatted cheerfully; this was not callousness, as official Chinese accounts later charged, but nervousness.

After a short flight from Shijiazhuang to Peking, she drove into South and Central Lakes and threw herself on her bed in panicky exhaustion. "I'm not afraid of anything," Jiang repeated compulsively. Yet she was afraid.

To a degree, Jiang was already an empress dowager regent. The emperor lay incapacitated and she was widely viewed as his political shadow. Yet rivals existed. Another possible successor was Hua

Guofeng, whom Mao seemed to have singled out in part because he physically resembled his own son Anying. To Jiang's consternation, Mao, one night after a talk with New Zealand Prime Minister Muldoon, apparently gave Hua a piece of paper on which he had written, "With you in charge, I'm at ease." And there was Deng Xiaoping, the anti-Mao alternative, officially in disgrace but influential in the military and a rallying force for all who hated the ultraleft.

Jiang, the empress dowager regent; Hua, the substitute son; Deng, the rebel waiting in the marshes.

At Mao's place the atmosphere was heavy with unbearable sadness. Lackeys wept for their chairman and also for themselves. Members of the Politburo came and went, taking turns at being on duty at the residence, hiding their maneuvers under a dark cloak of grief. For Jiang more than for anyone the tension was hard to bear, like an iron clasp around her skull.

She summoned extra helpers, then decided she could not put up with so many people. "Everyone not on duty, get out!" she cried, perplexing the new arrivals. She went into the bedroom to scrub Mao's back, gently exercise his limbs, and dust him with talcum powder. Then she rushed out, feeling, after all, that she must get her mind off that scene, and phoned the Ministry of Culture for some movies.

It was easy for Jiang's detractors to say she did wrong things in the next three days. "She shouldn't have turned the chairman over in bed," some of the medical staff complained. "His face turned blue and purple when she did so." How awful of her to tell doleful staff members, "You ought to try to cheer up a bit." The secretary who had taken Jiang's place in Mao's bed, Zhang Yufeng, later reported with horror that on September 6 Jiang "badgered Mao for money." The truth was that Jiang, no doubt with a twinge of guilt, tried to give Mao back money she had previously extracted from him.*

It was true that her behavior was brittle; she simply did not know what to do, and in truth there was nothing she could do for Mao and perhaps not much she could do for her own political future. But it was ridiculous to say she was "gloating" over Mao's imminent death; she more than Hua or Deng needed to have him live longer. It was her near-panic at what the morrow would bring that made her conduct brittle.

---

* The later diatribes against Jiang's conduct unwittingly proved what they set out to deny: She *was* the person closest to Mao during those last days.

On the evening of September 8, unable to contain her nervousness, she drove over to the New China News Agency. With some trusted staff she went to the earthquakeproof conference room and sent for this journalist or that editor. She feared there were "agents" in the agency who were under instruction to undermine her; she was hoping to create "supporters" who would stand up for her when the time of testing came. It was a pointless, damaging foray.

Jiang drove back unsatisfied to South and Central Lakes. It was late, but she did not go to bed. Lights were on all over the place. Medical workers huddled in silent groups. Most of the Politburo were present; so were Mao's two daughters and his nephew, Mao Yuanxin—but not his only living son, Mao Anqing, for Jiang had not wanted him told of the crisis, for fear of the effect on his mind. Busy pens, bent according to the political vibrations as best these could be discerned, were preparing an announcement for the next day. It began, "Chairman Mao has left this world" (shi shi le).

Among the wreaths at the catafalque, beside which hundreds of thousands of citizens shuffled, each one trying to cry harder than the next, was a large one of chrysanthemums and greenery with the inscription: "IN DEEP MOURNING OF THE REVERED MASTER TEACHER CHAIRMAN MAO ZEDONG, FROM YOUR STUDENT AND COMRADE IN ARMS JIANG QING."* Jiang did not mourn Mao Zedong as a widow, the way Deng Yingchao mourned Zhou Enlai. She had never thought of herself as simply Mrs. Mao, and she shuddered at the traditional Chinese idea that a widow is a bird with one wing. She mourned him as a co-worker.

Jiang made the wreath with her own hands, crying as she sat for hours, cutting the flowers with scissors, tucking them close together. Her political allies may have felt she should have used her time sharpening a knife to wield against Hua, Deng, and the rest.

The next week, a million people assembled at the Square of the Gate of Heavenly Peace as a vast mute chorus for the Peking opera of the funeral. Jiang Qing moved slowly onto the platform like a lofty galleon. The chiseled ivory face stood out against the beautifully pressed dark Sun Yat-sen suit. She stared straight ahead as a speech was intoned by Hua, its theme the greatness of Mao and the evil of Deng. Wang Hongwen, chairman of the funeral, leaned over

---

* Appended too were the names of Mao Anqing, Li Min, Li Na, Mao Yuanqin (son of Anqing), and Mao Yuanxin. There was a struggle over this name list between Jiang and some other family members. She obtained the inclusion of Yuanxin's name, over their opposition; they (especially Shaohua, wife of Anqing) won the inclusion of Anqing's son's name, over Jiang's opposition (it is possible Jiang doubted the boy was really Anqing's son). One notes that Li Na's daughter's name is not on the list; Chinese tradition would not require it.

to scrutinize the piece of paper in Hua's pudgy hand, as if to verify that the words were the same ones hammered out at the previous night's torrid Politburo meeting.

Jiang and her friends were not without strength. Forty percent of the Politburo backed her. Shanghai and much of Manchuria— China's two industrial bastions—were in the ultraleft camp; so were five or six of China's eleven military regions. And the aura of Mao hung over her more than anyone else.

Jiang's immediate opponent, during the excruciating month after Mao's death, was Hua. But she knew that Deng and his circle of supporters were the real problem. One of her first steps was to phone Hua to ask for an immediate meeting of the Standing Committee of the Politburo. "To discuss what?" Hua inquired. "I am not able to tell you," Jiang snapped. At the meeting she proposed that Deng be totally expelled from the Communist Party (he'd been allowed to keep his card "on probation"). But she did not prevail.

It was a warning sign that the coalition of ultraleftists and center-leftists had shrunk during 1976. The center-leftists (security chiefs such as Wang Dongxing, military chiefs such as Chen Xilian), sensing that the death of Mao would swing China to the right, step by step joined forces with Hua (powerful for the moment even though his power was that of a dispensable stalking horse), with the military mainstream, and with the moderates who were plotting from the marshes.

Wang Dongxing hesitated for some time before turning against Jiang. "Fortunately, Comrade Hua Guofeng and Marshal Ye Jianying were more decisive than I," he later said.

Feverishly Jiang Qing went through Mao's papers, helped by Mao Yuanxin, who warded off the anxious "secretary," Zhang Yufeng. Jiang especially wanted the original of a final instruction of Mao's that read something like, "Act according to the principles laid down." But Zhang Yufeng phoned Wang Dongxing and told him what was happening. This led to a terrible scene between Jiang and Hua—after Jiang and Yuanxin had already left Mao's residence with several documents in an envelope—during which Jiang shouted, "You want to get rid of me—what a return for Mao's kindness to you!"

Quietly each side marshaled a limited amount of military force. Jiang went to Baoting to rally the Thirty-eighth Army, while Mao Yuanxin ordered ten thousand troops to Peking from the Northeast.

Both sides prepared manifestos for the morrow of their victory. Jiang's "A Message to the Party and People" called Hua "anti-Party," proclaimed herself the Party chairman, Zhang Chunqiao the premier, and carried as an appendix an "official portrait" of the new lady chairman.

When the competing sides dealt with each other in meetings— now sullenly, now with frayed tempers—the topic mostly was Mao's words, especially the sentence, "Act according to the principles laid down." All but the ultraleft said Mao never wrote such a message. Hua, Ye, Wang, and the others said he merely wrote, "Act according to past principles"—a far vaguer instruction and one that did not imply, as Jiang's version did, that Mao had laid down some specific last-minute principles. (It was in search of this sentence, never uttered that afternoon, that Wang Hongwen had impatiently peered over Hua's shoulder at Mao's funeral.)

"Three of the characters are a fake!" Hua stormed at Jiang. "You and Mao Yuanxin simply wrote them in!"

"What a bloody liar you are," Jiang Qing came back, "and totally disloyal to the hand that fed you!"

Then Jiang went public, using her influence in the media, to have an article prominently published under her favorite camp-name, "Two Schools," that asserted "Act according to the principles laid down" was a genuine last-minute message of Mao's.

Hua and Ye and Wang (with Deng no doubt giving his views from his hideout at a hot spring near Canton) were furious with the "Two Schools" article. Supplemented by General Chen Xilian and Li Xiannian, a vice-premier, they met in a five-man conclave during the early morning of October 5. The meeting, held at the headquarters of the General Staff in the Western Hills outside Peking, discussed the challenge of the "Two Schools" article, of troop movements involving the Shenyang units and the Twenty-first and Thirty-eighth armies, and of an alleged plan by Jiang and her circle to extend their power the next day, beginning with a vast rally in Changsha that would criticize "the head of a new revisionist line, Hua Guofeng." The five men decided to cut the gordian knot of debate.

If Jiang Qing rose to power by Mao's body, it seemed she might fall from power by Mao's words.

Jiang's circle, meanwhile, came up with a document that revealed the mysterious "principles laid down," a real Mao "will" giving Jiang a clear mandate to rule. Whatever military moves Jiang had under way were incomplete at this time, but Ye and Hua took military steps; an infantry unit and two tank divisions were deployed near the Great Wall and Changpei; another army was mobilized in Peking's suburbs; the military commander in Canton was ordered to ready two divisions for immediate possible airlift to Peking; and Unit 8341 was briefed for an urgent task. One southern military leader, Xu Shiyou, banged the table at a meeting and shouted to his colleagues: "If you don't arrest that woman [Jiang Qing], I shall march north!"

The Chinese government had little legitimacy at this time. Two rival *coups d'état* were brewing; the only question was which would be mounted first.

Hua called a Politburo meeting for the evening of October 5. During this meeting at South and Central Lakes, the ultraleft proposed some appointments to vacant posts: Jiang as chairman of the Communist Party, Zhang Chunqiao as premier, Wang Hongwen as head of the parliament (National People's Congress). The new coalition listened with vague interest, taking note only in order to be able to accuse Jiang the next week of "usurping power" by these proposals. The meeting adjourned inconclusively, with an agreement to continue the discussion the following evening.

On the evening of October 6, Wang Hongwen arrived at the second conference room of the Central Committee building for the scheduled meeting. Security guards leaped from behind a screen, knocked him to the floor, and handcuffed him. Within five minutes Zhang Chunqiao and Yao Wenyuan each walked into the same trap, as Hua and Ye watched the "arrests" on closed-circuit television from a side room. Jiang Qing did not arrive for the meeting. Hua and Ye looked at their watches, then sent for Wang Dongxing.

An hour later, a posse of motorcycles and a military jeep glided through empty streets close to the Peking Zoo. Inside the jeep, Wang Dongxing pointed out to his three men a gray wall broken by a high iron gate. It was the Guanyuan Villa. Wang was nervous, unable to push away the sentimental memories that made his night mission seem dastardly. But the colonel and two captains, selected specially from Unit 8341's Thirty-seventh Detachment for this evening's extraordinary work, had their instructions and already were out of the jeep. At the gate they presented credentials that enabled them to replace the two sentries. Into the darkened villa they crept, knowing from careful study of its floor plan exactly which room they were to assault. Quiet as cats in their rubber sneakers, they found the light switches to the master bedroom, flicked them on, and burst into the elegant room with automatic rifles pointing toward the bed.

Jiang Qing sprang like a tiger from the sheets, eyes blazing, nightgown flying in all directions. "Don't move!" the troops shouted in unison. A moment of silence seemed like an epoch. Then Jiang slid to the floor, weeping loudly. Through her sobs the colonel said with a snarl, "You are under arrest!" Jiang turned her drenched face upward and shouted, "The chairman's body is hardly cold, and yet you have the gall to mount a *coup!*"

The *coup* was Hua's; Jiang's *coup* never was triggered. (Meanwhile, Deng waited by the phone near Canton for reports on who was eating whom.) Jiang's relation to the masses—her audience—didn't help her when she needed it; visits to her model village at Xiaojinzhuang counted for nothing beside her rivals' steps of political organizing. Ye Jianying and the other moderates, Hua the substitute son, and Wang Dongxing and his ex-leftists, acting with momentary cohesion as a tripartite force, took the risks. It paid off for them.

It seemed that Mao had been right when he said, "Jiang Qing is a paper tiger. One blow and she is punctured."

In the jeep, Wang Dongxing's face was cupped in his hands. "You won't believe me," he said later to a secret meeting, "but as I prepared the arrest of Jiang Qing I was deeply troubled; I felt I was being an ingrate toward her."

The clan was all, the individual nothing, just as in Empress Wu's time. So family members were made to share Jiang's fate. A squad went out to arrest Li Na; she went down with her mother, just as her half sister, Li Min, now rose like a helicopter because she had a *different* mother, the "shrew's" wronged predecessor. Mao Yuanxin, Mao's nephew, was taken into custody and roughly treated; he had drawn too close to "Young Auntie," and his uncle was no longer there to put that charge into proportion. And at Qinghua University Jiang's half sister, Li Yunxia, was bundled out of her son's house; no one at the campus has ever seen her since.

A rash of cartoons appeared with Jiang Qing's name written not in brushstrokes but in skeletal bones. The sixty-two-year-old widow was pictured as a witch, poking out her tongue, her left hand clutching truth, her right hand lies. She was shown before a mirror with a siren's tail, her lips crying out fellatio, checking her Western costume before a stage performance.

Some people who had hailed her as tomorrow's empress now scrawled cartoons of her as a rat. Others did not blush to walk around the streets of Peking shouting, "Ten Thousand Knives to the Body of Jiang Qing!" all the while holding aloft, with mindless shouts of adulation, photos of the man who had been her husband for thirty-eight years. From now on Jiang Qing was to be known as the White-Boned Demon.

In Canton, one cartoon had Jiang sitting back in a plush armchair reading a biography of Empress Wu, beside her a scatter of other books, including *Guide to Hong Kong Beauty Salons* and *Complete Account of Soviet Political Coups.* Here were suggested three traits of the evil, fallen Chinese woman: She was ambitious, she sought to beautify herself (and thus lead men astray), and she was in some way associated with China's enemies.

Songlin, the former wife of Mao Anying, had a message: "She tried to kill Chairman Mao throughout their marriage." Shaohua, wife of Anqing, reported: "It was Jiang Qing who drove Mao Anqing to mental illness." Li Min, Mao's daughter by He Zizhen, told China that Jiang Qing was a "counterrevolutionary." Wang Hairong, the daughter of Mao's cousin, marched at the head of anti-Jiang Qing demonstrations. *People's Daily* published a spate of articles in praise of Yang Kaihui, Mao's earlier wife.

The winners took all, including the corpse. Mao's body would not go to the reserved plot at Babaoshan after all. The new, truncated Politburo decided that a burial plan that linked Mao and Jiang as husband and wife was "invalid." Besides, these diffident heirs, Hua in particular, needed to hold fast to Mao's body no less than they needed to flee from his mind. A by-product of the arrest of Jiang—who favored burial at Babaoshan—was a decision to mummify Mao's body for eternal display in a mausoleum. To make "Mr. Mao" into an immortal was to cancel the very idea of a "Mrs. Mao."

8

"Shut Up, Jiang Qing"

I have never given in to an attack; this is one thing in
my life I am proud of.
                            —Jiang Qing to Tang Na, 1937

Nora: I must find out which is right—the world or I.
                            —From Ibsen's *A Doll's House*

Unlike the vast majority of Chinese who find themselves in prison,
Jiang not only never confessed but also never felt that she had anything to confess. This made unbearable the pompous interrogations,
and the insults that China, Incorporated rained down upon her. Her
first months behind bars were filled with fury and despair. She
found Deng Xiaoping's prison a worse experience than she had
found Chiang Kai-shek's prison forty years before.

"There's no one there," said a former inmate of Qin Cheng
Prison where Jiang was incarcerated, "but the king of hell and the
little ghosts." The prisoners, each one totally isolated, were given no
toothpaste lest they eat the tube in a suicide attempt, but Jiang in
her depression at the end of 1977 tried to end her life another way:
She banged her head against the cell wall.

The Marxist notion that to kill yourself is to let down the revolution meant about as much to Jiang as the old Confucian notion
that a woman must kill herself, out of shame, if a man (other than
her husband) should so much as cross the threshold of her bedroom.
Jiang's suicide would have been that of a romantic—the kind of suicide that occurred in China only during the brief era of individualism (after World War One) sandwiched between the dead hand of
Confucianism and the cold hand of communism.

But the provision of rubber walls to her cell and constant surveillance from an exterior peephole frustrated Jiang Qing's horrible
suicide plan.

Later, Jiang Qing's morale improved. "She is being looked
after and is eating well," Deng Xiaoping told a foreign visitor in

1979, and it seemed to be true. She received one and a half yuan worth of food each day, which is two or three times what the ordinary Chinese eats, and sometimes she had fish, meat, and milk, royal fare for Qin Cheng. Breakfast was rice porridge and *bao zi* (a dumpling). At lunch and dinner there were two dishes and a soup.

Jiang was fond of *bao zi,* whether sweet, with vegetable inside, or with meat inside. One evening a jailor caught her stealing two meat *bao zi;* she tucked them in her sleeves at dinner, planning to make a midnight snack of them. "Put those *bao zi* back!" cried a guard who had observed her. "You may take only what you are going to eat now." Jiang put the *bao zi* back, looking guilty.

For some time Jiang had access to newspapers. She even read the three-volume *Crimes of the Gang of Four,* which circulated among an elite during 1977. In February 1978 she wrote a letter to the Central Committee denouncing the compilation as a pack of lies.*

"I ate and slept well," Jiang said of the latter part of her pretrial confinement. She added a striking remark that alluded to an incident in ancient China. "Each day at the cock's crow I got out my sword [a quotation from a famous general who, having lost his kingdom, practiced daily readiness to recover it]. I tried to keep myself healthy and strong so that one day I could stride properly to the execution ground."

The curtained car wove out from Peking, past a sign, "Restricted Area, No Foreigners," by gently waving wheatfields and white poplars to the forbidding gate of Qin Cheng. Officials from the procurator's office climbed out, walked the length of a wall that bristled with iron barbs and electric wires, and came upon Jiang Qing. She was in the middle of her daily *tai ji quan,* the rhythmic snakelike exercise that tones the body and calms the mind.

"Take me into custody?" she blazed when the men of the procuracy made an announcement in bumbling bureaucratese about a change in Jiang's status. "I've been here for four years while nothing happened." Jiang was irritated that the officials referred to Qin Cheng as a place of detention (to cover up the awkward fact that Jiang should long ago have been either charged with a crime or released). "I can tell you, this is not a detention house. This is a goddamned prison." Her objection counted for nothing. "I am not a

* During the trial Jiang made no complaint about her overall treatment in prison, though in 1980 she was deprived of newspapers (for fear she would learn of the attitudes of the accused ten to each other), which annoyed her. "Even landlords, rich peasants, reactionaries, and bad elements are able to see newspapers. Why can't I?" she said.

criminal," Jiang added to her gray visitors, "I am a political prisoner." But this claim, too, met with an invisible bureaucratic smile.

Thus did Jiang Qing learn that she would face a full-dress trial, a judicial form of Peking opera that would serve as revenge for the victims of the Cultural Revolution.

"I am now not a member of the Politburo," she remarked to the officials, "I am merely the wife of Mao Zedong. And I have another role, I am the 'accused.' It means just that and nothing more—'accused.'"

After the procuratorial officials left, Jiang Qing glanced through the papers she had been given. She noticed the name order of the "Gang of Four": Wang Hongwen first, Zhang Chunqiao second, herself third. "Why am *I* not number one?" she cried to her prison guards.

Jiang Qing had been arrested at the end of the Mao era; by the time of her trial in 1980, China had entered the Deng era, with Hua Guofeng's interim rule fast becoming a memory.

It was Hua, as supervisor, and Wang Dongxing, as executive officer, who handled Jiang's case from her arrest in October 1976 until sometime in 1978. In custody, Jiang twice talked with Hua. "Confess and become an upright person again," advised this pedestrian man plucked from the pack by a dying Mao. Jiang Qing gave a grim little laugh. "Do you dare release me?" she mocked in a tone of vinegar. "Just release me, and in half a year I'll eliminate the lot of you." Hua found his tongue. "If you were released, people would assail you, and in half an hour you'd be shredded meat."

On another occasion Hua had the gall to say to Jiang: "It's your Party task to admit your errors; and also, in everything you say, to protect Chairman Mao."

By the end of 1978 Hua's position was slipping (and Wang had been purged), and it was the Deng ally, Chen Yun, who had interviewed Jiang when she sought to enroll at Lu Xun College forty-one years earlier, who had charge of Jiang Qing's case throughout 1979 and into 1980. Then Peng Zhen, Jiang's old foe from the Cultural Revolution, himself an alumnus of the very prison where Jiang now sat, handled the pretrial interrogations in the summer of 1980. Through it all the hand of Deng was drawing nearer to Jiang; she was a goose being prepared for his banquet of revenge.

Jiang Qing, austere in a black trouser suit, stepped forward to a wooden table in the office of the special prosecutor. At either side of her were two young soldiers, their nervous hands in white gloves that fluttered like frisky doves. At the table Jiang faced two clerks sitting before a thick document—her indictment. She stood calmly, her mouth resigned but not rough or old, occasionally leaning back slightly, her big feet planted confidently on the green carpet. The prosecutor summarized her "crimes." Jiang looked at him like a patient professor listening to a sophomore suggesting a paper topic that does not make sense.

Jiang bent over the table, took off her glasses, and as a white-gloved military hand held the document, signed it in her square characters. In China names are important, and a name had been arrived at for Jiang and her fellow defendants: "The Lin Biao and Jiang Qing Counterrevolutionary Cliques." She would be linked not only with her three Shanghai associates but also with five military colleagues of Lin's (who had been in prison nine years already) and with Chen Boda, Mao's aide who had naïvely thought the Mao-Lin alliance was solid and sincere.

Jiang took her copy of the indictment, rolled it into a scroll, which she held in her left hand as if it were a movie magazine, touched her hair gently with her right hand, and waited to see what the men of the law wanted next.

"She still appeared to her attendants so well preserved, " wrote Empress Wu's biographer of her looks at the age of sixty-eight, "that they did not realize she was aging. She used heavy makeup, and her fine features concealed the advance of old age." Jiang Qing at sixty-six was much the same. Her features seemed as nicely sculpted as ever, she groomed herself to the last degree, and her movements still were those of an actress aware that each gesture is being observed. As these men played their legal games, she, the lone woman, would fill the vacuum of meaning with a bit of style.

If Jiang was well groomed that winter day, it was because she knew the trial probably would be her farewell appearance. She was tired and discouraged; her health was spotty; her friends were gone. Yet she felt she must exploit this moment of drama. For four years she had lacked an audience; now she had a vast, fascinated one. She would show them the real Jiang Qing.

Politics or theater? Jiang Qing had played with fire at the intersection of the two for decades. She had plunged into Communist circles in Shandong and Shanghai in the course of furthering her acting career. She had used an actress's charm and flair to penetrate to the center of Yanan society. She had wielded the power she eventually garnered in the 1960s against theater people. Now, as the political powers of the day caught up with her, she sought to salvage her dignity by a last season of theater.

Did she want the state to appoint a lawyer to defend her? In a matronly tone Jiang discussed the matter. She wanted her lawyer to answer questions on her behalf in court. She insisted that he conduct the defense exactly as she laid down. And he must take it as a point of departure for her defense that the decisions of the Ninth and Tenth Communist Party congresses (1969 and 1973) were valid expressions of Chinese high policy for their time.

No Chinese lawyer would be permitted to accept these conditions. The point about the validity of the Party congresses was especially subversive of the special court's make-believe; it would have highlighted the distinction between "crimes" and "political mistakes," and it was the linchpin of the special court's case against Jiang that no such distinction existed. When the court smiled at her conditions, she smiled back at the court; she would defend herself. The lawyers who would not serve her as she wished she called "shady profiteers."

The arraignment of Jiang Qing had to be done three times, because the first two times Jiang "misbehaved" before the prosecutor, and the resulting film was not suitable for general exhibition. "How the hell would I know?" she kept answering in a rasping voice when asked a question. But on this cold afternoon of November 20, Jiang listened carefully, maintained her dignity, and cursed no one.

As it happened, Jiang had come to an agreement with the president of the court: The sessions would not be long, and if there were sessions on succeeding days she could stay within Peking, rather than make the long drive back to prison; in return she undertook to refrain from disrupting the procedures of the court.

Her disputatiousness hidden behind an actress's beautifully projected voice, Jiang explained that, no, she could not possibly respond as yet to the indictment. She had not had a chance to study it properly, she pointed out. Moreover, what she had been able to glance at seemed rather vague to her.

One part she had absorbed, and it displeased her. How could they identify her with Lin Biao! She took out a pen and wrote on that section of her copy of the indictment, "I don't agree."

The prosecutor had a few things to announce, but Jiang said, "Most of what you say I can't hear," in a tone of voice that did not suggest eagerness to have everything said again more loudly.

Jiang was led away to her cell, where she studied what official Peking now thought of her political career. Stripped of its verbiage, the indictment accused her of two broad sets of "crimes." She "persecuted" leaders, intellectuals, and ordinary people. And she tried to "usurp" the power of the Party and the state.

"The accused, Jiang Qing, conspired to prevent Deng Xiaoping's appointment as vice-premier in the fall of 1974." It was November 26, and the special court finally had assembled. The thirty-five judges and six hundred invited guests sat in neat array in the Ceremonial Hall of the Public Security compound on the Street of Righteousness. Jiang, dressed in a simple black suit, remained calm. Between the bars of the cagelike dock, her hands could be seen, fingers opening and closing in deliberate movements to aid relaxation. She was in command of herself. Her game plan was to be dignified and reasonable; and this first charge was an easy one to shrug off—surely the Chinese people could understand the difference between political struggle and the committing of crimes!

A witness took the stand. "Who suggested that you go to Changsha to warn Chairman Mao about the activities of Deng Xiaoping and Zhou Enlai?" The unhappy-looking man replied: "Jiang Qing made the suggestion." It was Wang Hongwen! Thirty-two years younger than Jiang, his eye on the future, he turned against her and confessed to every charge. The once-dashing Wang was almost unrecognizable: drooping shoulders, barest of crew cuts, the look of a sad spaniel on his handsome face.

For a while Jiang listened in silence to her young follower, moving her head gracefully from side to side at intervals. But later she became stiff, leaning forward, pressing her earphones tightly to her head, fixing Wang with large white eyes. Once during his testimony she asked loudly to be taken to the toilet. When, momentarily, Wang did not appear for the resumption of the session after a break, her proprietorial attitude toward him flashed back. "Where is he?" she barked. "Where *is* Wang Hongwen?"

As evidence for Jiang's anti-Deng and anti-Zhou activities, a deposition from Zhang Yufeng was read. This pretty secretary, present in Mao's study when he talked with Wang in Changsha, was the woman Mao appointed to handle Jiang's loans and grants from his funds. She was also Mao's favorite girl during the 1970s, picked up during a train trip, and now the mother of at least one Mao child. Jiang Qing sat upright and stared in front of her, square and white like a statue, as Zhang Yufeng's memories of the Gang of Four's efforts to twist Mao's arm were read by a prosecutor. It was just as well for Jiang's pact with the president of the court that Mao's girl dared not make a personal appearance.

When Nancy Tang and Wang Hairong, the two young courtiers of Mao's last years, came to the witness stand, Jiang began to wobble in her commitment to behave well. "We saw at once through the Gang of Four's schemes," Nancy Tang stated. Jiang blinked rapidly, her lips pursed; she tilted her head at an angle, inspecting the ceiling. "Chairman Mao was very angry with Jiang Qing," Wang Hairong related. The statue stirred to life; "I have something to say!" Jiang cried. But the president of the court would not let her speak.

"They are two little rats," Jiang hissed in a loud stage whisper, "two little rats who scurry back and forth between two boats."

"Did you," Chief Judge Zeng Hanzhou asked Jiang Qing, "on the evening of October 17, 1974 [the day before Wang Hongwen went to Changsha], call Zhang Chunqiao, Yao Wenyuan, and Wang Hongwen together at Villa 18 of Fishing Terrace?"

"No."

"What?"

"No—I know nothing of it."

"On that occasion what did you four discuss?"

"If I don't know about such a meeting," Jiang replied as she threw the judge a pitying look, "how can I tell you what was discussed at it?" She was still under control, and she was trying to be polite, but she refused to go along with most things that were suggested to her; her calm defiance was exasperating to the judges with their prepared scripts.

A trace of anxiety seemed to creep over Wang Hongwen's face. In confessing, he had two points in mind: The Gang of Four would never come back to power; and the more he confessed, the more leniently he would be treated. But Jiang's total denial of guilt brought a new atmosphere to the trial. Was Wang feeling a pang of doubt as to the moral and practical soundness of his strategy?

Not far from the special court, in a small room with a TV monitor set aside for VIPs, Deng Xiaoping was watching. The issue of Jiang's blocking his vice-premiership, hardly one for a court, was included in the indictment to give him personal satisfaction. Although the era of Deng was not being kind to Jiang Qing, the pair had not always been enemies. But Deng had been shrewder than she. And she had been imprudent toward him. "With a head that shape," she once remarked of the bullet-headed Sichuanese, "how could the hat of a high official stay steadily on him?"*

During trials the accused often try to behave well because they fear death and hope for leniency. But the premise of such conduct—that the authorities have a degree of reasonableness—did not exist in Jiang Qing's opinion. She knew that power is an addiction within the world of Chinese communism, and that truth and sentiment mean little. Total defiance was the only way, and Jiang possessed the fearlessness that was necessary to follow it. She did not believe Deng would execute her. It hadn't been done before to a top Chinese Communist; moreover, would that "fascist dwarf" dare to kill Mao's wife? Anyway, she did not fear death inordinately; she would rather lose her head, she said, than whimper before her enemies.

One could say that Jiang Qing chose the path of defiance because she realized her political future was entirely behind her. But her total character, consistent over sixty years, made defiance the only possible choice. For Jiang Qing, the only fixed reality was her own life and will. The real world was what she felt it to be. A line of action that inconvenienced her, or a point of view that failed to harmonize with hers, was as unnatural as fish in the trees, and she did not doubt that she could prevail against its absurdity.

At the special court, Jiang Qing refused to give in, and she stood alone. Asked if he was surprised that his former wife rejected all the charges against her, Tang Na replied: "Not a bit. Because she had loved Mao, she couldn't possibly confess."

On the morning of December 3, 1980, Jiang strode into the courtroom, smoothed her suit, touched her hair, and lowered herself onto her kitchen chair. In front of each prosecutor and witness sat a covered teamug; Jiang faced only a nest of microphones. Before the special court came to order she turned around to look at the public gallery. One woman dressed in green with a yellow scarf at her neck was staring at Jiang, and for a moment it seemed that the two women's eyes met. It was Wang Guangmei.

"Accused Jiang Qing, how did you know Comrade Wang Guangmei was a special agent of the Americans?"

"The newspapers of our government said so." Jiang's face was a wall of innocence, but her voice was hard and her lip curled.

The prosecutors hammered away at the claim that Jiang was

---

* An allusion to an elaborate, balanced hat worn by officials in old China.

chiefly responsible for the "persecution to death" of Liu Shaoqi and for his wife's twelve years in prison. Jiang clasped her copy of the indictment; in prison she had written in the margin of the section dealing with Liu and Wang: "Zhou Enlai was the head of the special group that doomed Liu and Wang."

Each witness came by with his bundle of dirty laundry, including the Lius' cook, Hao Miao, who had spent six years in jail since we met him last. "I want to make a statement!" Jiang's husky voice filled the auditorium. "Most members of the present Central Committee of the Party, and most of our government leaders, including you, Jiang Hua [president of the court], *competed* with each other in those days to criticize Liu Shaoqi. If I am guilty, *how about you all?*"

"*Shut up, Jiang Qing,*" a judge yelled. "*Shut up, Jiang Qing,*" six more judges chorused.

The prosecutors brought in strong evidence that Jiang Qing had supervised a search of the Liu-Wang home for incriminating materials. Interrupting President Jiang Hua, Jiang pulled off her glasses, held them at an angle in her right hand, and inquired of the court: "What's so strange about searching their house? Tell me, haven't you quislings searched *my* house by now?" Anyway, she added, "Doing away with the Four Olds [a policy laid down by the Central Committee in August 1966] inevitably leads to the search of homes. It was a revolutionary action."

A tape recording was played. A hushed courtroom listened to Jiang Qing speaking at the height of her power. "I can tell you now," she was crying to a performing arts meeting, "Liu Shaoqi is a great counterrevolutionary who is rotten to the core. . . . He should die a death of one thousand, even ten thousand cuts."

"Accused Jiang Qing, did you hear the recording clearly?"

"I'm afraid I did not."

The crackling tape was played again, bringing to the uneasy ears of the gallery the sounds of the era of the Cultural Revolution, when Jiang could do no wrong. Jiang pressed her earphones close. "It is indeed my voice."

Jiang said what the court hated to hear: "The arrests of Liu, Wang, and their people were done according to the authority of the time. The fact that these people were kept so long in prison—that really had little to do with me."

Tension rose. "Yes, my name is signed on some of these documents," Jiang went on, "but Chairman Mao and Premier Zhou gave the final approval. Why do you try to cover up for them?" The court offered no evidence that Mao at any time opposed Jiang's attacks on Liu and Wang.

Prosecutor Huang Huoqing said that under Article 36 of the Law of the National People's Congress (1954), deputies of the NPC (parliament) are immune from arrest or trial without a decision by the NPC or its Standing Committee. By what right, then, did Jiang Qing take away the freedom of Liu Shaoqi and Wang Guangmei? Jiang leaned back in her chair, head tilted upward, apparently humming.

The next day *People's Daily* began its report of the session: "The chief counterrevolutionary culprit Jiang Qing is an evil star who brought calamity to the country and the people. This evil star was brought to the people's court by two female bailiffs at 9:00 A.M. on December 3...."

Evil star or not, at the "Trial of the Ten," Jiang Qing was the only person who talked like a human being, the only one who reacted genuinely to the facts before her.

Jiang Qing's patience with her accusers ebbed further during the second week of December. Did she in cooperation with Kang Sheng prepare a list of Central Committee members who were to be opposed and deprived of office where possible? "You have a fact, but you twist it," Jiang snapped. "It was quite normal and legal to do such things in the lead-up to an important meeting of the Central Committee with big issues at stake."

A female judge cried: "At that time you were not even a member of the Central Committee!"

"Look ..." Jiang tried to explain.

"How could it be *normal*?" raged the judge. *"How could it be legal?"* (With a grand gesture Jiang Qing removed her hearing aid as the female judge shouted on.)

"I will tell you, if you give me a chance. Because I was a member of the Cultural Revolution Group, which was then the equivalent of the Central Committee." Even her enemies conceded it was a good answer.

Jiang's life in Shanghai during the 1930s was brought up. Did she order the tracking down of certain materials from the homes of Zheng Junli (best man at Jiang's marriage to Tang Na) and his wife, Huang Chen? "I would have to see the materials," Jiang replied, "before I could tell you if I had anything to do with tracking them down." Her tone was that of a confident girl addressing parents who did not have her measure.

"One moment you speak of photos," Jiang went on, "the next of notebooks, then of letters—it's very confusing to work out just what you mean."

As the prosecutors began to refer to her 1930s activities as "reactionary," Jiang Qing crouched tensely like a bear, staring at the bench. Then she sprang. "What *were* these reactionary activities?" she roared into the auditorium. The court did not say; of course, the sparks in the air arose not from political issues but from her personal life as Lan Ping.

Huang Chen herself entered the courtroom.

"My dear Huang,"* Jiang exclaimed as the widow of Zheng Junli—the director died in prison in 1969—took her place at the witness stand.

"I don't care to speak to you," Huang Chen replied curtly, then paused. "You were Lan Ping, weren't you? I tell you, the history of the 1930s is what you yourself wrote—it cannot be wiped out.

"It was because we knew about you in the 1930s," Huang Chen said, addressing not the bench but Jiang, "and because of that letter of yours [the one to Tang Na] that you wanted retrieved, that you broke up my family and caused the death of my husband. Oh, you are cruel!" Huang Chen was choking.

Jiang Qing's voice was soft as she switched into Shanghai dialect: "Dear Huang, really, I didn't know about that."

The former air force chief, Wu Faxian, his jowls like an old sheep's, his throat a Niagara of apologies, told the court that he had carried out much of the ransacking operation in the homes of the Shanghai artists in October 1966. Like the other military defendants, he seemed a broken man and agreed to everything the court suggested. "Jiang Qing is the chief culprit," he summed up, "and I'm her accomplice. . . . I hate myself."

Jiang Qing denied that she instigated the Shanghai ransacking operation, though the evidence against her was heavy.

A buzz ran through the courtroom as writer Liao Mosha took the stand. A friend of Jiang's in Shanghai days—she had lived in his house but later quarreled with him—Liao was imprisoned as an "enemy agent" for eight years as a result of the Cultural Revolution.

* The Chinese phrase Jiang used, *"Ah Huang,"* is a soft expression, almost like, "Huang, honey."

In his statement Liao linked his own sufferings with those of Liu Ren, whose widow sat in front of him as a judge of the special court.

"You and your kind committed countless crimes of all kinds," Liao said to Jiang Qing. "They are more numerous than the hairs on a human head." The writer paused to wipe tears from his spectacles. "The people of Peking hate you from their bones."

Jiang Qing finally lost control. "No more of your lies!" she shouted, springing to her feet. Liao's tearfulness, the chain reaction of emotion that it caused in the auditorium, and Liao's cunning appeal to the feelings of Liu Ren's widow had vexed Jiang beyond endurance.

"Sit down!" cried a male judge. "You have no right to speak!"

"I have the right to defend myself." Jiang pointed to her own chest. *"And* I have the right to expose you," she shrieked, pointing a finger at Liao. "That man [Liao] was involved in the 'Three Family Village,'* wasn't he? . . ."

"Stop. The accused will stop." A judge tried to make himself heard as Liao pounded the podium with one fist, clenched the other, and shouted, "You shut up!" to Jiang Qing. When Liao went on, crying and trembling, Jiang punctuated his talk with the shouts "Spy!" and "Revisionist!"

"I object!" yelled a judge to Jiang. "You are not allowed to continue!"

"Go ahead and object," Jiang replied, her temper now fully unpacked. "I'm already talking. What can you do about it?" She tossed back her head and gave a throaty laugh.

"You are committing new crimes!" the judge cried. Several other judges chimed in: "She continues to commit crimes!"

"Rubbish. You bring these traitors and bad elements [like Liao] here, alleging this, spouting that." Jiang banged her ears for emphasis. *"I don't want to listen to them! I have questions to ask!"*

The courtroom was melting into pandemonium. A female judge, Gan Ying, kept roaring that Jiang Qing was adding to her crimes.

"What the hell do you mean by crimes?" Jiang flung the words at her. *"You bitch."*

Chief Judge Zeng Hanzhou, his face crimson, ordered Jiang Qing removed from the courtroom. Two female bailiffs grabbed her

---

* A trio of writers, including Deng Tuo—and associated with Fan Jin, wife of Yu Qiwei, Jiang Qing's second husband—who had written boldly on the eve of the Cultural Revolution (see page 262).

by the shoulders. She struck both of them, but soon they locked her arms and frog-marched her from the special court. The public gallery applauded.

Jiang Qing's plan to remain rational and dignified had collapsed. Five sessions had worn her down. Two women judges were particularly unpleasant to her and did nothing to curb the audience's applause for hostile witnesses. Above all, Liao Mosha, a man of the 1930s, the most sensitive chapter in her past, who had helped her when she was in a tight spot in 1933 (and so reminded her of the humiliation of her dependence on men), had insulted her before the world.

By mid-December Jiang Qing had stolen the show at the Trial of the Ten and sent shock waves through the Chinese government. In the process she had deeply alienated a court that wanted the accused to declare themselves guilty before being declared guilty by the court.

Jiang Qing made herself a landmark in the history of communism. At Communist trials the accused is always guilty; allegation is unerringly echoed by confession. This is necessary to safeguard the arrogant trickery by which the Party is said to be both the repository of power *and* the fount of truth. So it was that in the Moscow trials of the 1930s the accused confessed to all charges, whether they were guilty of them or not.

No Communist Party can acknowledge the moral sovereignty of the individual. The truth is fluid, but the source of truth (the Party) is fixed. A Communist would not be a Communist if he or she did not confess when the Party pointed a finger of accusation.

Indeed, confession is as necessary to communism as to the Church. How else could the authorities explain the obstinate refusal of paradise to materialize—or, in the case of the religious mind, the sinful state of the world—except by cranking out the confessions of renegades (sinners) who endlessly sabotage paradise?

But Jiang Qing did not confess. She did not give away her mind to the self-appointed guardians of history; she held fast to her moral sovereignty as an individual.

If in the Communist view history is an escalator that goes upward, regardless of an individual passenger's steps in any direction, because the Party is in charge of its progress, this woman simply jumped off the escalator. Whatever else she was, Jiang Qing was not a good Communist.

Beyond the courtroom, Jiang Qing was winning a few points

(more than Deng Xiaoping expected) and losing a few. Most Chinese did not take the trial very seriously. Bewilderment at the powerful being brought low soon gave way to the casual jeers and cheers of a coliseum crowd. But Jiang's *spirit* evoked admiration. Zhang Chunqiao looked like a disheveled fortune-teller without a tongue; the army men resembled sixty-year-old shoeshine boys about to cry; Yao Wenyuan whined that he was in bad shape. By contrast, Jiang Qing was a fluent, self-reliant human presence, an entertainment on nightly TV, and in her willfulness a breath of fresh air in the closed box of the Communist system.

The authorities did keep the children in line. In the woods near the Summer Palace, a hundred schoolchildren arrived for a picnic, carrying shoulder bags, cooking pans, and bundles of firewood. In the midst of their preparations for lunch, a blast of a teacher's whistle turned the children's attention to large drawings propped up against the wintry trees. The Gang of Four were depicted in caricature; Jiang Qing was a rat. A teacher lectured on Jiang's evils. The children produced stones and paper bags filled with earth from their shoulder bags. The assault began. Each blow against "the rat" brought innocent cries of joy.

"How was I on TV?" Jiang Qing asked her prison guards after the pandemonium during Liao Mosha's testimony. They looked petrified. "What do you *mean,* you didn't watch? Guarding me is your job. How could you *not* watch?" Waiting for her next appearance, Jiang resolved to make Mao Zedong the rock of her defense.

The session was delayed as the Politburo debated why the White-Boned Demon had failed to conform to plan and what to do about it. Some leaders worried that her defiance impressed young people at least as much as it disgusted older, conservative people. Deng and Hua, having disagreed on many policy issues, were also at odds on this last big issue of how to deal with Jiang Qing. It was December 23 before the special court assembled to begin a climactic week of struggle with her. Almost nothing of these sessions was shown on TV.

Jiang started her long walk down the aisle of the auditorium, and the two female bailiffs reached out to take her arms. Furious with their twisting and pulling at the earlier session, Jiang resisted them. "Why did you pull my hair last time?" she snapped at them. Pushing both girls aside, she tossed her head high and strode unaided to her cage.

"Jiang Hua, may I ask you a question?" Jiang Qing looked at the president of the court over the metal rims at the top of her glasses. He seemed startled, and for a moment he was silent.

"Yes, you may."

"Is this place a court or a punishment ground?" Jiang sounded like a lawyer beginning the cross-examination of a witness. "Last time the bailiffs twisted my elbow. This caused me an internal injury and now I can't lift up my right arm." She placed her left arm gently upon her right. The judges shifted in their chairs. "Another thing, we have our pact, you know, Jiang Hua. I am respectful of the court, but you never permit me to speak, you *interrupt* me. The way you're going, you'll soon be calling for applause in the court as a weapon against me."

"Listen to me, Jiang Qing."

"I *am* listening to you!" But Jiang Qing had had her fill of listening. The voice was an older woman's, yet her whole life seemed to be expressed in its vigor, sensuality, and range; it was a slow, rolling sound with occasional surprises of tone. She had a matronly air as she moved her head from side to side, sitting back on her chair, her feet well forward in comfortable extension. But her sighs were youthful, and in profile her features seemed girlish. As she spoke, her right arm chopped up and down in a steady beat of emphasis.

"There are many issues from within the Party that you people simply don't know about. You see, in those years the *Communist Party* did the things you complain about. You put everything on *my* back. God, it seems I was a giant with three heads and six arms who worked miracles. I was *one leader* of the Communist Party. *And* I was the one who stood by Mao Zedong! Arresting me and bringing me to trial is a defamation of Chairman Mao Zedong!"

Each time she spoke of Mao, a judge cut in to stop her.

"Since you won't let me speak," Jiang said with an icy smile, "why don't you put a clay Buddha on my chair and try it instead of me?"

She was no clay Buddha. "I was Chairman Mao's wife for thirty-eight years," she went on. "I was the only woman who followed him onto the battlefield [a reference to the civil war of the late 1940s]." The court audience laughed. Jiang swung around and shouted: "Where were you all lying down then?" More laughter (her phrase "lying down," implying a comparison with herself lying down beside Mao, startled people).

Why was Jiang Qing getting away with rumbustious behavior, at times even seeming mistress of the situation? Because she was

Mao's widow, and because she spoke a part of the truth. The Chinese establishment felt sufficiently guilty—about the hypocrisy over Mao and the hiding of truth during the trial—that it preferred to snicker at her rather than to silence her totally.

Jiang threw a bombshell. "I will tell you something," she began to a hushed court, "about that night Mao Zedong wrote the words, 'With you in charge, I'm at ease' for Hua Guofeng." She looked around the auditorium as her spectacles became the focus of the camera lights. "That was not all Chairman Mao wrote to Hua. He wrote six more characters: *'If you have questions, ask Jiang Qing.'*"*

"I have had no political guiding line of my own," Jiang went on to a court that had fallen silent. "What I did followed Mao's line and the Party's line." She took a deep breath and turned her head slowly to fix her eyes on each section of the auditorium in turn. "What you are doing now is asking a widow to pay her husband's debt. To you all, I say I am happy and honored to pay Chairman Mao's debt."

Jiang Qing's trial was in part Mao's trial. The Communist Party had taken the easy way out, blaming Mao's mistakes on the Gang of Four, but Jiang destroyed the credibility of that explanation by showing that she often followed Mao's instructions.

If Pandora's box was not already open on the Mao issue, Jiang Qing's defiance opened it. She added to the plausibility of a "Gang of Five" theory, and in her insults against the entire "fascist" political system of China she pointed beyond the Mao issue to the even more delicate issue of the *system* that Mao (and others) built.

After Jiang Qing tore holes in the fabric carefully woven by the court, it became necessary to produce another fabric. "The Chinese people are very clear," prosecutor Jiang Wen responded some days later in a statement that came from China's top leadership, "that Chairman Mao was responsible ... for their plight during the 'Cultural Revolution.' He was also responsible for failing to see through the Lin Biao and Jiang Qing counterrevolutionary cliques."

Deng Xiaoping had chopped a few pieces off Mao to counter Jiang Qing's defense of herself.

"Chairman Mao again and again exposed and refuted Jiang Qing," the prosecutor declared. "For example, he said: 'She does not speak for me, she speaks only for herself. . . .' "

Jiang Qing could not stand this. "You're fascists, you're Chiang

---

* We cannot say whether Mao wrote the short version, the longer version, or any version. It is striking that *Zhong fa* 24, a most detailed documentation of the period from the government's point of view, contains no facsimile of Mao's alleged (shorter) note to Hua.

Kai-shek Nationalists!" she shouted. "You call black white. You find bones in eggs."

"I despise you, Jiang Wen," she went on, her voice a foghorn. "You are selling your strength so desperately to Deng Xiaoping. Oh, he'll certainly promote you—he'll give you a two hundred yuan reward, Jiang Wen."

A woman prosecutor intervened to defend Jiang Wen, and as usual Jiang Qing became even angrier than with the men. "God, you are far from beautiful," she said, sneering, to the woman. "In fact, you are as ugly as a hog!"

As pandemonium ensued, Jiang shouted out a final credo: "I am without heaven and without law [a law unto myself]!" Bells rang. Once more Jiang Qing was frog-marched from the Ceremonial Hall, as the public gallery clapped and the judges stared pale-faced at the opposite wall. "It is right to rebel!" she shouted as she moved down the aisle. "Down with the revisionists led by Deng Xiaoping!" she cried at the abashed assembly. "I am prepared to die!"

Order returned. "She refused to present her case within the framework of the accusations stated in the indictment," Chief Judge Zeng Hanzhou said, "but instead made use of the debate to make counterrevolutionary remarks."

People's Daily drew a veil over Jiang's words, contenting itself with listing her crimes again and calling for her execution. "A ten-year dream of being an empress has ended," it said in a summary. "Jiang Qing's ugly performance shows that she has not yet awakened from her feudalist dream of staging a comeback. Perhaps she will die unrepentant. Let her do so."

Jiang Qing's ordeal was over. The left wing of the Chinese Communist Party had been chewed up for its follies. Deng had exacted a revenge on behalf of those humiliated in the Cultural Revolution (and, as a bonus, drawn ahead of Hua Guofeng). A fumbling attempt had been made to stabilize the issue of Mao's legacy. But the trial will stand as Jiang Qing's, not Deng's or anyone else's.

Jiang Qing was not a political villain or a political hero. She was the star of the trial because she was simply herself (as no one else was—except perhaps the mute Zhang Chunqiao). "Which is right—the world or I?" Jiang, as Nora, once had asked. Jiang's self was sovereign, she was sure she was right, and so she put the Communist system on trial. She was not "for" the system or "against" it so much as at cross-purposes with it. She did not apologize to the

Chinese people for the Communist system. But her honesty in being herself showed up the system. The emperor's wife had blurted out that the emperor had no clothes.

Was Jiang Qing crazy? Or was the Communist system crazy?

"I have long hated Jiang Qing," a Chinese watching the trial murmured to his friend, "but now I hate her a bit less." Her defiance in itself was admired by many Chinese people who had grown cynical about the Communist system. To enjoy her insults against the court was to take an ounce of revenge against the system. A younger generation schooled to passivity by communism found in the aggressiveness of Jiang, a person shaped in the pre-Communist era, a heartening celebration of individual will.

In ancient times, an old monk decided to show a young monk the life of the street outside the monastery walls. As they walked, the young man stared at every girl they passed. "Don't look at those creatures," the old monk counseled, "they are man-eating tigers." Upon their return to the monastery, the old monk asked his disciple what was the most beautiful thing he'd seen in the world outside.

"Certainly the man-eating tigers!" replied the young monk.

Deng Xiaoping, the old monk of Chinese communism, has this problem with China's young generation. "Don't look at that creature," he says of Jiang Qing; but many people like to look.

Chinese women might well have sighed over Jiang's trial. No other woman rose as high in the Chinese Communist Party (nor in the Communist Party of any other country). She became one of the handful of most powerful women in China's four-thousand-year history. Yet she had not avoided being discriminated against as a woman. Having struggled all her life to transcend the housewife's role, Jiang had been tried in part as a housewife—who exceeded a woman's proper functions and led her husband astray.

For all the chatter about "capitalism" that filled the courtroom, it was the ghost of feudalism, not capitalism, that haunted the Ceremonial Hall on the Street of Righteousness. Jiang Qing was not really guilty of wrong ideas ("counterrevolution"), but of playing the wrong social role.

It took nearly a month for the Politburo to agree on a verdict for Jiang Qing. Meanwhile, the judges, who had no say in the matter, dispersed to their usual occupations; some even traveled abroad as the verdict was being weighed!

It was Peng Zhen, in Jiang Qing's heyday the embattled mayor of Peking, who brought Jiang the news of the verdict: "Guilty on all counts, a sentence of death ...." As soon as she heard the word "death," Jiang shouted to Peng: "It's no crime to make revolution!" Perhaps she thought she might be led immediately to the place of execution. But Peng Zhen had not finished his announcement: "... suspended for two years to see how she behaves ...."

Deng, at first in favor of a death sentence, had compromised with his nervous, guilt-ridden colleagues and agreed to spare Jiang's life. The army, the Mao loyalists, the remnants of the ultraleft would make too much trouble if "Mao's dog" were put to death. Some would whisper that she had been killed to silence a voice of unpalatable truth. Others would make a martyr of her. Above all, the leaders were conscious that they, as well as Jiang Qing, generally had failed to take a stand against Mao's errors; how could they execute his widow for the same failure?

On January 25, 1981, the guilty ten lined up within their cages at the special court, like beasts at a fence, to hear the verdicts publicly read. Zhang Chunqiao shared with Jiang the suspended death sentence. All the others were given lighter punishments.

A week later, Peng Zhen came to see Jiang Qing at Qin Cheng Prison. She made two requests: She would like to write her memoirs and to talk with Deng and Hua. Peng said the State Council would think about it.* He explained to Jiang that manual labor was compulsory, and Jiang, seeking to avoid its usual forms, said she would like to make cloth dolls. Peng replied that the State Council had no objection.

"She makes one doll in three days," said a prison source. "The dolls look good. As she stitches them she hums to herself. She likes listening to news broadcasts on the radio. At mealtimes she chats pleasantly with the woman jailors."

Peng Zhen felt it appropriate to reassure the world: "Jiang Qing will remain alive and we shall continue to feed her. She has only one mouth."

Later in 1981 and into 1982 Jiang Qing was less docile. She refused to write the obligatory monthly self-criticism (Wang Hongwen, in another prison, produced more than his quota of self-criticisms). She took to writing defiant statements on the prison walls. "I'm not afraid of having my head chopped off," she scrawled one day. The jailors washed the statement off the wall and warned

_____
* Jiang did meet at least once with Deng during 1981 (Hua had slipped from power); nothing is known of any manuscript she has produced.

her not to do it again. The next day she wrote up the same sentence. On her pretty cloth dolls she began to embroider her name; this put an end to the sale of her dolls, which began to pile up in a warehouse.

"She persists in behaving as a political and ideological enemy of our people," declared Peng Zhen.

Leaflets appeared in Peking and in Shandong Province that purported to come from Jiang's cell. In her texts, Jiang defended the Cultural Revolution, said she always had followed Mao, claimed that the Communist Party of Deng Xiaoping had gone off the rails, and vowed to return and save China. As preparations were made during the summer of 1982 for the Twelfth Congress of the Communist Party, Jiang addressed a letter to the Central Committee. "I would like to speak at the Congress," she explained. "I want to debate openly Deng Xiaoping and Hu Yaobang [Hua's replacement as Party chief] on questions of Party line, direction, and policy. If I can't do this, I would not be able to close my eyes when I die."

"If Deng won't debate," Jiang added, "he's a coward and a revisionist. Only if he debates me will he show himself a true Communist." It was the same Lan Ping who had told Tang Na: "Unless you correct your faults, you will not be worthy to say you once were my lover."

Jiang Qing received no reply to her letter; she spent the week of the Twelfth Party Congress sewing dolls and writing manifestos.

In January 1983 the two-year deadline on Jiang Qing's suspended death sentence was up. Although Hu Yaobang and Peng Zhen had during 1982 told the world of Jiang's recalcitrant attitude, the Communist Party said it had just carried out an investigation (as the law required!) to determine her attitude. "She has not resisted reform in a flagrant way." She had not repented. But she had not *not* repented—and so Peking got off the hook of having to execute Mrs. Mao.

In fact, Jiang Qing was as defiant as ever. "I regret nothing at all," she said to a guard. "I feel I have accomplished what I set out to do."

Beyond 1984?

Did Jiang Qing really still hope to emerge from prison and "save China"? She was a decade younger than Deng. She had not lost her concern for the future, as Zhang Chunqiao had, or her belief in the causes she fought for, as Wang Hongwen and the military culprits had. Nor had the trial demonstrated that Jiang did more than was normal among Communist Party leaders to "usurp" power and "persecute" opponents.

Yet in 1983 the obstacles looked overwhelming. Ultraleftist policies were discredited. Jiang Qing's supporters enjoyed no freedom of discussion or organization to prepare for a future change of mood. If the Chinese public was not necessarily convinced that Jiang committed "monstrous crimes," nor did it seem in favor of her cause; cynicism reigned, and that was not conducive to the only politics Jiang Qing knew—the politics of the Cultural Revolution. As for "escape" from prison—to where? That would be like trying to hide a giraffe on an antheap.

Ironically, Jiang Qing's prospects seemed to hinge not on ideology—much less on law—but on economics. If the Deng era brought impressive economic progress, the verdict against Jiang would not likely be challenged. But if modernization proved elusive, pro-Mao sentiment could return, Jiang Qing would be seen in a better light, and a younger generation of idealists plus disgruntled segments of the military might rally behind her. A mixed economic scorecard could see the government quietly give amnesty to Jiang Qing.

Yet the prospects were that Jiang Qing would spend her remaining years in prison, making dolls, declaring her innocence, and trying to set her jailors right on political questions.

One day, when the political cards have been reshuffled, a new Chinese government may declare with deep conviction that the case against Jiang Qing was, to quote Deng's deeply convinced words on Jiang's case against *him* during the Cultural Revolution, "the biggest unjust charge in Chinese Communist history."

Abbreviations in Notes

ACL   *Jiang Qing—Mao's Wife,* Taipei, Anti-Communist League
BJDS   *Beijing Dashen,* Taipei
CB   *Current Background* (U.S. Consulate General, Hong Kong)
CLG   *Chinese Law and Government,* White Plains, NY
CQ   *China Quarterly*
Cui I,   Cui Wanqiu: "Shanghai sui yue hua Jiang Qing," a series of arti-
II, III,   cles in *Bai xing ban yue kan,* HK, Nos. 16, 1/16/82, and after,
etc.   each fortnight, ending 8/16/82 (No. XII).
DGB   *Da gongbao,* Hong Kong
DW   Ding Wang: *Jiang Qing jian zhuan,* Hong Kong
FBIS   Foreign Broadcast Information Service
FEER   *Far Eastern Economic Review*
FN   Footnote
GTCH   *A Great Trial in Chinese History,* Peking
HK   Hong Kong
Hong   Zhou Yurui: *Hong chao ren wu zhi,* NY
IAS   *Issues & Studies,* Taipei
Ih. I   Kichinosuke Ihara: "Kosei no saisho no jinsei," in *Tezukayama daigaku ronshu,* 3/1976
Ih. II   Ihara: "Shanhai jidai no Kosei," *ibid.,* 5/1976
Ih. III   Ihara: "Kosei . . . Shanhai kara Enan e," *ibid.,* 4/1977
Ih. IV   Ihara: "Mo Ko kekkon mondai, 1," *ibid.,* 5/1977
Ih. V   Ihara: "Mo Ko kekkon mondai, 2," *ibid.,* 7/1977
Ih. VI   Ihara: "Mo Ko kekkon mondai, 3," *ibid.,* 9/1977
Ih. VII   Ihara: "Enan jidai no Kosei," *ibid.,* 1/1978
Ih. VIII   Ihara: "Kosei to Enan sei fu," *ibid.,* 4/1978
Ih. IX   Ihara: "Kosei no chosei: Senhoku tensen," *ibid.,* 7/1978
Ih. X   Ihara: "Goju nendai no Kosei," *ibid.,* 9/1978
Ih. XI   Ihara: "Kosei no bunkaku junbi, 1," *ibid.,* 9/1980
Ih. XII   Ihara: "Kosei no bunkaku junbi, 2," *ibid.,* 12/1980
Ih. XIII   Ihara: "Gendai chugoku no kogo—Kosei jiden," *Rekshi koron,* 12/1976
Ih. XIV   Ihara: "Witke to Kosei," *Mondai to kenkyu,* 3/1978
JPRS   *Joint Publications Research Service*
JQ   Jiang Qing
JQWY   *Jiang Qing tong zhi lun wen yi,* Peking

K & C	D. Klein and A. Clark: *Biographic Dictionary of Chinese Communism*
LL	Lao Long: *Jiang Qing wai zhuan*, Taipei
LP	Lan Ping
LSSP	*Li shi shen pan*, Peking
Lu	*Si ren bang yan xing lu*, HK, 1977
M	Ross Terrill: *Mao: A Biography*
MBYK	*Ming bao yue kan*, HK
NY	New York
NYT	*New York Times*
PD	*People's Daily* (in Chinese)
PK	Peking
PKR	*Peking Review* (later, *Beijing Review*)
QS	*Qi shi nian dai*, HK
RF	*Red Flag* (in Chinese)
RS	Edgar Snow: *Red Star over China*
RT	The author
SCMP	*Survey of China Mainland Press*
SF	San Francisco
SH	Shanghai
SW	*Selected Works of Mao Zedong*, 4 vols., in English
T	Taipei
TN	Information from a source close to Tang Na
URI	Zhong Huamin: *Jiang Qing zheng zhuan*, Union Research Institute
W	Roxane Witke: *Comrade Chiang Ch'ing* (Jiang Qing)
Wan sui	*Mao Zedong si xiang wan sui*, 3 vols., identified by date
WHCM	*What's Happening on the China Mainland*, T
YS	Zhu Shan: *Jiang Qing ye shi*, 2 vols., HK
ZB	*Zhong bao*, HK
ZG	*Zhong gong shou yao shi lue hui bian*, T (entry on JQ)
Zhang	Zhang Ganping: *Jiang Qing de chou shi yu yan wen*, HK
ZM	*Zheng ming*, HK (monthly)
ZW	*Zhan wang*, HK (fortnightly)

Dates and numbers of serial publications are given according to these examples:

6/1972   June 1972 (a monthly publication)

5/7/81   May 7, 1981

2–4, 1968 Volume 2, Number 4, 1968

Bibliographic Note

(Full details of items mentioned are given in the Reference Notes.)

A few skeletal biographical works in Chinese on JQ came out in the 1960s: Ding Wang's *JQ jian zhuan*, 1967; Zhong Huamin (Zhao Cong)'s *JQ zheng zhuan*, 1967 (translated as *Madame Mao* in 1968—page references are to this edition); Zhu (Chu) Haoran's brief but, for its time, accurate article in *CQ*, No. 31. These works are now largely superseded, Zhong Huamin's less so than the others.

Some generally reliable information quite early came from Russian sources (e.g., the memoirs of Otto Braun, *The Vladimirov Diaries*, Radio Moscow's biographical broadcast of 3/31/67).

During the Cultural Revolution (CR) bits and pieces concerning JQ's life spilled out (e.g., her own two works, *JQ tong zhi lun wen yi* and *Wei ren min li xin gong;* and *Guang yin hong qi*, 10/29/67, in *SCMP*, No. 4089). In addition, JQ's conduct as a politician is touched on in many of the basic CR materials; and it became an object of concrete observation and analysis by the better Hong Kong and Taiwan journals.

Meanwhile, the leading scholar of JQ's life and career, Kichinosuke Ihara of Tezukayama University, Japan, had begun to publish the first of his long series of articles (see Abbreviations).

JQ's autobiography as told to Witke in 1972 was a major addition to our knowledge, even though much new material has become available in the eleven years since Witke talked with JQ, and much has happened to JQ over that period (e.g., her struggles with Deng and Zhou, her rise to near-supremacy in 1974, the events following Zhou's death, her fall after Mao died, her imprisonment, her trial).

Semifictionalized accounts of JQ began to appear in the 1960s. Most must be disregarded as sources. The earliest book was Zhang Ganping's *JQ de chou shi yu yan wen*, 1969 (the author was a former Nationalist military officer), but much of it is based on fairly vague gossip. Two later "unofficial" (*wai shi*) accounts are worthy of attention. Lao Long's *JQ wai zhuan*, 1974, was actually written by Long Yuncan, a former official of the Investigation Bureau of the Department of Justice in the Nationalist regime. The sections on JQ's life in Qingdao and Shanghai contain new material that is probably in general accurate (presumably it comes in part from Nationalist interrogation of JQ in SH, and of her husband, Yu Qiwei, in Qingdao). As for *JQ ye shi* by Zhu Shan (a pseudonym), 1980, it is gossipy and biased, but for two periods of JQ's life, it is a valid source—the Yanan period and the stays in Russia (hardly surprising since the author is in fact Zhu Zhongli, the widow of the Communist leader Wang Jiaxiang, who was an important figure in Yanan and Chinese ambassador to the Soviet Union in the 1950s).

A preliminary task of the biographer of JQ in the 1980s is to seek to align those materials which existed by the time of her fall (e.g., Witke was apparently unaware of Ihara's work; Ihara's published work has not taken *JQ ye shi* into account, and some of it is pre-Witke).

The Chinese are not as good as the Russians at keeping secrets; their great weapon is the Chinese language—to keep information limited to Chinese-language materials is to keep it virtually a secret from the rest of the world. But the foreigner who can deal with Chinese probably can find out more about Chinese politics than a foreigner who knows Russian can find out about Russian politics (Moscow doesn't trust Russians outside Russia as much as Peking trusts its Overseas Chinese). Between JQ's fall and her trial, the period 1976 to 1980, much important material about her appeared in the more serious Hong Kong (and to a lesser degree, Taiwan) journals. References to these (e.g., *Ming bao yue kan, Zhong bao, Zheng ming, Qi shi nian dai, Issues and Studies, Zhong gong yan jiu, Zhan wang*) appear in my notes.

Over the same period (1976–80) the official press of China and the *neibu* (restricted) press put out important materials, which, if handled with care, throw new light. Examples (all referred to in detail in the notes): on JQ's family background, in *PD* and *Guang ming ribao;* on JQ's relations with Kang Sheng, in *Xin guan cha, IAS* (speech of Hu Yaobang), and elsewhere; on JQ's relation with "Sister Xu," in the *Zhong fa, PD,* 2/11/80, etc.; on the Mao-JQ family situation, the memoirs by the wives of Mao's two sons, Liu Songlin and Liu (Zhang) Shaohua, *JQ ye shi,* etc.; on JQ's identification with Chinese women rulers of the past (none of whose names she mentioned to Witke), *PD* and *Guang ming ribao* articles, *JQ shi qi shi dao ming de zheng zhi ba shou,* etc.; scattered memoir material on JQ, mostly by Bohemians writing about the 1930s or the Cultural Revolution period, e.g., works by Zhao Dan and Xu Zhuancheng, articles in the Shanghai magazine *Dian ying gu shi* and in the Hong Kong Communist newspaper *Da gongbao;* and the films of the trial, which I saw at the Ministry of Justice in Taiwan, which intercepted them via Fujian Province.

The Yanan period proved particularly susceptible to the uncovering of generally available but little-used sources (e.g., the memoirs of Chen Xuezhao and Si Malu); interviews with people in the People's Republic of China who knew JQ in Yanan (mostly anonymous); and hitherto unknown documents (e.g., Snow's explosive account of the breakdown of Mao's marriage with He Zizhen).

I have gleaned material through interviews in Taiwan and other places outside the People's Republic of China with people who knew JQ; e.g., Wang Tingshu, Warren Guo (Chen Ran), and Pei Mingyu in Taiwan; Kang Jian, Jack Service, Jack and Yuan-tsung Chen, all in San Francisco; Gerald Tannebaum in NY; and Zhang Suchu and other members of Zhang Zhizhong's family, in various countries.

In particular, interviews have enabled me to put JQ's three marriages prior to her meeting with Mao into their proper prominence in her life story; with Shandong classmates and associates for the Fei marriage; with a family member of Yu Qiwei for that marriage; and with a source close to Tang Na for JQ's third marriage.

The recent memoirs of Cui Wanqiu, who knew JQ in Shanghai, in *Bai xing ban yue kan,* are important. I have also benefited from sustained talks and comparing of notes with Mr. Cui in San Francisco.

Within the People's Republic of China, information gathering, beyond the materials already mentioned, had to be furtive and piecemeal (c.f., the attitudes of the bureaucrats as quoted in the latter part of my Prologue). However, numerous persons kindly helped; these persons vary from well-known figures (e.g., Ding Ling), to figures of note who were once friends of JQ (e.g., Su Fei), to persons at the grass roots who met or observed JQ at close hand on particular occasions (the names of these people have been withheld). It sometimes seemed that the more uncooperative official China was to my investigation of JQ, the more cooperative were the emerging voices of unofficial China. Some of these people were indefatigable, and indispensable to me, in locating materials, providing contacts, checking my translations, and especially in sharing their first-hand knowledge of the later JQ.

One day, perhaps, such collaboration between Chinese and foreigners will cease to be anonymous.

Reference Notes

1. Prologue: "I Was Mao's Dog"

Page

13–16   For detailed sources on the trial, see notes to Chapter 8; here, mainly *BJDS; ZM,* Nos. 19, 40; *LSSP;* TV Tape; *MBYK,* 12/19/80 (abbreviations are explained in notes to Chapter 8).

16   ("We've explained that") A senior Chinese diplomat to RT, Washington, DC, 7/8/81.

17   ("not very civilized") W, 50 (a paraphrase).

18   ("Let us not") *IAS,* 6/1980.

19   ("Personalities" and "It is all") Two Chinese officials to RT, PK, June 3 and 23, 1982.

19   ("deaf and blind history") E. Masi's *China Winter,* X.

2. Growing Up, Reaching Out (1914–33)

20   (frontquote) W, 55.

20–27   On the birth and Zhucheng, *Qiao bao yue kan,* HK, No. 3, 55ff. (includes a photocopy of a 1950 document in JQ's own hand that gives details of place, date, etc., of her birth); *PD,* 4/27/77, 5/18/77; Pei Mingyu to RT, T, 2/28/82; *Guang ming ribao,* 4/28/77; *MBYK,* 11/1979; W, 45; Chen Suimin's *Mao Zedong yu JQ,* 83ff.; *Xin guan cha,* PK, No. 1, 1981; Zhong Huamin (Zhao Cong) to RT, HK, 11/22/82; Ih. I, 35ff. Ihara, *ibid.,* 36–37, concludes Shumeng was born in Yibu county (can be called Qingzhou), based on some interviews with Shandong veterans; it is likely that this confusion arose from the fact that, according to new materials on Kang Sheng's life (*Xin guan cha,* Nos. 1, 3, 1981), county boundary lines changed around this time.

21   ("Your father") *PD,* 4/27/77. Records of the family have been subject to extraordinary distortion. (The problems are illustrated by the fact that there are serious sources that give her birthdate variously as 1910, 1912, 1913, 1914, and 1915—see Ih. I, 35.) The account of Shumeng's childhood that I give is an artistic piecing together of material from diverse sources which, in their detail, cannot be mutually reconciled. In outline the ambiguities are as follows: Some Chinese sources, mostly but not entirely outside China, say the girl was born Luan Shumeng, that her mother's family name was Li, and that Shumeng, in the light of the

divided family situation, gravitated to the Li side of the family and after having lost both her parents, lived for a time with grandfather Li in the city of Jinan.

However, *PD* and other Peking publications, which are often cavalier about changing their opinions but seldom so in regard to facts, say that the father's name was Li Dewen. Our subject herself has said her family name was Li.

In evaluating this contradiction one should bear the following in mind:

    (1) the information about the name Luan is from local sources over a long period of time and cannot easily be dismissed;

    (2) official Peking accounts have a strong bias toward establishing a class basis for JQ's temperament, and so toward discounting, or even suppressing, its psychological basis in the family's disordered state;

    (3) our subject has demonstrably distorted the story of her life at a number of points.

Perhaps Shumeng stemmed from both Luan and Li families. Certainly the relation between her father and her mother was more irregular than either she (for reasons of personal pride and political image) or the Chinese authorities (wishing to establish the class character of her moral shortcomings) state. It is possible that she was born out of wedlock—that her father was not Li Dewen, but a man named Luan from a household in which her mother worked; however, the evidence for these points is not enough to treat them as givens in our story.

22   Official Chinese sources exaggerate the father's prosperity (he was of "landlord" class, owning "120 *mu* of land" and a house of "14 rooms and 6 sheds," and *his* father was "a landlord owning more than 100 *mu* of land," *PD*, 5/18/77); our subject herself exaggerates the family's poverty (her father lived in "grinding poverty"; ". . . we were poor and had little to eat," W, 47), as do some Chinese sources based on oral material. See also DW, 12; *RS*, 522. The Chinese government's version of JQ's life is given in a *Zhong fa*, PK, 10/1977—*Pan tu JQ de li shi cui deng*.

One source (Pei Mingyu to RT, T, 2/28/82, see also *Ming bao*, 2/15/77) praises the father as cultivated, kind, and handsome, but it is possible that Mr. Pei, now 93 years old, is recalling Shumeng's grandfather; it seems that Shumeng sometimes led people to believe her grandfather was actually her father (Ih. I, 43).

PK sources flatly state nowadays that the mother was the "small wife" of the father (*Xin guan cha*, No. 1, 1981).

23   (prejudice against girls) M. C. Yang's *A Chinese Village*, 124–25. Female infanticide was far more common than male infanticide; see Marian J. Levy: *The Family Revolution in Modern China*, 226.

23   (father's remark) *Qiao bao*, No. 3, 55.

23   (bound feet) Wang Tingshu to RT, 2/23/82; Ihara's interviews with Zhang, Luo (Ih. I, 40); *Hong*, 232.

23   ("She hated") Wang Tingshu to RT, T, 2/23/82. Cf. the traditional saying "A small foot and an ocean of tears" (Smedley, ed., *Portraits of Chi-*

nese Women in Revolution, 35). In the city of Jinan, the authorities said that in 1929, 20%–30% of the women had bound feet (*Jinan shi zheng yue kan,* 10/1929, 138).

23   On Yunhe's half sister, Ih. I, 39; RT's interviews with persons at Qinghua University, 6/1982; W, 52 (where JQ speaks as if her half sister had the same mother as she).

23–24   (father-mother clash) W, 48. One may wonder about Shumeng's account of the broken tooth in light of the following report in a Shanghai magazine for 1936. The headline is "LAN PING LOSES a TOOTH and SHEDS BLOOD in SUZHOU." The article relates how Lan Ping (our subject's name in those years), in Suzhou for outdoor shooting of the movie *Blood on Wolf Mountain,* in which she had a role, "in a moment of carelessness, suffered two broken front teeth." (*Dian sheng,* 9/25/36, 986).

24   ("There was family") A well-informed Party veteran in PK.

24   (at father's farm) *PD,* 4/27/77. A concubine was not necessarily an outcast and could have a certain status in a family (Levy, 201). For a mother-daughter relationship to assume the prominence that it did in Shumeng's life was most unusual (Levy, 201, 183).

24–25   (Yunhe at school) W, 49; *Qiao bao,* No. 3; *Mao Zedong yu JQ,* 84; LL, Ch. 1.

25   (clothes) W, 49.

26   ("immoral") *PD,* 5/18/77.

26   (Shumeng on her mother) The interviewer was Roxane Witke, whose extraordinary sessions with JQ will be referred to throughout this book; W, 47–48. Some unconfirmable Chinese sources (e.g., *YS,* 1–2) say that one of the households was none other than the family of Kang Sheng (Zhang was the original name), later a Communist Party leader, a political associate and defender of our subject, and a principal evil genius of the Cultural Revolution. It is impossible to be sure that Kang Sheng and JQ met this way, but they did meet in Zhucheng, where JQ's house was near Kang's. Later, the two of them maintained a loyalty to each other that was most unusual in the upper reaches of the Party. (See *Xin guan cha,* Nos. 1, 3, 1981.)

26   Wolves scarcely exist in Shandong, but they heavily populate the literature of child psychoanalysis. Likewise, teeth as a symbol of hostility and conflict, recurrent in our subject's childhood memories, are common in children's unpleasant dreams. One doubts that either wolves or teeth played as big a role in her childhood as in her recollections of it.

27   On the move to Jinan, URI, 12ff.; *Qiao bao,* No. 3, 56; LL, 3ff.

27   ("A festive city") D. Buck's *Urban Change in China,* 171.

28   It is possible that the name Yunhe was given to her in Zhucheng, as JQ herself recalls, or by her grandfather, as stated by other sources. JQ says she "entered the world as Li Jin" (W, 45), but there is no other evidence for this. The name Li Jin, a grand, almost masculine, name, with the ring of a scholar to it, first crops up in the record much later, when she chose it as a name to travel under on visits to Shandong after 1949.

The name Li Qingyun occurs in Snow (*RS,* 459), who collected his information in the 1930s, as well as in Ching Ping and D. Bloodworth: *Heirs Apparent,* 6, the information in which comes from a well-connected Chinese woman, and in LL. Wang Tingshu (to RT, 2/23/82) said Yunhe was never known as Qingyun in their time as classmates. See also Ih. I, 38–39, relating testimony of Zhang Yizhi and others. According to PK's *Zhong fa,* JQ also used Li Yungu as one of her girlhood names.

28   (at school) Wang Tingshu to RT, 2/23/82 ("The name"); *Qiao bao,* No. 3; Wang Xuewen in *Fei qing yue bao,* T, 9/1974, 484; DW, 1; *Fei qing yue bao,* 6/1967; URI, 12. Many different names are given for the grandfather; he may have been called Li Ziming, a school official whom Yunhe some years later discussed with Cui Wanqiu (Cui VII, 17; Ih. I, 38).

29   JQ has said that she and her mother stayed two years in Tianjin (W, 52), but this is unlikely. It would have been impossible for her to complete eight or nine years of schooling, as we know she did (*Wan sui*–1969, 7/28/68), if she spent 1927–29 in Tianjin without attending school. Nor were the mother's relations with the father's family such that it is plausible for JQ's mother to have spent two years in the home of her ex-husband's daughter, when her own parents were far off in Jinan. It is even more unlikely that the half sister and her husband moved to Jinan—and our subject and her mother with them, as she states—in light of the evidence that in Jinan, the mother and daughter lived, as one would expect them to, with the mother's parents. (See also Cui I, 22.)

29   Among the many sources that say the mother died in 1928 or 1929 are *Qiao bao,* No. 3; DW, 1; URI, 13. On Yunhe sending money to her mother, W, 55, 56; she referred to her mother in a letter of 1936 to a future husband (JQ to Tang Na, in *Xin bao ban zhou kan,* SF, 10/6/79).

30   (FN) A. Smedley's *Portraits of Chinese Women in Revolution,* 8. Hundreds of prostitutes were registered as such with the city authorities, and hundreds more worked without registration. Particularly at examination time, when male candidates flocked to the city's inns from all over the province, prostitution was a prominent phenomenon in Jinan. One judge became so exercised by the situation at examination time that he arrested masses of prostitutes and sold them to peasants as wives by weight at the market price of pork for that day (*Jinan yue kan,* 9/1929 and 10/1929; Buck, 37).

30–31   (troupe) *Mao Zedong yu JQ,* 85; URI, 14ff.; *Xin guan cha,* No. 1, 1981; Kosuke Wakuta: *Watashiwa no chugokunin,* 105–06; Zhang, 7–8. Years later, in a speech, JQ went out of her way to make a reference to Shandong's "illegal theater troupes" (*Wei ren min li xin gong,* 11). For other possible explanations of Yunhe's disappearance, *Zhong gong ren ming lu,* T, 750; Ih. I, 44.

30–32   On Yunhe in Jinan, T. Minora's article in *Asahi Weekly* (in Japanese), 4/2/76; Si Ma Zhang Feng's article in *ibid.,* 11/5/76; Zhong Huamin (Zhao Cong) to RT, HK, 11/22/82. To see how bold Yunhe's behavior was, compare an account of usual girls' behavior, M. C. Yang, 63, 128.

30–31   (Yunhe's appearance) *Fei qing yue bao,* 6/1967, 65; *Qiao bao,* No. 3; Pei Mingyu to RT, T, 2/28/82.

32   On the wave of new progressive thought in Jinan, including that on marriage and divorce, the reminiscences of Cui Wanqiu, who went to school
in Jinan in the early 1920s (to RT, SF, 12/31/81, 3/5/82), and Zhong
Huamin (pen name of the author of URI) to RT, HK, 11/22/82.

One can see in the speeches of Jinan's mayor, and in other materials, evidence of the atmosphere of reform (on women's rights and social
equality generally) that influenced Yunhe (*Jinan yue kan*, 9/1930,
170–75 and *passim*). Also see the novel *Xuan feng*, set in Shandong at
this period; in it, one character, Fang Xiangqian, boasts to a friend
about the reforms, inspired by Russia, that were on the agenda:
"Since Russia went through the October Revolution," he said, "the social
revolution has been accomplished. Everyone works, everyone tills the soil, everyone eats, everyone is equal, everyone has freedom. Freedom to marry and
freedom to divorce. If your wife doesn't suit you, quickly divorce her, and get a
new one. The state has established nurseries, as soon as a child is born, send
him to the nursery, then you don't need to look after him, and you needn't have
anything to do with him! If you're sick, the state has established hospitals to
cure you free of charge. If you're old, the state has old folks' homes to care for
you until you die. In general, people in Russia have it made!" (From T. Ross's
translation, entitled *The Whirlwind*, 87.)

32–36 On Yunhe's life at the academy, Wang Tingshu to RT, T, 2/23/82; and
Wang's "JQ shi wo lao tong xue," *Da cheng*, No. 87, and a partially similar article in *Dao bao fang fen*, No. 6. See also Cui II, 23–24; Ih. I and
XIV; *Mao Zedong yu JQ*, 85ff.; W, 53–55; URI, 16; DW, 1 (role of Nora);
Da lu guan cha, 1/1973, 59. The most thorough treatment is in Ih. I, 46ff.;
Ihara (49) believes that Yunhe may have been Wang Tingshu's first love,
and I am inclined to agree. Wang's memory of her sexual attractiveness
is intense. Wu Ruiyan was Professor Wang Bosheng's wife. The allowance may have been six yuan (Wang Tingshu) or perhaps less (W, 53).

36   Yunhe told Witke that the girl was Yu Shan's sister (W, 53), but Wang
Tingshu insists it was Wang Bosheng's sister (Ihara to RT, Osaka,
1/25/82).

37–39 (Fei) DW, 3 (implies marriage) and Mr. Ding to RT, HK, 11/24/82; Cui
XI, 35; LL, 15ff.; *ZG*, 130; *DGB*, 11/2/80; Xu Zhuancheng's *Chao dan
yu shuiguo*, 190; Zhang, 10ff.; *Qiao bao*, No. 3; Pei Mingyu to RT, T,
2/28/82; Zhong Huamin to RT, HK, 11/22/82; *Xin Zhong guo ren wu
zhi*, T, 272; *Shinjitsu-ho*, Kobe, 5/15/76. One source (*Hong*, 232) gives
the young husband's name as Zhang, which may indicate a confusion
with the household of landlord Zhang, with whose son (Kang Sheng)
another source (*YS*, 1–2) asserts our subject had a girlhood link.

37   ("There was") Wang to RT, T, 2/23/82. Wang was surmising, based on
his knowledge of Yunhe's economic situation; he had no knowledge of
the Fei-Yunhe marriage.

38   ("When you marry") *Women in China*, ed. M. Young, 182.

38   The family was not "extended" in the sense of having aunts and uncles
in residence (such households were mainly limited to the upper classes),
but in the sense of a "stem family," in which one son establishes his family under the same roof as his parents (see Levy, 55).

We have given only the Fei family's side of the issue; JQ has never
spoken publicly of this first marriage.

Page

39–40   On Qingdao as a city, Buck, 173 and *passim*. On the intellectual atmo-
         sphere, *Da lu wen ti yan jiu ji,* No. 103, T, 423ff.

40   On Yunhe and Zhao, Wang Tingshu to RT, T, 2/23/82; *Hong,* 232–33;
         Ih. XIV (material from Zhang Yizhi); Shen Zongwen, then teaching at
         Qingdao University, confirmed that Yunhe was a worker in the library
         and not a student (Xu Kaiyu's *Our China Trip*—a private publication,
         114). According to Zhang Yizhi (Ih. XIV) JQ exaggerated her revolu-
         tionary activities in Qingdao when talking to Witke. See also *Zhong
         yang ribao,* T, 3/13/67.

41–45   On Yunhe and Yu, *Hong,* 233; close relative of Yu to RT, T, 2/24/82;
         RS, 459; *DGB,* 10/31/80; *YS,* 2ff.; Cui III, 35ff.; ACL, 14; LL, 34ff.; *Xin
         guan cha,* No. 1, 1981; Ih. I; *PD,* 2/13/58 (Yu joined the Party in 1932);
         ZW, No. 342, 26 (Chen Boda said JQ "joined the revolution" at the time
         of the "September 18 Incident").

41   Nym Wales's *Notes on the Chinese Student Movement,* 36. See also J. Is-
         rael and D. Klein: *Rebels and Bureaucrats,* 135.

43   Nym Wales to RT, 5/8/81.

43–44   Yunhe herself later spoke of having had to "pay off Li Dazhang," refer-
         ring to a top Communist official in Qingdao (W, 68). This sounds like a
         payment for Party membership, as Witke suggests, though it is also pos-
         sible that the money was a fine for indiscretions, or simply Party dues,
         which Yunhe portrayed as somehow discriminatory against her.

45   Snow, *RS,* 459, says Yu told him his uncle secured his release; the close
         relative in T confirmed this story to RT. *Xin zhong guo ren wu ji* (entry
         under Yu Qiwei) says JQ was arrested at the same time as Yu Qiwei, but
         this is mistaken.

45–46   "Back of tranquility lies always conquered unhappiness," ran one of
         Eleanor Roosevelt's favorite quotations. What has been said of Mrs.
         Roosevelt's upbringing could be said of Yunhe's: "Such documentation
         [of childhood difficulties] could be used trauma for trauma to 'explain'
         failure. Yet Eleanor Roosevelt 'succeeded,' in many ways triumphantly,
         in other ways, not without tragic overtones" (J. Erikson in *Daedalus,*
         Spring 1964, 792).

3.   ONSTAGE IN SHANGHAI (1933–37)

48   (frontquote) W, 55.

48–49   Arrival in SH is described in *Hong,* 234; Cui III, 36ff.; W, 69; *ZG,* 131;
         Ih. II, 41 (based on Zhang Yizhi, *inter alia*); URI, 19; *The Vladimirov
         Diaries,* 83. On Yunhe and Shi, H. Tsuji in *Kinema Jumpo* 4/1977 and
         5/1977; *Gong fei ren zhi,* T, 887; LL, 108ff. Wan, despite Yunhe's irrita-
         tion with him, probably helped her with SH contacts (Cui III, 36).

49   (FN) RT's *Flowers on an Iron Tree,* 47.

50   Kang Jian to RT, SF, 3/5/82.

Page

50–51   On the women's movement and the situation in SH, Lin Yutang: *My Country and My People,* 146ff., and M. B. Young, ed.: *Women in China,* essay by Leith and *passim.*

51   ("pinned") Cf. the reminiscence of a woman born in 1903 to a fairly comfortable family: "As for my old feudal family, the family into which I was born—they are to me but a dark and ugly memory, and to them I am but a fearful dream. . . . They once tried to pin me to a marriage bed with a millionaire that I might breed more creatures like themselves" (Smedley's *Portraits,* 26).

51   (FN) Lin Yutang, 146.

51–52   (Tian and brother) W, 70ff.; TN; Cui III, 37.

52–53   There are many reasons for doubting JQ's version of her motives in the spring of 1933: After Yu Qiwei went to PK, her relations with the Communist Party at Qingdao were not close; if the Qingdao Party had sent her south, she would not have had the inordinate trouble in "contacting the Party" in SH that she reports (W, 70ff.), nor would she have had to "renew" her Party membership in the new city; the people she first dealt with in SH, notably Wan Laitian and Shi Dongshan, were not Communists but men of the arts; Tian Han, the first left-wing notable she sought out, was not a logical bridge into Communist activities; if she really was told in an early meeting with Zhou Yang (a key Party figure in cultural matters) that she could be received as a Communist—as she claimed— then it is inconceivable that for much of the next four years she was "floundering" politically and still had to struggle to "contact" the Party; and her account of her Party connections in 1934 shows an unfamiliarity with Party procedures of the time. On Zhou Yang's view of JQ in the 1930s, see an interesting interview in *QS,* 9/1978.

53   Xu later was said by official Chinese sources to have become a traitor, perhaps because of her association with JQ (Ihara to RT, Osaka, 11/5/82; *PD,* 4/27/77). Be that as it may, she did suffer at the hands of the Nationalists, being arrested in SH in January 1935 (*YS,* 10).

54   ("There was no one") *DGB,* 11/1/80.

54   On money situation, *Hong,* 232; W, 75.

54–55   (Ai Gui) *PD,* 11/27/80.

55   (Liao) W, 74; *DGB,* 1/28/81.

55   (Tao) TN; Cui III, 36; W, 72.

55–56   (*"Babies"*) W, 78.

56   Organized dissent was possible, if dangerous, in Nationalist-ruled SH; in Communist-ruled SH after 1949, it was virtually impossible. On the difference, *Flowers on an Iron Tree,* 34ff. On JQ's nationalistic feelings, *Lu,* 69; Ih. III, 16ff.

57   ("She didn't") Kang Jian to RT, SF, 3/5/82. See also Radio Moscow 3/31/67, program on JQ (in Chinese).

57   ("If she came") Han Suyin's *My House Has Two Doors,* 473.

57–58   (trip to PK) One cannot accept her own statement that the Party, as represented by the League of Left-Wing Educators, transferred her to PK. Once in PK she fulfilled no Party purposes; if the point was to relieve her "plight" in SH, why not send her back to Qingdao, where her Party associations were? Indeed, how could she be confident of "making contact with the Party" in the tight atmosphere of PK any more than she had been able to in the slightly more open atmosphere of SH?

Huang Chen, the wife of Zheng Junli, has stated that while in SH, JQ continued an affair with "her former husband." If so, the man must have been Yu Qiwei. (*Now*, London, 12/5/80.) Also Vladimirov (82) has her in PK with Yu in 1934. And in the *Jun bu te wu ji guan*—Japanese authorities—materials, Yu is described, as of the mid-1930s, as being "married to Li Yunhe" (information from Zhu Haoran, Melbourne University, who has seen these documents). (See also W, 101; Cui III, 34.) It is known that Yu had spent time in SH in the company of people in the world of the performing arts (J. Israel and D. Klein: *Rebels and Bureaucrats*, 73). The authoritative memoir of Wei Zhaochang (*DGB*, 11/1/80) states that Yunhe became pregnant by Yu in PK.

58–59   (arrest, Wang incident) W, 88; Wang Tingshu to RT, T, 2/23/82.

60   ("Suddenly") *DGB*, 11/1/80.

60   There are two reasons to lean toward the second version of Yunhe's arrest and imprisonment: Communist and Nationalist accounts, which disagree about many periods of our subject's life, largely agree with each other on the prison period, diverging far from Yunhe's version; and years later she fought hard to try to ferret out and destroy any evidence relating to her arrest, imprisonment, and release. An account in *MBYK*, 10/1979, 47, based on Nationalist sources, states that she confessed, as do all accounts based on Communist sources, e.g., *YS*, 4–6. (See Cui III, 34, V, 36; Ih. XIV, 18.)

61   ("She was thin") Ih. III, 28. On her patriotic utterances at the time, *Lu*, 69.

62   A striking proof of the shift of priorities comes in her later letter to Tang Na (see page 98) in which, rejecting Tang Na's world of filmland, she says that unlike him she has known another world, a different phase in her life—which, with hindsight, she preferred to the theater.

62   The abandonment of the surname Li was probably not unconnected with feelings of guilt about the circumstances of her release from prison; cf., her enigmatic remark to Witke (129) that under the surname Li she "had become infamous in political circles." (See also *RS*, 522; *Hong*, 235.) "Ping" can also mean a kind of plant, and it is possible Wan Laitian had in mind its flowing, vigorous connotations in literature.

63   (rehearsal) Cui to RT, SF, 12/31/81; also Cui VI.

64–67   (Li) Zhang, 334ff.

67–68   (role of Nora) Cui VI and VII; TN; Cui and Mrs. Cui to RT, SF, 3/5/82; *Hong*, 235; W, 102, 497; (year of Nora) Cui VII, 35; Zhao Dan's *Yin mu xing xiang zhuang zao*, 17. It is quite clear between the lines of a memoir of Zhao Dan's, entitled "Remembering the Strict Teacher and Debater in Arms Zhang Min" (*Zhan di*, 3/1980, 8), that Zhao respected LP's work—as Nora and in other roles—and that his failure to mention her name, in an essay of 1980, was a mark of his good feelings toward her, since to mention her would necessarily have been to lambaste her.

69   (Zhang Geng), W, 102–103.

Page

69   (Wu Mei) *DGB,* 12/15/80 ("Wu Mei yu Lan Ping").

70   ("The difference") TN; ("ice cream") J. Leyda's *Dianying,* 102.

70   ("You see") Su Fei to RT, PK, 6/20/82.

70   Kang Jian to RT, SF, 3/5/82.

70–73 (At Dian Tong) *Jin ri shijie,* HK, 8/16/67; LL, 139ff.; Cheng Jihua's *Zhong guo dian ying fa zhan shi,* I, 619; TN; URI, 20ff.

70–71 (Yuan affair) Zhang, 93ff.

71   (FN) J. Leyda's *Dianying,* 64.

73   ("rotten apple") Chen Jiying to RT, T, 2/27/82; ACL, 10; Ih. III. She herself observed to W (107) that she was "vilified with all sorts of vulgar names and political slander."

73   Huang Chen says that her husband, the distinguished director Zheng Junli, introduced LP to her in 1936, an interesting indication that LP was making strides socially (*Now,* London, 12/5/80).

73–75 (Cui and LP) Cui VII, 36ff.; Cui to RT, SF, 11/28/82. For Cui's China Youth Party connection, Cui III, 37, and *Min zhu chao,* Vol. 31, No. 8, 14ff. Cf. *YS,* 6; *PD,* 4/27/77. On Yuan Lingyu, *Ming bao,* 5/8/77 and following days. Tang Na says LP could not sing the arias; Cui says she could.

75–80 (meeting with Tang) TN; *Dian sheng zhou kan,* 5/19/39, under the heading "A Secret Kept for Three Years" (reprinted in *MBYK,* 12/1976, under the heading "JQ de jiu wen"); *Hong,* 236. On the situation within Dian Tong, LL, 116ff.; Cheng Jihua, I, 239.

79   The *MBYK* commentator says LP had a "major role" in *Free Spirit.* This is not clear from the *Dian sheng zhou kan* account or from other evidence, but Ihara, visiting SH in 1981, found in an old movie magazine at the SH library an advertisement for *Free Spirit* which included a photo of LP.

84   According to *DGB,* 11/1/80, LP also had a small role in *Escape.* (See also J. Leyda's *Dianying,* 100, 400.) The movie Hong Shen objected to may have been *Shanghai Express.*

84   (FN—Ding Ling) Leyda, 381.

87   The quarreling is described in LP's "Wo wei sheme he Tang Na fen shou" (*MBYK,* 10/1977). Ai Gui's story is recounted in *PD,* 12/24/80. (Though TN's name is not mentioned, the man referred to is clearly TN.)

87–90 The 3/8/36 incident is recounted in "Wo wei sheme ..." and in W, 104–05. JQ's autobiographical account to Witke disguises her crisis with TN as a political and social crisis (she was "reviled" for her political beliefs, not for her personal behavior); she never once mentioned TN's name to Witke.

91   (Cui's words) Cui XI, and Cui to RT, SF, 12/31/81.

91   ("A strong") Chen Jiying to RT, T, 2/27/82.

92–94 (the wedding) *Dian sheng zhou kan,* 10/30/36 (see *MBYK,* 12/1976); *ZG,* 131; *Hong,* 236; TN; impressionistic account in LL, Ch. 10. Also *Dian sheng zhou kan,* 5/25/39; *DGB,* 11/1/80. Ihara's speculations (II, 53ff.) are now obviated.

93   (second party) *DGB,* 11/1/80.

Page

94   ("brink") *MBYK*, 10/1977; cf. W, 122 ("brink of suicide").

94   ("disharmonies") *Hong*, 236.

94   (Yuan's remark) "JQ xie gei Tang Na de 'jue qing shu' " (originally published in *Tao bao*, PK, 6/30–7/1/37), *Xin bao ban zhou kan*, 10/6/79.

95   ("Mention") *ZW*, No. 159, 23.

95   (FN) Ih. III, 16–17.

95   ("love-mad") URI, 24; see also *DGB*, 10/16/80.

96   On Jinan incident, *DGB*, 10/16/80, 11/1/80; *Xin Zhong guo ren wu zhi*, T, 272; LP's letter to Tang; *Zhong yang ribao*, T, 3/13/67; Cui XI. Ih. II, 65ff., presents some evidence that Tang's suicide attempts were not in deadly earnest. LP said he attempted suicide before she went north, but the chronology of the situation suggests otherwise—and that it was LP's departure from SH that helped drive Tang to despair. Some say LP went to Tianjin as well as to Jinan, but this cannot be verified. For Zheng Junli's role in the letter to Tang, see *PD*, 12/10/80.

97–100   (letter) *Xin bao ban zhou kan*, 10/6/79.

101   ("This is the year") Ih. III, 18.

101–02   JQ's conduct in movie circles, *Dian ying gu shi*, SH, 1/1981; *DGB*, 11/1/80; Zheng Yongzhi to RT, T, 2/27/82; URI, 20ff.; DW, 3ff.; Cheng Jihua, I, 611 and *passim;* Wang Tingshu to RT, T, 2/23/82. Although conventional Communist and Nationalist accounts both dismiss LP's acting talent, individuals who saw her repeatedly testify that she was very able: Hisakazu Tsuji in *Kinema Jumpo*, 5/1977; Kang Jian to RT, SF, 3/5/82; Su Fei to RT, PK, 6/20/82. By May 1937, even Zhang Geng was praising her ability (Cui VII, 36).

      Tang's role in LP's life in films is recalled in Xu Zhuancheng's memoir in *Hua qiao ribao*, NY, 9/27/80; also *DGB*, 10/16/80.

102–03   The Sai affair is based on *Nieh hai hua* (1906); H. McAleavy, ed., *That Chinese Woman* (1959); *Shou huo*, SH, 3/1980 (on Wang Ying); *Guang ming ribao*, 3/12/66; *YS*, 7; *DGB*, 10/16/80.

104–05   (Tang-LP encounter) *Xin bao ban zhou kan*, 10/6/79.

107   (Cui's words) Cui to RT, SF, 12/31/81.

107–09   (LP in *Lian Hua Pictorial*) *Xin bao ban zhou kan*, 10/6/79.

109   (FN) W, 138.

109   LP's "open living with" Zhang Min is reported in *MBYK*, 12/1976. Also URI, 22–23; *Hong*, 236–37; *Dian sheng zhou kan*, 5/25/39; *DGB*, 11/1/80; *ZW*, No. 159; *ZG*, 133; Zheng Yongzhi to RT, T, 2/27/82. (See also Ih. III, 14ff.) On Zhang Min's wife, *Heirs Apparent*, 3; *DGB*, 11/1/80. Apparently Zhang Min divorced his wife sometime in 1937–see *Shi bao*, SH, 6/15/37,

109   ("All those") A PK source.

110   ("I was not") W, 131.

111–13   ("Our Life") "Wo men de sheng huo," *Guang ming za zhi*, 2/25/37, reprinted in *ZW*, No. 366; *MBYK*, 4/1974.

112   JQ in later years led an attack on Stanislavsky's ideas; see *Che di pi pan Si Dan Ni 'ti xi,'* SH, 1971.

113   (Bergman remark) *International Herald Tribune*, 8/31/82.

Page
113   (Tang's words) TN.
114   ("Never forget") W, 423.

4. MAO'S HOUSEWIFE IN YANAN (1938–49)

123   (Frontquote) W, 449.
123   (at river) Jack Chen: *Inside the Cultural Revolution,* 157, and Chen to RT,
       SF, 3/5/82.
124   ("Lan Ping asked") Zheng Yongzhi to RT, T, 2/27/82. It has been writ-
       ten dozens of times that LP went to Chongqing on the way to Yanan, but
       it is clear now that she did not (TN; W, 145; *Xing dao ribao,* HK,
       1/30/77; *YS,* Ch. 2; Cui I; *Zhong yang ribao,* Chongqing, 9/15/39—de-
       tails on film *Zhong hua erh nu,* which does *not* include LP's name). The
       claim of Chen Jiying (to RT, T, 3/2/82) that he saw LP in Chongqing in
       1939 must be set aside. If LP feared movie work in wartime Chongqing
       would be tough, she was correct. "It was hard," said Kang Jian. "Work-
       ing and living conditions—collective accommodations and that sort of
       thing." (Kang Jian to RT, SF, 3/5/82.) Also Leyda, 118.
125   On Yu, Chen Ran (Warren Guo) to RT, T, 2/25/82; Cui III.
125   On Kang Sheng, *Xin guan cha,* No. 1 and No. 3, 1981; Hu Yaobang
       speech, in *IAS,* 6/1980.
125   Otto Braun himself (*Chinesische Aufzeichnungen,* 341; 248 of English
       edition) says his future wife traveled with LP, as does Snow in *RS,* 460
       (though Snow mistakenly says she traveled via Chongqing); see also
       Dian sheng zhou kan, 5/15/39, in *MBYK,* 12/1976, where the actress
       Ouyang Hongying (perhaps one of Mrs. Braun's names) was described as
       traveling with LP; Chen Ran, interview with RT, T, 2/25/82, says LP
       arrived alone at Yanan.
126   Sister Xu (Xu Yiyong, later Xu Mingqing) is extensively mentioned in
       nei bu (internal) publications attacking the "Gang of Four"; even Xu's
       handwriting is reproduced. There is a reference to her—as a "traitor"—
       in an article attacking the Gang of Four in *PD,* 4/27/77. See also Chen
       Xuezhao's *Yanan fang wen ji,* 81. RT has reason to believe that Zhu's *YS*
       is generally accurate about Xu's movements (she is represented by the
       character Chen Lanying, 14), though wildly prejudiced against her; for a
       postmortem on Xu's case, see *PD,* 2/11/82. It is quite possible, as is said
       in *YS,* Ch. 2, that through Wang Guanlan, LP had a brief meeting with
       Mao—in a group with others—soon after reaching Yanan.
128   (horse) W, 146. On Wu Zetian's horse riding, *Asahi Weekly* (in Japa-
       nese), 4/2/76.
129   ("all the leading") W, 146.
129   (Zhang's words) Zhang Guotao's *The Rise of the Chinese Communist
       Party,* II, 552. Years later, JQ claimed she "was not aware" at the time
       that Mao was traveling, one vehicle behind hers, in the same convoy
       from Luochuan to Yanan (W, 146).
130   A number of accounts give LP's arrival at Yanan as 1938: Jack Chen,

Page

157; *MBYK*, 12/1976; *IAS* 10/1980 (citing the dissident magazine *Beijing chi chun*, 3/1979); Vladimirov, 183; Cheng Jihua's *Dian ying . . .* , II, 10. However, the weight of evidence that she arrived in 1937 is irresistibly great: JQ's own story (W, 145); TN says she left SH in July 1937 and "went straight to Xian—she never went to Chongqing on the way"; Ding Ling to RT, 12/9/81; Zhu Haoran (his sister saw LP in Yanan) to RT, Melbourne, 12/26/81; Mrs. Zhang Guotao's memoirs (Yang Zilie: *Zhang Guotao fu nu hui yi*, 333ff.); the information communicated by Zhu Zhongli, the well-connected wife of Wang Jiaxiang in *YS;* Snow's *Random Notes on Red China*, 73; the new material on Kang Sheng in *Xin guan cha*, No. 1 and No. 3, 1981; PK's own post-fall account of her career, as in *PD*, 4/27/77; Xiao Ying's *Wo shi Mao Zedong de nu mi shu*, 70. Furthermore, the accounts of LP spending considerable time in Wuhan and Sichuan after leaving SH turn out to have holes in them.

130   On the situation in rural Shaanxi, M. Selden's *The Yenan Way*, Snow's *RS*, Smedley's *Battle Hymn of China*, Nym Wales's *Inside Red China*, 85 and *passim.*

130   On mixed motives, Si Malu's *Dou zheng shi ba nian.*

131   It is clear even in Witke that LP's political knowledge was sparse (e.g., 148–49, 178–79).

132   (FN) URI, 37. On women's situation in Yanan, "Revolutionnaires au foyer," in *Paris-Pékin*, No. 2.

132   (Zhu Guang) Warren Guo to RT, T, 2/25/82; Ih. VI, 37; *ZG*, 134; *Zhong gong yan jiu*, 5/1973, 51.

132–33   (Li Fuchun) Guo to RT, T, 2/25/82. It is likely that the "Old Fox," Kang Sheng, having been approached by LP as soon as he reached the loess hills from Moscow on November 24, 1937, nudged Sister Xu into writing a strong testimony, concealing the odd skeleton behind a silk screen. Party investigations were seldom done in a flash, however, and LP's status was to remain blurred for months; by early 1938, Kang was certainly a major "mountain" for Lan, and Xu's testimony may at that time have been augmented.

   After JQ's fall, Sister Xu denounced her, which eventually led to a substantial rehabilitation for Xu (see *PD*, 2/11/82). By 1977, however, Xu dared not say that Kang Sheng, by now regarded as a bad man, had encouraged and influenced her testimony on LP's behalf in 1937 and 1938.

133   ("She approached him") Ih. VI, 37–38, based on interview with Si Malu.

133   (Mrs. Zhang's words) *Lian he bao*, T, 1/31/77.

134   ("Li was reluctant") Guo to RT, T, 2/25/82.

134   ("Lan Ping didn't say") Guo to Ihara, 8/16/76 (Ih. VI, 41).

134   (at school), URI, 43–46; Wang Sicheng's *Mao fei Zedong zheng zhuan*, T, 7; *YS*, 37–38. See also *Xing hua liao yuan*, Vol. 6, 36–37 (article by Liu Wu); *Hong qi piao piao*, Vol. 16, 149ff. (article by Ma Ke). Evidence conflicts on the details of Mao's visits to the Party School and, later, to Lu Xun College.

134   ("sought her out") W, 153.

Page

135   On Lu Xun College, Chen Xuezhao's *Yanan fang wen ji,* 144ff.; Smed-
       ley's *Battle Hymn,* 99; H. Forman's *Report from Red China,* 87ff.; W,
       150 (denial of interest in the college).
135   (Yanan film studio) URI, 31ff.
135   ("She simply") Si Malu's *Dou zheng shi ba nian,* 55; *ZW,* No. 369, 17.
136   (Chen Yun) W, 149.
136   New light on the Kang Sheng-JQ relationship has recently been shed:
       Xin guan cha, Nos. 1 and 3, 1981; *ZM,* 8/1/80; *IAS,* 10/1980 (citing
       Beijing zhi chun) and 6/1980 (Hu Yaobang secret speech). See also
       Heirs Apparent, 4; URI, 39; Vladimirov, 100–01; *Kang Sheng si liao ji,*
       T, 1967, 9 and *passim; Dang dai,* HK, 9/1980.

              It now seems to be the Chinese government's view that Kang and
       JQ had a sexual relationship. Hu Yaobang said in a 1978 speech: ". . .
       the truth about JQ's depravity, degeneration, and promiscuous sexual
       relations is intolerably repulsive. I don't know how to describe her ob-
       scure personal relationship with Kang Sheng. We all know it, that is
       enough. Don't speak of it anymore" (*IAS,* 6/1980, 93). However, there
       is no clear evidence that Kang and JQ had a sexual relationship.
136   ("She was at") Guo to Ihara (Ih. VI, 41–42). On Xu Yixin, see also
       Yanan fang wen ji, 81, 144ff.; URI, 41ff.; ACL, 11; Ih. VI, 42 (fate of
       Sun Weishi); *ZW,* No. 369; *Xin Zhong guo ren wu zhi,* T, 273.
136   ("With Xu") *ZW,* No. 354.
137   (LP's life in Yanan) *Dian sheng zhou kan,* 5/25/39.
138   (Wales's words) Wales to RT, 5/8/81, and *Inside Red China,* 276; see
       also *M,* Ch. 9.
138–39 (hill incident) A source close to the Mao family.
139   ("I don't think") TN.
139–42 (He in Xian) Yang Zilie, *op. cit.,* 333ff. On He, *Paris-Pékin,* No. 2,
       102–04; *Hong qi piao piao,* No. 24; *Dong xiang,* HK, No. 14, 11/1979;
       Gong Chu's *Wo yu hong jun,* 142ff. ("crystals," "honey"); *ZM,* 7/1979;
       Liu Fulan's *Mao Zedong de mian mian guan,* 62–64; Anna Wang's *Ich
       kämpfte für Mao.* Liu Qunxian may have mistaken Lily Wu for LP.

              Apologists for Mao have postdated his marriage to He Zizhen to
       make it seem that he did not live with her before the death of Yang
       Kaihui (*YS,* 40, says it occurred in 1933!; and Han Suyin has put it at
       1931—*The Morning Deluge,* 265). But contemporary sources give the
       date of the marriage as 1928 (e.g., Gong Chu's *Wo yu hong jun,*
       142–45), including contemporary Communist sources (e.g., Xu Menqui
       in *Suijun xixing jianwenlu,* 94–96).
142–46 The account of the Smedley-He-Mao-Wu affair is based largely on a
       document in Edgar Snow's files entitled "The Divorce of Mao Zedong"
       and marked by him "not for publication," kindly shown to me by Lois
       Snow; a portion of it has been published in Japanese in *Chuokoron,*
       7/1954 (translated by Matsuoka Yoko). Also Wales's *Inside,* 176, 298;
       Braun, 342; A. Wang, *Ich Kämpfte . . . , passim;* Wales's *The Chinese
       Communists,* 250–53; Si Ma Zhang Feng's *Mao Zedong ping zhuan,*
       Vol. 2, 292ff., and 307ff. Mao also met with Wu in the cave of George
       Hatem and his wife, Su Fei (Braun, 249 of English edition).

Page

143   ("Mao often") *Battle Hymn,* 122.

146   Braun says Lily Wu was sent to Sichuan (343). See also *Inside Red China,* LX. Nym Wales says "Mao ordered Smedley to leave Yanan" (*Inside,* XLI, and *The Chinese Communists,* 250ff.). She says He Zizhen "hated" Smedley (Wales to RT, 5/8/81).

146   ("When she found out") Guo (Chen Ran) to Ihara, 10/22/74, Ih. V, 59–60.

146–47   (Yang and Mao) Yang Zilie, *op. cit.,* 338. A source present in Xian at the time told Liu Fulan (*op. cit.,* 65) that indeed He did not wish to return to Yanan.

147   (Lan on He) W, 160ff.

148   Snow visited Mao and He in Baoan (*Journey to the Beginning,* 167); see also the memoir of a bodyguard, Wu, cited in *ZM,* 11/1980, 39. Braun saw He in Mao's house in late 1937, when he witnessed the two of them quarreling in a "heavy argument" (343).

148   ("Depressive") W, 161. There is evidence that at the time, He's illness was not considered serious (Liu Fulan, 64; Ih. V, 59).

148–49   Braun, 249 of English edition.

149   (He Yi and her husband) Zheng Xuejia in *IAS,* 11/1973, 65; Liu Fulan, *op. cit.,* 58; Ih. VI, 57; A. Wang, *op. cit.* (strike).

149   ("sex maniac" and "Chairman is becoming") W. Guo's *Analytic History of the Chinese Communist Party,* Vol. III, 520–21; Guo to RT, T, 2/25/82.

150–51   (Li, Cai, He Long, FN, etc.) "Revolutionnaires au foyer," in *Paris-Pékin,* No. 2. (The Huang Kegong case is parallel to those cases in societies of the Hispanic world where "legitimate defense of honor" can almost excuse a man killing a woman who has spurned him. See, for example, the account of the trial of the Brazilian playboy Raul Fernando do Amaral Street, in *The Press,* 12/1981, 16.) On marriage as a luxury of the power-holders in Communist Yanan, see Jin Dongping's *Yanan jian wen lu,* 151. On the Jiangxi period, see Hu Chi-hsi's "Mao Zedong, la revolution et la question sexuelle," in *Revue Française de Science Politique,* Vol. 23, No. 1, 1973.

151   ("Shanghai corrupts") Lu Qiang's *Jing gang shan de ying xiong,* 28.

151   ("colorful") Braun, 343. On the controversy in general, Si Ma Zhang Feng's *Mao Zedong ping zuan,* Vol. 2, 307ff., and 367ff.; *Kang Sheng si liao ji* (1967); *ZM,* 8/1/80 ("Kang Sheng he Mao Zedong"); Braun, 343 (vouching for LP's Party background); *ZM,* 11/1980, 38–40; *IAS,* 10/1980, 85; *Xing dao ribao,* HK, 11/4/70; *Xin sheng wanbao,* HK, 1/26/67.

151   ("The leader") Si Malu to Ihara, 8/26/75, in Ih. VI, 50.

153   (Kang Sheng on drums) *Xin guan cha,* No. 1, 1981, 36.

153   (Kang Sheng's use of Anying) *IAS,* 6/1980, 94. See also the semifictional *Zhang,* Chs. 14–17. Some sources (*Jin ri shijie,* Vol. 35, No. 7) say Zhou Yang played a role in securing the Mao-JQ match.

153   (appeal to Stalin) *ZM,* 11/1980.

153   (telegram) *ZM,* 11/1980, 39.

153   ("Chairman Mao and I") *South China Morning Post,* 11/27/76.

Page
153   ("Without Lan") Zhou Jingwen's *Feng ba shi nian,* 120.
154   ("go back to") E. Rice's *Mao's Way,* 108.
154   (threats) W, 157.
154   ("is verified") Guo, *op. cit.,* 398 (Chinese). Snow's document errs in placing the divorce too early; also in stating that He Zizhen was banished from Yanan—she cleared out of her own accord.
       That Mao wrote to He in January 1938 about coming back to Yanan makes it clear that they were not yet divorced. Snow's document wrongly relates the divorce to the Lily Wu incident, when in fact it came as a result of Mao's attachment to LP. It may well be that He asked Mao for a divorce during 1937, but that he was unwilling to agree to it—until he fell in love with LP and wanted to marry her. It seems reasonable to argue, as Si Ma Zhang Feng does (Vol. 2, 192), that had He Zizhen, who was known and respected by the old cadres, remained Mao's wife, it is hard to imagine the occurrence of the Cultural Revolution, which was directed against those old cadres (whom JQ disliked as a group). It is not certain that LP was to stay out of politics for precisely thirty years; Wales says it was twenty-five years (*The Chinese Communists,* 252).
155   (FN) *IAS,* 6/1980, 92.
155   ("They oppressed") *ZM* 11/1980; FBIS 12/29/80.
155   It was after he stage-managed the Mao-JQ settlement that Kang Sheng rose to hold three important posts simultaneously: Director of the Central Committee's Work in Occupied Districts, Chief of the Political Security Bureau, Minister of Social Work in the White Areas (*Kang Sheng si liao ji*). In general, he eclipsed and replaced Wang Shoudao at the heart of the Party secretariat.
155–56 D. Barrett's *Dixie Mission,* 64.
156   (Wang Ming's words) *Menggu xiao xi bao,* Mongolia, 6/15–29/1974.
157   ("worshiped") W, 187.
157   ("We were puzzled") Service to RT, SF, 8/5/82; also Braun, 250 of English edition.
158   On reluctance of some intellectual women to marry leaders, see ACL, 14–15.
158   (FN) TN.
158   (Nym Wales [H. Snow] remark) *Inside Red China,* 167.
159–60 (Mao-LP house) Ih. VII, 36–37; *M,* 141; Barrett, 29; *Yanan fang wen ji,* 98–99; *Xing luo liao yuan,* Vol. 4, 134ff.
160   On the name change, URI 50–51; Cui I; *ZW,* No. 173; W, 155; Ih. XIV, 20; Rice, 106. JQ was not well versed in old poems; she was not in a position to propose a name that stood on a footing with Mao's; in previous name changes, she had been guided by someone more literary minded than she; and her statement that she chose "Jiang" in order to put her original surname, "Li," completely behind her is strange in view of the fact that her daughter and stepdaughter were both given the name Li.
       The Tang poem is "Dream of the Fairy Princess Playing Her Lute," by Qian Ji, one of Mao's favorite love poems, to which he alluded in several of his own later verses. Its last lines run:

Page

>The music stopped, the fairy princess vanished
>There remained only a few mountain peaks,
>   high above the river, bright and green.

Zhu Zhongli (Zhu Shan) has it that LP changed her name to JQ, under Sister Xu's influence, when registering at the Eighth Route Army office in Xian. Such timing, suggesting extreme calculation on JQ's part in an effort to obliterate her Bohemian past, could explain why she has been defensive when questioned about the change of name from LP to JQ (if Mao gave her the name JQ, one would think she would be happy to say so). On the other hand, it is not difficult to imagine Zhu Zhongli, who is so pro-Mao and anti-JQ, hiding from the reader any information suggesting that Mao himself gave JQ her name.

160–61   (JQ at home) *Zhong guo gong ren*, No. 24, 1958; Barrett, 83; *RS*, 460; *Inside Red China*, 75; Vladimirov, 37, 157, and *passim;* Chen Chang-feng's *Gen sui Mao zhu xi chang zheng*, 102; Payne's *Chinese Diaries, 1941–1946*, 355.

161   That JQ exaggerated the length of time she spent at Nanniwan is suggested by the fact that Roman Karmen saw her in Yanan on 5/25/39; if she went to the wasteland sometime in January, as she says, she could not have stayed a full six months, as she claims (W, 168, 171).

162   On maternity in Yanan, *Paris-Pékin*, No. 2, 97; *Yanan jian wen lu*, 152.

162   On He's two youngest children, *Dong xiang*, 11/1979; Ih. VII, 39ff.; W, 165.

163   Li Na and Li Min were not the original, "baby names" (*xiao ming*) of the two girls, but the *da ming* or *xue ming* given to them when they were several years old. Their original *xiao ming* were Jiao Jiao (Li Min) and Mao Mao (Li Na). (These are names given in *ZM*, 4/1979; *ZG*, 135 says Li Min's *xiao ming* was Mao Mao.)

163   (visitors) *Zhong guo gong ren*, No. 24, 1958; Ih. VII, 41; Zuo Shun-sheng's *Jin san shi nian jian wen za ji*, 92.

163   Payne's *A Rage for China*, 42ff.

163–64   (Russians) Vladimirov, 53ff., 293 ("Without").

164   Forman's *Report from Red China*, 178.

164   (medical couple) Ih. VII, 41.

165   Braun, 344 (German edition); Alley to RT, PK, 6/18/82.

165–66   Roman Karmen's *God v Kitae*, Moscow, 1941, 108.

166   (Zhou-JQ riding incident) *Dang dai*, HK, 9/1980, 55.

166   ("Ever since") "Ye bai he hua an guan zhan ji," in an edition of *Ye bai he hua*, Chongqing, 1943, preface.

166–68   (dancing) Service to RT, SF, 3/5/82; Snow's unpublished "The Divorce of Mao Zedong"; Zhang Dongcai's *Sancho Nosaka and Mao Zedong*, 46; Si Ma Zhang Feng, appendix, 556; Forman, 96–97; Barrett, 51; Wales's *Inside Red China*, Book Three; Ih. VII, 53; *Yanan yi yue*, 155–56; Vladimirov, 223. Apparently the Japanese version of Vladimirov, from which Ihara quotes (Ih. VII, 53), is fuller than the Chinese and English versions, neither of which contains all of what Ihara quotes about dance parties.

168   Ding Ling, of whom Mao was fond for a time, was stubborn, like He and

Page

   unlike JQ. Ding Ling was proud of her writing talent, He of her revolutionary seniority; JQ, without such grounds for pride, was more flexible toward Mao. On Ding Ling, *Yanan de nu xing,* 12ff., and Ding Ling to RT, Wellesley, Mass., 11/17/81.

168 ("not impossible") *Yanan de nu xing.*

168 (Wang) *Paris-Pékin,* No. 2, 8.

168 ("Comrade JQ") *Zhong guo gong ren,* No. 24, 1958.

168–69 (visits to opera) Vladimirov, 103, 215; Payne's *Chinese Diaries,* 352ff.; Ih. VII, 47ff.; *Yanan yi yue,* 59ff.

169 (Wang Ming visit) Dick Wilson's *Mao,* 250.

169 (Zhang Zhizhong) Information from family members in PK and T.

169–70 (documentary film) Si Malu's *Dou zheng shi ba nian,* 124. JQ's later remark, *ZW,* No. 352; URI, 251.

170–71 (Li Liuru) Article by Wang Meilan in *Zhan di,* 6/1980. Chen Xuezhao greatly admired Li and applied a line from Anatole France to him: "Les hommes qui se montrent tels gentils m'ennuient rarement" (*Yanan fang wen ji,* 100).

171 (FN) Yang Lien-sheng in *Harvard Journal of East Asian Studies,* 1961, 56–57.

172 Vladimirov, 293, 83, 366.

172 (influence on Mao's talks) *Zhong yang ribao,* T, 5/4/77; W, 185.

172 ("Opinions") B. Compton's *Mao's China,* 4. Vladimirov says she "resigned" from Lu Xun College, but W (173) appears to indicate she had continuing duties at the college.

173 Wang's choice of title is discussed in Timothy Cheek's unpublished "The Fading of the Wild Lilies," Cambridge, Mass., 21.

173 ("JQ battles") W, 295.

173 Barrett, 83.

173 (Orlov) Vladimirov, 320.

173 Service to RT, SF, 3/5/82.

174 Zuo Shunsheng's *Jin san shi nian jian wen za ji,* 91–92.

174–76 (visit to Chongqing) *ZW,* No. 366, 52; *Kuai bao,* HK, 11/28/65; Ji Jian's *Mao gong zheng chuan fen lie nei mu,* T, 1969, 268; *Xing dao ribao,* HK, 6/15/70 (article by Wang Zheng); *Zhong gong yan jiu,* T, 5/1973, 52; *Xing dao ribao,* 1/30/77 (corrective afterthoughts by author of URI); interviews in Ih. VII, 65; *M,* 181–82; Zhang Suchu to RT, Cambridge, Mass., and Donald Zhang to RT, T, 3/1/82.

   JQ's visit to Chongqing (for decades never mentioned in any PRC publication) was, after it became an issue at her trial, eventually referred to in *PD,* 12/10/80, "dental treatment" being given as the purpose of her trip. It seems, from the reports of the trial, that while in Chongqing, JQ made contact with Zhao Dan and Gu Erhyi (*ibid.*). JQ wrote a warm letter to Zhao Dan in 1946 (*DGB,* 12/14/80).

175 (scandal) Nationalist sources (see Wang Sicheng, 8–9) have the facts mixed up. A composite picture is made of the two daughters, their ages are given wrong, and it is falsely stated that one daughter left Chongqing for Yanan. Still, one cannot dismiss the story totally, given Mao's nature and the ways of Chinese politics; it remains an unconfirmed re-

Page

port. What JQ may have said about Mao's meetings with Miss Zhang we do not know, but she did remark that General Zhang's defection "was not so surprising, perhaps . . ." (W, 219).

176   (call to Tang) *Hua qiao ribao,* 9/27/80 (article by Xu Zhuancheng); TN.

176   (Mao and Tang) TN.

176–81   (North Shaanxi campaign) W, 192ff.; Jiang Qinfeng in *Hong qi piao piao,* 3, 338ff.; Yan Changling's *The Great Turning Point,* 92–94; Ih. IX, 58ff.; *Zhong gong yan jiu,* 5/1973, 52 (political assistant, not instructor).

177   ("coward") W, 200; *YS,* 111.

177   ("colorful clothes") *Dou zheng shi ba nian,* 123.

177–78   ("I am the one") *BJDS,* 83.

179   ("Vice-Chairman") Si Ma Zhang Feng's *Zhou Enlai ping zhuan,* 346–47.

180   (Yu Shan affair) Wang Sicheng, 8–9; Cui XI, 29–30; Zhang, Ch. 22.

180   ("reactionary") W, 53.

180   (Empress Wu) C. P. Fitzgerald's *Empress Wu,* 50.

180   (Tang) *Hua qiao ribao,* 9/27/80; TN. The account of Tang's later life in Ih. II, 66ff., is largely incorrect.

5.   LETDOWN (1950s)

182   (frontquote) *Wei ren min li xin gong,* PK, 1967, 2.

182   On the arrival in PK, *M,* 195ff.

183   ("Will the") J. Kinoshita in *Sekai,* Tokyo, 9/1963.

183   (JQ on Russia trip) W, 225.

183–84   (Yu affair) A close relative of Yu Shan to RT, T, 2/24/82; on the role of Liu, Ih. X, 58–59; "Mo takuto Sono shi to Jinsei," *Bungei Shunju,* 1965; Zhang Dajun, ed., *Zhong gong ren ming dian,* HK; on the dates of the *Amethyst* Incident and JQ's trip to Yalta, *SW,* IV, 403, and W, 226.

184   (FN–Liu Shaoqi) *Dadao Liu Shaoqi: guan yu Liu Shaoqi dang an cai liao de chuli* (Qinghua University, 1967).

184   The most detailed account of an alleged Mao fling around this time happens also to be an account of an alleged JQ fling. It is in the memoir *Mao Zedong de qing di,* by Cheng Qianwu, T, 12/1951. According to this account, Mao had an affair with a Miss Lin who was a secretary on his staff, while JQ had one with Lin's boyfriend, Yu, an official at the offices of the China-Russia Friendship Association. The whole drama ended when Mao came in unexpectedly while JQ was with Yu. Although JQ quickly hid Yu in a cupboard, Mao saw Yu's cap on a chair. A scene resulted, and the Mao-JQ marriage was greatly damaged. However, there are aspects to the memoir which detract from its overall credibility.

184   Su Fei to RT, PK, 6/20/82; TN.

185   (at station) G. Tannebaum, then Song's aide, to RT, NY, 9/10/81.

185–86   (the apartments) *PKR,* 9/23/77; W, 224; Mao's daughter-in-law has spoken of the separateness of the living arrangements, *ZB,* 5/1980, 80.

Page

186 (Anying to JQ) *ZB,* 8/1980, 10.

186–87 (Yangs) *PKR,* 10/14/77; BBC, Far East, 5617, B11, 9/17/77.

187 (bodyguard) Chen Changfeng's *Gen sui Mao zhu xi chang zheng,* 85.

187 (new arts organization) URI, 70ff.

188 (seeks job) Testimony of Yang Yizhi, Premier Zhou's secretary at the time, in *New Statesman,* London, 1/20/67; *Lian he bao,* T, 1/26/67; Xuan Mo in *Zhong gong yan jiu,* 5/1973, 54; *Xin sheng wan bao,* HK, 2/13/67. She acknowledged Zhou's help in *Wei ren min li xin gong,* 9.

188–89 (Wuxi trip) W, 226ff.

190 (FN) W, 232; see also *JQWY,* 207. On film committee, *PD,* 7/12/50; P. Clark: "Heroes Without Battlefields," Ph.D. thesis, Harvard, 56ff.

191 (Wu Mei) *DGB,* 12/15/80.

191–92 (Zhao, Zheng) TN.

192 (opera reform in Yanan) *Yanan yi yue,* 123ff.; *ZW,* No. 342, 27.

192 (Mei) *SCMP,* No. 4089; Ih. X, 69–70; *SCMP,* No. 3996, 4; *JQWY,* 206; *ZW,* No. 341, 24.

193–94 (*Inside Story*) URI, 72ff.; W, 234ff.; Yao Wenyuan in *RF,* 1/1967; *PKR,* 4/7/67; Ji Benyu in *RF,* 5/1967; Yao Ke's article in *MBYK,* 5/1967; Ih. X, 69ff.

194 ("We haven't") *SW,* V, 151.

194–97 (*Wu Xun*) *SW,* V, 57–58 (emphasis added to Mao's words by RT); *Zu guo yue kan,* 5/1968; W, 238ff. ("no one listened"); Ih. X, 81ff.; *SCMP,* No. 3996, 4; *Da lu wen ti yan jiu ji,* No. 103, T, 462ff.; *JQWY,* 207; *RF,* 1/1967 (Yao article); *Wu Xun li shi diao cha ji,* PK, 9/1951. Mao's editorial, *PD,* 5/20/51, contains a list of the articles that had criticized *Wu Xun,* but mentions no article by JQ (the *SW* text is an abridged form of the editorial). See also *PD,* 5/20/51, 5/30/51, 6/30/51, 7/23/51. On comparing *Wu Xun* with *Inside Story,* ACL, 21; URI, 78; Ih. X, 83. On Tao Xingzhi's praise for Wu Xun and other points, P. Clark, 79ff.

198–99 (in Hubei) W, 227ff.; Ih. X, 88ff.

199–200 (new job) W, 255; Ih. X, 88–89; *JQWY,* 183.

199 (nature of General Office work) A confidential source in PK.

200 JQ's formal removal from the film committee and the China-Russia organization was effected only in 1954 and 1955, respectively (URI, 81–82; ACL, 22).

200 (Zhou's remark) *JQWY,* 208; *SCMP,* No. 3996. On Zhou and JQ see also *ZW,* No. 341, 24; *QS,* 9/1978.

201 (Mao and JQ at receptions) A Burmese leader to RT, Rangoon, 11/15/79; and Ambassador Mononutu to RT, Jakarta, 12/1/79.

201 (Liu's words) *Hong,* 242.

202 (visit to Zhang) Personal communication from one of Zhang's daughters.

202 (Zhai) Zhai Zuojun's *Zai Mao zhu xi shen bian,* Wuhan, 54. See also *ZW,* 156, 22–23.

203 (Li) *Zhan di,* 6/1980.

203 ("taken away") W, 256.

203–04 (abortive cultural projects) *JQWY,* 209; *SCMP,* No. 3996, 5/25/67.

Page

204   (women in 1950s) Delia Davin in *Modern China,* 10/1975, 365.

204   (Russia) *Women in China,* 156ff.

204   (three slots for women) S. Leith in *Women in China,* 47.

204–05 (private and public spheres) D. Munro in *The China Difference,* ed. by RT, 37ff.

205–06 (Zhang) Zhang Suchu to RT, Cambridge, Mass., 6/1980, and her memoir in *Living in China,* New World Press, PK, 1979, 195, 227.

206   (appearance of women elite) Quan Ruxiang to RT, Cambridge, Mass., 8/1980.

206   ("I did not") W, 55.

207   (Zhou, Liu, and JQ's trip to Russia) Ih. X, 55–56. Ihara discusses the possibility that JQ was fulfilling a diplomatic purpose (Ih. VIII).

207–13 Stay in Russia is based largely on *YS* (its author, Zhu Zhongli, was the wife of the Chinese ambassador in Moscow at the time), Ch. 10, 15, 16, and *passim;* and W, Ch. 10.

214   (FN) *Gong ren ribao,* 12/2/80.

214   (Chen Yi's role) *Mao Zedong de mian mian guan,* 58–64.

214–19 JQ's family feuds are based in part on the memoirs by Songlin and Shaohua in *ZM,* 4/1979, 44ff., and *ZB,* 5/1980 and 8/1980.

215–16 On Anying's life and character, *ZW,* No. 156, 22ff.; Songlin's article in *Ren min wen xue,* 2/1978; *M, passim; CB,* No. 900, 5ff.; *Gong ren ribao,* 7/18/61 (memoir by Hao Guanghua); *PKR,* 10/14/77; D. and N. Milton's *The Wind Will Not Subside,* 155 (tribulations after 1927); *IAS,* 5/1980; Rice, 95, 531; L. Pye's *Mao,* 209, 218.

215   (Anying on cult) O. Vladimirov and V. Ryazantsev's *Mao Zedong,* Moscow, 54.

216   Lin Yutang's *My Country and My People,* 148.

216   To Witke, JQ expressed no personal feelings over Anying's death, and she got the date wrong—it was not October but November 25, 1950, at 9:00 P.M., according to Songlin.

216–17 (Li Yunxia) Information from persons who were her neighbors after she left the Mao-JQ household; *YS, passim;* the Songlin and Shaohua memoirs.

219–20 (*Dream*) *SCMP,* No. 3996; W, 276ff.; Ih. X, 92ff.; *SW,* V, 150–51; *JQWY,* 209; *M,* 295 (FN).

221   (Khrushchev) W, 262; *Khrushchev Remembers* (*Last Testament*), 322, where Khrushchev recorded his appellation of JQ as a "mattress."

221–23 (Yuanxin, He Yi) *YS,* 139.

223   (Wang affair) *YS,* 194; Songlin and Shaohua memoirs.

223–25 (Anqing) *ZM,* 4/1979; Songlin and Shaohua memoirs.

225   (at Beidaihe) Zhang Suchu to RT.

226   (Lin's visit) *Mao zhu xi de gu shi,* by Xu Haidong *et al.,* 93–94.

226–27 (Anqing) In some accounts (e.g., *ZB,* 8/1980), the physician's name is Mao Hongying.

227   For Songlin, Mao in his letter used her alternate name, Sizhai, and for Li Min, the nickname Jiao Jiao (*ZM,* 4/1979).

227   It was typical of JQ's penchant for publicly interpreting her personal feuds in terms of political struggle that she told Witke it was *Chiang Kai-shek's Nationalists*—not resentful family members—who spread

the notion that JQ had added to Anqing's health problems (W, 164).

227   (Mao's letter) *Qing nian yi dai,* SH, 9/1979.

227–28   (in Wuhan) *DGB,* 7/1/57; *Mao Zedong sheng ping ziliao jianbian,* 325. On the poem, see *ZW,* No. 356.

228   (Song reception) Tannebaum to RT, NY, 9/10/81.

228–30   (fourth trip to Russia) W, 268–270; *YS,* 205ff.

229   (FN—Mao failing to contact JQ) It was to a reporter that Witke told this story, *Washington Post,* 11/10/75; JQ's activities in Qingdao in the summer of 1957 are described in *Mao Zedong sheng ping ziliao jianbian,* 368; see also Ih. X, 98–99. (The fanciful tale about Mao failing to visit JQ is repeated by Richard Harris in *London Times,* 10/13/76.)

230   (Moscow incidents) *YS,* 207–208, 210.

231   (Mao and the Yangs) *ZB,* 8/1980; BBC, Far East, 5617, B11, 9/17/77; Mao's *Nineteen Poems,* 1958; *M,* 255ff.

231   ("Of my") *CLG,* 1–4, 1968, 39.

231   (JQ "hated" Shaoshan) E. Masi's *China Winter,* 223.

232   (FN—clothes) *ZW,* No. 359, 11.

232   (Mao on health) *Wan Sui*—1969, 1/24/64; W, 259.

232   (JQ at Li Lisans') *ZB,* 8/1980.

232–33   (in Henan) *PD,* 7/1/58.

233   Huang Jing's obituary is in *PD,* 2/13/58.

234   (Liu, Chen wives) ACL, 15.

234–35   (He Zizhen, Zhu De and dance) *YS,* 244f.

235   (Hangzhou villa) A source close to JQ; Julie Nixon Eisenhower's *Special People,* 178–79.

235   Pearl Buck to RT, Rutland, Vermont, fall 1972.

235   ("Sex") W, 449.

6.   Recovery and Revenge: Politics as Theater (1960s)

237   (Zhou) W, 270.

237   (doctors) *ZB,* 9/1980; W, 302; *SCMP,* No. 3996, 7.

238   (poem) *Mao Zedong Poems,* 1976, 40; JQ's error is revealed by Chen Chuxin in *Dong xiang,* HK, 2/1981. For an erotic view of the poem, Zhang, 238. See also *Zu guo yue kan,* 5/1968 (article by Zhong Huamin).

238   ("I'm a doctor") an ex-Red Guard in PK.

239   (photos) *PD,* 9/25–9/30/62; R. Macfarquhar in *CQ,* No. 46.

240   ("They treated") *M,* 290.

241   ("Our doctors") *CLG,* 9–3, 1976, 117.

241   ("Each person") *Wan Sui*—1969, 6/16/64.

242   (visit to Canton) *China Youth Daily,* 8/26/61. On JQ's link with Lin, *Hong,* 244.

242   ("I am fond") *IAS,* 8/1978, 94.

242   ("butcher's knife") *Lu,* 2.

243–51   On JQ's theater reforms, *JQWY; SCMP,* No. 3996; W, Chs. 16, 17; URI, 83–149; *Heirs Apparent,* 11 and *passim;* Ding Wang's *Wang Hongwen Zhang Chunqiao ping zhuan,* 5 and *passim; Jing gang shan* (Red

Page

Guards), 5/25/67; *PD,* 2/13/77 and 12/24/80. An attempt is made in
China Reconstructs, 5/1977, 2ff., and in *JQ shi qi shi dao ming de zheng
zhi ba shou,* PK, 5, to argue that the theater reforms were mainly *not*
JQ's doing.

244   (JQ's link with Ke) Ding Wang's *Wang . . . ,* 171ff.; *Dong xi fang,* HK,
1/15/81; *Dong xiang,* HK, 2/1981.

244   (Yang sketch) *Dong xi fang,* 1/15/81; *China Reconstructs,* 5/1977, 6.
The sketch was in the form of a Suzhou *pingdan,* a ballade form; on
this, see E. Masi's *China Winter,* 337.

244   (FN—dancing) *Shou huo,* SH, 1/1980, 116ff.

244–45   On JQ's links with Zhang and Yao, see *Guang ming ribao,* 1/27/77,
1/14/77, 6/18/77; Ding Wang's *Wang . . . ,* 171ff.; *FEER,* 10/14/68.

245   (Tian Han play) Ding Wang's *Wang . . . ,* 172.

246   ("boiled water") URI, 104.

246   ("Don't think I'm here") *SCMP,* No. 3996, 8.

246   ("PK chauvinism") Ding Wang, ed., *Zhong gong wen hua geming,* Vol.
5, 318.

246   ("mostly rubbish") W, 419.

246   ("Hate," "spring," "resolve," "Never forget") W, 420, 422, 423, 421.

247   (JQ and Tong) W, 420ff.

247   ("We became") W, 416.

247   ("Red Lantern") *SCMP,* No. 3996, 9ff.; W, 408ff.; *ZW,* No. 348, 23ff.

248   ("I have seen") *My House Has Two Doors,* 517.

248   (JQ's speech) *JQWY,* 21ff.

248   (festival incident) W, 311.

248   (Mao's remark) URI, 94.

249   (Song) URI, 289.

249   (Liu's, Peng's, Deng's remarks) RT's *The Future of China,* 268; *SCMP,*
No. 3996, 6ff.; *CB,* 842, 12; *Da lu wen ti yan jiu ji,* No. 103, T, 495; *ZG,*
140; *Zhong yang ribao,* T, 7/16/67 and 7/17/67.

249   (banquet) W, 313.

249   (Peng's and Liu's words) A Red Guard source in PK. See also Ding
Wang, ed., *Beijing shi wen hua da geming yundong,* 318.

250   Sources for JQ's dance reforms: *SCMP,* No. 3996; W, 425–37; *JQWY,*
passim; URI, Chs. X, XI.

250   (Deng's remark) RT's *The Future of China,* 269.

250   ("forced reflection") URI, 109.

250   ("Mao's praise") URI, 123; *JQ shi qi shi dao ming de zheng zhi ba
shou,* 19.

250–51   On the music reforms, *RF,* 5/23/67; URI, 124ff.; W, 386–90.

250   (violinist and Zhou Yang) Jun Jing in *Zhong guo wen xue,* No. 3,
1967.

251   (FN) W, 392–404; *JQWY,* 82ff.

251   ("processing plant") W, 397.

251   (price of radios) A PK broadcaster to RT.

251   ("shining pearls") *SCMP,* No. 3996, 12.

252   ("study to be") *IAS,* 1/1979, 108; (Mao on Sun) *Wan Sui*—1969,
5/20/58.

Page
252   ("A bit of fighting") *SCMP,* No. 418, 3.
252   ("Nor should we") W, 407.
252   (overcoat, library) W, 56, 100.
252   ("student") See page 368.
253–54 (Hai Rui) *Wen hui bao,* 11/10/65; JQ's *Wei ren min* . . . , 11–12; Ding Wang's *Wang* . . . , 177ff.
255   ("Look") Mao's *Poems.*
255   (Luo issue) *M,* 310–11; W, 311–12.
255–56 (army appointment) *SCMP,* No. 3996, 5; W, 318; *JQWY,* 4 (Lin's words); *Shi bao,* 8/28/67; *Hong,* 246, calls JQ the "liaison officer" between Mao and Lin. In the *Wan Sui* volumes, talks and dialogues of Mao's between 1949 and 1968, it is in 1966 that JQ first appears as an *interlocateur.*
256   ("they have less") S. Schram, ed.: *Chairman Mao Talks to the People,* 120.
256–57 (at rally) A. Grey on BBC *Panorama,* 4/18/77.
257   ("The peasants") G. Bennett and R. Montaperto: *Red Guard,* 214.
258   ("armed intellectuals") the phrase is from K. Heiden's *Der Fuehrer,* 19.
259   ("I was") *Wei ren min li xin gong,* 1; *JPRS,* 52658, 43.
259   (correspondence in fluctuations) *IAS,* 8/1976, 87; *ZW,* No. 143, 24ff.
259   (flattery) *SCMP,* No. 4172; *Heirs Apparent,* 15; *ZW,* No. 311, 13 and No. 339, 17; *ZG,* 151.
260   (wives) *SCMP,* No. 4182, 10, 8. See also *Zhong yang ribao,* 7/16/67 and 7/17/67.
260   (Zhang) *IAS,* 4/1981, 100.
260–61 (Song) Tannebaum (the aide) to RT, NY, 9/10/81.
261   (Tao) *ZW,* No. 137, 11; Ding Wang, ed., *Dou zheng zhong yang ji guan dang quan pai,* Vol. I, 505.
261–62 (Fan Jin) *Zhong guo qing nian bao,* 6/7/66; *Zhong gong wen hua geming,* Vol. 5, 411–12; URI, 50–52; *Beijing ribao,* 4/16/66; Cui III, 35; *K & C,* 393; *PD,* 11/30/80; Rice, 274, 550; information from a close relative of Yu Qiwei.
262   (Li Min and Fan) Rice, 448.
262   ("We must take") *SCMP,* No. 216, 4; *JPRS,* 52658, 45–46.
263   (Information on JQ's movies in the 1950s and 1960s) Chen Yuan-tsung to RT, SF, 3/4/82.
263   (entertains Zheng) *Now,* 12/5/80; TN. JQ even received her old rival Wang Ying, in 1955 (*Shou huo,* SH, 3/1980, 148ff.); cf. *ZW,* No. 339, 17.
263   ("nothing to do") *JQWY,* 159.
263–64 (Zhou Yang) W, 159.
264   (Yang) W, 328; Rice, 273.
264   (wives) W, 336; *MBYK,* 12/1980 (Tao and Deng wives); NCNA dispatch, PK, 12/12/80 (Xu and Nie wives). On JQ's fascination with revenge in literature, see *Nan bei ji,* HK, No. 126, 53, and *PD,* 3/12/77.
264   (Wang) URI, 246.

Page

265   (football player) Zhang, 359.

265–68   The account of Zheng and the others is based on Huang Chen's story in *Now,* London, 12/5/80; *PD,* 12/10/80, 12/27/80; *Si ren bang shi dian ying shi ye de si di,* PK, 199ff.; *Guang ming ribao,* 12/10/80; *DGB,* 12/25/80; FBIS, 12/9/80 and 12/10/80; material divulged at JQ's trial and passed on by those present (see Notes for Chapter 8). On JQ's relation with Ye Chun, *Lu,* 8–10.

268–69   (Tang's words) TN.

269   ("You must") W, 328; the Red Guard impressions and the account of the PK University visit are from interviews by RT with two former PK University students. See also W, 297; *Wan Sui—*1969, 7/28/68.

269   (on capitalism) JQ's *Guan yu wen hua da geming,* 21.

269   ("hang" and "fry") *ZG,* 152.

269–70   (speech to military) JQ's *Wei ren min . . . ,* 1ff.

270–71   (high school students) JQ's *Guan yu . . . ,* 27–28; *ZW,* No. 137, 11.

271   Camus: *Notebooks 1942–1951,* 90.

271   (Shanghai actor) Tannebaum to RT, NY, 9/10/81.

271–72   (Tan) A PK source (name changed).

272–74   (Chen, and account of campus speech) A former PK University student (name changed); Cathy Ye (former Red Guard) on BBC's *Panorama,* 4/18/77.

275   (Songlin, Li Min, and Yuanxin) *ZM,* 4/1979; *ZB,* 5/1980; *ZW,* No. 340, 26.

275–76   (Li Na) *YS,* 280–81; *PD,* 12/10/80; *Hong,* 246; *ZW,* No. 361, 27 and No. 159, 24.

276   (Li Ganqing) *ZW,* No. 402, 27; information from the Inspection Bureau, Department of Justice, Taipei; see also Jinan Radio, 11/28/80 (FBIS, 12/23/80).

276–86   On Wang and JQ, *ZM,* 12/1979 and 1/1980; Li Tianmin's *Liu Shaoqi,* T, 5–6 and *passim; PD,* 12/4/1980; R. Baum's *Prelude to Revolution,* Ch. 4; Madame Sukarno to RT, Jakarta, 6/8/83; *ZG,* 153; W. Hinton's *Hundred Day War,* 101ff.; W, 311, 333–34; R. Alley's *Travels in China,* 137–39; URI, 118ff., 250ff.; *ZW,* No. 200, 19–20; L. Dittmer's *Liu Shaoqi and the Chinese Cultural Revolution,* Chs. 4 and 5; *Guang ming ribao,* 12/4/80; *JPRS,* Red Guard Samples, 8/1/67.

277   (FN) C. P. Fitzgerald's *Empress Wu,* 32.

280–81   (FN) *CB,* No. 848, 2/27/68.

281   ("Her father") URI, 235.

281   (Liu Tao) *ZM,* No. 26; C. B. Kok's *Duan tou tai xia zhi JQ,* 146.

282   (Shao) FBIS, 12/4/80, L1.

282   ("Spare her") *Gong ren ribao,* 12/6/80, 2. On how Mao used JQ, *Shi dai pi ping,* Vol. 24, No. 7, 11.

283   (cook) *GTCH,* 41.

283–85   (Liu Yunruo) A PK source acquainted with Yunruo. See also *ZM,* 12/1979, 20ff.

286   ("That monstrous") *JPRS,* 52658, 39; *ZG,* 153.

286   ("When Liu") *SCMP,* No. 4181, 10.

286   ("This big traitor") *PD,* 12/4/80.

Page
286   (her greetings) W, 324; URI, 290, 294.
286   ("Clowns") URI, 278.
287   ("Time is up" and "Old Kang") URI, 262, 273.
287   (on guns) URI, 282; *ZW*, No. 359, 26.
287   (deceit) *M*, 320; W, 362, 348, 365.
287   ("arduous struggle") *SCMP*, No. 4076, 3.
287   ("Comrade Yang") Si Ma Zhang Feng's *Zhou Enlai ping zhuan*, 7. See
       also Li Tianmin's *Zhou Enlai*, T, 343.
288   (FN—words on Zhou) *M*, 327.
297–98 (midnight meeting) *Wan Sui*—1969, 7/28/68.
298   (FN) *M*, 319–20.
299   On her moderation, URI, 146, and postscript; W, 317; *ZW*, No. 272,
       11.
299   (FN—Witke's words) W, 317–18.
300   (Ninth Congress) Schram's *Chairman Mao Talks to the People*,
       283–84; Rice, 467ff.; *M*, 332ff.
300   ("Don't get giddy") *Zhong yang ribao*, T, 11/4/72; *ZW*, No. 261.
300   ("I never approved") *Chairman Mao Talks to the People*, 298; *ZW*,
       No. 356, 23.
300–301 (at park) W, 371.

7.   BID TO BE EMPRESS (1970s)

302   (frontquotes) W, 295; *IAS*, 9/1977, 104; Wakuta, 176.
302   (at Summer Palace) W, 371 (Witke refers to "White Cloud Palace,"
       but there is none such at the Summer Palace; *bai*, white, must have
       been misheard for *pai*); a source at the theater-restaurant. It was true
       that Lin's circle constantly stressed Mao's ideas, while stressing Lin as
       a figure; e.g., *PD*, 12/3/68 (Yan Zhongchuan's article about the need
       to follow the "splendid example of Vice-Chairman Lin and be loyal to
       Chairman Mao's revolutionary line.")
304   (Mao to Malraux) C. L. Sulzberger's *The Coldest War*, 11.
304   ("I was quite uneasy") *Zhong yang ribao*, T, 11/4/72.
304   (Suzhou conversation) *YS*, Ch. 23. On other occasions, JQ spoke of
       Lin's "eternal healthiness" (*yong yuan jian kang*), *PD*, 12/28/80.
304   ("Protect JQ") *Heirs Apparent*, 15; *ZG*, 151.
304   ("If there's anyone") *PD*, 12/28/80, *ZB*, 9/1980, 10.
304   ("our Party's") *PD*, 12/28/80.
304–05 (promotion and Lin's explanation) *PD*, 12/28/80.
305   ("For JQ") A PK source; *Lu*, 8.
305   (Lin to Huang) *IAS*, 6/1980, 95.
305–08 On the Mao-Lin-JQ relationship and Lin's demise, *M*, 332ff.; *PD*,
       11/27/80; *ZB*, 9/1980; Si Ma Zhang Feng's *Wenge hou de zhong gong*,
       170ff.; *Lu*, 8ff.; *YS*, Ch. 23.
305   ("The Cultural Revolution") A source in PK.
306   ("Each time" etc.) *PD*, 12/28/80 (article by Yu Youhai).
306   (photo of Lin) *Lu*, 8–9; *Zhong guo she*, 1/1977, 50ff.; *PD*, 5/28/77.

Page

306   ("even if") *YS*, 273.

306   (JQ in Qingdao) *Lu*, 10.

306–07   (Ye-JQ talk; melons) *PD*, 12/28/80, article by Yu Youhai; *DGB*, 12/29/80.

307   ("Let him go") C. Murphy in *National Review*, NY, 6/8/73. In slightly different words, this is confirmed in the drama performed in China during 1982, entitled *Jiu shi san shi jian*.

307   ("If Lin Biao") *IAS*, 2/1979, 2 (part of *Zhong fa*, No. 37).

307–08   (Canton dinner) A source within China, and *YS*, 273. Later JQ repeated some of these points to Witke (W, Ch. 15).

308   On Zhou's relation to the fall of Lin, *M*, 343, 366–67.

308   (assertion of individuality) J. Hightower, in *Journal of the History of Ideas*, No. 22, 1961, 164.

308–15   Wu Zetian and other women politicians of the past, Qu Jianyi's *Zhong guo li dai nu zheng zhi jia;* Jian Ziqing's *Zhong guo li dai xian neng fu nu ping zhuan*, T, especially Ch. 55; Nan Gongbo's *Zhong guo li dai ming nu ren*, HK; L. S. Yang's "Female Rulers in Imperial China," *Harvard Journal of East Asian Studies*, 1961, 47–61. A good biography of Wu in English is C. P. Fitzgerald's *Empress Wu* (quotations from pp. 20, 44, 47, 76, 129). On Wu's love life, Eric Chou's *Dragon and Phoenix* (quotations from pp. 27–30). Major pro-JQ articles on Wu, Lü, and others are in the Shanghai leftist journal *Xue xi yu pi pan*, 8/1974, 11/1974 (two articles), 1/1975 (two articles); major anti-JQ articles on the same topics are in *PD*, 2/8/77; *Guang ming ribao*, 2/8/77, 3/20/77, 4/7/77; *China Reconstructs*, 6/1977; *Lu*, 1–3; *JQ shi qi shi dao ming de zheng zhi ba shou*, 36 and *passim*. See also *Asahi Weekly* (in Japanese), 4/2/76, 54ff.

311   ("Even under communism" and Wu, Lü) *Lu*, 6–7, 2.

312   ("Women are the true revolutionaries") Fitzgerald, 109.

315   ("By 1971") Han Suyin's *My House Has Two Doors*, 517; other visits, her chapter in *Huai nian Mao Zedong*, HK.

316   ("The Court was already") Fitzgerald, 44.

316   ("quiet revenges") J. Alsop's *FDR: A Centenary Remembrance*, 157.

317   Information on Mao's relations with Zhang Yufeng from two well-placed PK sources. On other Mao affairs, Wang Sicheng's *Mao fei Zedong zheng zhuan*, and Cheng Qianwu's *Mao Zedong de qing di*, T, 1951. Cf. the novel *Coldest Winter in Peking*, 261.

317   Information on JQ's relation with Zhuang is based on three well-placed sources within China, and *Dang dai*, HK, 2/15/81. See also *PD*, 5/28/77, 2; *IAS*, 9/1977, 96 and 2/1979, 97.

317   ("Why shouldn't") *My House Has Two Doors*, 609–10.

317–18   (helicopter) *ZM*, 7/1/80.

318   (FN) Wang Ming's *Mao's Betrayal*, Moscow (in English), 38ff.

318   (nurses) *ZB*, 9/1980; another version of the incident, or perhaps a parallel incident, is in *China Reconstructs*, 6/1977, 6.

318   ("The absolute monarch") Fitzgerald, 32.

319   (Wu's cat) Fitzgerald, 143.

319   (monkey) A source within China; also *Lu*, 115; *YS*, 224 and *passim*.

Page
319   (cutting pages) A source in PK.
320   ("Even Mao") Huang Hua to RT, NY, 3/25/74.
320   (FN) A private communication from Quan Ruxiang (Brandeis University) and Phillip West (University of Indiana).
321   (FN) TN.
321–22 A Chinese government postmortem on the Witke interviews, including Mao's reaction and Zhou's words, is in *Zhong fa*, No. 37, Pt. 12 (in *IAS*, 5/1979).
322   (advice, lotus, worship, "teacher," skirts) W, 444, 187, 445, 287.
323   (king of counterrevolution) *IAS*, 2/1979, 97.
323   (Japanese) *ZW*, No. 275, 6.
324   ("It's better") *QS*, 12/1976; *IAS*, 7/1979, 97.
324   ("My body") *M*, 381.
324   PK's claims are in *Zhong fa*, Nos. 16, 24, and 37, all reprinted in *IAS* during 1978 and 1979.
324–25 ("She's poking") *IAS*, 7/1979, 97; *QS*, 12/1976.
325   ("JQ has" and "JQ wants") *Zhong fa*, No. 24 (in *IAS*, 9/1977).
325   ("It's time") *London Times*, 12/17/74.
325   (Exchange of letters) *IAS*, 9/1977, 102ff.
326–27 On JQ's 1974 activities, *WHCM*, 10/31/74; *PD*, 5/18/74, 5/27/74, 7/16/74, 7/31/74, 9/3/74, 9/10/74, 9/20–9/30/74, 10/5/74, 10/20/74; *RF*, 7/1974; Han Suyin in *Huai nian Mao Zedong; Xue xi yu pi pan*, 11/1974 (on Lü), and 1/1975 (on Wu); *IAS*, 9/1977, 11/1977, 7/1979, and 7/1981, 23; Ding Wang's *Wang . . .* , 27ff.; *ZM*, 4/1982, 68ff. Of the drive against Lin and Confucius, JQ remarked: "I have been standing at the forefront, commanding the battle" (*IAS*, 9/1977, 91). See *M*, 381ff.
326   (Wu) *Xin Tang shu zhuan*, 76, *lie zhuan*, 1.
327   ("That summer") Tannebaum to RT, NY, 9/10/81.
327   (poem) *Lu*, 6; *PD*, 11/26/76; *Zhong fa*, No. 24 (in *IAS*, 9/1977, 104); *Zhong guo she ying*, 5/1978.
328–29 (Han Fei) *Guang ming ribao*, 7/23/74; *WHCM*, 9/30/74.
329   ("The current struggle") *IAS*, 10/1978, 105.
329   ("Zhou") *PD*, 11/27/80. On Zhou's difficulties at this time, *RF*, 4/1974 (the article "Kong Qiu—The Person" is an attack on him); Kissinger's *White House Years*, 1059; *M*, 385ff.; *Xin guan cha*, Nos. 1 and 3, 1981 (collusion between JQ and Kang Sheng); *Zhong fa*, No. 37, Pt. III (in *IAS*, 9/1978). As the drive against Lin and Confucius began, JQ exclaimed at a meeting: "I've got Premier Zhou into a fix, and he doesn't know what to do" (*IAS*, 9/1977, 91).
329   ("black art") *PD*, 5/22/77.
329–31 (*Song of the Gardeners*) *Zhong fa*, No. 37, Pt. 8, Sect. 4 (in *IAS*, 3/1979); *IAS*, 4/1979.
331–32 (Xiaojinzhuang) *Guang ming ribao*, 10/10/74; *PD*, 11/26/76; *JQ shi qi shi dao ming de zheng zhi ba shou*, 36; *ZB*, 9/1980.
332–34 Visit to oil rig based on eyewitness account of a worker in Tianjin.
333   (Deng's remark) RT's *The Future of China*, 268; JQ on Deng and oil, in *Zhong fa*, No. 37, Pt. 10.

Page

334–35 Material on the dress is based on accounts from a woman living in Tianjin at that time, and another in PK. Also *Eastern Horizon,* 2/1981 and 4/1981; *Lu,* 112; W, 291; *My House Has Two Doors,* 609ff.; Wakuta's *Watashiwa no chugokunin,* 174ff.

335–37 (Imelda Marcos' visit) An account to RT by a member of the Philippine party; *Guang ming ribao,* 10/10/74; *NYT,* 9/30/74 and 12/23/74; *PD,* 9/20–27/74; *WHCM,* 10/31/74.

336 (JQ's 6/1974 speech in Tianjin) Ding Wang's *Wang . . . ,* 30; *Guang ming ribao,* 3/3/77; *Lu,* 6.

337–39 Material on JQ's life-style comes from several sources within China, and the following: *ZB,* 9/1980; *Lu, passim;* Wakuta's *Watashiwa no chugokunin,* 159ff.; *YS,* 229, 236, 235, 215ff.; *Lu,* 112; *ZM,* No. 13; *Zhong yang ribao,* T, 5/4/77.

339 (film) *ZB,* 9/1980.

339 ("Push the national economy forward" affair) *Zhong fa,* No. 37, Pt. 8 (in *IAS,* 5/1979).

341 ("Why did you?") *RN: The Memoirs of Richard Nixon,* II, 39. Other sources on the Nixon visit: W, 379, 389; *PD,* 2/21–25/72; *NYT,* 2/22–26/72.

342 (Indian soldier) W, 273.

342 (Li) *Li Zongren gui lai,* Changchun, 150.

342 (Cambodian banquet) Letter to RT from the ambassador present, dated 2/25/82.

343 (snails) *IAS,* 5/1979.

343 (JQ on capitalist culture) W, 325, 154.

343 (Daqing equipment, oil exports) *Zhong fa,* No. 37 (in *IAS,* 5/1979).

344 (liking for *Jin ping mei*) W, 154.

344–46 (Fragrant Hills speech) *ZW,* No. 321; Chen Suimin's *Mao Zedong yu JQ,* T, 174ff.; *M,* 388ff.

346–47 (Li Min, Songlin, and Anqing and his wife) *ZB,* 5/1980 and 8/1980; *ZM,* 4/1979; *IAS,* 5/1980, 91ff.

347 (Li Yunxia) Interviews by RT with former neighbors at Qinghua; *YS,* 146, 149–50.

348 (Mao Yuanxin) *IAS,* 10/1977, 11/1977, and 1/1979 (Zhang Tiesheng); *Zhen xiang,* HK, No. 28; *M,* 382, 418; *Empress Wu,* 138ff. (Wu Chengsi). Wakuta (130) makes an unconvincing case that Yuanxin is the son of JQ and Xu Yixin.

348–49 (Mao's words to Li Na) T. Scharping's *Mao Chronik,* 192. Also *YS,* 280–81; *Zhen xiang,* HK, No. 28, 16ff. (Li Na had to approach her mother through Yuanxin).

349 Foreign Communist leader to RT, 12/24/81.

349–50 (Wang and Tang) *IAS,* 9/1977.

350 (Wang visits Mao) *QS,* 12/1976; *Ming bao,* 10/26/76.

350 (Mao to Chen) *Ming bao,* 10/29/76.

351 (money) *Zhong fa,* No. 24 (in *IAS,* 11/1977); *ZB,* 9/1980; W, 443.

351–52 ("I am old") *QS,* 12/1976.

352–53 ("Pioneers") *Zhong fa,* No. 37 (in *IAS,* 3/1979).

353 (Mao's quips) RT's *The Future of China,* 120.

Page

353   ("arm") *Lu*, 68.

354   (carping remarks) URI, 159.

354   ("Don't cook up") *Zhong fa*, No. 37, Pt. 2 (in *IAS*, 2/1979).

354   ("Because I did not want") *Zhong fa*, No. 37, Pt. 2 (in *IAS*, 2/1979).

355   (JQ on Deng and Mao) *Zhong fa*, No. 24 (in *IAS*, 10/1977).

355–56   (JQ at Dazhai and Mao's response) *Zhong fa*, No. 37, Pt. 6 (in *IAS*, 4/1979); *Ming bao*, 10/27/76; *China Reconstructs*, 2–3/1977; *Lu*, 67; *ZB*, 9/1980.

356–57   (Kang Sheng affair) *Zhong fa*, No. 24, Pt. 3 (in *IAS*, 10/1977); *Xin guan cha*, 2/10/81, 36.

357–59   On Zhou's death, *M*, 404ff.; observations of foreign diplomats then in PK; *QS*, 12/1976 (Shenyang soldier, Canton crowd); *Paris-Pékin*, No. 2, 40 ("Little Chao").

358   ("I was a person") *Zhong fa*, No. 37, Pt. 2 (in *IAS*, 2/1979).

358   (Zhu's words) *Zhong hua zhoubao*, 12/27/76. For background on the Zhu-JQ hostility, *Shi dai pi ping*, T, Vol. 24, No. 7, 10.

358–59   (TV scenes) *QS*, 12/1976.

359   On Deng's defeat, RT's *The Future of China*, Ch. 4.

359   ("sally launched") *Zhong fa*, No. 24, Pt. 3 (in *IAS*, 10/1977).

359   ("fascist") *Zhong fa*, No. 37, Pt. 2.

359   (Nixons) *PD*, 2/24/76; *London Times*, 2/24/76; *ZW*, No. 339, 16.

360–61   (Tiananmen incident) *M*, 414ff.; *PD*, 4/8/76; *QS*, 2/1977; *Tiananmen ge ming shi chao*, HK, 32, 41, 50; *DGB*, 11/27/78, 2.

361   (FN) *Empress Wu*, 98.

361   (anniversary of Cultural Revolution) *IAS*, 9/1978, 96.

361   (history course) *Zhong fa*, No. 37, Pt. 6.

362   (New Zealand prime minister) R. Muldoon's *Muldoon*, 130. On JQ's key role at this time, China Information Service (Taipei), No. 77–881.

362   (Kang Sheng) *Zhong fa*, No. 24, Pt. 3 (in *IAS*, 10/1977).

363   Mao said of himself that he was part monkey and part tiger; see *M*, *passim*.

363   (grave) *China News*, T, 11/5/75.

363   (poem) *Manchester Guardian*, 11/7/76.

363   (bedside meeting) *Ming bao*, HK, 10/26–30/76; BBC, Far East, 5335, 10/12/76; J. van Ginneken's *The Rise and Fall of Lin Biao*, 318; *QS*, 2/1977; Si Ma Zhang Feng's *Wenge hou de zhong gong*, 548ff.; *Guang ming ribao*, 12/5/76; *Gong dang wen ti yan jiu*, Vol. 7, No. 1, 28.

364   (three visits) *IAS*, 11/1977.

364–65   (Xiaojinzhuang) *PD*, 11/26/76; *IAS*, 2/1979, 98; ("drop of sperm") Wakuta, 176.

365–66   (JQ at Dazhai) *ZB*, 9/1980; *Zhong fa*, No. 24, Pt. 4 (in *IAS*, 11/1977); *China Reconstructs*, 2–3/1977; *Eastern Horizon*, HK, 3/1977; *JQ shi qi shi dao ming de zheng zhi ba shou*, 34ff.

366–68   (Mao's last days) *Zhong fa*, No. 24, Pt. 4 (in *IAS*, 11/1977); *Ming bao*, 11/26–30/76; Ding Wang's *JQ yu Beijing zheng bian; ZW*, No. 361, 28, and No. 362, 11 (Hua as Mao's alleged son).

368–69   (wreaths and funeral) *CQ*, No. 68, 880; E. Masi's *China Winter*, 98ff.; *M*, 422ff.; R. Garside's *Coming Alive*, 137. Of course, Mao may also

Page

have instructed, as HK Communist sources claimed, that "at his funeral she not be accorded any mention as his wife" (*NYT*, 10/22/76).

369   ("I am not able to tell you") *ZB*, 8/1980, 9. On the politics of JQ's fall, RT's *The Future of China*, 110ff.; the Wang and Zhang exposés in *Paris-Pékin*, No. 1 and No. 2; *QS*, 12/1976 and 2/1977; *Ming bao*, 10/26–30/1976; *Zhong fa*, No. 24 (in *IAS*, 11/1977); *ZM*, 11/1980, 38ff.; *Gong dang wen ti yan jiu*, Vol. 7, No. 1, 26ff.; Singko Ly's *The Fall of Madam Mao*.

369   ("Act according") *Zhong fa*, No. 24 (in *IAS*, 11/1977, 105ff.).

369   (JQ-Hua scene) RT's *The Future of China*, 123.

370   ("Three of the characters") *Zhong fa*, No. 24 (in *IAS*, 11/1977).

370   ("Two Schools" article) *Guang ming ribao*, 10/4/76.

370   These same five men who met in the Western Hills were the leading figures at the "Victory Rally" after JQ's fall, on October 24 (*London Times*, 10/25/76).

371   ("If you don't") *Ming bao*, 11/3/76.

371–72   (JQ's arrest) *ZB*, 9/1980, 18ff.; *QS*, 12/1976; *Paris-Pékin*, No. 2 (Wang Dongxing's secret speech), No. 1 (Zhang Pinghua's secret speech); *MBYK*, 11/1976, 3ff.; Ding Wang's *JQ yu Beijing zheng bian; Le Monde*, 10/21/76 (Mao Yuanxin); *ZM*, 10/1978, 32ff.; *My House Has Two Doors*, 637. Accounts vary as to whether Yao was arrested upon arrival at the second conference room, or at his home.

372   ("JQ is a paper") *PD*, 9/8/77.

373   (White-Boned Demon) *JQ shi qi shi dao ming de zheng zhi ba shou*, 21.

372–73   (cartoons) RT's *The Future of China*, 114, 130ff.; Masi's *China Winter*, Ch. 5; interviews with Chinese observers; *London Times*, 11/19/76.

373   (words of Songlin, Shaohua, and Li Min) *ZB*, 5/1980 and 9/1980.

373   (Wang, Yang) *London Times*, 10/22/76; *PD*, 12/8/76.

8.   "Shut Up, Jiang Qing"

374   ("There's no one") *Lian he bao*, T, 11/18/80; *IAS*, 6/1979, 112ff. On JQ in prison, *ZB*, 9/1980; *MBYK*, 12/1980; *ZM*, 8/1978; *Nan fang ribao*, 11/23/80; *QS*, 12/1980; *Zhong guo ren quan*, 2/1979 (*JPRS*, 73421).

374   (suicide attempt) *London Times*, 11/24/76; *ZM*, 8/1978, 15; *Free China Weekly*, 2/6/77. On suicide, W, 321; R. Witke and M. Wolf: *Women in Chinese Society*, 111ff.; unpublished papers on suicide in Chinese history supplied to RT by J. Spence of Yale University; Lin Yutang, 141. Mao Dun and Ding Ling both wrote about suicide before 1949 and were criticized after 1949 for having done so indulgently.

374   ("She is being") A PK source.

375   (*bao zi*) *Nan fang ribao*, 11/23/80, 3.

375   (FN) *ZM*, No. 19.

375–76   (exchange with procuratorial officials) *ZM*, No. 19.

376   ("not number one") *ZM*, No. 13, 7/1980, 26; *JPRS*, 73421.

376   (Hua) *ZW*, No. 447, 24; *Zhen xiang*, HK, No. 28; *ZB*, 9/1980.

Page
376–90 Principal general sources on JQ's trial are: RT's inspection at the Investigation Bureau in Taipei of audiovisual records of the trial, intercepted through Fujian (TV Tape); *Li shi shen pan,* PK (*LSSP*); interviews in China and the U.S. with Chinese present at the trial; *ZM,* 1/1981; *QS,* late 1980 and early 1981; *ZB,* late 1980 and early 1981; *China News Analysis,* HK, No. 1199; *PD* throughout the trial from 11/20/80 until the verdict on 1/25/81; *MBYK,* 12/1980 and 3/1981; *IAS,* 1/1981 and 6/1981; *Beijing da shen,* T, 1981 (*BJDS*); *A Great Trial in Chinese History,* PK (*GTCH*). Text of indictment is in English in *PKR,* No. 48, 1980, in Chinese in *LSSP,* 17ff. See also *CQ,* No. 85. On linking of JQ and Lin, see *QS,* 12/1980, and an unpublished thesis by Zhu Lili at Mucha, Taiwan, entitled *Lin Jiang ji tuan shen pan de qian yin yu hou guo.*

377   ("She still") Fitzgerald's *Empress Wu,* 145.
378   (lawyer) *MBYK,* 12/1980; *GTCH,* 26–27; *PD,* 12/24/80.
378   ("I don't agree") *ZM,* No. 40.
379–80 (Changsha incident) *ZM,* No. 40; *GTCH,* 46ff.; TV Tape; FBIS, 11/28/80, L1–L4; *BJDS,* 25ff.; *PD,* 11/27/80.
380   ("They are two") *ZM,* No. 40, 19.
380–81 ("With a head") Si Ma Zhang Feng's *Deng Xiaoping fu zhi mo,* 198.
381   (Tang's words) TN.
381–83 (Liu-Wang session) FBIS, 12/4/80, 12/5/80, 12/8/80, 12/9/80; *GTCH,* 33ff.; TV Tape; *BJDS,* 34ff.; *PD,* 12/4/80, 12/6/80; *IAS,* 1/1981 (searching houses).
382   On the trial as an expression of law, *IAS,* 7/1981.
383   ("evil star") *PD,* 12/4/80. It is interesting, and sad, to see how much JQ's trial resembled pre-Liberation trials (see Smedley's *Portraits,* 29) and that of Sai Jinhua (see *That Chinese Woman,* Ch. 17). Sai had to kneel before the magistrates while Jiang Qing was allowed to sit on a kitchen chair. Sai was in her thirties when tried while Jiang was in her sixties. Still, the two trials had much in common. In neither case was there any question of the rule of law. Politics dominated the trial. And the accused was adjudged to have used her feminine charms to attain a niche in public life when she should have stayed home and knitted.

        Both Sai and Jiang Qing were able to hold their heads up; their lives were consistent; they refused to succumb; they were not cardboard shadows but genuine articles.

383   (list) *GTCH,* 51ff.; FBIS, 12/18/80.
383–86 (Huang, Liao, and 1930s issues) *BJDS,* 53ff.; *GTCH,* 58ff.; *PD,* 12/10/80, 12/13/80; FBIS, 12/8/80, 12/9/80, 12/10/80, 12/12/80, 12/15/80, 12/16/80, 12/18/80; TV Tape. For background to the Liao-JQ hostility, *DGB,* 1/28/81.
387   (children) *FEER, 11/28/80.*
387   ("How was I" and "Why did you") *ZM,* No. 40.
387–90 (sessions of 12/23, 12/24, and 12/29) TV Tape; *BJDS,* 71ff.; *GTCH,* 101ff.; *Christian Science Monitor,* 12/30/80; *PD,* 12/24, 12/25 ("A ten-year dream"), and 12/30; *ZM,* No. 19 (complaints to Jiang Wen) and No. 40; *MBYK,* 12/1980; FBIS, 12/23/80, 12/24/80, 12/29/80; *FEER,*

Page

1/2/81; *PKR,* 1/12/81 ("She refused"); *IAS,* 6/1981, 44 (Mao quote); *DGB,* 12/30/80.

391   ("I have long") A PK citizen who attended the trial.

391   (monk story) *ZW,* No. 401, 7.

391–92   (sentencing) *Zhen xiang,* HK, No. 28; TV Tape; *IAS,* 1/1981 and 6/1981; *GTCH,* 128ff.; *BJDS,* 415ff.; *FEER,* 1/16/81; *ZM,* No. 40, 22ff.

392–93   (prison and the commutation) *Zhen xiang,* HK, No. 28; *Lian he bao,* T, 8/16/81; *QS,* 3/1981; *NYT,* 1/24/83, 1/26/83; *PD,* 1/26/83; *International Herald Tribune,* 9/1/82; *Zhong yang ribao,* late summer 1982 (clipping in RT's possession is undated).

392–93   (dolls, radio, "I'm not afraid," name on dolls) *Lian he bao,* T, 8/16/81, 1/26/83, 1/24/83; *NYT,* 1/24/83.

393   (Peng) *NYT,* 1/24/83.

393   One of JQ's leaflets, addressed to the "Proletarian revolutionary fighters of the whole Party and whole nation," which was inserted in letters leaving Shandong Province, is in RT's possession.

393   ("I would like") *Zhong yang ribao,* T, 9/26/82.

393   ("She has not") *PD,* 1/26/83; *NYT,* 1/26/83. Cf. *Zhong yang ribao,* T, 1/26/83 and 1/27/83.

393   ("I regret") Wakuta, 203; *Lian he bao,* T, 1/24/83; *International Herald Tribune,* 9/1/82.

394   ("The biggest") *IAS,* 6/1981, 46.

Index

Terrill, Ross

The white—boned
demon

DATE DUE

0

MAR 2 3 1984